CW01506628

# 797,885 Books

## are available to read at

## www.ForgottenBooks.com

Forgotten Books' App
Available for mobile, tablet & eReader

ISBN 978-1-331-52272-0
PIBN 10201411

This book is a reproduction of an important historical work. Forgotten Books uses
state-of-the-art technology to digitally reconstruct the work, preserving the original format
whilst repairing imperfections present in the aged copy. In rare cases, an imperfection in
the original, such as a blemish or missing page, may be replicated in our edition. We do,
however, repair the vast majority of imperfections successfully; any imperfections that
remain are intentionally left to preserve the state of such historical works.

Forgotten Books is a registered trademark of FB &c Ltd.
Copyright © 2017 FB &c Ltd.
FB &c Ltd, Dalton House, 60 Windsor Avenue, London, SW19 2RR.
Company number 08720141. Registered in England and Wales.

For support please visit www.forgottenbooks.com

# 1 MONTH OF
# FREE
# READING

at

## www.ForgottenBooks.com

By purchasing this book you are eligible for one month membership to ForgottenBooks.com, giving you unlimited access to our entire collection of over 700,000 titles via our web site and mobile apps.

To claim your free month visit:

www.forgottenbooks.com/free201411

* Offer is valid for 45 days from date of purchase. Terms and conditions apply.

English
Français
Deutsche
Italiano
Español
Português

# www.forgottenbooks.com

**Mythology** Photography **Fiction**
Fishing Christianity **Art** Cooking
Essays Buddhism Freemasonry
Medicine **Biology** Music **Ancient**
**Egypt** Evolution Carpentry Physics
Dance Geology **Mathematics** Fitness
Shakespeare **Folklore** Yoga Marketing
**Confidence** Immortality Biographies
Poetry **Psychology** Witchcraft
Electronics Chemistry History **Law**
Accounting **Philosophy** Anthropology
Alchemy Drama Quantum Mechanics
Atheism Sexual Health **Ancient History**
**Entrepreneurship** Languages Sport
Paleontology Needlework Islam
**Metaphysics** Investment Archaeology
Parenting Statistics Criminology
**Motivational**

# SPEECHES

BY

# LORD CURZON OF KEDLESTON.

# SPEECHES

BY

# LORD CURZON OF KEDLESTON,

VICEROY AND GOVERNOR-GENERAL OF INDIA.

———

## 1898-1901.

———

Haec est in gremium victos quæ sola recepit,
Humánumque genus communi nomine fovit,
Matris non Dominæ ritu ; civesque vocavit
Quos domuit ; nexuque pio longinqua revinxit.

*Claudian.*

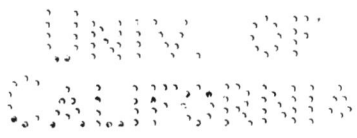

———

CALCUTTA :

THACKER, SPINK & Co.

——

1901.

CALCUTTA :

PRINTED BY THACKER, SPINK & CO.

HENRY MORSE STEPHENS

# CONTENTS.

511666

# PART I.

SPEECHES DELIVERED BEFORE
LEAVING ENGLAND,
1898.

# Speeches delivered before leaving England, 1898.

---

### DINNER GIVEN BY OLD ETONIANS.

*28th October,* 1898.

[On Friday evening, the 28th October, 1898, a dinner was given by old Etonians at the Café Monico to Lord Curzon of Kedleston (Viceroy-Designate of India), the Earl of Minto (Governor-General-Designate of Canada), and the Revd. J. E. C. Welldon (Bishop-Designate of Calcutta). Lord Rosebery, who presided, proposed the toast of " Our Guests." In the course of his speech he said :—

Lastly, I take the case of our friend who is going to undertake the highest post of the three, because after all it is one of the highest posts that any human being can occupy. He goes to it in the full flower of youth, and of manhood, and of success—a combination to which everyone must wish well. Lord Curzon has this additional advantage in his favour—that he is reviving a dormant class, the Irish peerage. (*Laughter and cheers.*) Some might think that that implied some new legislative or constitutional development on the part of Her Majesty's Government, but it would be out of my place to surmise that to be the case. But, at any rate, sure I am of this—that Lord Curzon of Kedleston has shown in his position at the Foreign Office qualities of eloquence, of debating power, of argument, which have hardly been surpassed in the career of any man of his standing. (*Hear, hear.*) I cannot say—it would be difficult to say—that he has done so in defence of difficult positions, because that would be at once to raise a political issue of the very gravest kind. (*Laughter.*) But I am quite sure that no Under-Secretary has ever had to defend in the House of Commons any but positions of difficulty, and I think the foreign situations are always of that character. I am quite sure that when Lord Curzon has had to defend these situations he has defended them with not less than his customary success. He has devoted special study to India. I believe he has even entered into amicable relations with neighbouring potentates. He will pass from his home of Kedleston in Derbyshire to the exact reproduction of Kedleston in Government House, Calcutta. We all hope that in his time India may enjoy a prosperity which has of late been

denied to her, and that immunity from war and famine and pestilence may be the blessed prerogative of Lord Curzon's Viceroyalty. (*Cheers.*)
Lord Curzon of Kedleston, who, on rising, was received with loud cheers said :—]

*Lord Rosebery, My Lords, and Gentlemen,*—This gathering to-night, composed as it is of old school-fellows, old friends, of men who have inherited the same traditions and are loyal to the same collegiate mother, is a compliment which I am sure the happy trio who are fortunate enough to be your guests are never likely to forget. But if there is anything that could enhance the special significance and value of that compliment, it would consist in the fact that Lord Rosebery has consented to occupy the chair and in the speech to which we listened a short while ago. (*Cheers.*) It will ever be memorable to me, whose public life has been associated with one political party, that at this turning point in my fortunes, my health has been proposed by one who has been the leader of the rival political party. (*Cheers.*) And it will be memorable to all of us, your guests this evening, that as we are starting forth for our different spheres of work, the farewell to which we have listened should have proceeded from the lips of an ex-Prime Minister of England. (*Cheers.*) Surely there is something of good omen in this combination. For after all we each of us are going out to occupy, if the expression may be permitted, a different thwart in that stout craft of Empire of which Lord Rosebery once pulled the stroke oar. (*Hear, hear.*) From his lips we have all of us, on many occasions, imbibed the lessons of an Imperialism, exalted but not arrogant, fearless but not rash (*cheers*), an Imperialism which is every day becoming less and less the creed of a party and more and more the faith of a nation. (*Loud cheers.*) I have said that we are especially fortunate in our hosts and in our Chairman. But may I, for myself, also claim a particular good fortune in the person of one of my fellow-guests ? When 20 years ago Welldon and I lived together in Paris, in the house of a French apothecary, to study the French language (*laughter*) ; when, at a later date, we crossed together the United States of

America, and together viewed the glories of Niagara and the Yosemite ; when on another occasion, in the company of a dear friend, also present to-night, the head-master of Haileybury, we rode together across the mountains and valleys of Greece, little did we think that the day would one day come when at the same time he and I should be going forth to the same great continent, to take our share in that noble work which I firmly believe has been placed by the inscrutable decrees of Providence upon the shoulders of the British race. (*Cheers.*) I congratulate India upon having obtained such a successor to the See of Heber and of Cotton (*Cheers.*) I congratulate myself that I shall have as my spiritual and episcopal master one of my oldest and dearest of friends.

Lord Rosebery has spoken in gracious terms of the circumstances under which I have accepted this appointment. There is a passage in the writings of Thomas Carlyle which in this connection has always haunted my mind. This is what that acute but rugged old philosopher said :—

" I have sometimes thought what a thing it would be could the Queen in Council pick out some gallant-minded, stout cadet and say to him, ' Young fellow, if there do lie in you potentialities of governing, of gradually guiding, leading and coercing to a noble goal, how sad it is they should be all lost. See, I have scores on scores of colonies. One of these you shall have as vice-king. Go you and buckle with it in the name of Heaven, and let us see what you will build it to.' "

Well, though these words were spoken of the West Indian colonies, I think that, *mutatis mutandis*, they are equally applicable to the East Indian Empire ; and they indicate to me the spirit of courage, but yet of humility, of high aspiration, but still more of duty, in which any man should approach such a task. (*Hear.*) I have often seen during the past few weeks my acceptance of this office attributed to a variety of causes—to personal ambition, to the disappointment of Parliamentary hopes, to failing health.

(*Laughter.*)  My own experience of public life, such as it
has been, leads me to think that the simplest explanation
of the phenomena of human action,—human beings being
more or less always cast in the same mould,—is likely to be
the most correct, and that the recondite is apt to be the
fallacious as well as the obscure. (*Laughter.*)  Is it permissible, therefore, for me to say in this company of old
school-fellows and of personal friends that, whatever may
have been the views of those who thought me worthy of this
office, I gladly accepted it, because I love India, its people,
its history, its Government, the absorbing mysteries of its
civilisation and its life ?  I think it was first while I was
at Eton that a sense of its overwhelming importance dawned
upon my mind.  There we were perpetually invited by a
body of assiduous and capable mentors—I need hardly say
that I allude to the Eton masters (*laughter*)—and we
responded with greater or less reluctance to the appeal,
to contemplate the pomp and majesty, the law and the
living influence, of the empire of Rome.  We had at Eton
in my day, and I hope it still flourishes, an institution
called the Literary Society, of which, I believe, my friend
Welldon was one of the first presidents, and in which I
afterwards had the honour to follow in his footsteps.  To this
society, from time to time, came down eminent men to
preach to us about the wider world outside.  Among those
distinguished persons who came in my day was Sir James
Fitz-James Stephen, but just returned from India—the father
of my dear friend, Jim Stephen, the " J. K. S." of the
literary world, that brilliant but meteoric intellect that all
too soon plunged into the abyss and was lost from view.
(*Hear, hear.*)  Sir James Stephen came down to Eton and
told the boys that listened to him, of whom I was one, that
there was in the Asian continent an empire more populous,
more amazing, and more beneficent than that of Rome ; that
the rulers of that great dominion were drawn from the men
of our own people ; that some of them might perhaps in the
future be taken from the ranks of the boys who were listening

to his words. Ever since that day, and still more since my first visit to India in 1887, the fascination and, if I may say so, the sacredness of India have grown upon me, until I have come to think that it is the highest honour that can be placed upon any subject of the Queen that in any capacity, high or low, he should devote such energies as he may possess to its service. (*Cheers.*)

But may I carry my suggestion one step further? May I not say that the growth of the ideal of duty has been the most salient feature in the history of our relations with India during the past hundred years, and still more during the reign of the present Queen? (*Cheers.*) A century ago India in the hands of the East India Company was regarded as a mercantile investment, the business of whose promoters and agents was to return as large dividends as possible, and the larger, of course, the better, to the pockets of their shareholders at home. In the course of these proceedings many of those men amassed great wealth, almost beyond the dreams of avarice—wealth, the display of which was apt to be vulgar, and the source of which was often impure. Indian posts, low as well as high, were the spoils of political patronage at home, and were exclusively distributed according to the narrowest and most selfish exigencies of party polemics in England. We have only to look to the treatment of Warren Hastings to realise how little the welfare of India was thought of in comparison with the loss or gain to Whigs and Tories in London. I do not say that we have altogether extricated India from the perils and the contamination of the party system; I do not say that our administration of that great Empire is altogether free from blemish or taint. But I do say that it is informed with a spirit of duty, and that it is edified and elevated by that influence. I do say that we think much of the welfare of India and but little of its wealth (*hear, hear*); that we endeavour to administer the Government of that country in the interests of the governed; that our mission there

is one of obligation and not of profit ; and that we do our
humble best to retain by justice that which we may have
won by the sword. (*Cheers.*) May we not, indeed, say
that at the end of the 19th century the spectacle presented
by our dominion in India is that of British power sustained
by a Christian ideal ? (*Cheers.*)

What then is the conception of his duty that an outgoing
Viceroy should set before himself ? I have no new or
startling definition to give, but the light in which it presents
itself to my mind is this. It is his duty, first and foremost,
to represent the authority of the Queen-Empress, whose
name, revered more than the name of any other living
sovereign by all races and classes from Cape Comorin to
the Himalayas, is in India both a bond of union and the
symbol of power ; and to associate with the personal
attributes that cling about that name, the conviction that the
justice of her government is inflexible, that its honour is
stainless, and that its mercy is in proportion to its strength.
(*Cheers.*) Secondly, he should try to remember that all
those people are not the sons of our own race, or creed, or
clime, and that it is only by regard for their feelings, by
respect for their prejudices—I will even go so far as to say
by deference to their scruples—that we can obtain the
acquiescence as well as the submission of the governed.
(*Cheers.*) Thirdly, his duty is to recognise that, though
relatively far advanced in the scale of civilisation compared
with the time of Lord Wellesley, or even Lord Canning,
India is still but ill-equipped with the material and industrial and educational resources which are so necessary to
her career, and so to work that she may, by slow but sure
degrees, expand to the full measure of her growth. And
lastly, it is to preserve intact and secure, either from internal
convulsion, or external inroad, the boundaries of that great
and Imperial dominion. (*Loud cheers.*)

This, I would venture to suggest, is the conception which
every outgoing Viceroy sets before himself. He is probably
unwise if he attempts to fill in the details too closely in

advance. The experience in which he must be sadly lacking at the start, but which will come to him in increasing
volume day by day, will, with slow and sometimes with
painful touch, fill in the details as he proceeds. For after
all—and I speak to those, if there are any here present,
who have travelled in the East and have caught the
fascination of its mysterious surroundings—the East is a
University in which the scholar never takes his degree.
(*Hear, hear.*) It is a temple in which the suppliant adores
but never catches sight of the object of his devotion. It is
a journey the goal of which is always in sight but is never
attained. There we are always learners, always worship-
pers, always pilgrims. I rejoice to be allowed to take my
place in the happy band of students and of wayfarers who
have trodden that path for a hundred years. I know that
I have everything to learn. I have, perhaps, many things
to unlearn. But if the test of the pupil be application,
and if the test of the worshipper be faith, I hope that I may
pass through the ordeal unscathed, (*Cheers.*) At any
rate, I have among the long list of names inscribed on the
back of this *ménu* the example of three immediate Eton
predecessors to guide me—of Lord Dufferin (*cheers*), whose
Indian Viceroyalty was but the culminating point in a
career which for over 30 years has been the property less of
himself than of his country (*cheers*), of Lord Lansdowne
(*cheers*), who left India amid greater manifestations of
popularity and of regard and esteem than any departing
Viceroy since the Mutiny (*cheers*), and of my immediate
predecessor Lord Elgin (*cheers*), who has confronted a time
of storm and stress with a fortitude and a composure which
are worthy of the high name that he bears and of the race
from which he is sprung. (*Cheers.*) I know that with
these distinguished predecessors I cannot hope to compete.
But there is one characteristic which I share together with
them, and which we derive from our common part in the
Eton heritage, and that is the desire to be true to the honour
and the credit of that ancient foundation. (*Cheers.*) I am

not so foolish to-night as to utter any vain prophecies, or to indulge in any illusive hopes. But I shall be satisfied if I can carry out the work which they have begun, and if at the end of my time it can be said of me that I have not been unworthy of the traditions of the greatest and the noblest of schools. (*Loud cheers.*)

## DINNER AT THE ROYAL SOCIETIES' CLUB.

### 7th November, 1898.

[Lord Curzon of Kedleston, Viceroy-Designate of India, was entertained at dinner on the 7th November, 1898, by the Royal Societies' Club at their Club House in St. James's Street. Sir Clements Markham, K.C.B., President of the Club, was in the chair, and proposed the toast of the guest of the evening.

In reply, Lord Curzon spoke as follows :—]

*My Lords and Gentlemen,*—Among the parting compliments which have been offered to me before leaving England, there is none which I have accepted more readily, or which I have enjoyed more keenly, than the honour of this evening. For here I have the privilege of meeting and being entertained by a number of gentlemen who are interested in many branches of scientific enquiry, and not least in that one with which alone I can claim to have any practical connection, *viz.*, the science of geography. (*Hear, hear, and cheers.*) It is a commonplace of public life that we all of us have our innocent distractions (*laughter*) ; which, however little we may excel in them, we pursue with an enthusiasm which is at least sincere. A dreadful book was published in London last year in which eminent personages were invited to state what were the amusements with which they occupied their leisure hours. (*Laughter.*) One man said photography ; another man preferred golf (*hear, hear*) ; a third indulged with exhilaration in the composition of some noxious gas ; and a fourth would take his morning dip in the Serpentine. (*Laughter.*) My own distraction for many years has been the study of the geography of Asia in its political and commercial as well as in its physical aspects ; and I can truthfully say that the distinction which in all my life I have most valued, outside the domain of politics, has been that which I received a little more than three years ago from the hands of the Chairman of this evening, *viz.*, the Gold Medal of the Royal Geographical Society. (*Cheers.*) I am afraid that my practical contributions to that science have been small when compared with the illustrious names among which mine is privileged to appear ; and that they in no sense deserve the lavish encomiums which they have received. But I would ask you to remember that they have been achieved under stringent and difficult limitations both of time and opportunity, inasmuch as they have all been contained within the period in which I have held a seat in the House of Commons. If I have not succeeded in reaching the Pole in a balloon (*laughter*) ; if I have not even lived for a number of years among a mythical cannibal tribe in the heart of Australia (*laughter*) ; I have yet endeavoured to compensate for these deficiencies by the assiduity with which I have piled upon the library shelves a number of solid and thoroughly indigestible tomes. (*Laughter.*) I believe that among the Royal Societies of London the Royal Geographical Society, with which alone I have a close acquaintance, is by its educational, its literary, and its exploratory work doing a great service to the nation. It is with a sense almost of stupefaction that I look back upon the geographical knowledge that was taught to me while a boy at school, and on the disgraceful literary productions in which it was enshrined. (*Laughter.*) All this is now changed. A knowledge not merely of topography, but of the physical features of a country, its hydrography, and its ethnology, all of which are essential to an understanding either of its history, or of its problems, is becoming widely diffused, and will eventually, when we have ceased to write Latin elegiacs, or Greek iambics, be regarded as a necessary part of a liberal education. Meanwhile exploration has become more strictly scientific. Works of travel are not mere dilettante narratives of romance. The *fin de siècle* explorer undergoes a preparation of months, sometimes of years, in advance. He acquires the languages of the countries to be visited, he learns the use of instruments, he masters the literature of his problem. Botany, geology, archæology, meteorology—all these occupy his attention.

When he starts forth he is, from the point of view of scientific equipment, *totus teres atque rotundus.* When he comes back he writes a volume, usually of unnecessary length (*laughter*), which adds not merely to the entertainment but to the knowledge of mankind. I may quote as an illustration of this kind of traveller and this sort of work my friend the now famous Swedish explorer, Dr. Sven Hedin, whose great work, recently issued, represents not only years of labour in the territories which he visited, but years also of studious preparation in advance.

The President has spoken in gracious and complimentary terms of my appointment to the high office which I am about to take up. I have said on a previous occasion that I am glad to go to India ; and my main reason for being so is the fact that India has always appeared to me to be the pivot and centre—I do not say the geographical but the political and Imperial centre—of the British Empire. To my mind we are before and beyond all else an Asiatic dominion ; and I venture to think that the man who has never been east of Suez does not know what the British Empire is. Here in Europe we occupy a few small islands that are scattered on the surface of the Northern Sea. We possess a number of carefully selected and well adapted points of vantage along the highways of commerce in the Mediterranean : and we have also a Navy so formidable that it constitutes us the most powerful maritime nation in the world. (*Cheers.*) Elsewhere, in the American Continent, and in the Atlantic and Pacific Oceans, we possess great tracts of territory, amounting in some cases to the size of continents, which are peopled by men of our own blood, flying the same flag, and enjoying the sovereignty of the same Queen. (*Hear, hear.*) Such possessions have been acquired, and such colonies have been founded, not of course on the same scale but on a smaller scale, by other nations. But it is in Asia, and in India, that the great experiment is being made. (*Hear, hear, and cheers.*) It is there that we are doing a work which no other people has ever attempted to do before, and by the doing of which we shall be judged in history. There lies the true fulcrum of dominion (*cheers*), the real touchstone of our Imperial greatness or failure. (*Hear, hear.*)

Why were we first tempted into Egypt? Because it lay on the route to India. What was the reason of our old traditional policy as regards Constantinople and the Turkish Empire? Because their possession by a hostile power was held to be a danger to our Eastern dominions. Why do we maintain an expensive establishment in Persia and exercise a supreme control over the Persian Gulf? Because the former is on the road to India, and because the waters of the latter mingle with those of the Indian Ocean and open a path to Indian shores. What was the origin of our Colonies at the Cape? Because we went by that way to India. Why do we subsidise the Amir of Afghanistan, and why have we twice or three times sent military expeditions into that fateful country? Because it is a glacis of the Indian fortress, on which we cannot afford to permit the lodgment of an enemy. Why are we interested in the forlorn and inhospitable wastes of the Pamirs? And why have such perilous diplomatic controversies arisen in connection with territories so intrinsically abominable and vile? Because they command the northern passes into India. Why did we guarantee the main part of the kingdom of Siam? And why do we take so keen an interest in the fortunes of that picturesque country and in the policy of its enlightened monarch? Because it is one of those border States that are co-terminous with British territory in India and that separate the Indian frontier from a rival European State. Why, in conclusion, do men talk so much about the Upper Yangtse and about Szechuan and Yunnan? Because those provinces are contiguous with Upper Burma, that is, with India itself. I might pursue this subject indefinitely, but I think I have said enough to show how the casual stone, which was thrown into the sea of chance by a handful of merchant adventurers

200 years ago, has produced an ever-extending circle of ripples, until at the present moment they embrace the limits and affect the destinies of the entire Asiatic Continent. (*Cheers.*) I am one of those who think that the Eastward trend of Empire will increase and not diminish. In my belief the strain upon us will become greater and not less. Parliament will learn to know Asia almost as well as it now knows Europe ; and the time will come when Asiatic sympathies and knowledge will be, not the hobby of a few individuals, but the interest of the entire nation. (*Cheers.*)

It is because of the intensity of the conviction with which I hold these views, that all my travels and studies and writings, such as they have been, have been connected with the theme of India and the neighbouring countries. No pleasure has been greater to me than that of wandering along the frontiers of our Indian dominions and of observing the manner in which we there discharge our Imperial task. In doing so I have learned something of the character and temperament of the Native tribes. Those wild clansmen have an individuality that is entirely their own. We have sometimes, I may even say often, been compelled to fight them. We have never fought them gladly, and we have always sheathed the sword with pleasure. For there is a manliness in their patriotism and a love of independence in their blood that is akin to our own. If I were asked what appears to me to be the secret of the proper treatment of those tribes, or of Oriental races in general, I would reply that it consists in treating them as if they were men of like composition with ourselves. I do not mean to suggest that they have the same views, the same scruples, the same precepts, or the same codes as ourselves ; in many instances the diametrically opposite is the case. But there is a common bond of manhood between us, the element of the human in humanity, which holds us together, and is the true link of union ; and it is the recognition of that bond, and the sense of fellowship that it engenders, that have been the secret of the success of every great Frontier officer that we have ever had. (*Cheers.*)

I know that there is a widespread belief in this country that the Oriental is a solemn and reflective creature from whom we are separated by oceans of moral and intellectual difference ; and nowhere has this idea been better expressed than in the magnificent verse of Mathew Arnold, in which he described the contact of the Empire of Rome with the East and the issue of that collision :—

> " The East bowed low before the blast
> In patient deep disdain ;
> She let the legions thunder past,
> And—plunged in thought again."

There is no doubt a great deal of truth in that. It is the note of the Oriental as contrasted with the Western temperament. But I venture to say that, however true it may be of the inhabitants of the soaked and low-lying plains, it is not true, or at any rate it is much less true, of the Highlanders on the outskirts of our Indian dominions. There we find a light-hearted and festive temperament ; we meet with laughter and dancing and song ; above all we recognise the power of a well-organised and well-delivered joke. (*Cheers and laughter.*) When I look back upon some of my experiences, and remember the dinner that Captain Younghusband and I gave to the poor Mehtar of Chitral, afterwards murdered by his brother, or when I recall my many conversations with the Amir of Afghanistan, I recognise that the saving grace of humour is just as much a property of Orientals as of ourselves, and that the man who wants to find a key to their heart and to their sympathies will do well to employ that weapon. (*Cheers.*)

I have also been much struck on my Frontier travels by the character and the work of the young British officers who are there engaged in positions of responsibility or command. It may be thought, perhaps, that I have a natural and even selfish propensity towards youth. (*Laughter.*) So I have. (*Cheers.*) I should be the last to deny it, and I hope I may retain it even when I am old. For of one thing I am certain, that the old men who have rendered

best service to their country have been those who have also
been capable of stimulating, encouraging, and utilizing the
services of the young. (*Cheers.*) It may also be thought
that youth is synonymous with impetuosity. (*Laughter.*)
Nevertheless I have found in those regions just as keen a
sense of responsibility, as cool a judgment, and as wise a
forecast among the young men as I have among their
seniors. In a sense it is even more so in proportion ; since
the young officer who exceeds his instructions, or who takes
the bit between his teeth, has no previous reputation to save
him from the consequences of disaster. We employ, and
we rightly employ, the grey-beards in our councils and in
positions of supreme control ; but on the outskirts of civilization we require the energy, the vitality, and the physical
strength of youth. I look forward with enthusiasm to
being the colleague and the leader of those young men, and
I wish them God-speed in the work that they have undertaken. (*Loud cheers.*)

Then, again, upon the Frontier one sees something at
first hand of the native soldiers of the Indian Empire. I
wish those brave men were better known at home. From
time to time, at a Jubilee celebration or otherwise, we see
detachments of them in the streets of London. But, for
the most part, their services are rendered and their gallantry
displayed in fields that are far removed from the public
gaze at home ; and I doubt if our people here, or if the
nations of Europe have any idea of the magnificent Native
army that we possess. I can only attribute to this ignorance
the utterly inadequate response that has been made to the
appeal for the Indian Heroes' Fund, which was organised
for the relief of the families of those who fought so bravely
for us in the Frontier campaigns of last year. Those men
laid down their lives for us, fighting, in some cases, against
men of their own race, of their own religion, sometimes
of their own family, with as much strenuousness and loyalty
as if they had been British redcoats defending a British
home. (*Cheers.*) But in proportion to the ignorance which

prevails upon this subject is the duty which rests upon those who know to speak. When it is said that we hold India by the sword, be it remembered that that sword is two-thirds forged of Indian metal ; and that in reality we defend her frontiers and fight her battles by the aid of her own sons. (*Loud cheers.*)

My Lords, the march of science and the improvements in steam communication are every day bringing India nearer to ourselves. From one point of view that is a great advantage ; for in proportion as we know more, so shall we misunderstand less, and there will be less chance of mistakes and blunders and crimes. But there is something to be said on the other side also. In the old days a man who went out for an Indian career, whether as Viceroy, or Governor, or in some subordinate post of administration, went out for the work of a life-time. It took him, in fact, no inconsiderable part of a life-time to get there. When Clive went to India in 1742 he was more than a year upon the way ; when Warren Hastings first went out in 1750 he spent from eight to nine months upon the journey, and when he finally returned in 1785 his passage occupied four months and was regarded as exceptionally quick. The average interval between the issue of a despatch and the receipt of a reply was $1\frac{1}{2}$ years. The consequence was that men settled in India, so to speak, for a life-time. They were continued in positions for which they were fitted. They came home for a holiday perhaps once in their career. Right into the course of the present century a Viceroy occupied the Viceregal chair for a period of ten years. There were great advantages in that system. There grew up from it a solidarity of interests between the rulers and the ruled, and a sympathetic and intimate knowledge which was an immeasurable gain in the development and pacification of the country. Nowadays all that is changed. The journey to India is accomplished in a fortnight. An Englishman in India may enjoy six weeks in London, and will be back at

his post in three months from the date at which he left it.
The telegraph repeats to him every morning the news and
the excitements of Europe. Of course this has a freshening
effect upon his intellect ; but it has a disturbing effect also.
The consequence is that he looks less to India and more to
home. He does not merge the European in the Asiatic
interest ; but is the temporary exile who is always looking
to his return home. This is the tendency, perhaps an
inevitable tendency, of our modern system, but it is one
the serious side of which it would be well to recognise.
Anyhow, the term of the Viceroy is fixed. By a practice
which has become almost invariable he cannot leave the
shores of India for five years. During that time he is a
prisoner, though in my case it will be a happy imprisonment,
behind the bars of that gilded cage. Whether the period
of five years is a long enough time for him to do his work ;
whether in that period he can make any lasting impression
upon the tremendous problems that come before him, or
upon the vast populations committed to his care, is a
question which I shall be better able to answer five years
hence than now. Anyhow, they are certain to be the
most crowded and responsible years of his life. As he takes
up the task there comes upon him a feeling that there is
much in it that is altogether beyond his powers, and exceeds
perhaps his most extreme desires. But I believe that he
may confidently rely upon the indulgence and the toleration
of his fellow-countrymen, who are just to their servants
beyond the seas, and that they will echo the God-speed
which you have given to me to-night. (*Loud cheers.*)

## PRESENTATION OF AN ADDRESS AT DERBY.

*25th November*, 1898.

[In the Drill Hall at Derby on Tuesday, the 25th November, 1898, Lord Curzon was presented with a congratulatory address on his appointment to the Viceroyalty of India. The presentation was the outcome of a public subscription among the people of Derbyshire, of which county Lord Curzon is a native, the seat of the Curzon family being at Kedleston, 5 miles from the county town.

In the course of his reply to the address Lord Curzon spoke as follows :—]

There is one aspect of this gathering and presentation which has been a source of great pleasure to me ; and that is that they have been in the main divorced from party politics, or indeed from any political association. I confess that when I was appointed to the post which I am about to fill, I had little right to expect the generous wealth of indulgence with which my nomination was greeted. Owing to the fact that I have recently occupied a rather prominent position in political controversy, that I have been a target into which a good many arrows have been shot, and that I have also myself perhaps fired a certain number of arrows into the targets of others, it would not have been surprising if my appointment had been very severely criticised in the Opposition press. The fact that it has not been so is not due, I am well aware, to any conviction that I am a fit man for the post, but it is due to the feeling of the country that any man going forth to take up that burden is entitled to its unanimous suffrage and support. On the glaring and well-nigh solitary eminence upon which the Viceroy of India stands, it is his duty for five years to represent his Sovereign and his country, to carry on the traditions of a long line of illustrious predecessors, and to convey to the minds of the countless millions who are subject to his sway the conviction that justice and bene-ficence are embodied in his example and are reflected in his rule. (*Cheers.*) If I were asked what are the two qualities which appear to me to be most essential for the adequate discharge of those duties, I would reply 'courage and sympathy '—(*cheers*)—courage to grapple with the many problems that arise in Indian Government, problems which bewilder by their complexity even more than they overwhelm by their dimensions ; sympathy with the Moslem, the Sikh, the Parsee, the Hindoo ; sympathy with every race and class and creed, from the Native Prince who occupies a throne that is assured to him by his loyalty to the sovereign power, to the humble peasant who drives his furrow through the soil in mute reliance on that remote over-mastering power, of the existence of which he is but dimly conscious, but which is to him the security of his industry, his property, and his life. (*Loud cheers.*) I have been speaking of the qualities that are required for that office. I do not claim to possess them. I may be incapable of ever acquiring them. But surely it is better to have ideals and to fail to reach them, than not to have ideals at all. (*Cheers.*) In one respect I feel that, although my wife and I are going to be separated for many years from Derbyshire associations, and from all the connections of the county, of home, and of friends, yet something of Derbyshire we shall carry with us, or something of Derbyshire at any rate we shall find when we land at Calcutta. You will have read in the papers that Government House, Calcutta, was built by Lord Wellesley upon the model or upon the ground plan of the old home of the Curzon family at Kedleston. (*Cheers.*) It is strange by what small events and by what petty coincidences the current of life is shaped and turned. For it is certainly true that it was the fact of that resemblance that first turned my thoughts to the question of the Government of India ; and when I left the doors of Government House in Calcutta on the first and only occasion on which I have visited it in 1887, it made me feel that some day, if fate were propitious and I were held deserving of the task, I should like to exchange Kedleston in England for Kedleston in India. Now that that has come to me, I feel it a great help to know that I carry with me to my new home in that country the good wishes and feelings of those who

have known me for so long in my old home here.  It
will be some time before my wife or I will be among you
again, but while away no higher ambition shall actuate
me than the desire, if I cannot do anything to add to
the glory, at least to do nothing to detract from the
credit, of my native county. (*Loud and continued cheers.*)

LUNCHEON GIVEN BY THE DIRECTORS OF THE
PENINSULAR AND ORIENTAL STEAM
NAVIGATION COMPANY.

*2nd December*, 1898.

[On the 2nd December, 1898, Lord Curzon of Kedleston, Viceroy-Designate of India, was entertained at luncheon by the Directors of the Peninsular and Oriental Steam Navigation Company at their offices in Leadenhall Street. Sir Thomas Sutherland, M.P., Chairman of the Company, presided, and proposed the health of Lord Curzon, who, in reply, spoke as follows :—]

*My Lords and Gentlemen,*—There are several reasons for which I accepted with particular pleasure the invitation of your Chairman. In the first place, I regard it as a high compliment that I should be entertained by the Directors of this great Company, whose name and reputation are known wherever the English language is spoken, and whose Chairman occupies so honourable a position in the mercantile and Parliamentary world, and that there should be present this afternoon so many gentlemen distinguished for their interest or stake in important branches of Indian commerce and industry. Secondly, I congratulate myself that this is a luncheon and not a dinner ; since if there is one thing that can be predicated of a luncheon in contra-distinction to a dinner, it is that a long speech at the former would not only be a private infliction, but would almost amount to a public scandal. (*Laughter, and hear, hear.*) In the third place, I must congratulate my hearers as well as myself that this is positively the last occasion upon which I shall make any public utterance before I leave these shores. (*Laughter.*) I am conscious of a certain tedium in the spectacle of a too long protracted farewell. It is rather like the case of an invalid who is afflicted with some incurable disease, and of whom all hope has been given up, but who still lingers on as if loth to die. There is also a certain air of unreality in a series of speeches delivered about an office and a duty which have not yet been taken up. On the other hand, I have to say in self-defence that I have only been driven to this course of conduct by the insistent hospitality of my friends

(*laughter*) ; and that just as the stomach for fighting of the
old Homeric warrior does not appear to have been at all
impaired by the long speeches that he and his adversary
exchanged on the field of combat before they set to, so I
hope that the compulsory loquacity into which I have been
forced during the past few weeks may not altogether
incapacitate me for action when the time for action arrives.
(*Hear, hear.*)

My Lords and Gentlemen, the Peninsular and Oriental
Company is a great factor in the Imperial connection
between this country and India. (*Cheers.*) I do not refer
merely to the comfort of your ships and the application to
them of all the latest resources of mechanical invention,
nor to the thoroughly and almost exclusively British
character of the establishment that you maintain—although
I may say in passing that I have never voyaged between
this country and India in any other vessels, and that I
hope not to depart from that course (*hear, hear*)—I
refer rather to the efficiency of your organisation and the
character of your service, which are every year bringing
India and England nearer together, and are producing
a solidarity between those parts of the Empire which a
few years ago would hardly have been dreamed of. I was
talking only yesterday to a gentleman who went out to
India on the Staff of Lord Ellenborough less than 60 years
ago. He told me that he left London in November and
did not arrive in Madras till the middle of February. I
should not myself object to such an interval of repose
(*laughter*) ; at the same time it is important in the public
interest to know that one can leave these shores, as I shall
shortly do, and in little more than a fortnight can step
on the quays of Bombay. This close and ever-increasing
connection between India and England has its disadvan-
tages as well as its advantages ; but on the whole the latter
outweigh the former. First among them I would place
the increased defensibility of India, which we owe to the
vast improvements in steam communication. There used

to exist a short time ago a school of opinion, and I daresay
that it exists still, who held that India can only be secured
by overland lines of communication, and by vast trunk
railways traversing entire continents. That belief has
been explanatory of a good deal of our Asiatic policy in
the past. I have never myself been inclined to share those
views. I have always thought that if British troops were
required for India, they must in the main be sent not by
land but by sea ; and that it is in the improvement of our
steam services, and the shortening of the sea route by
every means that science and wealth can effect, in the
maintenance of our unquestioned supremacy in the
Mediterranean, and in the retention of the use of the Suez
Canal, that the true security of our connection with India
consists, rather than in any speculative schemes such as I
have sometimes seen sketched out in the Press. In that
work the Peninsular and Oriental Company has rendered,
and is still rendering, a great and Imperial service, deserving
both of the confidence of the Government and the
gratitude of the nation. (*Hear, hear, and cheers.*)

The Chairman has incidentally referred to India in the
interests of business men as a field for commercial enterprise
and for the investment of British capital in the future.
My own belief is, though I am desirous to avoid
prophesying, that at no very distant date we shall see a
great and perhaps an unexpected development in this
respect. (*Hear, hear.*) No doubt any such advance has
been retarded in recent years by the financial cyclone
through which India has been passing, and by the consequent
dislocation of the whole mechanism of business. But
if we could establish in India anything like stability of
exchange—a great problem to which any outgoing
Viceroy must turn his attention—I believe that confidence
and interest in Indian investments will revive, and that
capital will flow more freely to her shores. In trade and
finance it may perhaps be regarded as a counsel of perfection
to expect any other motives than those of interest and

expediency to be the public guide. But in everything connected with India the consideration of duty and of obligation to me is paramount (*hear, hear*) ; and I am positively amazed when I hear, as I have often done during the past year, appeals made to the Government and to Parliament to lend the credit of this country, and to scatter the money of our tax-payers, in vast and speculative undertakings in foreign countries, with effete governments and tottering institutions, while our own great Dependency of India, so rich in her capabilities, so undeveloped in many of her resources, as well as incomparably more imperious in her claims, is calling—nay, is even clamouring—for our attention. (*Hear, hear.*) I read only a few days ago an astonishing statement made by a foreigner who professes to be a student of English public opinion. He said that every Englishman of authority or knowledge wished to be quit of India and to be rid of that encumbrance. (*Oh !*) I will not argue the case here from the standpoint of moral obligation or of Imperial responsibility, although that is the aspect from which I should prefer to regard it. I will not repeat here my familiar thesis that India is the pivot of Empire, by which I mean that outside the British Isles we could, I believe, lose any portion of the dominions of the Queen and yet survive as an Empire ; while if we lost India I maintain that our sun would sink to its setting. But here, as business men, you will pardon and sympathise with me if I look at the matter also from the sordid point of view of pounds, shillings, and pence. Let us for a moment compare the trade of India with that of our Colonies. I find that the total sea-borne trade of India for 1896-97, which was an unprosperous year, almost equalled that of the whole of our Australian Colonies, and was much greater than that of our South African and North American Colonies combined. Indeed, it constituted nearly one-tenth of the trade of the whole British Empire, and was more than one-third of the trade of the whole Empire, outside of the United Kingdom. (*Hear,*

*hear.*) These are astounding figures ; and if any deduction is to be drawn from them it is certainly not the conclusion that, even regarded from the point of view of self-interest, our Indian Empire is a matter to which we can afford to be indifferent. On the contrary, I believe that India is a vital interest, not merely to the Imperialist whose senses are dazzled by the pageantry of dominion, nor to the philosopher who watches that most absorbing of all problems, the contact of Eastern with Western civilisation, nor even to the moralist, whose aim is the regeneration of those many millions, but to the British working-man, who is presented with an enormous market, and to the Indian working-man, who finds this great outlet for the produce of his labour. (*Cheers.*)

The next thing that strikes me about Indian trade is the extraordinary recuperative power of that country, a faculty which she seems to share with the more familiar cases of France and Japan. There has quite recently been a devastating famine in India; and yet in the first six months after the complete disappearance of famine, namely, from April to September 1898, India exported by sea more produce than in any previous half year ; 31 per cent. more than in 1897, and 14 and 15 per cent. more than in 1891 and 1894, which were the previous years of largest export. I venture to think that these figures are encouraging, not merely to the shareholders of the Peninsular and Oriental Company (*hear, hear*), but to everyone who takes an interest in India. (*Hear, hear.*)

There is another fact which I may mention which also concerns yourselves. Sir George Chesney, in the last edition of his classical work, alluded sadly to the fact that six years ago there were only 18,000 miles of railway completed in India, and that less than 500 miles were opened and only 136 miles sanctioned in 1892. There are now 20,841 miles open and 4,298 in course of construction. Long before I leave India I hope that the total railway mileage will have exceeded 25,000 miles. (*Cheers, and hear, hear.*) You will, I am sure, join me in congratulating my illustrious predecessor,

Lord Elgin, on the manner in which, despite arduous obstacles, he has in this and in other respects successfully laboured for the development of Indian resources. (*Hear, hear.*) With facts and figures such as I have placed before you, there seems no reason to despair in looking to the future of Indian commerce and finance. I at any rate shall lend whatever efforts I can to the furtherance of that end. I rejoice to think that I shall serve under a Secretary of State who has made so close a study of the problems, and is so interested in the welfare, of that great Dependency ; and I am happy to think that I carry with me the good wishes of the very representative audience whom I have had the privilege of addressing this afternoon. (*Cheers.*)

# PART II.

SPEECHES DELIVERED IN INDIA,
1898-1900.

# SPEECHES

BY

# THE VICEROY AND GOVERNOR-GENERAL OF INDIA.

———◆———

## ADDRESS FROM THE BOMBAY MUNICIPAL CORPORATION.

### 30th December, 1898.

———

[Lord and Lady Curzon of Kedleston arrived in Bombay Harbour on the morning of Friday, the 30th December, 1898, and landed about 7 o'clock. Their Excellencies were very warmly received by all classes of the community. They were accompanied by—

> Mr. W. R. Lawrence, C.I.E., Private Secretary,
> Lieut.-Col. A. E. Sandbach, R.E., Military Secretary,
> Capt. R. J. Marker, A.-D.-C.,
> Lieut. the Hon'ble A. V. Meade, A.-D.-C., and
> Lieut. Lord Suffolk, A.-D.-C.

On landing at the Apollo Bunder Lord Curzon was met by the Commander-in-Chief of Bombay, the Members of the Governor's Council, the Judges of the High Court, and a large number of officials. The Municipal Corporation of Bombay, with the Hon'ble Mr. Bhalchandra Krishna Bhatawadekar as President, were also in waiting, and presented an address of welcome to His Excellency, which was as follows :—

We, the President and Councillors of the Municipal Corporation of Bombay, esteem it a privilege to be the first public body to welcome you on landing on the shores of India, as in previous years we have welcomed many of your illustrious predecessors. We consider ourselves fortunate that, in according this welcome, we are able to convey to your Lordship the keen and intense gratification with which all classes of the people, over whose destinies our beloved and revered Sovereign has been pleased to appoint you to rule as Her Imperial Majesty's representative and Viceroy, have hailed the announcement of your fixed determination that in discharging the great trust reposed in you, you will be guided ' by regard for their feelings, respect for their prejudices, and even deference to their scruples,' and, above all, by a frank and generous recognition of 'a common bond of manhood and the element of a common humanity.' We may take leave to assure your Lordship that no people are more responsive than the people of this country to kindness and sympathy, and that no policy is better calculated than the noble and statesman-like policy enunciated by your Lordship to deepen and intensify the earnest and devoted loyalty which the whole Empire entertains for its august Queen-Empress. The

simple reason which your Lordship has stated as the reason which induced
you to accept what is undoubtedly the most onerous and responsible post
under the British Crown, has not a little touched the heart of the country,
and your words that you accepted it because you 'loved India, its people,
its history, its Government, the absorbing mysteries of its civilization
and its life,' are cherished throughout its length and breadth with revivify-
ing gratitude and hopefulness. The country has indeed passed through a
time of heavy affliction and dire distress, when it has been in sore need of
every possible sympathy and consideration. Famine, plague, war, and
earthquake have ravaged the land and impaired its prosperity. Our own
Presidency has, perhaps, suffered most, and our local and provincial
resources have been drained almost to the verge of insolvency. At the same
time, the city has, in the vital interests of commerce and of intercourse
with foreign countries, been obliged to undertake no less gigantic a work
than the sanitary improvement and reconstruction of almost the whole of
it. We venture to hope that our appeals for liberal treatment are likely to
meet with a generous response from the Government of India, and we
respectfully venture to implore your Lordship's aid to start us again on a
renewed career of vigorous progress and improvement, to which this
Presidency has been for more than two years a stranger. In conclusion, we
pray that long life and health may be given to you and Lady Curzon, whom
we cordially welcome along with you, so that you may be enabled to
discharge the duties of your high office with credit to yourself, with honour
to your country and its Sovereign, and with lasting benefit to the millions
entrusted to their care.

    Lord Curzon replied as follows :—]

*Mr. President and Gentlemen of the Municipal Cor-
poration of Bombay,*—I accept with pleasure the address
which you have just read out to me, and I have been struck
by the cordiality and eloquence of the terms in which
it is expressed. No Viceroy can set foot on these shores,
which are to be his home, and the scene of his labours,
for five years, without a keen and almost overpowering
sense of the importance of the vista that opens before him,
or without a corresponding gratefulness for the first
words of welcome that fall from the lips of those over
whose fortunes he is about to preside. (*Cheers.*) To me
it is some slight alleviation of the anxiety in which any
man must be placed at such a moment, that I do not come
altogether as a stranger to your country, and that the
intimate concern which I have long entertained in its
people and problems, and which will be commensurate

with my life itself, is based not exclusively upon hearsay, or upon reading, but upon some small personal acquaintance with India. (*Hear, hear.*) This is the fifth time that I have gazed from the sea upon the majestic panorama of your city of palaces and palms ; and if my previous visits have been those of a private traveller only, they have yet given me an interest, which official experience can but enhance, in your city—itself so worthy a gateway to a land of enchantment—and in its occupations, so typical of the busy industry to which the peoples of India have turned under the security assured to them by British rule. I am glad to note that in this address you speak of the " earnest and devoted loyalty which the whole Empire entertains for the Queen-Empress." My first sentiment in accepting this great office when it was bestowed upon me, was one of pride that it has fallen to my lot to be one of the Governors-General—the fifteenth in number, but I would fain hope not the last—in her long and illustrious reign. (*Cheers.*) Such a recollection fires a wonderful train of memory, for it brings before one a stately procession of names, many of which have passed into the Valhalla of history, and it recalls a period at the commencement of which India was but a scattered dominion, while at its close it is a relatively homogeneous Empire. But it also awakens in the breast of an incoming Viceroy an ardent sense of duty, for it inspires him with the desire to emulate those distinguished predecessors, and to act in a manner not unworthy of that august and benignant Sovereign whom he is privileged to represent. I believe that loyalty of which you speak to the person and the throne of the Queen-Empress to be as widespread as it is profound and sincere. In my eyes it is more than any other factor the bond which holds together in harmonious union the diverse races and creeds of this country, and which secures to them the blessings of internal peace and tranquillity ; and during my stay in India I shall spare

no effort, so far as in me lies, to fortify, to diffuse, and to
encourage that feeling. I have seen it somewhere stated
that I am expected, on this the first occasion that I
speak on Indian soil, to say something of the principles
which are likely to be the basis of my administration. I
hold myself dispensed from any such obligation for more
reasons than one. In the first place, I have, before
leaving England, given halting expression to the spirit,
at any rate, in which I approach this undertaking, and
the fact that you have in your address quoted with
approval some of the sentiments to which I then gave
utterance, leads me to think that I need not repeat them
now. In the second place, it would be presumptuous
to assume that any one Viceroy enters upon his office
with a conception of its duties more generous or more
exacting than his predecessors. (*Hear, hear.*) Each of
them, as he has landed on this quay, has doubtless felt
that he has been summoned to no mean calling, and has
mentally resolved that justice and magnanimity, that
sympathy and prudence, shall be the keynotes of his
administration. I remember that a great countryman of
mine, on being sent to take up a mission, not indeed
comparable with this, but one that brought him into
contact with religions and races different from his own, in
a remote and difficult country, said that he went out to hold
the scales even. Such might be no contemptible motto for
a Viceroy of India. (*Hear, hear, and cheers.*) For with
what a mosaic of nationalities and interests he is confronted ;
with his own countrymen, few in number, and scattered far
and wide under a trying climate in a foreign land, and with
the manifold races and beliefs, so composite and yet so
divergent, of the indigenous population, in its swarming
and ever-multiplying millions. To hold the scales even
under such conditions is a task that calls indeed for supple
fingers and for nerves of steel. But there is another reflection that leads me to place some restriction upon anything that I may say about the future. No one can be

more conscious than myself that the verdict to be passed upon my administration depends not upon glittering promise, or fair prophecy now, but upon actual performance later on. (*Hear, hear, and cheers.*) The time for rejoicing is not when a man putteth on his armour, but when he taketh it off. (*Hear, hear.*) I thank you for your friendly greeting, because no man can be insensible to the encouragement of a generous welcome. But I shall be tenfold better pleased if, when I weigh anchor from these shores, and when all eyes are turned towards my successor, any of you who are now present can come forward truthfully to testify that during my time I have done something, if it even be but little, for this land, which, next to my own country, is nearest to my heart.

Gentlemen, in your address you call my attention to the fact that, during the past few years, India has been subject to the triple scourge of war, pestilence, and famine, and that your own Presidency has suffered sorely from the ravages of the two latter in particular. In England our hearts have gone out to you in your trouble—our purse-strings have, as you know, been unloosened on your behalf. (*Hear, hear, and cheers.*) The unceasing and devoted efforts of your rulers—of the present illustrious Viceroy, and in this place of your Governor, whose application to the onerous work imposed upon him by the plague has excited widespread gratitude and admiration (*cheers*)—have, I believe, enabled India to cope with these trials in a manner more successful than on any previous occasion. (*Cheers.*) In this great city the patience of your people, the voluntary co-operation of your leading citizens, and the natural vitality of your resources, have greatly assisted in the work of recuperation ; and I would fain believe that the corner has now been turned and that an era of reviving prosperity is already beginning to dawn. (*Cheers.*) To that movement it will be my agreeable duty to lend whatever impulse I can ; and it is with feelings of sympathy that I regard, and shall take an early opportunity of enquiring into, the great undertaking to which, with so marked a combination of courage and wisdom you are about to address yourselves in Bombay. (*Hear, hear.*) In conclusion, it only remains for me to thank you for the gracious welcome that you have extended, along with myself, to Lady Curzon. (*Cheers.*) She comes to this country with predispositions not less favourable, and with sympathies not less warm, than mine ; and with me she looks forward with earnest delight to a life of labour, but of happy labour, in your midst. (*Loud cheers.*) Allow me, Sir, to thank you in conclusion for the address, and for the handsome and artistic casket in which it is enclosed. (*Loud and prolonged cheers.*)

## ADDRESS FROM THE BOMBAY CHAMBER OF COMMERCE.

### 30th December, 1898.

[A deputation of the Bombay Chamber of Commerce, headed by the Hon'ble Mr. R. H. Macaulay, the Chairman, waited on Lord Curzon at noon on the 30th December, 1898, and presented him with an address of welcome. Mr. Macaulay read the address, which, after welcoming His Excellency and congratulating him on his appointment as Viceroy, said that his past career, the study he had already devoted to Oriental questions, and his recent public utterances, assured them of the ability and industry he would devote to his duties, and of the noble conception of those duties he had set before himself. It expressed the hope that a sound and automatic currency, either silver or gold, would soon be established, and stated that the attraction of British capital to the country was one of the beneficial results anticipated from a gold standard. It urged, however, that more than stability of exchange was required, and that the Government of India should treat more generously, and adopt more expeditious methods in dealing with, those who were ready to devote time and capital to the development of the resources of the Empire. It also expressed the hope that means might be devised to render some portion of the balances in the Government Treasuries available for trade purposes, at all events in times of monetary pressure. His Excellency's special and personal attention was claimed to the scheme for the construction of the Nagda-Muttra Railway, which the Chamber wished to be included in the Government programme as being of paramount importance to Bombay merchants. Finally a hope was expressed that His Excellency's term of office might be one of peace and progress, undisturbed by any such grave calamities as those which his predecessor had faced with such manly fortitude.

Lord Curzon replied as follows :—]

*Mr. Chairman and Members of the Bombay Chamber of Commerce*,—It is with peculiar pleasure that I have received at your hands, Sir (in whom I recognise an old schoolfellow and friend of my own), the address which you have just read, and the courteous and instructive contents of which I desire to acknowledge. I say " with peculiar pleasure " because, in this great industrial and trading city, which along with a beauty all its own, reminds me of some of the great hives of manufacture and labour in my own country, it seems befitting that the views of the mercantile classes should be placed before me by the authorised exponents of those interests ; and because my experience elsewhere has already brought me into frequent and agreeable contact with

Chambers of Commerce. As Under-Secretary of the Foreign Office at home, and as head of the Commercial Department there, I have, during the past three years, been placed in constant communication with analogous organisations in England ; and I have learned to what an extent the views of Government may be shaped, and their action assisted, by the advice, the authority, and the trained information which such bodies are in a position to afford. I doubt not that a similar experience awaits me in India, and to any representations that you, or associations of like character and influence, may care, from time to time, to address to me, I can promise in advance a respectful and interested attention. You have been good enough to congratulate me upon my appointment to the high office which I am about to assume. I accept your congratulations ; and may I in return ask you to be the recipients by proxy of the thanks of Lady Curzon and myself for the magnificent welcome which we have met with to-day at the hands of all sections of the population of this great city. The continuous miles of people in the streets, and the enthusiasm with which they greeted us, were incidents that will live long in our memory, and that will never fail to revive delightful recollections of Bombay.

Gentlemen, your address proceeds to bring before my notice a number of subjects in which you are keenly interested, but upon which, while you are from the nature of your experience and your occupations qualified to form and to express definite opinions, I shall be doing no injustice to your imaginations if I say that you do not at this stage expect any similar declaration from myself. A Viceroy setting foot in that capacity for the first time upon these shores can hardly be expected, and would be singularly ill-advised, within four hours of his landing, to make a pronouncement upon such abstruse questions as Currency reform, the attraction of British capital to India, the utilisation for commercial purposes of the cash balances temporarily accumulated in the coffers of Government, and the particular railways which ought, or ought not, to be included in the programme of construction. Upon these matters I shall, of course, profit by the counsel of your Governor, and by the advice of the expert colleagues by whom I shall presently be surrounded ; and while studying them, I shall bear in mind the authoritative character of the representations which you have made.

Gentlemen, it only remains for me to endorse the hopes with which you conclude your address, that a period of returning peace and prosperity, of which I think that there are already some signs, may await this recently afflicted country. A sensational administration is the last prospect that any incoming Viceroy can desire, and, although the cup of destiny is filled by other hands than his, he may yet, with a clear conscience, promise, during his term of office, the fullest devotion of which he may be capable to the domestic interests, and to the material development, of the vast populations committed to his care.

## ADDRESS FROM THE PROPOSED SCIENTIFIC RESEARCH INSTITUTE.

### 31st December, 1898.

[On the afternoon of Saturday, the 31st December, 1898, Lord Curzon of Kedleston received a deputation from the Provisional Committee of the Imperial University, or Research Institute, proposed to be established in India for the purpose of post-graduate instruction in the higher scientific and technical branches of learning. The address which the deputation presented said that there had been a long-felt want of a higher course of post-graduate instruction in scientific research for the best students of the Universities, which would enable them to help in the industrial development of the country. About two years before, Mr. Jamsetjee N. Tata had decided to offer property representing a capital of Rs. 30,00,000, and calculated to yield a yearly income of Rs. 1,50,000, on trust for an Imperial University, or Research Institute, which would, with the help of the Government, the Native States and the public generally, supply this want; and after consulting his friends, he had made his offer to Lord Sandhurst under certain conditions. The Provisional Committee had prepared a draft Bill for the approval of the Government of India, together with a scheme of studies and estimates of the probable expenditure. The scheme divided the studies into (1) scientific and technological; (2) medical and sanitary; (3) educational and philosophical; the estimated initial expenditure was about Rs. 15,00,000, and the annual charge Rs. 30,000. Mr. Tata's offer could go but a little way, but it was hoped that if the Government promised support, and the scheme was fairly placed before the Native Princes, the several Local Governments, and the public generally, it would meet with such support as to ensure the chance of its being started at an early date. The address further asked for a grant-in-aid and suggested the amalgamation of the Dholpur Health Institute and the Punjab funds with Mr. Tata's scheme. The Committee expected to issue their appeal shortly, and already the rulers of two large Native States had been approached and were likely to help, but it was felt that the success of such an appeal depended no less on his Lordship's interest and sympathy than upon the measure of support the Government of India might feel inclined to extend to the institution.]

Lord Curzon of Kedleston, in replying to the deputation, said he had carefully examined the representation, and though he could, of course, give no final answer to it, he could, at all events, assure them that the object they had in view had enlisted his warm sympathy. In the first place, he desired to recognise the great generosity and public spirit which Mr. Tata had shown in contributing so magnificent a sum for the promotion of a great public purpose. He himself, though he could lay claim to no special knowledge of the subject, had learnt, in the course of some years' study of Indian questions, that there were gaps at both ends of the educational system of India, and it was the gap at the upper end which Mr. Tata by his generosity was anxious to supply. While he warmly sympathised with the object of the scheme, there were certain considerations upon which, without the least hostility to it, or without committing himself to any unfavourable opinion in regard to it, he was desirous of eliciting information. In the first place, he desired to know if the Committee were satisfied that when they had got together a number of professors with high salaries there would be a sufficient number of pupils for them to teach. He would be the last to say anything against paying professors on the most liberal scale ; at the same time it would be disappointing to have a number of liberally paid professors lecturing to empty classes. Then, again, a good deal had been heard about the number of students turned out by the Indian colleges who found it difficult to obtain remunerative employment. Were the Committee satisfied that, after a number of qualified chemists and scientists had been trained in the proposed institution, any posts would be available for them? He noticed that a reference was made in the memorial to the part that it was hoped the Native Princes would take in assisting the scheme, and something was said about their co-operation with the Government of India. He should like to know what was in the mind of the Committee in relation to this aspect of their scheme, for anything like an effort on the part of the Government of India to influence the Native Princes to contribute to it might be misunderstood. Then there was one branch of the proposed Institute described in the scheme as philosophical and educational, about which he had some misgivings. Was it proposed to expend Rs. 60,000 a year upon salaries of professors to teach such subjects as methods of education, ethics, psychology, history, archæology and so on ?

[Mr. Justice Candy responded to the invitation which his Lordship had given for information on certain points of the scheme, and explained in regard to his Lordship's inquiries as to the educational and philosophical branch, that the idea of the Committee was to give, in the first instance, completeness and rotundity to the scheme, and, therefore, although they scarcely hoped to carry it out at once, they thought it best to include these subjects. His personal opinion was rather in favour of giving more limited scope to the scheme, but the Honorary Secretary was very enthusiastic on this point, and no doubt would later on give to his Lordship the desired information in regard to it. As to the danger of having professors with only an insignificant number of pupils, it was intended only to carry out the scheme by degrees, and as the funds came in, and they quite hoped that as the institution developed, the number of students would increase There were many directions in which he thought employment could be found for the students who were turned out by the institution ; the medical and sanitary service, for instance, would supply a useful career for students in that branch. As to the way in which it was intended to approach the Native Princes, the Committee never contemplated a direct appeal by the Government ; what they hoped was that the Government would express its sympathy with the objects of the scheme and give it their sanction The appeal would then be made by the Committee, who, of course, would look only to the perfectly free and voluntary contributions of the Chiefs.

The Rev. Dr. Mackichan explained that the philosophical and educational branch had been included in the scheme because it was desired to give the institution the character of a University, and it was felt by those members who held that view that the institution would be wanting in that character unless those subjects were included. Dr. Mackichan answered his Lordship's enquiry as to the possibility of finding employment for the students who had passed through the institution by saying that, so far as his experience went (and he had had long experience in collegiate education in Bombay), the graduates of the Bombay University were able, either in the Government service, or elsewhere, to find employment.

Other members of the deputation also offered explanatory remarks, it being further stated that the Dewan of Mysore had written to Mr. Tata stating that he had a fund of about five and a half lakhs at his disposal, which he hoped to be able to apply to the purposes of the scheme, and Mr. Tata entertained hopes of being able also to secure a further sum out of a large bequest which the late Maharaja made for charitable purposes.]

ADDRESS FROM THE TALUKDARS OF OUDH.

*10th January,* 1899.

[On Tuesday, the 10th January, 1899, a deputation of the Talukdars of Oudh waited on the Viceroy with an address of welcome. The deputation was headed by the Hon'ble Maharaja Sir Partab Narayan Singh, K.C.I.E., of Ajudhya, who read the address. The address offered a hearty welcome to Lord and Lady Curzon, and remarked that His Excellency's experience of statesmanship in England, his familiarity with questions of foreign policy, and his deep interest in Eastern affairs, made them confident that he would grapple successfully with the many difficult problems, political and social, every ruler of India had to face, and that his administration would add still greater lustre to his high office. The common bond of loyalty to Her Majesty united the various nationalities of the country, and their actions had shown that this sentiment was deeply seated in their own hearts ; they trusted His Excellency would strengthen the bond. His Excellency had come to the country when it was in a state of peace, but the task of develop-ing the internal resources of the country called for even greater statesman-ship than the showy triumphs of war, and he might feel assured of receiving from the Talukdars at all times that loyal support which they had given to His Excellency's predecessors.

His Excellency the Viceroy replied as follows :—]

*Maharaja of Ajudhya and Gentlemen, Talukdars of Oudh,*—It was within my knowledge before I landed in India that among the agreeable duties awaiting a new Viceroy upon his first taking up the reins of office, is that of receiv-ing a deputation from the Talukdars of Oudh. That body, conspicuous for its representative and influential character, is always among the first to welcome the Representative of Her Majesty the Queen-Empress, and your appearance here to-day is an indication that your attitude remains unaltered, and that, in commencing my administration, I shall receive at your hands the same support which you have consistently accorded to my predecessors.

My studies of Indian history have rendered me fairly familiar with the history of your body, from the time when your relations with the British Government were re-adjusted by the skill and impartiality of Lord Canning, down to the legislation of more recent years. Throughout this period the Talukdars of Oudh have been animated by the same spirit of loyalty and of good sense, which I think it is no exaggeration to say has now assumed almost the fixity of a tradition.

The work of internal administration is, as you justly remind me, one that applies as searching a test to the capacities of statesmanship as the more dramatic issues involved in external policy. There is no standing still in the growth of nations ; and the adaptation of the conditions and environment of life to the increasing stature of a people is a task that calls both for vigilance and foresight. I hope to devote much of my time and energies to this task, the importance of which is measurable by the enormous numbers of those whose welfare it affects in the crowded but often obscure by-ways of industry and toil.

I am grateful to you for having included Lady Curzon in the welcome which you have extended to myself.

## ADDRESSES FROM THE MYSORE FAMILY.

*11th January,* 1899.

[At 3-15 P.M., on Wednesday, the 11th January, 1899, a deputation of the members of the Mysore Family attended at Government House and presented an address of welcome to Lord Curzon. The Hon'ble Sahibzada Mahomed Bakhtyar Shah, C.I.E., headed the deputation and read the address, which welcomed His Excellency, remarking that he had been called to undertake the Government of India at a time when the ball of success in the political world in England seemed to be at his feet, and when a career of the highest distinction seemed to be assured to him there. While His Excellency's predecessors had all been actuated by a sense of duty in assuming office, none had been led to do so for a nobler reason than that which had actuated him, the love of India. His noble words had struck a corresponding chord in the hearts of the members of the Mysore Family, who confidently trusted that his tenure of office would be marked by measures productive of the highest benefit to the Empire. His Excellency's predecessor had had to deal with external and internal difficulties, but it was hoped that Lord Curzon's tenure of office would be marked by continuous peace and by the ever-increasing prosperity of the people. In conclusion, a hope was expressed that His Excellency would regard with compassion the members of the Mysore Family, and that his administration might lead to the further stability of British rule, and to the happiness and contentment of the people.

The Ladies of the Mysore Family also took advantage of the occasion to address Lady Curzon. They referred to the days of their Royal ancestors and congratulated themselves on having secured shelter under the ægis of the British Sovereign. It was a matter of special pride to them that the supreme Ruler of India was of their sex ; and they hoped that His Excellency would show the same kindness to the family as they had invariably received at the hands of his predecessors. The address concluded with the prayer that His Excellency might have a peaceful and prosperous reign, and that Her Excellency might be so blessed as to be able to support and strengthen him in his arduous duties.

The Viceroy replied to the addresses as follows :—]

*Gentlemen,*—It gives me much pleasure to meet the members of so distinguished a family as that to which you belong, and to receive at your hands the cordial words of welcome which have just been read out to me. Previous Viceroys have been approached by you on the occasion both of their arrival in this country, and of their subsequent departure ; and it is only a few days ago that I was reading a report of the friendly interchange of courtesies that has recently passed between my predecessor and yourselves. I hope that the same happy relations may prevail between us, and that I may have further opportunities of improving the acquaintance, which I have already made, with the leading representatives of your ancient line.

Of such experience as I have been enabled to gain by travel in foreign lands, a good deal has been acquired in Eastern countries, and among peoples who are co-religionists of your own. For that faith, and for those who practise it, I have always entertained the highest respect ; and my residence in India will, doubtless, strengthen those feelings, at the same time that it will give me opportunities of testifying an equal interest in all classes and creeds in the Indian continent.

I must, before I conclude, add a few words of acknowledgment on behalf of Lady Curzon to the ladies of your House, for the gracefully-worded address in which they have expressed to her their good wishes and aspirations. It is her desire to follow the noble example set by our gracious Sovereign, whose heart has always gone forth to her subjects in this great Dependency, and who has entered with equal sympathy into the joys and sorrows of the women of India.

Gentlemen, I thank you again for the two addresses.

ADDRESS FROM THE MUNICIPAL CORPORATION OF CALCUTTA.

*11th January*, 1899.

[A deputation of the Municipal Commissioners of Calcutta waited on the Viceroy at Government House at 3-30 P.M. on Wednesday, the 11th January, 1899, and presented His Excellency with an address. Mr. W. R. Bright, Chairman of the Corporation, read the address, which, after welcoming His Excellency, said that he had been called to undertake the Government of India at a time when the ball of success in the political world in England seemed to be at his feet, and a career of the highest distinction assured to him there. While His Excellency's predecessors had all been actuated by a sense of duty in assuming office, he had been led to do so by the love he bore to the country, and, on behalf of the people of Calcutta, the address said that His Excellency's noble words of affection had struck a corresponding chord in their hearts, and they hoped his tenure of office would be marked by measures productive of the highest benefit to the Empire. His predecessor had to deal with external and internal difficulties, but it was hoped that His Excellency's tenure of office would be made memorable by continuous peace on the borders, by the ever-increasing prosperity of the people, and by attention to the problems connected with their well-being. The address expressed confidence that His Excellency would carefully and sympathetically consider the provisions of the Municipal legislation then under the consideration of the Bengal Government, which involved "wide and far-reaching changes and a system differing from the lines of municipal self-government which had been followed in Calcutta during the last quarter of a century."

Lord Curzon replied to the address as follows :—]

*Mr. Chairman and Gentlemen of the Municipal Corporation of Calcutta,*—I have already had the pleasure of being introduced to you on the occasion of my arrival at the Station at Howrah ; and your words of welcome now are but a more formal echo of the friendly reception which you accorded to me then. To a new Viceroy the opening days of his life at Calcutta cannot fail to be fraught with a deep interest ; for, after his long journey from England, here at length he finds himself at the seat of Government and the capital of the Indian Empire, amid surroundings that have been rendered historic by the labours and services of many generations of illustrious Englishmen. It is a spot which long before his term of office has expired, will have become invested in his eyes with all the familiarity and with many of the attractions of home. Here, too, he is brought for the first time into contact with the trained counsellors, by whose assistance he is destined during that period to profit so largely, and with the leaders of a community whose assiduous enterprise has made this city an immense emporium of commerce and one of the leading ports of Asia. From all these points of view Calcutta must be to any Viceroy a place of exceptional and enduring interest.

The opening remarks of your address might lead one to suppose that my resignation of political life in England upon acceptance of the post which I now have the honour to fill involved in your opinion some self-sacrifice. Such is far from being my own view of the case. There is no office in the Government of the Queen-Empress which, in my judgment, should more appeal, I will not say to the imagination, but to the sense of duty and the patriotism, of any of her subjects, than the charge of her great Indian Dependency. I will venture further to say that there is no post in Her Majesty's gift which arouses in a higher degree her personal solicitude and concern. Great in my eyes as were the fascinations of Parliamentary life at home, it was, therefore, in no spirit of self-denial, but with an eager, though humble, anxiety to render some service to Her Majesty and to a country which should be as dear to all Englishmen as it is to the heart of their Sovereign, that I surrendered my seat in the House of Commons in order to devote the best years of my life to the task which had for long been its favourite pre-occupation.

In your third paragraph you speak of the internal and external troubles with which my predecessor, Lord Elgin, was confronted, and which a consensus of opinion, both in India and abroad, concurs in recognising that he met with no common fortitude and sagacity. You then proceed to express a hope that my period of office may be devoid of similar complications, and may be marked by efforts directed to the well-being and prosperity of the people. Such is my own earnest aspiration and desire. But even a limited knowledge of India has confirmed the impression, which I might have derived from the experience of previous Viceroys, that prophecy in Asia, the home of surprises, is a rash and perilous thing, and that the most praiseworthy intentions are liable to be frustrated by the unforeseen, and not always controllable, compulsion of events. I therefore refrain either from promise or from prediction. But I record my ready agreement with your underlying proposition, which I take to be that what India requires is a period of tranquillity for the steady development of her resources, and for the examination, and if possible the removal, of such obstacles as may be found to retard the smooth path of her progress.

I have not yet had time to make myself acquainted with the full details of the municipal problem to which you conclude by inviting my attention. At a later stage it will doubtless come before me ; and I will give to it the thoughtful consideration which its intrinsic importance demands.

Gentlemen, in accepting your address allow me to thank you for the encouragement which it conveys, and to express the hope that during my residence in Calcutta I may be so fortunate as to retain the confidence of the Municipal Commissioners of this great city.

## ADDRESS FROM THE BRITISH INDIAN ASSOCIATION.

### 11th *January*, 1899. ·

[At 4·15 P.M. on Wednesday, the 11th January, 1899, a deputation of the British Indian Association, headed by their President, Maharaja Sir Narendra Krishna Bahadur, K.C.I.E., waited on the Viceroy at Government House with an address. After prefacing the address with special words of welcome to Their Excellencies, the Maharaja proceeded to read the address, which expressed satisfaction at the success of the British arms on the Frontier, and gratitude that the distress of the people during the famine had been mitigated by British philanthropy, by the vigorous administrative measures of the Government, and by the devotion to duty of the Government officials. It deplored the fact that plague had not disappeared from the country. The misapprehension regarding the plague policy of the Government had been shown to be entirely unfounded, and the address expressed appreciation of the conciliatory attitude taken and the generous sympathies shown by the Government in the time of trial. It must have been gratifying to His Excellency that the country was then enjoying profound tranquillity and was in a fairly prosperous condition—the fruits of the good government for which the Association was deeply grateful to the Queen. His Excellency's noble public utterances had given intense gratification, and administrative success of the highest order was confidently anticipated during the period of his rule. Various administrative problems of great difficulty but of extreme importance would be presented to His Excellency for solution, but his loving words led to the hope that no violent changes affecting religious and social organisations, which were not likely to carry the people with the Government, would be made during His Excellency's administration. The interests of landed proprietors and the preservation of the old and influential families of the Province would doubtless receive the Viceroy's careful and sympathetic consideration. There was a consensus of opinion that the scheme conferring the benefits of self-government had so far yielded fairly satisfactory results : whether the basis of the scheme should be widened, the system of representation re-formed, the elective franchise given in proportion to the importance of the individual, were leading questions which would claim His Excellency's earnest attention.

The Viceroy replied as follows :—]

*Gentlemen,*—The address which you have just presented to me, and which I gratefully acknowledge, adds a contribution of no small value to the generous volume of welcome which has been accorded to me upon my arrival to take up the post of Viceroy of India.

It is, I think, the first address that has reached me from an exclusively Indian source ; and it furnishes me, therefore, with the opportunity of conveying my thanks not merely to yourselves but to the many thousands of your countrymen, who throughout India have combined to testify in so marked a manner their loyalty to the Queen-Empress by the reception which they have accorded to her representative.

The Queen has herself enjoined me to profit by the first occasion of expressing her sentiments of warm interest in her Indian subjects; and I shall not assume any undue prerogative if I say that the intensity of those feelings is only matched by the reciprocal attachment and veneration which they have aroused in the bosom of the Indian peoples towards their gracious Sovereign.

I derive additional pleasure from the presentation of your address owing to the fact that, as long ago as 1891, when I was Under-Secretary of State for India in England, I was made acquainted with the influential and representative character of your Association and with the excellent work which it has done.

Your address contains a brief epitome of the recent vicissitudes through which the Indian Empire has passed. Those vicissitudes, comprising, as they have done, the almost simultaneous trials of frontier warfare, plague, and famine, have laid a heavy tax upon the resources of the country and the patience of its inhabitants. The teachings of previous experience and the results of long preparation enabled the Government of Lord Elgin to encounter the famine with greater success than on any previous occasion; and the manner in which these periodical visitations, inseparable from the Indian climate, are now met, constitutes in itself no mean justification of British rule.

The plague has not been similarly stamped under foot; but the methods adopted for its eradication have, I believe, been shaped into the requisite harmony of sanitary precaution with respect for natural susceptibilities.

You call my attention to the interests of the landed proprietors and the preservation of the old and influential families of the province of Bengal. My own inclinations,

whether in England or in India, are conservative in respect
of the land, because I hold that a territorial proprietary long
associated with the soil, trained in its management, familiar
with its traditions, and conscious of its responsibilities, is
an element of stability in a community.    In this respect my
views are but a reflex of that which has been the constant
policy of the British Government in India, and notably in
this Province of Bengal.

The future of self-government in municipal institutions
is, as you justly observe, a question which will claim my
attention.    It would be presumptuous in me as yet to make
any opinion derived from Western experience the basis of
an induction as to the principles or methods which may be
feasible here.    The measure of the growth of any civilized
community is, however, its capacity to assume within safe
and well-ascertained limits the responsibility for its own
regulation ; and in India as elsewhere, there is required for
this problem of political and social evolution not merely the
goodwill of the deponents of power, but the aptitude of the
depositories for the exercise of the functions that may be
committed to their care.    In Eastern countries which are
lacking in the traditions of self-government, the rate of
progress is relatively slow ; but the future historian of India
will record that, during the 40 years which have elapsed
since the direct Government of India passed to the Crown,
it has been steady and sure.

*Gentlemen,* I am much obliged for your address, and
I should like to add one word of personal thanks to
Maharaja Bahadur Sir Narendra Krishna for the graceful
additional phrases of welcome with which he preceded the
printed address, and also for his kindness in remembering
that to-day is my birthday, and in according me his own
felicitations and those of your important Association.

## ADDRESS FROM THE JAIN COMUNITY.

### *11th January*, 1899.

[A deputation from the Jain community waited on the Viceroy at Government House at 4-30 P.M., on Wednesday, the 11th January, and presented an address of welcome. The address referred to the part played by the Jain community in the great civilising work in India during the last 150 years, and remarked that no subjects of Her Majesty were more loyal. One of the noblest features in British rule in India was toleration in religious matters and His Excellency's utterances in England encouraged the hope that, during His Viceroyalty, similar neutrality would be observed.

The Jains, hitherto slow in availing themselves of the benefits of Western learning and science, were now alive to the importance of occidental learning, and were ready to work more earnestly for the advancement of the best interests of the country ; and they hoped that their aspirations and efforts would meet with encouragement and sympathy from the Viceroy.

The Viceroy replied as follows :—]

*Gentlemen,*—Among the various communities who have addressed me since my arrival in India, there is none whose words of welcome awaken a more responsive echo in my breast than the Jains. I am aware of the high ideals embodied in your religion, of the scrupulous conception of humanity which you entertain, of your great mercantile influence and activity, and of the ample charity that has characterised your public and private dispensations. Previous travels in India have also familiarised me with many of your temples, in whose architectural features I have observed a refinement that reminded me of the great days of Asiatic art.

I rejoice to think that under the ægis of British Government you enjoy full toleration for the practice of your faith, and the necessary security for the pursuance of your honourable avocations.

The office to which I have been called will not be one of labour if I continue to receive the sympathy which has been so spontaneously accorded to me, upon my arrival, by all classes in this country.

In the career of any Viceroy, there will be inevitable fluctuations, both in the tide of fortune and in the impulses and attitude of men. But I hope that, whatever form these may take, the feelings of genuine regard which I venture to think prevail between the peoples of India and myself at the opening of my term of office, may not be shaken or impaired.

## LEGISLATIVE COUNCIL.

### 13th January, 1899.

[In opening the proceedings of the first meeting of the Governor-General's Legislative Council at which Lord Curzon presided after his assumption of office, His Excellency addressed the Members as follows :—]

*Your Honour and Gentlemen,*—In taking my seat for the first time at this table, I should like to say, before we advance to the proceedings of the morning, what an honour I conceive it to be to preside over this distinguished and representative body, which is entrusted with the legislative work of the Government of India. I think I may claim a peculiar interest in the work of this Council for the reason that I happened to be the Minister, as Under-Secretary of State for India, who, in 1892, under the Secretaryship of State of Lord Cross, had to conduct through the House of Commons the Indian Councils Bill of that year. To that Bill we owe the enlarged constitution, and, as I believe, the extended usefulness of this Council, and of the kindred, though smaller, bodies in the other parts of India ; and it is, therefore, with exceptional pleasure that I find myself presiding here over a body which I assisted to launch into the later stage of its existence, and in which I feel myself entitled, therefore, to entertain a more than official concern. I hope, Gentlemen, that our deliberations may be characterised by the dignity which has always attended the proceedings of this Council, and that they may redound to the advantage of this country and of its peoples. For my own part, I doubt not that I shall receive at your hands, as my predecessors have always done, the help which your greatly superior experience in Indian matters must put you in a position to afford.

## ADDRESS FROM THE MAHOMEDAN LITERARY SOCIETY OF CALCUTTA.

### 13*th January*, 1899.

[A numerous deputation of the Mahomedan Literary Society of Cal cutta waited upon His Excellency the Viceroy at Government House on Friday, the 13th January, at 4 P.M., and presented an address of welcome.

The address, which was read by Khan Bahadur A. F. Abdur Rahman, after welcoming His Excellency, referred to the foundation and objects of the Society, to its relations with previous Viceroys, and to the Secretary of State's opinion that it represented the best form of Mahomedan feeling in India. The Mahomedan community, it said, deemed it a special gratifica- tion that, beyond his deep and accurate knowledge of Indian affairs, His Excellency had been afforded exceptional opportunities of contact with Mahomedan princes and potentates, and had thereby acquired an intimate knowledge of Moslem history and character in different parts of the world : this. coupled with His Excellency's admittedly high qualities as a statesman, would go far towards enabling him to steer a safe course through the many difficulties inseparable from the administration of India. He might rest assured that, should occasion arise, the Mahomedan commu- nity would not be backward in their duty or fail in their allegiance. They congratulated His Excellency upon assuming office at a time when the clouds had all but vanished, and when the unbroken peace reigning throughout the land would enable him to promote internal peace and financial improvement, and they hoped that when he laid down his office he would be able to point to a reign of prosperity and unqualified success. The address further expressed the hope that His Excellency would receive favourably any representations they might make, particularly those touching the question of the amelioration of the condition of Mahomedans.

The Viceroy replied as follows :—]

*Gentlemen*,—I have already received several addresses from important bodies and associations since my arrival in Calcutta, but I do not know that among them any has been couched in language more felicitous, or has breathed senti- ments more manifestly sincere, than yours. Perhaps the fact that you are the Committee of what I observe is styled a Literary Society may account for your proficiency in the former respect. Your experience of the goodwill and just administration of the British Government has, I hope, inspired the feelings of loyalty and devotion to which I allude. I am acquainted with the history of your Society, which indeed is only a little younger in years than myself, and with the admirable exertions of your late founder. A combination of the resources of Western knowledge and discovery with the teachings of Oriental learning is, as you say, the indispensable condition of an intellectual equipment which shall enable the cultured Mahomedan to hold his own in the competitive struggle of the modern world. Perhaps the Mahomedans of India have been for a while somewhat handicapped in the race by an inadequate supply of the facilities requisite for such a training ; although the great institution founded, after a life-work of honourable activity, by the late Sir Syed Ahmed, and kindred efforts organised, or supported by yourselves, should enable you to recover the lost leeway, and to claim your share in the development of the inheritance of your forefathers. At the same time I am glad to hear you speak with legitimate pride of the wealth of Oriental literature as being included in your curriculum, because the acquisition of the resources of modern science, indispensable though it be, should blind no student to the substantial merits of the philosophy, the poetry, and the ethics of bygone times. Imperfectly as these may conform to the standards of a more progressive age, they have yet contributed no inconsiderable quota to the moral elevation, as well as to the intellectual enjoyment of mankind. To any Mahomedan Literary Society therefore, and more especially to yourselves, whose prestige and influence are so high, I would say, pursue your modern studies, but do not altogether neglect your ancient prophets and guides, and remember that the fountains of an obsolete erudition have not infrequently distilled the precious drops of truth.

*Gentlemen*, no one with the smallest knowledge of India can be ignorant of the great part that has been played in its past by Mahomedan dynasties, Mahomedan literature, and Mahomedan customs. No one with the least appreciation of the present can ignore the powerful and stable element contributed to Indian society by the existing Mahomedan States and communities. I have, as you remark, been so fortunate as to visit on various occasions the courts of most of the principal Mussulman potentates of Asia, and I have, perhaps, thereby acquired some slight insight into the working of your institutions, as well as into the practical application of your religion. I am also aware that Her Majesty the Queen-Empress, whose representative in India I am privileged to be, is the Sovereign of a larger number of Mahomedans than any monarch in the world. All these considerations are an explanation of the peculiar interest which I feel in your community, and of the satisfaction which it gives me to receive your congratulations.

I accept your statement that upon any occasion of appeal I may implicitly rely upon the faithful allegiance of the Mahomedans of India. But I rejoice to think that the happy harmony existing between the various races and religions of this country, which is the glorious outcome of Her Majesty's reign, and the loyalty which is common to them all, are likely, should any emergency ever arise, to enlist in her enthusiastic service not one section alone, but the whole of the peoples, and the votaries of every creed, who own her sway.

It will be with the utmost pleasure, and with profound respect, that I shall receive from you during my tenure of office any representations that you may care to address to me ; and I confidently rely upon such communications to assist me in the task of government, as well as to broaden both my acquaintance and my sympathies with the Mahomedans of the Eastern world.

## ADDRESS FROM THE BENGAL NATIONAL CHAMBER
## OF COMMERCE.

*23rd January,* 1899.

[A deputation of the Bengal National Chamber of Commerce headed by Babu Joy Gobind Law, the President, waited on the Viceroy on the afternoon of the 23rd January with an address. The address said that the community represented by the deputation were most grateful for the advantages and benefits of British rule, which enabled them to pursue their avocations unmolested by foreign aggression or internal dissensions, and so they cordially welcomed His Excellency, as the personification of Her Majesty's authority. The responsibilities of His Excellency's office had been magnified by the recent occurrence of a series of calamities : which owing to the efforts of his predecessor had disappeared or were disappearing, but the enfeebled people of India had been anxiously praying, in view of the coming change in the Viceroyalty, for a statesman with a steady and capable hand and a sympathetic heart, and their prayer had been granted. It was no small matter for congratulation that just on His Excellency's assumption of office signs of returning prosperity were everywhere visible and commercial prospects were brightening, as shown by the sudden rise in the price of Government promissory notes, as well as in that of the shares of numerous joint stock companies.

Among the subjects which would pre-eminently invite His Excellency's attention were the re-establishment of a sound and automatic currency in India ; a permanent provision, so far as might be practicable, against the recurrence of famine by the extension of railways and irrigation works ; and scientific and technical education by the establishment of a sufficient number of technical institutions, whereby the people might be enabled to advance on the lines of agricultural and manufacturing progress and to develop the resources of the country. To those deeply interested in the trade of the country His Excellency's assurance on the subject of railway extension was most welcome. The address concluded with the hope that His Excellency would, by fostering educational and industrial development, and by helping to develop the commercial resources of the country, secure lasting contentment and ever increasing prosperity to the people of India, and so raise in a united and contented India an invincible barrier against all foreign aggression.

His Excellency replied as follows :—]

*Gentlemen,*—I beg to thank you for your address. I will not repeat what I have said, in reply to somewhat similar addresses with which I have been honoured by other representative bodies since my arrival in India, concerning both the circumstances of the country and the requirements of the hour. That India has suffered severely from recent afflictions, and that the task of recuperation should be the first interest of Government, are propositions of universal acceptance, to which I have previously signified my assent. The realization of any such ambition, while subject to vicissitudes which none of us can control, will nevertheless be greatly assisted by the harmonious co-operation of all parties and classes ; and the theory of a common interest in the national progress is one which, though it is in the nature of a truism, I commend to the attention of all sections of the population, native and foreign, as capable of very practical application, both in the efforts of individuals and in the action of the larger units which compose our corporate existence.

In your address you call my notice to a number of subjects which excite your own interest, and which should appeal to mine. I am not disposed to cavil either at the contents or at the order of your enumeration. Relief from the financial uncertainty and fluctuations which have for so long hampered the Government and interfered with trade, by a currency reform which shall give stability to our monetary system, is in my opinion the first step, though I am far from saying that it is the sole step, towards economic and commercial revival in India. While this difficult problem is still under investigation by an expert Committee in London, it is useless, and would be premature, for me to forecast the issue. Nevertheless the symptoms, both here and in England, appear to be not unfavourable to an ultimate realization by the Indian Government of the objects with which the policy now in course of operation was initiated by them a few years ago.

Concerning Railways and Irrigation, I find that my Railway programme has to a large extent been fixed for me in advance by the sanction, which has already been given, to the contemplated expenditure of the next three years. Irrigation, which in my eyes is a problem of not inferior importance, will be one of the first subjects to receive my patient study. A great deal is said in India—

but, as it appears to me, there has hitherto been much more said than done—about scientific and technical education—a topic to which you also allude. I have a word to say to you on that matter in a moment.

I have so far dealt with the subjects which you have yourselves selected for recommendation to me. Will you now allow me to reciprocate the compliment by making some counter-observations to you? Acquainted as I am with the immense resources and teeming population of Bengal, and familiar as I have long been with the quick and receptive intelligence of its peoples, I felt confident on coming here that in this city and province I should find abundant evidence of the application of those advantages to industrial and mercantile exploitation on a large scale. I cannot say that the investigations which I have so far made have altogether confirmed those anticipations. If I take the number of joint stock companies registered in India, I do not find that there has been during the last decade the same development, either in number or in capital, in Bengal, that there has been in Bombay, while in ratio to the total population, which is four times greater in Bengal, it has been considerably less. In joint stock enterprise in Bengal it appears further that native capital plays as yet only a very subordinate part.

If I look to cotton mills, I find similar results. Whereas in 1880 there were 6 mills in Bengal as compared with 44 in Bombay, in 1897 the number had risen to 10 only in Bengal, but to 114 in Bombay ; and whereas in Bombay a large majority are under native, or Parsi management, in Bengal only four are managed by natives, and not one of the latter is a native of Bengal. Jute, it may be said, however, stands to Bengal in much the same relation as cotton stands to Bombay, and affords, therefore, a fairer field of observation. While I am glad to note that the number of jute mills, of which enterprise Bengal enjoys a practical monopoly, is slowly but steadily increasing, I yet find that of the 33 mills in Bengal only one is at present under native management.

In Bengal and Bombay there is the same number of
paper mills, but the capital, the number of employés, and
the production of the Bengal mills are, largely owing to
Government patronage, much greater than in Bombay. On
the other hand, while the mills in the Bombay Presidency
are all owned and worked by natives, those in Bengal are
all owned and worked by Europeans.

You speak in your address of the latent mineral
resources of this country, and I assume, therefore, that you
are alive to their great possibilities, and to the call for their
exploitation. I have accordingly examined the statistics of
coal-mines ; and while I find that six-sevenths of the mines
now worked in India are in this province, yet it appears
that, out of the 50 principal mines, 19 only, and those the
smaller and less important, are owned and managed by
natives.

Finally, I revert to the question of scientific and technical education, and to your recommendation that a sufficient
number of technical institutions should be established to
meet the needs of the people. I concur with you as to the
supreme importance of this aspect of education in India ;
but I would point out that for its successful prosecution is
required, not merely the consent of Government to found
the desired institutions, but also the willingness of pupils
to enter their courses when founded. I have alluded to the
great development of mining in Bengal ; and the opportunities thereby afforded for technical acquirements are already
great, and are constantly increasing. Nevertheless I regret
to find that the mining scholarships in the Sibpur Engineering College are not popular, and that only one student has
elected to undergo a mining course since the scholarships
were established ; although ample encouragement might be
derived by other competitors from the fact that this solitary
aspirant obtained employment on the East Indian Railway
as soon as the period of his training had expired. An even
richer field of employment has, I believe, been opened by
the increasing application of electricity to so many of the

purposes of industry and labour. And yet in spite of attempts to induce students who have taken their B. E. degree to undergo a special training in electricity, only one pupil in the same College selected this course, and he did not complete his instruction. Mechanical proficiency of any kind is sure, in these days of applied science, of its immediate rewards ; and I should like to see the youth of India not merely turning to the lore of books, but qualifying themselves for the strenuous crafts and professions of industrial life.

*Gentlemen,* I have not made these observations to you in any spirit of criticism, much less of reproach. Such an attitude on my part would have been at once ungenerous and unbecoming. But the opportunities of speech that are presented to a Viceroy on occasions such as this, are but ill utilised by him if, while they are taken advantage of by the bodies or persons who are addressing him to state what are their aspirations or desires, he does not with equal frankness submit such reflections in reply as may be present in his own mind. I give utterance to them on the present occasion, because I feel on the one hand that the future development of Bengal largely hinges upon the turn that is given to the professional studies of its rising population, and because in your Chamber of Commerce, which has so frequently and with so much advantage been consulted by the Government, I recognize an agency possessing the power, if it also has the will, to communicate the requisite impulse, and to assist the Government in its supreme task of developing at once the resources of the country and the welfare of its inhabitants.

ADDRESS FROM THE TRADES' ASSOCIATION OF CALCUTTA.

*31st January*, 1899.

[At 3-30 P.M., on the 31st January, a deputation of the Calcutta Trades' Association waited on the Viceroy at Government House and presented him with an address of welcome, which was read by Mr. McGregor, the Master. It referred to His Excellency's previous experience of India, which would be of service in many intricate questions, and expressed the hope that during his Viceroyalty the resources of the country would be largely developed and that peace and tranquillity would prevail. The Association had noted with satisfaction Lord Curzon's belief in the stability of exchange and that the wealth of England should be largely attracted to India, as these would lead to an opening out of her resources and to increased prosperity. India, they said, possessed all the requisites of a self-supporting nation, as shown by its various industrial enterprises. There was an impression that the Government were disposed to obtain their requirements direct from England without first ascertaining whether they could be supplied locally on equally advantageous terms ; but they felt sure that His Excellency would foster local industries and enterprise to the fullest possible extent and so dispel this impression.

The Viceroy replied as follows :—]

I am glad to receive at your hands, Sir, at the termination of what I believe has been a successful year of office, this address of welcome from the Calcutta Trades' Association. Your society represents, as I am informed, with much ability and discretion, the manifold trading interests of this city ; and, as such, it is brought into contact with, and must have an intimate knowledge of, many aspects of industry and business.

I am certainly of opinion that English money should be attracted to India, and that Government should do what lies in its power to encourage that movement. The opposite theory which I have seen argued, *viz.*, that the employment of British capital in India constitutes a drain upon the natural resources of the country, I regard as a mischievous delusion. Capital, both British and Native, is, in my opinion, required for the development of India. Native capital is somewhat shy, and requires to be coaxed. It is not as yet habituated, at least in Bengal, to large ventures, and is satisfied either with landed investment, or in smaller fields with the high rate of interest upon loans which is procurable here. British capital is, therefore, a *sine quâ non* to the national advancement ; and it is, I believe, sound economic policy, as well as good citizenship, to desire that India should become one of its chosen fields of investment, and that this great and expanding dominion should attract some portion of that wealth which appears to be equally at the disposal of the petty and venal republics of the Western hemisphere and the moribund kingdoms of the East.

You tell me that India possesses all the requisites of a self-supporting nation. I am afraid that, at present at any rate, this is the language of hopeful anticipation rather than of demonstrable fact. I have spoken of the absence, or of the timidity of capital. Do we produce silver ? How much native iron ore is smelted in Indian furnaces ? Do not the only rolling mills in India work up imported iron ? I take note of your phrase, therefore, as an aspiration rather than as an assertion, but it may help to widen our outlook and to stimulate our energies for the future.

You proceed to say that there is an impression that a disposition exists on the part of the Government to obtain their requirements from England without first ascertaining whether they can be supplied on equally advantageous terms on the spot. I am glad that this is only an impression ; because an impression is something that is capable of effacement, unless it be well-founded. I have looked into the matter, and I have not so far found sufficient justification for the belief. As long ago as 1883 the Government of India issued special orders to the Local Government to purchase, whenever possible, in the local markets articles of *bonâ fide* local manufacture, and, unless price or quality compelled a different choice, invariably to give the preference to Indian over European manufacture, such preference to extend also to articles locally manufactured from raw material imported from Europe. A schedule was at that time drawn up of all the objects that might be so preferred, and on more than one occasion since, notably in June of last year in the case of articles of iron and steel manufactured in India from imported material, that list received a considerable extension ; while certain firms of high standing, some of whom are, I believe, members of your Association, were selected as qualified to tender for the Government contracts in articles of steel and iron. I find, indeed, that of all the stores purchased by Government, a proportion of one-third, amounting to a total value of 154 lakhs, or over one million sterling, was in 1896-97 procured in India. These consisted of iron, copper, hardware and cutlery, explosives, cotton and silk fabrics, and many other sorts of goods. When the Viceroy drives in a Calcutta-made carriage, with Calcutta-made harness, and writes his notes for this speech on paper manufactured in a Bengal mill, it cannot be said that he exhibits any reprehensible indifference to the patronage of local industry or enterprise. When the British soldier goes into action, or performs his regimental routine in India, in clothing and in foot gear that come from Indian factories, his energies are directed to the defence of an interest the produce of which he carries upon his own person.

So far, therefore, from holding that there is ground for lament, I think, on the contrary, that there is much cause for congratulation, and that India is daily asserting her reasonable pretensions in louder and more insistent tones. While I am here—and I think I may safely say for long afterwards—she will receive from me, in the prosecution of these ever-growing claims, the whole of my sympathies, and as much as may be given to me of strength.

*Gentlemen,* may I thank you, in conclusion, for this singularly beautiful casket, as happy in its symbolism as it is elegant in its execution ? It is a specimen, I understand, of local design and manufacture ; and it reflects, if I may say so, infinite credit upon a handicraft in which I have long been keenly interested, namely, the native silver work of Hindustan.

## ADDRESS FROM THE CENTRAL NATIONAL
## MAHOMEDAN ASSOCIATION.

*31st January,* 1899.

[A numerous and representative deputation of the Cenːral National Mahomedan Association waited on the Viceroy at Government House at 4 P.M., on the 31st January, and presented him with an address of welcome. The Mussulmans of India, they said, yielded to none in their loyalty to the Queen, and were eager and anxious that the expectations awaken in the public mind by His Excellency's recent utterances might be fully realised ; having regard to His Excellency's many eminent and statesman-like qualities, they had no doubt but that he would be equal to the great task imposed upon him. The three questions of perennial importance to the cause of Mahomedan advancement in India were those relating to their education, their employment by the State, and their adequate represent. ation in the Legislative Councils, District Boards, etc. ; it was hoped that these questions would have His Excellency's consideration and sympathy. In connection with Mahomedan education, he would no doubt lend the countenance of Government to the movement for founding a Moslem University in India in memory of Sir Syed Ahmed. Another grave question was that relating to *wakf* properties, the chief source of support and sustenance to a large number of Mahomedan families in the country ; and His Excellency's attention was called to the interpretation which the law. as administered, had legalised in respect of such properties, which had excited alarm in the minds of Mahomedans and regarding which the Association would shortly submit a memorial.

The Viceroy replied as follows :—]

*Gentlemen,*—Your words of welcome to me, upon my arrival in India, and entry upon the arduous duties of my office, are characterised by a sympathetic warmth to which my heart would be dull did it not respond. The first essential, in my opinion, to the orderly rule of a community of one race and religion, and still more of a community of many divergent races and religions, by a governing class of another origin and faith, is the recognition by both parties of that fellow-feeling which substitutes mutual respect for distrust, co-operation for antagonism, and kindliness for social indifference. There are many departments of life, both public and private, in which this spirit may manifest itself with advantage, whether in the official association which the free spirit of British Government opens with so liberal a hand, irrespective of birth or creed, to those who are well qualified among its citizens, or in the more modest but not less obligatory amenities of every-day subsistence.

I apply these reflections, Gentlemen, to a consideration of the topics to which you have especially called my attention. The education of Mahomedans and their employment in the higher as well as in the lower ranks of the State's service, and their adequate representation on public bodies in a scale proportionate to their numbers and capacity, have long been features of the declared public policy of the Government of India ; but the attainment of these ends will also be facilitated by the mutual recognition of the feeling which I have described. My enquiries have acquainted me with the fact that, ever since the days of Lord Mayo, there has been a continuous effort on the part of the State to extend the educational facilities offered to the Mahomedans of India, by encouragement to their language, by additions to the teaching faculty, and by financial aid ; the object being not to create for you exceptional advantages in the struggle of life—for this your own sense of proportion and fairness has never led you to claim—but to remove the drawbacks under which you formerly laboured and to provide for you an open approach to a fair field. For I imagine that upon these principles we shall all be agreed—namely, that the patronage of the State must be regulated in the main by public competition, and by the reward of merit ; and that the true law of progress is not the depression of the educational standard to humour the limitation of the individual but the elevation of the individual to the level of modern competition. In this effort, which has been met by a corresponding activity on the part of the Mahomedans of India, a considerable and gratifying advance has already been made. The latest figures which I have been able to procure show me that, in 1892, when the percentage of the Mahomedan population to the entire population of India was 21, the percentage of Mahomedan scholars in public educational institutions was 19—no great disparity ; while in this Province of Bengal the percentage of Mahomedan population was 32, and that of Mahomedan scholars 25. I believe that these, on the whole, very creditable figures are not as yet reproduced in the higher stages of education, in the professional, technical, and art colleges. But the impulse has been communicated, the movement has begun, and there is no crying "halt" in the modern march of enlightenment and emancipation.

Subject to the principles which I have laid down, I believe that the share given by the State to Mahomedans in its public service, is both just and generous. For the posts which are decided by public competition, descrimination, or selection, is obviously impossible ; but in the case of posts which are filled by Government, by nomination or otherwise, the object is to secure that fair and proportionate representation which you legitimately claim. When the Public Service Commission reported some years ago, it was found that of 2,588 persons engaged in executive and judicial work 1,866, or 72 per cent., were Hindus, and 514, or 19 per cent., Mahomedans ; proportions that very nearly corresponded to the actual proportions of Hindus and Mahomedans in the total population of India at that time, which were respectively 75 and 20 per cent. A revised calculation would probably show figures even more favourable to your community.

Of the representation of Mahomedans on local bodies and District Boards I cannot speak from first hand knowledge ; but Local Governments are expected, in their appointment of nominated Members, to have regard to the due representation of classes and interests otherwise unrepresented ; and I believe that they acknowledge and act up to this obligation. In the Legislative Councils I find that there are two Mahomedans in the Councils severally of Bengal, Bombay, and the Punjab ; and one each in the Councils of Madras and the North-Western Provinces. I have also the advantage of one Mahomedan Colleague upon the Legislative Council of the Government of India. These figures are not fixed, and there is no reason why they should not in your case, as in that of other constituent classes, correspond to the expanding capacity and power of the community. I may summarise what I have said by the remark that the symptoms of Mahomedan advance, educational and otherwise, seem to me to be encouraging ; and by reminding you that while your efforts are watched with a friendly eye by Government, the future rests for the most part in your own hands.

I have not alluded, Gentlemen, to the question of *wakf* properties, because I understand that you propose shortly to address a memorial to me on that subject. As regards a Moslem University in India, if it is intended to carry to a further stage the work already undertaken by the Aligarh College, which has so abundantly justified its existence by the production of a number of first class men, it is a project to which all must wish well.

I am pleased, Gentlemen, to have had the privilege of meeting you to-day ; and I hope that the Deity whom we equally revere may look with blessing upon our respective labours.

ASIATIC SOCIETY.

*1st February,* 1899.

Speaking at the annual meeting of the Asiatic Society on Wednesday night, the 1st February, the Viceroy said that it gave him great pleasure to be present on that occasion. He had come there not in his official garb as patron of the Society, but as a student and writer who had himself profited by its publications, and who was intensely interested in its work and welfare. He was glad to have heard the interesting inaugural address of Mr. Risley, and the account by Mr. Bendall of his recent researches and discoveries in Nepal. The latter was a country of great interest, in which he doubted not that original discoveries would await the future explorer and student. Mr. Bendall's remarks on two subjects in particular had confirmed his own observations in Asiatic travel. The parallelism which Mr. Bendall had noticed between some of the features and practices of Roman Catholicism and of the Buddhist religion in Nepal had been observed in many other countries, and was one of the commonplaces of Oriental travel. He had himself made some study of monastic life and institutions in China, and had made a careful note of the many points of resemblance between the ritual, the theogony, and to some extent even the dogma of the two religions. Perhaps it was this coincidence that in some degree explained the easy entry of the Roman Catholic propaganda into those Asiatic countries. The combination of a sort of nature worship with an æsthetic regard for the beauties of natural scenery had also greatly struck him in Korea, and he gave an account of the annual mission of the State embassy from Soul to pay homage to the Long White Mountain in the north. As regarded the work of the Asiatic Society of Bengal, although he knew that it consisted mostly of voluntary effort, and that they did not spurn the help of amateurs, he yet did not personally regard its work as the mere academic exercise of students. He looked upon it rather as part of the duty which we owed to India. Planted as we had been by Providence upon the throne of the Indies, we were trustees for the world of a literature, an archæology, a history, and an art that were among the priceless treasures of mankind. For nearly 3,000 years there had been a succession of kingdoms, dynasties, races and religions in India, all of them leaving relics of some sort, many of them relics of the highest value, which it was incumbent upon us to examine, to elucidate, and to conserve. It was sometimes said the official in India had nowadays no time for independent study or research. "No time" was always the excuse of idleness, and the busiest man was usually he who had most time at his disposal. He did not, therefore, accept that plea as an excuse for any relaxation in the efforts which so many distinguished members of that Society had made in the past, and during his term of office he meant to do whatever lay in his power to encourage research, to promote study, and to safeguard the relics of the past as a part of our imperial obligation to India.

ADDRESS FROM THE ZEMINDARI PUNCHAYAT.

*3rd February,* 1899.

[A deputation of the members of the Zemindari Punchayat waited on the Viceroy at Government House at 4 P.M., on the 3rd February, and presented an address of welcome. The address was read by the Hon'ble the Maharaja of Durbhanga, who headed the deputation.

The address dealt with the want of a proper system of education among the classes whose interests the deputation represented, and stated that the Western method of judicial administration had been found to be incompatible with the national instinct of the people of India, so that one of the objects of the Association had been to encourage arbitration and mediation in the settlement of disputes through the medium of Punchayat Institutions. The address further expressed the hope that the development of the agricultural and industrial resources of the country and the improvement of the material condition of the people would always find a prominent place in His Excellency's thoughts.

The Viceroy replied as follows :—]

*Gentlemen,*—Many of the expressions in your address, which I gratefully accept, along with the beautiful silver casket in which you have placed it, recall, both in kindliness of tone and in generosity of sentiment, similar passages which I have already acknowledged and commented upon in addresses from other bodies. You will not, I am sure, think me guilty of any insensibility to the flattering character of your welcome if, without reiterating the warmth of my own sympathies and the sincerity of my desire to act up to the high responsibilities imposed upon me, I pass at once to an examination of the points which you bring more specifically under my notice.

I understand that you are dissatisfied with the system of education prevailing at both ends of the social scale with which your property and interests bring you into connection. Of the education given to the ryats, you report that it is inadequate and unsuited to their actual avocations of life. These avocations I take to be in the main the pursuit of agriculture ; and I, therefore, assume that you desire a system which shall better qualify the rural classes for the industry which it will be their life's occupation to pursue. I believe that this also is the view of the Government of India. In recent years great efforts have been made to analyse and to supply the deficiencies in existing systems of elementary education ; and much progress has been made, for example, in the provision of more suitable text-books in what are called object lessons, and in physical instruction. Upon this I have to make two observations : the first that Government ought not to be left to grapple with this problem alone, but that the initiative and effort of private individuals and bodies should be freely placed at their disposal ; the second, that in teaching agriculture we must not lose sight of the still greater importance of training the faculty to understand what agriculture is. The basis of any practical education must be the acquisition of such knowledge as will enable a man to use his senses, to exercise his reason, and to have some intelligent understanding of that which he is required to perform.

As regards the education of the higher ranks, you record your opinion that, as at present pursued, it fails to qualify its pupils for their proper stations in society, or for participation in public life. Now it is true that the system of public school training, as we call it in England, is not indigenous in this country, and is not at once adaptable to the traditions or habits of Oriental society. Nevertheless the Raj Kumar Colleges in various parts of India are now established on a firm footing, and appear on the whole to be producing excellent results. Here, again, I would call your attention to the fact that in England this class of education has been supplied almost entirely by private initiative and without the assistance or support of the State. Should, however, there be any suggestions in this respect which are present in your own minds, and which you think capable of translation into practice, I shall be glad if you will appoint a committee of your own body, with whom I would associate an educational officer to assist in formulating your views for my further consideration.

In your ensuing paragraph you deprecate Western methods of judicial administration as foreign to Oriental instincts and as unfortunate in their results. I have never myself felt any personal attraction towards the law courts of any country, whether Eastern or Western ; and while the lawgiver who evolves order out of chaos has been justly regarded in all ages as a great man, I think that an even greater would be he who could persuade his fellow-creatures to abstain from drinking too deeply of the wells of justice. The thirst is frequently not appeased until it has entailed some exhaustion to the constitution of him who drinks. Litigiousness, however, has always struck me as the result not so much of the temptations of law courts as of the temper of peoples ; and I do not know that it would be altogether correct to say that litigation, according to Western rules, has been found in practice to be abhorrent to the instinct of Eastern peoples. However that may be,—that simple cases should not be taken to the law courts, but should be settled by arbitration, or by some other outside method ; that the costly and dilatory procession of appeals should be discouraged ; and that society should learn to regard the courts as a refuge, and not as a relaxation—these are propositions which few will be found to deny. Your *punchayat* institutions are, I gather, accustomed to deal with questions of a particular character rather than with the cases, or disputes, that commonly end in a reference to courts of justice. But that the Government are keenly interested in the employment of arbitration as a substitute for judicial proceedings, is shown by the Arbitration Bill which has only lately been introduced by one of my colleagues, the Legal Member of Council. I conclude with the hope that the interest thus testified may be met by a corresponding inclination on the part of the people.

*Gentlemen,* I thank you for your good wishes in the career of pleasurable responsibility that lies before me.

IMPERIAL ANGLO-INDIAN ASSOCIATION.

*7th February,* 1899.

[A deputation of the Imperial Anglo-Indian Association waited on the Viceroy at Government House on the 7th February at 3-30 P.M. and presented an address of welcome, which was read by Mr. L. P. Pugh, Barrister-at-Law. The address explained the position of the community represented by the deputation, but said that, though that community might have claims to which His Excellency's attention might afterwards be drawn, their only present desire was to heartily welcome His Excellency and Lady Curzon to the country. A hope was therefore expressed that their Excellencies would enjoy health and strength, that His Excellency would be free from administrative anxieties, and that at the end of his term of office he would have the joy of knowing that the land had been abundantly blessed while he ruled over it.

The Viceroy replied as follows :—]

*Gentlemen,*—Your address differs from every other that has so far been presented to me in this important particular—that while, as you say, there are topics of special interest to you which you might have brought to my notice, anomalies or drawbacks that you might have pleaded to have redressed, urgent measures that you might have desired to recommend, you have refrained from pressing your views upon any such points, and have been content to swell the volume of generous acclamation which has greeted the assumption on my part of the Viceroyalty of India with a contribution which I count as inferior in interest or importance to none of those that I have previously received.

Allow me in the same spirit, Gentlemen, to thank you for your welcome, so gracefully extended to Lady Curzon as well as myself ; to assure you, in my capacity as head of the Government, of my confidence in your loyalty,—a loyalty which, as you remind me, you have not been slow to testify by personal service in the past,—and to wish well to your exertions and interests in the future.

You rightly observe that the community which you represent occupies a unique position, midway between the social extremes of Indian society. In my judgment this is a position which, while not unattended with difficulty, and while accompanied by apparent disqualifications, is yet endowed with some positive advantages. There are many functions in a social economy like that of India which can be best performed by those who have ties of blood with both the European and the indigenous peoples ; and who to the bringing-up and associations of Englishmen, add the familiarity with native character, language, and habits of thought which descent from an Indian parentage, whether recent or remote, can scarcely fail to impart. In particular it seems to me that these faculties should find a ready field of employment in the mechanical industries which are being developed with so much rapidity in modern India, and not least in Bengal. The fact that, on the one hand, Anglo-Indians, by their education and mode of life, are in touch with the European proprietors or managers of such enterprises, while, on the other hand, they must have a closer understanding of the interests and feelings of the native artizans than a foreigner can ever acquire, should render their services in many cases as foremen, or as intermediaries in some capacity or other between the two ranks, of great practical value. I am informed by those who can speak from an experience of many years that such has in many instances proved to be the case. I invite your attention, therefore, to this arena of honourable occupation for Anglo-Indian youths, and I would respectfully represent to your Association that great dignity, and no reproach, attaches to manual labour ; and that the community that succeeds best in the world is that which most speedily determines its true adaptation to the environment in which it is placed.

### ADDRESS FROM THE INDIAN ASSOCIATION.

*7th February,* 1899.

[At 4 P.M. on the 7th February a deputation of the Indian Association waited on His Excellency at Government House and presented an address of welcome. It was read by the Hon'ble Baboo Surendra Nath Banerjee, the Secretary of the Association, and was of considerable length. After expressions of loyalty, of cordial welcome to the Viceroy, and of hopes regarding his administration, it stated that local self-government was already firmly rooted in Indian soil, and that the proposed legislation in regard to the municipal administration of Calcutta had given rise to feelings of anxiety and alarm ; it urged the separation of Judicial and Executive functions in the administration of criminal justice, and the wider employment of natives of India in the higher offices of State ; and it stated that the questions of primary and technical education would not fail to engage His Excellency's full attention  His Excellency's expressed sympathy with the cause of education and his appreciation of its bearing on the development of the country had been gratefully noted, and it was hoped that his name would be associated with the necessary administrative measures to ensure to India the full measure of her growth.

The Viceroy replied as follows :—]

*Gentlemen,*—The address which you have been good enough to present to me covers, I think, a wider field than any of those which it has been my agreeable task to receive and acknowledge during the past month. At the same time it is not one whit behind them in its sympathetic expressions of welcome and in the good wishes which it formulates for my administration.

I need not either allude to or recapitulate expressions which have occurred in previous speeches of my own and to which you have paid the compliment of quotation. I do not know that sentiments gain in intensity, even though they may earn a wider publicity, by frequent repetition ; and I will therefore content myself on the present occasion with saying that I hold by what I have previously said, both of my anxiety to serve this country and its peoples, and of my deeply-rooted conviction that as Great Britain succeeds or fails in India, so to a large extent will she be judged by the High Court of history.

If there is sound reason for not repeating this afternoon what I have so often been called upon to say elsewhere, I have been supplied by yourselves, Gentlemen, with an equally valid reason for not advancing on to new or debatable ground. In your fourth paragraph you justly remark that it would be altogether out of place on an occasion like this to discuss the great public questions of the day, and that you would not be justified in soliciting an expression of my opinions with regard to them at so early a date. I observe with pleasure that your disclaimer in the former respect has not prevented you from conveying to me with considerable amplitude and with abundance of argument, your own views on several of those topics. I say " with pleasure," because while you deprecate discussion or the premature extraction of any pronouncement from me, it must yet be an advantage to me to be made acquainted, as early as possible, with the attitude that is adopted towards these subjects by the important Association to which you belong. I take note therefore of what you say with regard to Local Self-Government, to the separation of Judicial and Executive functions, and to the employment of natives of India in the service of the State ; and while deferring to your canon that any utterance on these questions is not at present called for from me, I may yet be at liberty to add that they are topics which have constantly occupied my attention, and will no doubt, while I am in India, frequently come under my eye. I would observe, however, that they are questions, some of which are of a controversial character, and admit of a good deal of debate ; and which are not settled, even though they be advanced, by a consideration of one side of the case only. It will be my duty to look into both sides and to decide, so far as decision is called for, impartially, and without fear or favour. In the discharge of this duty I cannot always expect to carry with me the assent, or even the approbation, but I hope that I may at least never forfeit the respect, of the community which I regard it as so high an honour, while energy and hope are still strong within me, to serve.

## CONVOCATION OF THE CALCUTTA UNIVERSITY.
### 11th *February*, 1899.

[The Annual Convocation of the Calcutta University, for the purpose of conferring degrees, was held in the Senate House of the University on Saturday afternoon, the 11th February, at 3 P.M. The Viceroy, as Chancellor of the University, presided, and was accompanied by Lady Curzon. The hall was filled with graduates and the general public, amongst whom were many ladies. His Excellency was received at the entrance by the Vice-Chancellor (Sir Francis Maclean) and the Fellows and Members of the Senate, and conducted to the daïs, where he took his seat with the Lieutènant-Governor of Bengal on his right and the Vice-Chancellor and the Bishop of Calcutta on his left. After the degrees had been presented by the Vice-Chancellor, the Viceroy, who on rising was received with applause, addressed the assembly as follows :—]

*Mr. Vice-Chancellor, Ladies and Gentlemen,*—Among the most honourable, and certainly not the least pleasant, duties that devolve upon a Viceroy, is that of presiding as Chancellor at the Convocation of this University. If I may venture to say so, to me the task is one of peculiar gratification and interest, for I will not conceal from you that I am a University man to the core of my being ; and that deep down in me, behind the mask of the official immersed in public affairs, and beneath the uniform of State, there lurks an academic element, ineradicable and strong, connecting me with my old University days, and affecting me with a natural sympathy towards those who, although in different circumstances and under a different clime, can also claim connection with a University. (*Applause.*) It has been reserved for you in fact to put the crown upon an otherwise imperfect academic career. I have been an Under-graduate of a University, a Bachelor of Arts, a Master of Arts, a Fellow of a College, and a Member of Convocation. But a Chancellor I have never been until to-day, and perhaps when Sir Francis Maclean and I some years ago entered Parliament together— a situation which is not very productive of academic repose —we little thought that a day would one day arrive when, clad in fine raiment, we should appear upon a daïs side by side as the Chancellor and Vice-Chancellor of a University.

I must be allowed to congratulate you upon having secured the services of Sir Francis Maclean as your Vice-Chancellor. (*Applause.*) That a Chief Justice of the High Court of Calcutta should be the *de facto* head of your Governing Body, seems to me a very fitting exemplification of the harmony that should prevail between two cognate branches of human knowledge and learning. And may I be allowed also to congratulate myself upon a discovery which I have made from a study of the proceedings on previous occasions, namely, that while but few observations are expected from me this afternoon, the real burden of the performance will fall upon shoulders that are so well fitted to bear it ; in other words, upon the Vice-Chancellor himself. Though I am but a new-comer in this country, I am yet not so ignorant of its educational system as not to know that when I speak of my own connection with a University in England, I am speaking of something very different from the University which prevails here. A residential and teaching University such as Oxford or Cambridge, with its venerable buildings, its historic associations, the crowded and healthy competition of its life, its youthful friendships, its virile influence upon character, its *esprit de corps*, cannot, either in Great Britain or in any country, be fairly compared with an examining and degree-giving University such as yours. They are alike in bearing the same name, and in constituting parts of the machinery by which in civilised countries all peoples work for the same ideal, namely, the cultivation of the higher faculties of man. But they are profoundly unlike in the influence that they exert upon the pupil, and in the degree to which they affect, not so much his profession, as his character and his life. Nevertheless, inevitable and obvious as these differences are, there may yet be in an examining University, and there is in such institutions in some parts of my own country, and still more abroad, an inherent influence, inseparable from the curriculum through which the student has had to pass before he can take his degree, which is not without its effect upon character and morals, which inspires in him something more than the hungry appetite for a diploma, and which turns him out something better than a sort of phonographic automaton into which have been spoken the ideas and thoughts of other men. (*Applause.*) I ask myself, may such a thing be said with any truth of the examining Universities of India? Now, at first sight, it may appear that I shall be met with an overwhelming chorus of denial. I shall be told—for I read it in many newspapers and in the speeches of public men—that our system of higher education in India is a failure; that it has sacrificed the formation of character upon the altar of cram ; and that the Indian Universities turn out only a discontented horde of office-seekers, whom we have educated for places which are not in existence for them to fill. Gentlemen, may I venture to suggest to you that one of the defects of the Anglo-Saxon character is this, that it is apt to be a little loud both in self-praise and in self-condemnation. When we are contemplating our virtues we sometimes annoy other people by the almost pharisaical complacency of our transports. But equally, I think, when we are diagnosing our faults, are we apt almost to revel in the superior quality of our transgressions. There is, in fact, a certain cant of self-depreciation as well as of self-laudation. I say to myself, therefore, in the first place, is it possible, and is it likely, that we have been, for years, teaching hundreds and thousands of young men,—even if the immediate object be the passing of an examination, and the winning of a degree,—a literature which contains invaluable lessons for character, and for life, and a science which is founded upon the reverent contemplation of Nature and her truths, without leaving a permanent impress upon the moral as well as the intellectual being of many who have passed through this course? (*Applause.*) I then proceed to ask the able officials by whom I am surrounded, and whose trained assistance makes the labour of a Viceroy of India a relaxation rather than a toil, whether they have observed any reflection of this beneficent influence in the quality and character of the young men who enter into the ranks of what is now known as the Provincial Service. And when I hear from them almost without dissent that there has been a marked upward trend in the honesty and integrity and capacity of the native officials in those departments of Government, then I decline altogether to dissociate cause and effect ; I say that knowledge has not been altogether shamed by her children ; and grave as the defects of our system may be, and room though there may be for reform, I refuse to join in a wholesale condemnation which is as extravagant as it is unjust. (*Applause.*) But, Gentlemen, when I admit the existence of imperfections, you may say that, as head of the Government, it is my duty to define them, and still more to find a remedy. May I remark in reply that though I have been here long enough to find out that everything is not perfect, I have not been here long enough to dogmatise as to how perfection may be attained. Perhaps in succeeding years I may be able to express opinions which will be less presumptuous than they would be at the present time. On the whole I believe the present system to be faulty, but not rotten, and I feel that cautious reform, and not wholesale reconstruction, should probably be the motto of our action. (*Applause.*) There is one consideration, however, by which I am forcibly impressed. I find myself the Chancellor of this University in virtue of my office as Viceroy of India, and I draw from this fact the not unnatural conclusion that the Government of India assumes some direct responsibility, not merely for this University, the functions of which I am informed, extend over the Central Provinces, Burma, Assam, and Ceylon, as well as Bengal, but also over the entire system of which this University is the exemplar and head. At the same time I am not certain that the Supreme Government applies as close an attention to, or exercises as genuine a supervision over education as it might do. There is no separate Educational Department in the Government of India, as we have in England, with an organization and a staff of its own. There is no official charged with the ministerial or

secretarial management of education alone. May it not be that
we have been somewhat remiss ourselves in the task, and
that we have been expecting the plant to flourish when we ·
have not sufficiently exerted ourselves to trim aud prune its
branches? (*Applause.*)  This only I will say before resuming my seat to-day, that the whole subject of education in
this country, in which I think are involved both the reputation of England and the future of India, will, during my
term of office, have my earnest attention, and that I shall
hope annually to attend at this Convocation, and to show
myself not unworthy of the honourable post which I am
permitted to fill.  (*Applause.*)

It remains only for me to congratulate those who have
received their degrees this afternoon, and to call upon the
Vice-Chancellor to deliver his address.

(His Excellency was warmly applauded on resuming his seat.)

COUNTESS OF DUFFERIN'S FUND.

*3rd March,* 1899.

[The Fourteenth Annual General Meeting of the Countess of Dufferin's Fund took place in the Town Hall on Friday, 3rd March 1899. The Viceroy, who was accompanied by Her Excellency Lady Curzon, occupied the chair. The attendance was unusually large and representative.

The Hou'ble Mr. C. M. Rivaz, C.S.I., presented and moved the adoption of the Report, the motion being seconded by the Hon'ble Maharaja Rameshwara Singh, Bahadur, of Darbhanga. His Honour the Lieutenant-Governor of Bengal moved a vote of thanks to the Viceroy for presiding, which was seconded by Khan Bahadur Moulvi Mahomed Yusuf.

His Excellency then, addressed the Meeting as follows :—]

*Ladies and Gentlemen,*—As this is the first occasion on which I have had an opportunity of evincing my interest in the work of this Fund, I should like to say what a pleasure it is both to Lady Curzon and myself to carry on the work which has been initiated and patronised by our predecessors. I say Lady Curzon and myself, because I must, in fairness, place her in this as in all other matters, in a different and in a superior category to myself. (*Applause.*) It is she who is the Lady President of this Fund, succeeding in that post the three eminent ladies who have preceded her, and who have, I believe, distinguished themselves by the business aptitude with which they discharged the duties of that office; it is she who visits the hospitals; it is she who presides over the Committee which is responsible for the control of this now gigantic organisation; and, so far as I can ascertain, the only function which she does not perform, and from which I think, if I may express an opinion, she wisely abstains, is that of making the speeches on this annual occasion. (*Laughter.*) That function she devolves upon the shoulders of others—the business-like speech she entrusts to the capable hands of Mr. Rivaz ; the ornamental speech she assigns to me. (*Laughter.*) Now, Ladies and Gentlemen, I have not in the short time that I have been in this country had time to acquaint myself with all the minutiæ of the work of this Association in its various branches, and indeed had I done so, and come here this afternoon with a speech packed with details of a laudatory character, the words would have been taken out of my mouth by the speeches delivered by those who have preceded me. But my position being perhaps somewhat different from theirs, I should like to say that my attitude towards this Association and its work is determined by wider outside considerations to which you will perhaps allow me in passing to refer.

There was once a time, now lost in the mist of ages, when the Aryan race, to which both the British people and the bulk of the Indian peoples belong, started forth from their ancestral home and commenced those wanderings which have taken them to such opposite corners of the world. Where that home was nobody knows, and I am not going to hazard a guess. If I did so I should probably find some scholar rising up in some corner of this building to confute me. (*Laughter.*) There are some who say it was in the valley of the Oxus, in the plains of Bactria, or in the uplands of the Pamirs. If it was in the latter, it must have been in a very cold region. (*Laughter.*) There are others who fix the locality in Mongolia or Sarmatia ; in fact there are as many theories as there are students, and much study in this case as in others, leads to weariness of the flesh. However, wherever that home originally was, from it diverged the two great branches of the Aryan stock. Since then the European branch on the one hand, and the Asiatic branch on the other, have passed through many vicissitudes of fate, and fortune, and power. While the kingdoms of Asia were powerful, Europe was still uncivilised. Later on as Asia crumbled, Europe became more strong. At length came a time when the Aryan branch from Europe came back to this country to rule its own kith and kin. They came back as conquerors but as benefactors also ; they came to govern the Asiatic branches of the Aryan family, but they brought gifts in their hand, and they said to these people, " See here, we have for long sojourned in the West, where we have acquired much knowledge and made many discoveries, and we come back to you-to ask you to take a share of these blessings." (*Applause.*)

Now, what were the boons which they brought, and with what have we come to you in India as gifts in our hand ? We have brought to you our religion, our law, our literature, and our science. About some of these gifts some doubts may be legitimately entertained. As regards our religion, there are some who accept it, but there are others—and they are a far larger majority—who prefer their own ; and inasmuch as religion amongst all intelligent persons and races is a matter of free thought and free choice, and should never be imposed by force by one people upon another, we leave you to choose, or to adhere to what you will. (*Applause.*)

As regards our law, we have arrived at a happy compromise. You had a law of your own, which was not so much the work of independent legislators in the past as it was the slowly ripening product of the experience of many centuries and the necessities of your country. We have, I think, done much to amalgamate the two systems—the British and the Indian—and in this way the stately outlines of British jurisprudence have been filled in with the details suggested by the experience and needs of the East.

Then as regards our literature, I think it has taught you many good and ennobling lessons, and I know it has brought you enlightenment, and has taught you the true significance of moral and intellectual freedom. (*Applause.*) But there are here, as in most cases, two sides to the shield, and there are some who argue that, while it has done much to elevate, it has also in some cases done something to unsettle and to disturb.

And now I come to the last boon, which is science, and medical science in particular ; and about this I say that no two opinions can possibly be entertained. There may be prejudices, and there may be scruples arising from long custom, or from ignorance, or from other causes, but doubts there cannot possibly be ; and I say this, that if we had come back to you from the West with our medicine in our hand,

and with that alone, we should have been justified in our
return. For what is this medical science that we bring you?
It is no mere collection of pragmatical or experimental
rules ; it is built on the rock-bed of pure and irrefutable
science ; it is a boon which is offered to all, rich and poor,
Hindu and Mahomedan, woman and man ; it lifts the
*purdah* without irreverence ; and it is so far as I know, the
only dissolvent which breaks down the barriers of caste
without sacrilege. Medical science, indeed, is the most
cosmopolitan of all sciences because it embraces in its
merciful appeal every suffering human being in the world.
Now, our Anglo-Indian poet Rudyard Kipling—and I claim
him as Anglo-Indian, though he is also the property of
the world—our Anglo-Indian poet, in his latest poem—and
I hope and pray, and I am sure you will join in that prayer,
that it will be by no means his last—has thus written :

> " Take up the white man's burden,
>   The savage wars of peace,
>   Fill full the mouth of Famine,
>   And bid the sickness cease."

Well, this part at any rate of the white man's burden,
this portion of the bounty of the Aryan of the West, has
not been ignored by the British in India, and in my view
every hospital that we build in this country, every doctor
that we train, every nurse that we turn out, every patient
that we cure, is a part of the service that we owe to India,
is an element of our duty in this country, is a part of the
home-coming gift which the Aryans of the West have
brought back to their kith and kin. (*Loud cheers.*) For
these reasons it is, Ladies and Gentlemen, that I take so
keen an interest in the work of Associations such as this.

I gather from what I have heard this afternoon, and
from the Report which I have in part studied, that this
Association is steadily winning the confidence of all classes
of the people ; that it is slowly but surely wearing down
the prejudice which it had to encounter, and that it has
already relieved an enormous amount of human suffering.

I am glad to see from the figures supplied to me that it does not interfere with the usefulness of already existing institutions. Had it done so, there would have been cause for jealousy, and there might have been friction; but I find that the class of those whom it aids lies, for the most part, outside those affected by already existing institutions, and that whereas the women who were treated in hospitals and dispensaries in India officered by women are rapidly increasing in numbers from year to year—from 100,000 in 1888, to 600,000 in 1893, and to 1,377,000 in 1897—the figures for women who were treated in Government hospitals and dispensaries in India, officered not by women but by men, are increasing in a similar ratio—2,126,000 in 1888, 3,171,000 in 1893, and 3,756,000 in 1897.

I think these figures are re-assuring, because they show that the two great systems can work side by side without interfering with the work of each other. Speaking in Calcutta, and in the presence of the Lieutenant-Governor, I wish also to offer my congratulations upon the excellent work done in Bengal. The Lieutenant-Governor spoke of this—as he appears to do of all matters of the kind—with almost unnecessary modesty, and he attributed no part of the credit to himself, but ascribed it all to the generosity of those who have subscribed to the fund. But my experience is that people do not subscribe unless there is some conciliatory and popular person to induce them to do so. I know very well in my own case that where I would give one man one rupee, I would give another man twenty, and I am quite sure that the personality of the Lieutenant-Governor, and the interest which he and Lady Woodburn, as well as Mr. Gayer, the Honorary Secretary of the Bengal Branch, have taken in this work, have very largely been responsible for the excellent results obtained. (*Applause.*) I am glad also to notice that in other parts of the country the rulers of some of our Native States—of Cochin and Travancore, as well as of Jeypore, Gwalior, Hyderabad, and Bikanir—have done much to assist the Association with scholarships during past years. I hope these efforts will be continued on their part, and will be imitated by others.

In conclusion, therefore, Ladies and Gentlemen, I would say to my own countrymen, " Persist in your efforts in connection with this Association—efforts all the more honourable from the fact that they are voluntary and unpaid —persist in these efforts because it is part of the service that you owe to the country in which you live, and in which lies your work." (*Applause.*) And I would say to the great and wealthy men of India—" Come forward and show your interest in this great and truly philanthropic work ; give to it from your ample means, exercise what influence you can to support this Association, encourage young women to study and to embrace a medical career, open your homes to the blessings of medical science, which is not the monopoly of one nation, but the handmaiden of all." I am sure that we all listened with interest to the speech of the Maharaja of Darbhanga this afternoon. May I say that it is a pleasure to all of us to observe the manner in which he at this very early age of his tenure of his new dignity, is following in the footsteps of his lamented and admirable brother ? We rejoice that Native gentlemen of high rank, position, and means should come forward to help us, and I hope that the example and encouragement set by him may be followed by others.

I hope, Ladies and Gentlemen, to have many other opportunities, while in India, of showing my interest in the work of this Fund. I have to thank you for the very gracious references to Lady Curzon, and to assure you on her behalf, as she cannot do it herself, that her heart is in this work, and that during the time she is in India she recognises the tie that binds her as a woman to the women of India, and that she will do whatever lies in her power to alleviate and to brighten their lot. (*Loud and continued applause.*)

SUGAR DUTIES BILL.

*20th March*, 1899.

[In the Viceroy's Legislative Council held on the 20th March the Hon'ble Sir J. Westland moved that the Bill to further amend the Indian Tariff Act, 1894, be. taken into consideration. To his remarks of the previous week explaining the character of the Bill he added a reference to a memorial from the sugar planters of Mauritius praying for legislation of the character of the Bill under consideration. After a discussion and the addition of a clause restricting the application of the Bill in certain cases, he moved that the Bill, as amended, be passed. His Excellency the President then said :—]

Before I put the question that this Bill be passed into law, I should like to make a few observations with regard to it. I have been glad to notice the complete unanimity that has prevailed with regard to the Bill in this Council — representative as it is of so many diverse and important interests. The Hon'ble Mr. Mehta indeed would have preferred that this Bill should have been referred to a Select Committee—a contention to which I think that an adequate reply was given by the Hon'ble Sir James Westland. I also understood him to urge that it might have been desirable that further enquiry should have taken place with respect to the subject-matter of this legislation. Well, I have always heard it made a reproach against the Indian Government that it is perpetually conducting enquiries, and very seldom acting upon them ; and that reproach I, at any rate, during my time of administration here, desire to escape.

The answer to my Hon'ble friend Mr. Mehta is that we have been conducting enquiries for a whole year past. We have received representations from every leading Chamber of Commerce in the country, and from most, if not all, the important firms connected with this industry. We have addressed observations to, and received replies from, the Governments of all the provinces and districts of India concerned. We should have had, if my Hon'ble Colleague's advice had been followed, to wait for the best part of another year before we introduced this legislation. We regarded the case as urgent, and we were not prepared to accept such a delay. At the same time I am glad to notice that the Hon'ble Mr. Mehta, although he delivered this criticism on a point of detail, did not withhold his assent, which I am certain that he is prepared to give, to the general principle of the measure. Then we have had on a previous occasion and again to-day a statement approving the Bill from the Hon'ble Mr. Allan Arthur, the distinguished representative of European mercantile interests in this capital ; and finally we have had two speeches from the Hon'ble Mr. Chitnavis and the Hon'ble Mr. Ananda Charlu, which I take it we are entitled to regard as typical of the opinions that are held by those important sections of the Native community which they represent at this table. I am therefore, I think, justified in saying that at any rate within these walls complete unanimity has prevailed with regard to the principle of the Bill.

This complete unanimity here reflects an almost equally complete unanimity outside. There are, it is true, certain interests and certain Chambers of Commerce—Bombay and Karachi I may name—in which those interests are strongly represented, which have not entirely concurred in the necessity for countervailing duties at this stage. Those representations are entitled to due consideration, but it is to be noted that they do not come from the areas where the sugarcane is grown, where the refineries exist, or where the real effect of the bounty system is felt. They represent in the main the interests neither of the producers nor of the consumers, but of the importing merchants. On the other hand, if I regard either the representations to which I have already referred, and which have been received by us from the Local Governments, or the reception which our proposals have met with alike in the English and the Native Press of India, I do not hesitate to say that few measures have ever passed through this Council with a greater weight of qualified and homogeneous opinion behind them.

Now the first point that I desire to emphasise is this—that it is in the interests of India, and of India alone, that this legislation has been proposed by us, and that I have authorised the introduction of this Bill. It may be that our Bill may ultimately affect the action of other countries. It may more immediately touch the interests of certain of our own Colonies as well. The Hon'ble Sir James Westland in his speech to-day has alluded to the representations that we have received from the Colony of Mauritius, a Colony in which, in view of the enormous Indian population that is there engaged in labour, we here are bound to take a close interest, and whose welfare we should be glad, I am certain, consistently with our own, to subserve. It may be that this Bill will set an example of far-reaching significance. By some it may even be regarded as a factor in the Imperial problem. It is from such points of view that we may expect the measure to be examined, and perhaps criticised, in the British Parliament in London. I do not deprecate such examination, or such criticism, conscious that it will not weaken, but will rather strengthen, our case. All I have to say here is that our conduct has not been determined by those considerations. We are exercising our own legislative competence, of our own initiative, though with the sanction and concurrence of the Secretary of State, to relieve India from an external competition, fortified by an arbitrary advantage, which can be shown to have already produced serious consequences upon our agriculture and manufactures and which, if unarrested, is likely to produce a continuous and a dangerous decline.

There is another point upon which I must, in passing, say a word. I have been glad to notice that no one in this Council has ventured upon the argument that we are guilty of an economic heresy in our proposal to meet bounties by a countervailing duty. Bounties are in themselves an arbitrary, and in my opinion a vicious, economic expedient designed in exclusively selfish interests. They are inconsistent with free trade, because they extinguish freedom, and they reverse the natural currents of trade. To meet them by a countervailing duty is to redress the balance and to restore the conditions under which trade resumes its freedom. I do not think that we need pay much attention, therefore, to the mutterings of the high priests at free trade shrines. Their oracles do not stand precisely at their original premium. This is not a question of economic orthodoxy or heterodoxy ; it is a question of re-establishing a fiscal balance which has been deflected for their own advantage and to our injury by certain of our foreign competitors.

Moreover, if the utilitarian basis upon which the doctrines of free trade are supposed in the last instance to rest, *viz.*, that they regard the interests of the greater number, be examined, out of their own mouths would the prophets of those doctrines, in India at any rate, be condemned. For here we are dealing in the case of the sugar-industry with a population the vast majority of which are not consumers of a cheap imported article, but are themselves producers of the raw material, and in their capacity as consumers consume for the most part the article which they have themselves produced and worked up. In other words, the conditions that prevail in England are completely reversed. The majority in England consists of poor consumers to whom it is indispensable that the price of sugar should be low. The minority consists of capitalist producers. On the other hand, the majority in India consists of poor producers whose industry is at stake ; the minority consists of well-to-do consumers of refined sugar who are not likely, in my judgment, to be affected seriously, if indeed they are at all affected, by enhanced prices resulting from our legislation, but who, if they were, could not claim that their interests should override those of the overwhelming majority of the population.

I shall not recapitulate the figures which have been laid before you with so much ability and clearness by the Hon'ble Sir James Westland when he introduced the Bill at our last meeting ; but let me remind you of the facts which have been established in this discussion. They are these :--firstly, that there has in the last few years been an enormous increase in the importation of beet-sugar into India from Germany and Austria—a fact which is unquestionably due to the loss by the American market of those countries in consequence of the imposition of countervailing duties by the Government of the United States in 1897 ; secondly, that in the same period the rupee price of sugar in this country has seriously fallen ; thirdly, that there has been a contraction in nearly every part of India in the area under sugar cultivation, the total reduction being estimated at as much as 13 per cent. ; fourthly, that there has been a widespread and a still unarrested closing of native refineries, a phenomenon which is capable of one explanation, and one alone ; for while it may be argued that the decline in the total area under cultivation may be partially due to other causes, such as famine and the low prices resulting from famine, that this is not the case in respect of the factories which have been closed is demonstrated by the fact that in districts where cultivation has increased, or remained stationary—in other words in districts which have remained unaffected by famine—the refineries nevertheless have been, and still are being, shut.

From these facts it appears to me to be impossible to draw any other conclusion than that this decline in an Indian industry—in which I have seen it stated that two millions of people are employed, and in which the value of the annual crop has been estimated at nearly twenty million sterling—is due to the importation of beet-sugar at a price below the natural cost of production *plus* the cost of transport, in other words, to the unrestricted competition of a bounty-fed article.

Now this is a state of affairs which neither the Government of India nor I, as the head of that Government, from whatever point of view we may regard it, can contentedly accept. If we look at it from the point of view of the agriculturist, we cannot sit still and look on while he is impoverished by the economic exigencies of Continental nations. If we regard it from the point of view of native manufactures, what would be the meaning and value of the speeches which I have made since I came to India about the encouragement of native enterprise, if I were to acquiesce in the tacit suppression of this promising branch of indigenous industry? We ought, on the contrary, I think, to stimulate and to encourage its development by every means in our power. Finally, if I approach the question from the point of view of the Government, while we should be strangely constituted if we could contemplate with equanimity the preventible growth of an agrarian and industrial grievance, which must sharply react upon the general prosperity of the people, we should also be poor stewards of our own estate if we were to acquiesce in a condition of affairs that must detrimentally affect both the land assessments and the canal returns, and in this way jeopardise the ultimate revenues of the State.

These are the grounds—which I have endeavoured to state in their wider rather than in their narrower aspect—that have induced the Government of India to introduce this Bill, and that enable me confidently to recommend it to the acceptance of this Council and of the public.

[The motion was put, and the Bill was passed.]

CALCUTTA VOLUNTEER RIFLES. ·

*22nd March*, 1899.

[On Wednesday afternoon, the 22nd March, His Excellency the Viceroy inspected the Calcutta Volunteer Rifles and distributed the prizes. The proceedings took place in the grounds of Government House and were witnessed by a large number of spectators. After distributing the prizes His Excellency addressed the Corps as follows :—]

*Colonel Jenkins, Officers, Non-Commissioned Officers and Men of the Calcutta Volunteer Rifles,*—Among the many unaccustomed but agreeable duties which I have been called upon to perform since I took up my present office, the function in which I have been privileged to take part this afternoon is not the least strange. In the first place, I, who am essentially a man of peace, find myself for the first time in my life a Colonel, although it is true only an Honorary Colonel. Perhaps, however, when I remember that your actual Commandant, Colonel Jenkins, whom I have pleasure in congratulating upon the admirable work that he has effected in the re-organisation of your Corps, is also sometimes, in the few moments that he can spare from military duties, to be seen in a civilian and even a judicial garb, I may feel rather less uncomfortable than I otherwise should in my novel position. I am also told that it is my duty to make you a speech ; and I am astonished to find that on similar occasions in previous years my predecessors, who were also like myself men of peace, although one of them, Lord Lansdowne, has subsequently blossomed into a Minister for War, delivered to the Calcutta Volunteers rather lengthy and very eloquent orations upon the advantages of Volunteer forces in general, and the merits of this Corps in particular. I assure you that on the present occasion I shall be more merciful.

We are frequently told that it is the duty of all patriotic citizens to be willing to shed the last drop of their blood for their country. I accept this obligation ; and also the chronological sequence which it seems to involve. It is the business of the army, I apprehend, to shed the first drop : of

the Volunteers, including the Calcutta Volunteers, to shed
the second : and of the Viceroy, whether he be an Honorary
Colonel or not, and of the civil administration to shed the
last.

I gather that since the last occasion when this Corps
was inspected by Lord Elgin in the grounds of Government
House, a great change has taken place in its organisation.
At that time—-I am speaking of 1895—the old Administrative Corps of Presidency Volunteers still existed, including
in its composition the Calcutta Light Horse, the Cossipore
Artillery Volunteers, the Calcutta Volunteer Rifles, and
the Eastern Bengal State Railway Volunteers. This organisation I understand to have been superseded by the
present Corps, consisting exclusively of infantry. Meanwhile I gather that the old Presidency Volunteer Battalion
has, under the energetic auspices of Colonel Jenkins, both
changed its character and expanded its numbers and range.
What may be called a departmental organisation has been
applied to it, with great advantage, as it seems to me, both
to the practical utility and to the *esprit de corps* of the entire
battalion.

The amalgamation thus effected by Colonel Jenkins will,
I hope, give a new lease of life and activity to this most
important organisation. It is in my opinion greatly to be
desired that the youths and young men of Calcutta should
voluntarily undertake these duties. Their service is an
evidence of public spirit and of private unselfishness which
entitles them to the encouragement and patronage of the
State. It places every man in this Corps in the responsible
position of being not merely the guardian of his own household, but a factor in the defensive system of the Empire.
As such, I regard it as an honour to be connected with your
Corps, in whose welfare I shall feel a continuous and a
growing interest.

It remains only for me to congratulate you upon the
work of the past season and upon the success of your prize
meeting, at which I learn that my prize was won by the

extraordinary and record score of 291 ; to notice the efficiency of the Armenian boys in their drill in the Lieutenant-Governor's competition ; to compliment your Commander upon the efficiency of his Corps, and yourselves upon the energy of your Commander ; and to wish you every good fortune until we meet again.

[Colonel Jenkins then called for "three cheers for His Excellency the Viceroy" and for "three cheers for Her Excellency Lady Curzon," which were very heartily responded to by the Corps.]

## FAREWELL DINNER TO SIR JAMES WESTLAND AND MR. M. D. CHALMERS.

### *23rd March,* 1899

[On Thursday evening, the 23rd March, His Excellency the Viceroy entertained the Hon'ble Sir James Westland and the Hon'ble Mr. Chalmers at Government House at dinner on the eve of their departure from India. The Lieutenant Governor, the Commander-in-Chief, the Bishop of Calcutta and many of the leading officials of the Government were present, besides many ladies. After dinner His Excellency proposed the toast of the Queen, which was drunk with the usual honours. His Excellency then proposed the toast of the guests of the evening in the following terms :—]

*Your Honour, Your Excellency, Ladies and Gentlemen :*—We meet to-night upon an interesting occasion, although it is not without a tinge of melancholy and regret. I have invited you all here this evening to join with me in bidding good-bye to two public men—colleagues of some of us, friends of all—who are about to leave India, and to devote their great abilities to some other branch of the public service. Of course it is an accident that places me in the position of being their host upon this valedictory occasion, and that lays in my hands the delicate task both of composing their Indian epitaphs, and of wishing them success in whatever incarnations they may choose to adopt in their future career in the West. (*Applause.*) No one, probably, in this room is less qualified than myself to do justice to such a task, for while I yield to none in admiration of the virtues and the qualities that have raised them to their high station, and that have endeared them to all, I must own that until three months ago it was only by reputation that I personally was acquainted with those qualities and with those virtues. Perhaps, at the same time, my brief familiarity with them, whilst it may disable me from speaking with the authority which others in this room might claim, may enable me to feel as well as any how great is the loss which the Government of India, and I, who am the head of that Government, sustain in their approaching departure. (*Applause.*) Now, ladies and gentlemen, there might not appear to be any remarkable exterior resemblance between the careers of Sir James Westland and

Mr. Chalmers, but, at the same time, there is one point of strange and peculiar identity between them. Neither of these gentlemen has been able in the course of a long and varied career to shake off the wonderful and inexplicable, but absolutely irresistible fascination of India. (*Applause.*) Mr. Chalmers first came to this country—although no one who regards him will believe it—as much as 30 years ago. He came as a member of the Civil Service, but he left again in 1872. At a subsequent period he dispensed justice with equal ability upon the Rock of Gibraltar, and in the Borough of Birmingham (*applause*) ; but for him, as for so many others, the East was always calling, and it is not surprising, therefore, to learn that, in 1896, he came back to this country as Legal Member of Council, a procedure by which it is hardly necessary to say that the loss of Birmingham was converted into the gain of Bengal. (*Applause.*) Now, let us look at Sir James Westland. (*Laughter.*) In the middle of his career, for some reason unknown to historians, Sir James Westland retired to the *otium cum dignitate* of a pastoral existence in the colony of New Zealand. (*Laughter.*) But, ladies and gentlemen, it was no good. (*Laughter.*) A man cannot fight against his destiny, and, like Cincinnatus of old, Sir James Westland was presently called back from the plough, or whatever may have been the New Zealand equivalent of that implement (*laughter*), to the guidance of the fortunes of this country. (*Applause.*) Well, in the face of these precedents affecting these two gentlemen, who knows, and who can say, in what capacity, or as the Avatars of what future revelation, they may again reappear in our midst? (*Laughter.*) We may see them again in the flesh in India. (*Laughter.*) I devoutly hope, and believe, that we shall, but even if we do not, it is certain to me that their disembodied spirits will hover over the Department in which they have presided, and will communicate a stimulus and an inspiration to those who are their unworthy successors. (*Applause.*)

Now, ladies and gentlemen, may I touch a little more closely, with your permission, upon the careers and the services of these two gentlemen who are our guests this evening? it is with profound respect that I must speak of the career of Sir James Westland, which began in India at a time, now nearly 40 years ago, when I myself was in what is popularly known as the nursery. Sir James Westland's career has been a remarkable career, and it has been remarkable for its continuity and consistency as much as for any other feature. It has come to my knowledge, for instance, that almost the first act of merit performed by Sir James Westland when he came to India was the writing of a report on the cultivation of sugar, whilst it is a matter of public knowledge that his last act has been the passage of a Bill to prevent the extinction of that useful article. (*Laughter and Applause.*) It may, therefore, be said of his career as it can of no other within my knowledge that it has been equally sweet at the beginning and at the end. (*Laughter.*) It reminds me, indeed, of the famous oration of the great Chatham, who made a speech in the House of Commons which he commenced with the words " Sugar, Mr. Speaker," and when he was greeted with the irreverent titters of the honourable members around him, he proceeded to reiterate with increased animation and anger the word " sugar," until eventually he ended by saying " Sugar, Mr. Speaker, who will dare to laugh at sugar now ?" Now it is in connection with the Financial Department of the Government of India that Sir James Westland's chief services have been rendered. He entered that department as Under-Secretary in the year 1870. He became Accountant-General, Comptroller-General, Financial Secretary, and ultimately Financial Member of Council. In 1881 as Financial Member of Council he devised the system of accounts which is the basis of the present financial organisation of the Government of India. In 1895 he converted the Indian Debt, with the result of an annual saving of nearly fifty lakhs of rupees to the revenues of the State. For full five troublous years he has been the Chancellor of the Exchequer of our Government, and, during that time, he has

been a vigilant guardian of the public purse. (*Applause.*) He
has seen his lean years, but I suspect that sometimes in the
night watches, like Pharaoh of old—an historical character
to whom I would not compare him (*laughter*), except in
this respect that he has known sometimes how to harden his
heart—in the night watches, I am convinced he has seen
visions of the fat years that were to come ; and so it is that
he now retires, I will not say in the odour of sanctity,
because that is incompatible with the sphere of finance
(*laughter*), but at any rate in the comfortable atmosphere
that is engendered by the production of a record surplus
and by the acclamations of a contented people. (*Applause.*)
Ladies and gentlemen, these are no light services, and no
man is capable of rendering such services who has not an
equal familiarity both with the conditions of India and with
the principles of finance. It is to my mind one of the
proudest features of our system that we are enabled to
enlist in the service of India the most capable intellects of
our time, and among such men no man assuredly has
rendered more patriotic, or more far-reaching services to
the Government of India than our guest of this evening.
(*Applause.*) He has been, as I have said, a vigilant guardian
of the public purse, but behind the almost impenetrable
orthodoxy of his superficial aspect there has been, if I may
say so, concealed a temperament which was open to every
petition of mercy and never resisted the dictates of common
sense. (*Applause.*) He now retires from the service of the
Government of India, conscious of the great work which he
has performed, and by which his successors will profit. On
behalf of the public service of this country, of which it is
my pride to be the head, I acknowledge these great services.
I bid God-speed to Sir James Westland as he leaves this
country, and I hope that, in another and not less useful
sphere, India may continue to profit by the abilities which
he has so freely spent upon her behalf. (*Applause.*)

Mr. Chalmers has been for a less time a Member of the
Indian Government, but any one who has heard, even for

the short time that I have done, his logical and trenchant utterances in the Legislative Council of the Government of India, or who has read the masculine record of opinions with which he favours us on paper, must be conscious of the fact that strength goes out of the Government of India because of his departure. (*Applause.*) He has now been summoned to England to draft the laws which a wise, or an unwise, Parliament insists in impressing upon a happy or an unhappy people. (*Laughter.*) It is said that there is no Act of Parliament which is passed, through which it is not possible to drive a coach and four. I believe that to be absolutely true, but, in the presence of Mr. Chalmers, it will only be gallant to assume that that is the fault not of the Lawyer but of the Politician. (*Laughter.*) I hope that sometimes, in the sombre recesses of Whitehall, Mr. Chalmers will look back upon the three years that he spent in listening to the manuscript eloquence of his colleagues in the Legislative Council of the Government of India (*laughter and applause*), and that he will console himself for the bad laws that he is called upon by Government to draft for the Parliament of England by remembering the good laws that he drafted on his own responsibility for the Government of India. (*Applause.*)

These, ladies and gentlemen, are the two friends and colleagues to whom we are met here this evening to say farewell. It is permissible for me to add in the case of Sir James Westland that we equally dedicate our gratitude and our respect to Lady Westland and to her two daughters (*applause*), who during the time that they have been here have made so many friends and will leave such happy memories, and that if I cannot speak of the past or the present of Mr. Chalmers in tones of similar domestic eulogy, it is yet to be hoped that in the more populous and social clime to which he is about to revert, he will make amends in the future ? (*Laughter and applause.*)

Ladies and gentlemen, I ask you to drink the health of our guests of this evening, Sir James Westland and Mr. Chalmers.

[The toast was very cordially received. Sir James Westland and Mr. Chalmers both responded to the toast.]

FINANCIAL STATEMENT, 1899-1900.

*27th March*, 1899.

[The Hon'ble Sir James Westland, Financial Member of Council, introduced and explained the Financial Statement, 1899-1900, in the Governor-General's Legislative Council, on the 20th March, and the discussion on it took place on the 27th idem. The discussion was opened by Sir James Westland, who was followed by the Maharaja of Darbhanga, Mr. Rees, Mr. Smeaton, Mr. Spence, Nawab Faiyaz Ali Khan, Mr. Mehta, Mr. Allan Arthur, Mr. Chitnavis, Pandit Suraj Kaul, Mr. LaTouche, Sir Griffith Evans, Mr. Ananda Charlu, Mr. Rivaz, Sir Arthur Trevor, Sir Edwin Collen, and the Lieutenant-Governor of Bengal. Sir James Westland replied at length, touching upon the various points raised. His Excellency the President then summed up the discussion as follows :—]

I AM glad to think that I need not detain my Hon'ble Colleagues by remarks of any great length. The discussion to which we have listened has been far from devoid of interest ; but although it has elicited differences of opinion, such as may legitimately be expected, it has, on the whole, been marked by an unusual unanimity of sentiment, due, no doubt, in the main to the prosperous circumstances in which we find ourselves, but nevertheless gratifying both to the Government and to the Financial Member, with whose last Indian Budget we are dealing. The official life of Sir James Westland, to whose affecting farewell we have none of us listened without emotion, has been, as he has just told us, indissolubly bound up with the finances of India. This is the seventh Budget that he has introduced into the Legislative Council of Government. Few Chancellors of the Exchequer in England, where the conditions of public employment are more permanent, have introduced a greater number. I doubt if any Indian Chancellor of the Exchequer has introduced so many.

In neither country, I imagine, has any guardian of the public purse been confronted in the course of his official career with more marked vicissitudes of fortune than has Sir James Westland. He is happy, I think, in this—that his fat years have followed upon his lean years, instead of preceding them ; and I can well believe that the anxieties and worries which have distracted him in times past are now forgotten in the glow of honourable satisfaction with which he can regard the termination of his labours, and can congratulate India, not less than himself, that he leaves her upon an ascending plane of mateiial and economic progress.

If the Finance Member in India is chided and reproached for his misfortunes in bad times, at least he should not be robbed of his share of the credit for better days ; and I am sure that Council will cordially join me in assuring Sir James Westland of our grateful appreciation of his long and arduous labours, and in wishing him equal success in whatever work he may set his hand to in the future.

With regard to his speech, to which we have just listened, I would also say this—and I would say it from personal knowledge—that he has represented himself as a much less charitable individual than he really is. To myself it is, I confess, a source of no slight pleasure that the first Financial Statement to which I should have listened in this Council has been one of so gratifying a description. My belief, more than once expressed on previous occasions, in the economic vitality of this country, in the solidity and range of its resources, and in its capacity for an industrial expansion far beyond what has hitherto been deemed possible, is confirmed by the experience of the past year. I recognise that the circumstances have been exceptionally favourable. War has fortunately ceased upon the frontier. There has been a high and an almost uniform rate of exchange. There has been a notable expansion in certain industries. The harvests have been abundant. On the other hand, there have been corresponding sources of depression and alarm in the recurrence of plague, which neither the resources of science nor the utmost administrative vigilance have so far succeeded in defeating, and which has made heavy inroads upon the Imperial as well as upon the Provincial Exchequers. That the net result of these contending influences should yet be a balance of $4\frac{3}{4}$ crores is indicative to my mind not merely of uncommon powers of recuperation, but of a marvellous latent reserve of strength.

We have been criticised in these circumstances for not having proposed a remission of taxation ; and that criticism has found capable expression in more than one quarter at this table to-day. I quite understand, and I do not in any degree deprecate, such criticism. It is the natural and legitimate desire of tax-payers all over the world to obtain relief from what they regard, or at least represent, as their burdens, and to feel the passion for relief swelling in their bosoms in proportion to the apparent existence of the means for satisfying it. I doubt not that the payers of income-tax would have welcomed an extension of the scale of exemption. The Hon'ble the Maharaja of Darbhanga pleaded their cause with great ability, and was anxious for the extension of that scale from R500 to R1,500 ; the Hon'ble Mr. Charlu took much the same view ; and the Hon'ble Mr. LaTouche pleaded for some relaxation of the same system. I may add also that it is equally the desire of Governments not merely to earn the popularity that may result from a remission of taxation—although my experience is that popularity so won is a very ephemeral asset—but also in the interests of good government itself to reduce the burdens upon the people. But there are considerations in this case, both normal and exceptional, which decided us to take the opposite course.

The normal consideration of which I speak was that of ordinary caution. Though I have spoken of the astonishing recovery of the past year, though I believe it to represent a much more than transient improvement in the resources of the country, and though Sir James Westland budgets for a surplus of nearly 4 crores in the coming year, I am yet too conscious of the part played by what I may describe as the swing of the pendulum in the economic world to be willing to sacrifice any portion of a hardly won advantage by being in too great a hurry. The Hon'ble Sir Griffith Evans has reminded us that India is a land of surprises, and these surprises are liable to start into existence equally in the spheres of politics and finance. Even in the more sober atmosphere of England we have had during the past year a startling instance of this phenomenon ; for whereas, in the plenitude of our wealth and substance, the Government of which I was a member a year ago agreed to a remission of taxation by which we forfeited in the case of one duty alone a sum of nearly 1½ million sterling without, so far as I remember, exciting any gratitude from anybody, within the space of a year the balance has so completely swung round owing to unexpected calls that, if what I read in the papers be correct, there will be no cause for surprise should the forthcoming Budget contain proposals for the recovery of considerably more than was then remitted. To reduce taxation in one year and to re-impose it in the next is a condition to which Governments have frequently been driven by unforeseen events. But it is one which it is better to avoid by an excess of prudence at the time than to meet with whatever ingenuity at a later period.

The special circumstances which, more even than these general considerations, decided us against any remission of taxation in the forthcoming year are known to all. It is not unlikely that we may be invited before long to inaugurate momentous changes in the financial system of the Indian Empire. What these changes may be none of us as yet know, and we reserve our entire liberty to examine and consider them when they are submitted to us by Her Majesty's Government as the result of the expert enquiry now proceeding in London. But it must be obvious to the least informed that the prospects of any such change as we may decide to undertake must depend very largely upon the position and the credit that we enjoy at the time in the eyes of the world ; that they will be enhanced by the evidences of financial strength to which a large balance and expanding resources are the best testimony ; and that they might be correspondingly imperilled by any stringency or insecurity here. We may be called upon to take steps that will affect the entire future of Indian trade and finance. We cannot afford, therefore, to slacken our hold upon any implement that may conduce to their success.

There is another respect in which we may be thought to have carried caution to excessive lengths. The Hon'ble Member has framed his estimates for next year upon the basis of a $15\frac{3}{4}d.$ rupee. This has been variously explained as typical of the prudence of one whom I may perhaps without offence describe as ' an old financial hand,' or as prompted by a chivalrous desire to present a larger surplus than is apparent on the surface to his successor. I understand that both interpretations have been repudiated by the Hon'ble Member to-day. May I however add—and I do not think that I shall err on the opposite side of optimism in so doing—that this under-estimation, for so I think it may be called, must not be taken to indicate the least want of confidence on the part of the Indian Government. For my part I have every belief that the rupee will retain throughout the ensuing year the same position that it has done during the past ; and I may even go further and say that I shall be disappointed if we . are not able to invest the $16d.$ rupee with a greater durability than any which it has hitherto attained.

I am glad to have heard in the speeches of those Hon'ble Members who have special knowledge of the circumstances and needs of outlying Provinces, notably in the speech of the Hon'ble Mr. Rees speaking for Madras, and I think, if he will allow me to say so, speaking for interests rather more wide than the railways of Madras, and in the speech of the Hon'ble Mr. Spence speaking for Bombay, a generous recognition of the assistance that has been rendered by the Government of India to those of the subordinate Governments who have been in distress. For a few months before the Budget is finally made up, and while the lips of the Finance Member are still sealed, he is the object either of passionate objurgations or of piteous appeals from those who think that they are going to get less than their

due share of the Imperial superabundance, and who in the
agony of their apprehension not infrequently appeal to the
large-hearted impartiality of the Viceroy to rescue them
from the niggardly prepossessions of the Finance Member.
Such at least has been the experience of Sir James Westland and myself during the past few weeks. Meanwhile the
Finance Member holds his counsel, and behind a front of iron
conceals a melting heart. The result is that, now that the
figures have transpired, it is I believe generally admitted
that we have dealt liberally with our suffering brethren.

The Hon'ble Mr. Mehta indeed argued that inadequate
treatment had been given to his Province of Bombay.
Now let me assure him that I have specially interested
myself in the fate and fortunes of Bombay. I have been in
frequent correspondence with its Governor on the subject,
and I have been most anxious that financial justice should be
tempered with some financial mercy. I believe that the
Government of Bombay are themselves on the whole content
with the treatment meted out to them ; and I was glad to
find that the Hon'ble Member, although he commenced his
remarks in a tone of criticism, ended them in a spirit of
generous, and I might almost say of wholesale, congratulation. The ordinary grants, as I may call them, that we have
made to the Provincial Governments, in relief of the heavy
burdens which have been laid upon them by the direct charges
of plague and famine, amount to 42 lakhs. We have given
to them in addition an extraordinary sum of 70 lakhs, a gift
which, while it is no criterion of ordinary opportunities or
deserts, and while it must not be interpreted by them as a
precedent upon which they can rely, is yet, I hope, fairly
proportionate on the present occasion both to our abundance
and to their needs. The Provincial Contract System is one
for the successful working of which a good deal of consideration is required at both ends of the scale ; and I hope that
the Provincial Governments while they press upon us the
obligations of munificence, will not lose sight of the corresponding obligation of economy.

I am entirely in agreement with some of the remarks that fell from the Hon'ble Mr. Arthur with respect to the present high rate of telegraphic charges. I regard that rate as inimical to trade, as being a barrier to the evergrowing intercourse between India and the mother country, and as being obsolete and anomalous in itself. I have already considered the question, and I may say that I have placed it in a category of twelve important questions, all of them waiting to be taken up, all of them questions which ought to have been taken up long ago, and to which, as soon as I have the time, I propose to address myself. What these questions are I do not propose to relieve the curiosity of Hon'ble Members by now informing them. It is conceivable that I may have to add a thirteenth to their number in respect of the appeal of the Hon'ble Sir Griffith Evans with regard to the Small Cause Court Judges in the mofussil. That is a question with which I am necessarily not myself familiar, but, while I understand the Finance Minister to have answered him on the point of finance, the impression left on me by Sir Griffith Evans' remarks was this, that he was arguing the case not from the point of view of pay but from that of character. It is from that point of view that the question is deserving of the attention of the Indian Government, which attention I shall be glad to give to it. But another question has been raised by an Hon'ble Member sitting at this table which I am unable to add to the dozen already alluded to. I am unable to add to it the suggession of the Hon'ble Mr. Chitnavis that I should acquiesce in the reduction of the British soldiers in India. I can assure him that no such proposal will form part of the programme of the Government of India during my time.

As regards Railways, Sir James Westland has indicated in his Budget Statement that for the moment our motto is *estina lente*, although this must not be taken to mark any policy of revulsion from that which has lately been pursued. There are times, however, at which it is desirable to go a little slower than the maximum pace. I am, however, rather in sympathy with what fell from the Maharaja of Darbhanga concerning the encouragement of light gauge feeder railways; and since I came here I have authorized the construction of some hundreds of miles of such lines. I should say in this context that one of the subjects to which I propose to turn my attention while at Simla is the whole question of the policy of Government in respect of railways in India, and our attitude towards private enterprise in particular. I am not satisfied with a condition of affairs which lays the Indian Government open to the charge—whether it be true or false I have not as yet the knowledge that enables me to pronounce—of indifference to the offers of assistance that are made to it, and of hostility to the investment of British capital in the country. We may hope much from fixity of exchange if we can succeed in establishing it. I should be glad if the Government could at the same time by its own attitude encourage what I hope may before long be a pronounced inclination towards India of the financial currents in the mercantile world.

The subject of Irrigation is one that appeals very closely to my concern. We are all familiar with the aphorism about the service of the statesman who can make two blades of grass to grow where only one grew before, and in India we do not need to be reminded of the direct and almost immediate benefit to the agrarian class that results from an increase in the area of cultivation. I shall not embark upon any discussion of the rival advantages of irrigation and railways, because such a discussion would not be germane to this debate, and is in reality futile. The Government of India has never been inclined to balance its duties in these respects one against the other, and would, I think, be unwise to do so. Nevertheless the annual allotment of 75 lakhs which has for some time been made to irrigation might, I think, with advantage be extended; and I have persuaded Sir James Westland in his estimate for the forthcoming year to give me another 10 lakhs for that purpose. I had asked for more, and he would have been willing to give me more. But a scheme of irrigation is not a project upon which you can start quite as expeditiously or as easily as you can upon a railroad. In the first place, the best areas for the purpose have already been utilised. Fresh schemes are likely to be less profitable, and therefore require more consideration, than their predecessors. In the next place, very careful surveys require to be made, levels have to be taken, a staff must be got together, an investigation of existing rights has in all probability to be undertaken. It is not the case, therefore, as is sometimes imagined, that as soon as the cheque is drawn, it can at once, so to speak, be cashed in terms of tanks and canals. For these reasons it has been found that we are not in a position in the forthcoming year to spend more than an additional 10 lakhs upon irrigation ; although in succeeding years, if our finances continue to flourish, I hope that we may present to you a more extended programme. I am about, in the course of a visit to the Punjab, to inspect the great irrigation works that have been taken from the Chenab River, and which were favourably alluded to in the speech of the Hon'ble Pandit Suraj Kaul, and I shall hope to learn a good deal there both concerning the present system and as to future requirements.

It only remains for me to thank you for your co-operation in the labours of the session which is now about to conclude, to terminate this discussion, and to announce that this Council is adjourned *sine die.*

ADDRESS FROM THE MUNICIPAL COMMITTEE OF LAHORE.

*30th March*, 1899.

[A deputation of the Municipal Committee of Lahore waited on the Viceroy on Wednesday, the 30th March, at 11 A.M., at Government House, Lahore, and presented him with an address of welcome. His Excellency was attended by the members of his staff and accompanied by the Lieutenant-Governor and his staff. Mr. G. C. Walker, Deputy Commissioner of Lahore, who headed the deputation, read the address, which, after expressions of welcome, went on to remark that since the last occasion on which a Viceroy visited the Punjab, India has been visited by famine and plague. The Punjab, though more fortunate than other provinces, has not altogether escaped ; but the plague has been confined and the effects of the famine mitigated by the action of Government. Throughout these troubles there had been continued evidence of the solicitude of the Govern. ment for the welfare of the people, which they were anxious to recognise. It was hoped that during the Viceroy's stay at Lahore some conclusion would be arrived at as to the Punjab Frontier policy, in any decision regarding which the people of the province would heartily co-operate. Attention was drawn to the efforts for improving the sanitation and water-supply of the city and its surroundings, for which objects Govern. ment assistance in the form of favourable loans was necessarily looked for. Another loan of five lakhs was now desired, which, if granted at the same rate as the existing loan, would make the annual charges for interest nearly Rs. 80,000. It was represented that Government might lighten the burden by reducing the interest on the existing and coming loans by at least one per cent. Finally, the address drew attention to the very rapid progress of education in the province, and suggested that so few careers being open to youths with a purely literary education, steps might be taken to give effect to the remedy suggested by Lord Dufferin by establish. ing or assisting institutions for the encouragement and extension of technical education.

His Excellency the Viceroy replied as follows :—]

*Your Honour, and Gentlemen,*—I am glad at this early stage of my period of office to have the pleasure of visiting the historic and important city of Lahore. Every Viceroy must desire to become as soon as possible acquainted with the Punjab, and with its capital. A good deal of the success, and the greater part of the tranquillity of his administration, will be decided by what passes during his term upon the frontiers of this Province. In its leading city he will observe the relics of a kingly past ; he will be brought into contact with a race that still begets not merely men, but heroes ; and he will have the opportunity of consulting with the officers upon whose tact and experience the management of what are more than provincial interests in the main depends. If in my case these experiences are not entirely novel, they do not render it any the less agreeable to me to return as Viceroy to a locality which I have more than once visited as a student, and which has always possessed for me a peculiar fascination.

We are in the habit, in England, of celebrating important anniversaries in our history, with the object either of recalling great events, or of commemorating great men. I cannot fail, therefore, to notice upon the present occasion that yesterday when I arrived in Lahore was the exact 50th anniversary of the day on which the Treaty was signed, by which the Punjab was included in the dominions of the British Crown. Were the Governor-General now living who concluded that Treaty, he might indeed congratulate himself upon the issues of his policy, and upon the reception accorded half a century later to his eleventh successor in that high office.

While I sympathise with you in the sufferings from famine and plague which have in recent years visited the Punjab in common with so many other parts of India, I may yet congratulate you upon having escaped far more lightly than some of them have done. As head of the Government I cannot be insensible to your gratifying recognition both of the efforts of the administration in India, and of the generosity of the British public. They have not merely contributed greatly to the mitigation of your hardships, but they have testified to a unity of interest and sentiment which it is my desire to encourage in both countries.

In the fourth paragraph of your address you assure me of loyal support from the inhabitants of this Province in the pursuance of a policy that shall at once protect and pacify your frontiers. This is not the occasion for any pronouncement upon frontier affairs. It will be sufficient for me to say that my desire is to keep India safe, to re-spect tribal independence, to be friendly to those who will be friendly, but firm towards those who attack without provocation. No man can forecast what may happen in a region so fertile in surprises as the Indian border. But I shall perhaps not err if I record my own conviction that frontier politics are not an exact science, and that their prudent management is less dependent upon hard and fast rules than it is upon methods and manners, and still more upon men. The ideal frontier is that in respect of which its own sons are largely enlisted in its defence.

In the next place you call my attention to the efforts which you have long been making, and are continuing to make, for the improvement of the drainage and water-supply of your city. I have been brought up in England as a member of a political party whose leader once prescribed for it the motto " *Sanitas sanitatum omnia sanitas.*" I have, therefore, what I may almost call a hereditary political prepossession in favour of such exertions ; which, I may observe, are even more urgently called for in the conditions of an Eastern climate, an Eastern soil, and Eastern habits of life, than they are in the West. Having thus appealed to a predisposition upon which you can safely rely, you proceed to ask me to evince my sympathies by reducing the rate of interest upon a loan which you have already contracted with the Government, as well as upon another for which you are about to apply. That the Government do not take altogether the same view of the question as yourselves, is apparent from the fact that you included the same appeal in your address to Lord Elgin five years ago. Its repetition in substantially the same form now would seem to indicate that you have not been able to convince the Supreme Government in the interim. It will of course be both my duty and my pleasure to consider any fresh application that may reach me from your Government, which is the proper channel of communication ; nor will there be any predisposition on my part to treat such an appeal from the exclusive standpoint of official or financial pedantry. I must, however, point out to you on the one hand, that in every country in the world State loans to Local Bodies are only granted upon a margin beyond the actual burden incurred by the State, because its credit is to a certain extent diminished by this hypothecation of its resources ; on the other hand, that there is a growing tendency in India to regard the State as a milch-cow, whose duty it is to provide universal sustenance, whereas the real function of the State as a money-lender is to lend in quarters which cannot borrow on their own account, rather than to supplement and prop up an independent and already existing credit.

You conclude by inviting my attention and support to the provision of technical education in the Punjab, either by the founding of suitable institutions, or by the gift of grants-in-aid. By technical education I understand you to mean the sort of education that will fit a man for the professions of life rather than for the arm-chair or the study. In this respect I concur with your aspirations, and I have ascertained that the Local Government already supports a Medical College, a Veterinary College, a School of Art, and a number of Industrial Schools, and that the number of pupils under technical training .in the Punjab exceeds 2,000.

There are two observations, however, which I am tempted to make in this connection. In England such matters as technical education are largely taken up and pressed forward by Municipal Corporations. May I ask if the Lahore Municipality have taken any independent steps on behalf of the interest which they have so much at heart ? The second observation is this—that technical education is not exclusively a State obligation, but may be largely assisted by private enterprise. I have heard of one such Industrial School at Rawal Pindi in this Province, but of one alone. Grants-in-aid are available on easy terms for any similar institutions that may be founded ; and if the demand be as urgent as is represented, there should be little difficulty in enlisting public or private generosity up to the point at which the State may legitimately be called upon to assist.

In conclusion, allow me to thank you, Gentlemen, for your loyal address, which I understand it is intended to enclose in a specimen of the silver work of Lahore. I would give a great deal to revive the ancient art industries of this once ingenious and artistic country.

PUNJAB CHIEFS' COLLEGE.

*1st April,* 1899.

[ On Saturday forenoon, the 1st April, the Viceroy presided at the annual prize giving at the Aitchison (Punjab Chiefs') College, Lahore. The proceedings took place in the Central Hall of the College, in which a large audience was assembled, including many ladies, civilians, and native gentlemen of Lahore. The students of the College numbered about 70. The Viceroy was received at the College by the Lieutenant-Governor, who after he had conducted His Excellency to a seat on the daïs, opened the proceedings by thanking His Excellency for presiding on the occasion. The authorities of the College, he said, augured happy results from the renewal of Viceregal interest in the College, which had done some good work in the past and had promise of greater development. They trusted that in time the College would attain that position in the educational institutions of the Province and that amount of popularity with the Punjab Chiefs designed for it by its founder, Sir Charles Aitchison. Sir M. Young then called on Sir Benjamin Bromhead, the Governor of the College, to read a report of the history and aims of the institution. This having been done, His Excellency distributed the prizes to the students, two of whom subsequently read addresses of welcome to His Excellency in Persian.

The Viceroy then spoke as follows :—]

*Your Honour, Ladies and Gentlemen,*—It has been a great pleasure to me to visit this College, and to present these prizes to-day in this beautiful Hall which forms so noble a feature of the stately building in which we find ourselves, and which appears to me to be so well suited to the purposes for which it has been raised. I confess I did not know that included in the pleasure which I was to experience this morning would be the compliment of finding myself addressed in Persian by two original poets. However, I can assure them that although I could not from my ignorance of the language estimate the full measure of the compliment, I am yet very much gratified at the manner in which they have paid it.

*Ladies and Gentlemen,* I think that after the interesting address which has been read to us by Sir Benjamin Bromhead, it is not incumbent on me to say much either as to the foundation or as to the objects of this institution. We know that a little more than 12 years ago the foundation stone was laid by the then Viceroy, Lord Dufferin, in the presence of one of the sons of the Queen—the Duke of Connaught. This College takes its name, as we have been told, from Sir Charles Aitchison, the Lieutenant-Governor of the Punjab, whose features in marble we see before us, and whose long and active interest in the objects with which this School was founded, as well as in those of the similar Mayo College at Ajmere, is known to you all. The funds with which the College was endowed were partly subscribed by the Punjab Chiefs and partly given by the Local Government assisted by a subvention from the Imperial Government, and the aim with which it was founded was to supply the benefits of what we call a public school education in England to the young men of princely or noble family in the Punjab. Now, the question may be asked, what are the benefits of that which we describe in England as the public school system ? And inasmuch as I am an old public school man myself, and to a certain extent, therefore, the product of that system, I am perhaps entitled to give you a reply.

The public school system, as we understand it in England, is one which is designed to develop simultaneously and in equal measure the mind, the body, and the character of the pupil. We undertake to educate our young men at these schools in England for the position or profession in life which they are destined to fill. We endeavour to train their physical energies so as to give them a manly bearing and to interest them in those games and pastimes and pursuits which will both conduce so much to their health and add so greatly to the pleasure of their lives. And above all, by the ideals that we set before them, by the high example which we endeavour to inculcate in them, and by the attrition of mutual intercourse with each other from day to day, we endeavour so to discipline their character that they shall be turned, not merely into men, but into what in England we call gentlemen. (*Applause.*)

In England this system of which I am speaking has attained a perfection unequalled in any other country.

Boys are drawn to our English public schools from every class in the community that possesses adequate means. Two of the Queen's grandsons are at this moment being educated at Eton, which is the greatest of our English public schools There the boys of the school mingle with each other on terms of perfect equality. They board together in the same house, they take part in the same classes, they play games together, they are taught not merely by their masters but by the high standard that prevails in the school and among the boys themselves, to be honourable, chivalrous, and just. They form friendships with each other that last for a lifetime, and when they go forth to take their place in the world, they are proud and fond of the school, and their first and principal desire is to do credit to the institution which has done so much for them. (*Applause.*)

Let me give you an illustration of the strength of the feeling of which I am speaking. A few months ago when I was appointed to the office which I now hold, there were appointed almost at the same time two other old Etonians to posts of great distinction under the Crown. One of these was Dr. Welldon, the present Metropolitan of India ; the other was Lord Minto, who has gone as Governor-General to Canada. All three of us, as I have said, were old Eton boys, and when our appointments were announced almost at the same time it befel that a number of old Etonians—over 200 in all—joined themselves together to give us a parting dinner, and to bid us farewell. At that dinner there were men of over 70 years of age and men of not more than 20. There were Viceroys, and Judges, and Commanders-in-Chief. There was a Prime Minister in the chair. There were also men of modest careers and of unambitious lives. But every one of those old Etonians who met there was animated by the same feeling of love for the school which had sent them all forth ; by pride that she was still fulfilling her mission ; and by hope for the success of those who were going out to carry her name into the uttermost corners of the world. (*Applause.*)

That, boys of this College, is the spirit engendered by the public school system in England. That is the spirit that we want to introduce into this country of India. I am aware that there are many difficulties in the task. In England the public school system which I have been describing has been the gradual growth of many centuries. It is the natural outcome of the free institutions and of the liberal sentiments of the British nation, and it has been easy to establish in a country where the territorial aristocracy is both recruited from and finds its chief strength in the confidence of the remaining orders of the people. But here, on the other hand, all is different. The public school system is an exotic in India. It is not a natural growth in this country. It has to contend with many obstacles such as prejudice and custom, and it has to fight against the barriers of caste. It is only by slow degrees, therefore, that we can expect it to take root in India. Nevertheless, from the reports which have been submitted to me, and which have been drawn up from year to year by the Governor and Principal of this College, and by the Inspector who conducts his annual enquiry, I derive the impression that substantial progress is being made towards the ideal which the founders had in view.

I am glad to note that the educational standard is steadily improving, and that the boys are reported to be industrious and well behaved. (*Applause.*) I am also glad to observe that they take part in games with more zest than they were at first disposed to do, and I hope that inclination will be encouraged, because games and gymnastics make boys nimble and active and strong ; they also bring boys very much together, and they stimulate a healthy spirit of emulation. I was pleased also to hear what the Governor said about riding. I think every boy in this College, or at least a large majority of the boys, in a country like India, ought to learn to ride, and to ride well. (*Applause.*)

Now, I have a word to say to you young men and boys of this College. If you will allow me to make to you a few personal observations, I would say this : Do not fritter away the time that you pass at this College. It is a very precious time ; and believe me that you will rejoice later on for every moment here that you have spent well, and you will bitterly regret every moment that you have wasted. Make friends with each other, because the friends that you make here will be your friends in prosperity or adversity in after life. Do not regard the education you get in this College as a sort of State machinery provided by the Government in order to enable you either to pass Entrance Examinations at the University or to obtain Government posts later on. There are a great many of you who will never obtain Government posts, and who are not fitted to obtain them, and a larger number who will never take a University degree at all, and are not required to take a University degree. The education you receive here is intended for the most part to qualify you to fill with distinction and honour the positions in life to which your birth will naturally raise you when you leave this College. (*Applause.*)

Many of you young men and boys, as I have just said, are of good birth and of high rank, and these are qualifications which obtain—and I hope that they may long continue to obtain— respect in a conservative country like India. But you have no right to be conceited or haughty because of your birth or rank. There is a certain honourable pride which a man may take in high birth, and which it is legitimate for him to feel only on one condition—that he is inspired thereby to dutiful ambitions. We have a motto in England which runs as follows—*Noblesse oblige*—and the meaning of that is that noble birth requires a man to be noble, and to act nobly; it means that high rank carries with it duties as well as privileges, and that when you go forth into the world you must so comport yourselves as to be worthy of your position. Otherwise you will forfeit, first, the-confidence of your fellow-countrymen, and finally, the position itself. (*Applause.*)

Next, I have a word to say to any Chiefs of the Punjab who may be here present, and if none are here to-day, it is possible that my words may reach them through the medium of the Press. If they were here I would speak to them in the following terms :—

This Aitchison College has not been founded in our interests. It is not a device that has been constructed by Government in order to bring either credit or advantage to the British Raj. It is an institution that has been founded in your interests, and in the interests of your families, and your fortunes. You ought, therefore, Chiefs of the Punjab, to give to this College greater support than you have hitherto done. You ought, with scarcely an exception, to send your sons and grandsons and male relatives to this College, and you ought to endeavour to turn it into that which was the ambition of its founders, namely, that it should be the Eton or the Harrow of the Punjab. (*Applause.*)

Believe me, Chiefs, if you are here present, that the days are gone by when a hereditary aristocracy, however noble its origin or however illustrious its service, can sit still with folded hands and contemplate the glories of its past. If you are to hold your own in the estates which you enjoy by virtue of your position, and in the confidence of the people, you must come forth from your isolation, must grapple with the facts of life, and show that you are fitted by character and merit for the position which every one is ready to concede to you. You must march alongside of knowledge instead of toiling helplessly and feebly behind it ; you must reinforce the claims of high birth by equally high attainments. You must realise above all that destiny is not a passive influence that lies in the lap of the gods, but is an active instrument that is in your own hands to shape as you will. (*Applause.*)

I have ventured to give these words of advice to the boys and young princes and nobles of this College and also to the wider circle of the Chiefs of the Punjab outside. May I be allowed to say that I have done so in no spirit of censorship, or dictation, or command ? I have spoken to you both because, as a student, I am interested in the manly and splendid traditions of this famous Province of the Indian Empire (*applause*) ; because, as Viceroy, I have a claim to the support of every man in this country in my efforts to make India prosperous and strong ; and because, as your friend, I desire that in future generations, and in an era of peace, you should retain, not by rank alone but by pre-eminence of influence and character and worth, the position which you won for yourselves in the more stormy days of old. (*Loud and continued applause.*)

ADDRESS FROM THE COLONISTS OF THE CHENAB DISTRICT.

*3rd April,* 1899.

[The Viceroy, attended by his personal staff and accompanied by the Lieutenant-Governor of the Punjab and his staff, Colonel Montgomery, Settlement Commissioner, Mr. Wilson, Chief Secretary, Punjab Government, and Captain Popham Young, Colonization Officer, arrived by special train at Lyallpur, the head-quarters of the Chenab Irrigation District, on Monday afternoon, the 3rd April. His Excellency had inspected in the morning the headworks and plans of the Chenab Canal at Khanki, where he was met by Mr. Higham, Inspector-General of Irrigation, Mr. Beresford, Chief Engineer, Punjab Irrigation Department, and other Canal Officers. At Lyallpur His Excellency was received at the railway station, which was brilliantly decorated, by the principal Civil and Irrigation Officers of the district and, later on, at Captain Young's bungalow, was presented with an address of welcome by a large body of Colonists. The address was read by Mahomed Hyat Khan, C.S.I., and welcomed His Excellency to Lyallpur—"one of the latest triumphs of British philanthropy, organising power, and engineering skill, where we (the Colonists) have congregated to dwell as the specially favoured subjects of the Government." The Punjab, they said, had ever been conspicuous for its steadfast loyalty and unswerving devotion to Government, and they acknowledged with gratitude the generosity of Government in granting the people this land, thereby providing them with increased means of earning a livelihood by agriculture. They concluded by making certain requests, to which the Viceroy referred specifically in his reply, which was as follows :—]

*Nawáb Mahomed Hyát Khán and Gentlemen,*—I am only sorry that I cannot address you in a language that most of you will understand, but I daresay that my remarks, although made in English, will be translated afterwards, and will be communicated to the large body of those who do not understand them in the form in which I speak.

A new Viceroy coming out to India learns many interesting lessons and sees many surprising things. Among the most novel and gratifying of these is the operation of that great system of Irrigation which in England we dimly know has filled up immense blanks upon the map of India, has made the wilderness to blossom like a rose, and has provided sustenance and livelihood to millions of human workers. What we do not and cannot know there is the sort of experience that I have been able to derive to-day from a

visit to the actual scene of one of these beneficent reclama-
tions, and from a study of the reports and information
presented to me in connection therewith. The Punjab has
been one of the main fields of this particular application of
the energies and resources of the Government of India ; and
it may interest any of my fellow-countrymen in England
under whose eyes these words may subsequently fall to
know that at the present time in the Punjab alone we have
constructed 4,500 miles of main and branch canals, not
including 10,500 miles of smaller distributaries ; that the
total area irrigated by these means, which, in 1868, amounted only to one million acres, in 1878 to 1,300,000 acres,
and in 1888 to 2,300,000 acres, has risen, owing to the
startling progress of the last decade, to 5,200,000 acres in
1898 ; that the value of the crops which the irrigated area
produces is estimated at 10 millions sterling ; that the total
capital outlay on the Irrigation Works of the Punjab has
been nearly 6 millions sterling ; and that the net revenue
was over 90 lakhs of rupees, or £600,000 in 1898, or a
return upon the capital expenditure of 10½ per cent.
Though statistics are commonly said to be prosaic and dull,
I venture to think that in these figures, with their astonishing upward march, and with the evidences of sound finance
with which they teem, there is an element of romance that
almost surpasses in its dramatic surprise the more solid
interest attaching to a far-sighted and successful effort of
Imperial administration.

And now I turn to the particular project and locality
which have tempted me here to-day, and which I have spent
a pleasurable morning and afternoon in examining. When
I am informed that four years ago the place in which I am
now speaking, and which has the appearance of a flourishing township and mart of agricultural produce, was a barren
and uninhabited jungle ; and that there are now 1,000
separate villages in a settlement that, eight years ago,
existed only on paper, I confess that I doubt whether the
records of the far West, where towns are said to spring up

like mushrooms almost in a night, can show any result more wonderful or more gratifying. Here was an area of $2\frac{1}{2}$ million acres of what is known as waste land. The big dam across the Chenab was commenced in 1889. It was finished in 1892. At the end of the year that has just closed 1,000,000 acres have already been brought under irrigation ; there has been a capital outlay of $2\frac{1}{2}$ crores, or $1\frac{1}{2}$ million sterling ; the net revenue in 1898 was 16 lakhs of rupees, or a return of nearly $7\frac{1}{2}$ per cent. Now that the annually irrigated area has reached a million acres, it is estimated that the total value of the crops raised in a single year equals the capital cost of the entire works; and I have little doubt that the ultimate returns on the expenditure will nearly, if it does not quite, double the present amount. On the land thus reclaimed has been planted a large and prosperous peasant population with allotments of from 20 to 30 acres each, upon which they enjoy perpetual and heritable rights of occupancy. Other portions of the land have been bestowed as rewards upon pensioners of the Native Army, and upon yeoman grantees, or have been sold or leased to capitalists. There is believed to be a population of over 200,000 persons now in a district which six years ago was almost without an inhabitant. Where at that time emigrants could with difficulty be found for what appeared to be a precarious venture, there is now almost a rush of would-be settlers ; and great care is required in sifting the numerous applications for grants. I have only to look about me in order to note the air of contentment and affluence that everywhere prevails. If ever there was a case in which has been realised the ambition of statesmen as described by our English poet—

> " To scatter plenty o'er a smiling land,
>  And read their history in a nation's eyes,"

it would seem to be in this favoured corner of the Province of the Punjab.

I observe that in your address you attribute this remarkable triumph to British philanthropy, organising power, and engineering skill. I am glad that you have included the two latter among the causes of success : for it is certainly true that no small share of the credit is due to the able officers who devised or have superintended the execution of this magnificent scheme, among whom I may mention Colonel Ottley, Colonel Jacob, and Mr. Preston ; to the Engineers who have carried it out, and who, with a precision of detail never before attempted, have brought the water literally to the door of each tenant as he has entered upon his holding ; and to the Colonization Officer, Captain Popham Young, who has accompanied me here to-day, and who both by his ingenious and successful sub-division of squares upon principles that have been equally acceptable to the settlers and helpful to the administration, by his institution of the admirable system of *panchayats* for settlement by arbitration of your local disputes, and by his paternal influence over the colonists, has done so much for the rapid development of this Indian Utopia. Let me also, for my part, include in the tribute of our well-merited praise the sturdy and sensible men of the Punjab who, leaving their old homes, have girt up their loins, and have marched forth with confident courage to this new land of promise.

While expressing your thanks for the benefits which you thus enjoy you conform to what appears to be the hallowed practice of all Indian deputations by asking for a little more. Your first request is for a military cantonment at Lyallpur. I sympathise with your martial ardour ; but I am informed by my military advisers that there are other places better suited for the proposed dispositions.

Next you ask for certain pecuniary advantages. The first of them is a remission of the ground rent that is levied on all town lands in the Settlement. I do not think that this is a reasonable request, and I see no chance of its being granted. The second is that the revenue thus raised may be credited to the Municipalities for local use. Now I must point out to you that the fund realised from the sale-proceeds of sites has already been handed over to the

Municipality of Lyallpur; and while I am willing to consider any fresh appeal on its own merits, I must observe that in one respect you go far to justify the character of the precocious infant by opening your mouths rather wide in your early years. Thirdly, you ask for quicker trains, and better goods sidings and stations. All these will come in good time. You must not be in too great a hurry.

You conclude by asking me to give you some special service to perform in discharge of your gratitude to Government. I appreciate the offer, and the spirit in which it is made. But for the present the only service that I would impose upon you is that of developing the colony of which you are the parents, of living in peace and concord with your neighbours, and of setting an example of loyal citizenship to other parts of this great and flourishing Province. (*Applause.*)

ADDRESS FROM THE KHALSA DIWAN, LAHORE.
*5th April,* 1899.

[On the 5th April, at 12-30 P.M., a deputation of the members of the Khalsa Diwan, headed by Sirdar Bulwant Singh, the President, waited on the Viceroy at Government House, Lahore, with an address, which was read by Jowahar Singh, Chief Secretary of the Khalsa Diwan. The address welcomed His Excellency, not only as the head of the Government, but as the representative of a beloved and adored sovereign, for whom the Sikhs had shed their best blood. Many of His Excellency's predecessors, the address remarked, had felt and expressed the mutual attachment subsisting between the British and the Khalsa. It was not necessary to assure His Excellency that, next to their duty to the Ten Gurus, the highest ambition of the Sikhs was to serve their beloved Queen-Empress. This feeling was reciprocated by their British fellow subjects. Allusion was made to the raising of a memorial by the Government, and another by the Anglo-Indian community, in honour of their brothers who fell fighting at Saragarhi, in the recent Tirah Campaign. Among the many benefits which the community had received during Her Majesty's reign, particular mention was made of the Khalsa College, which had been secured through the patronage of the Government and the rulers of some of the Native States. His Excellency's attention was called to the unsatisfactory character of Dr. Trumpp's translation into English of the Sikh scriptures, and an appeal was made to him to have a correct translation made.

The Viceroy replied to the address as follows :— ]

*Gentlemen :*—In responding to the address which was presented to me a few days ago by the Municipality of Lahore, I spoke of the Punjab as the home of a race that produces not merely men but heroes. When I used that phrase I did not know that I should have the pleasure before I left this city of meeting a representative body of the nationality to whom it obviously applied. The incident of Saragarhi, to which you refer in your address, is one of several that were in my mind in making the remark in question. There are many qualities required to constitute the ideal soldier : bravery, endurance, a certain aptitude of intellect, and discipline ; but I am not sure that above them all I would not place that unfaltering devotion to duty and heroic disregard of self that impels a man to die at his post, as the Sikhs at Saragarhi did, unmurmuring and even happy, fighting against overwhelming odds. Of this virtue the

Sikh soldiers of the army of the Queen have given many an illustration in fifty years of fighting for the British Raj, since the time, now nearly forgotten, when they fought so well against us ; so that the name of your race has become almost synonymous in the English language with traditions of desperate courage and unflinching loyalty. On Monday as I walked about the new settlement of Lyallpur, upon which have been planted as colonists a number of pensioners of the Native Army, I was received by veterans of your race upon whose bosoms hung the Queen's medals that recorded their prowess in China, in Abyssinia, in Egypt, in Burma, and in Afghanistan—no mean synopsis of the range of action of the Sikh soldier. Long may he retain his martial character, and never may the day arise when the British Government in time of need cannot rely upon his staunch and unquestioning service.

I think you know that we are neither unconscious of, nor ungrateful for, this long and honourable record of Sikh allegiance. If proof were needed I might refer to the monument which is about to be erected at Amritsar by the Government of India in memory of the Sikh soldiers of the 36th Regiment who gave up their lives at Saragarhi in 1897 ; while the popular appreciation of that heroic incident will be shown by a further memorial to be erected by public subscription at Ferozepur. These two monuments will testify to later ages at once the valour of your race and the gratitude of mine.

Nevertheless in the modern world military virtues, however pre-eminent, are not the only requisites to the preservation of national existence, and you have wisely realised that if you are to hold your own with the more populous and erudite communities among whom you are placed, you must provide your families with an education comparable with theirs. I am pleased to learn that the Khalsa College, which was founded in the time of Sir James Lyall, has already attained to a high standard of excellence ; and I hope that it may continue to receive the active support of the Sikh Princes of the Punjab, and may turn out a number of young men, who, like Lord Lawrence in the famous statue which stands in this city, may be competent to wield the pen, at the same time that their other hand rests confidently upon the hilt of the sword.

You have quoted in your address a passage from a recent speech by myself in Calcutta, concerning my desire to preserve with the utmost care and reverence in India the memorials and relics of the past ; and I am naturally, therefore, interested in the subject of the translation of your scriptures into the English language, to which you call my attention. I regret that the translation which was undertaken nearly 30 years ago, at considerable expense, by the Government, has been found to be so unsatisfactory ; and I rejoice to think that a more correct and scholarly version is likely before long to appear. Such a work, however, appears to me emphatically to belong to the class of undertakings that are best supported by those whose interests are principally concerned ; and if the Princes and nobles of your race are anxious that an accurate reproduction of the Granth should be available in the English tongue, I cannot doubt that they will without difficulty provide the inconsiderable funds required for that purpose.

In concluding my reply, may I take advantage of the opportunity thus afforded to me—to express my recognition of the gratifying reception that has been extended to me by all classes and creeds upon this my first visit as Viceroy to the capital of the Punjab ?

ADDRESS FROM THE SIMLA MUNICIPALITY.

*6th April,* 1899.

[The Viceroy, accompanied by his staff, arrived at Simla on Thursday afternoon, the 6th April, and was received by a large number of officials, at Viceregal Lodge, the 15th Sikhs and the Simla Volunteers forming Guards of Honour. The President and Members of the Simla Municipality were also in waiting, and presented an address cordially welcoming His Excellency and Lady Curzon to Simla, and expressing a hope that Lord Curzon's Government would continue to show the same interest in the welfare of Simla as his predecessors had done, more especially with regard to the matters dealt with by the " Simla Extension Committee," the improvements recommended by which were not possible without the financial aid of Government. The Committee also expressed their grati- fication at Her Excellency Lady Curzon having assumed the Presidentship of the National Association for providing medical aid to the women of India, and they hoped that the interest in local charities and institutions evinced by their predecessors would be continued by Their Excellencies.

The Viceroy replied as follows :—]

*Mr. President and Members of the Simla Municipal Corporation :*—It gives me much pleasure to accept your kindly assurances of welcome upon my arrival at Simla. The relations between a Viceroy and the people of this place, where it has become the practice for him to spend considerably more time than at any other spot during his stay in India, must necessarily be of a very intimate character. In the case of each of my predecessors without exception, since Simla became the summer head-quarters of Government, they have further been marked by a cordiality which no effort on my part will be spared—although I am convinced that effort will be unnecessary—to maintain on the same high level of mutual concord and esteem. Simla is in a peculiar sense not merely the official residence of the Viceroy during the hot weather, but his country home. For here he divests himself—if not of the cares of office ; that is I fear never possible in India—at least of some of the trappings of State ; and amid your beautiful mountains he may almost succeed in mistaking himself for an Anglo- Indian Horace retiring from the noise and smoke of Rome to the peace of the Tiburtine hills.

But there is one criticism not uncommonly passed upon the summer migration to Simla of the Viceroy and the Government of India which I should like to meet. It is sometimes supposed that after three or four months of more or less serious official labour at Calcutta they stampede at the first touch of the sun to Simla, and that there, like the weary mariners in the *Lotos Eaters*, they

>  . . . . . . "live and lie reclined
> On the hills like gods together, careless of mankind."

In other words, Simla is spoken of as though it were the holiday resort, the Indian equivalent to a marine villa, or suburban retreat, of an Epicurean Viceroy and a pampered Government. I can assure you that it is from no such point of view that I regard it. At Calcutta during the winter months there are so many calls upon the Viceroy's time arising both from the session of the Legislative Council from the visits of Native Princes or important personages, from the large number of persons whom he is anxious to see, or who have a claim to see him, from the ordinary stress of office work, and from the heavy, though agreeable social obligations that are inevitable in the crowded Capital of the Indian Empire, that he has barely time to get through the work of each day as it comes round, and never has time to think. Were this strain, which is constantly increasing, to be borne without intermission during the summer months in the low-lying delta of Bengal, I do not hesitate to say that no Viceroy in the world—and Viceroys are not as a rule drawn from a class already acclimatised to this country— could withstand it, or could do justice to his work. It is in order that he may have time to think, time to enquire exhaustively into the many questions calling for solution, time to mature his policy and programme for the forthcoming year—that he comes up to Simla to find here the larger leisure which is denied to him either at Calcutta, or when on tour, and an atmosphere which is more conducive than that of the plains both to mental and to physical energy. Simla is in fact the workshop in which during the summer months are fashioned the materials of the fabric, be it well constructed or badly constructed, of each Viceroy's Indian Administration. If it be objected that while these considerations are valid enough in their application to him, they are less valid in relation to the large subordinate staffs of the Departments who twice yearly are called upon to perform the same migration, I would reply, so far as I am at present competent to form an opinion, that the head of the Administration, if he is to be a head in anything but the name, must have the officers and the staff of the various Departments in close proximity to himself, so that they may be the immediate instruments of the policy of Government. In former times. when the telegraph wire and the railroad were in their infancy in India, the most serious dislocation of business as well as interminable delays were caused by the long absences of the Governor-General on tour leaving his colleagues behind him. Although tours are a most instructive and important, and in my opinion an absolutely essential, part of the Viceroy's yearly routine, and although the previously existing drawbacks have been immensely reduced by the two scientific agencies which I have named, I yet take leave to doubt whether the work of the Government of India can be as effectively conducted while the Viceroy is separated from his counsellors and agents as when they are united, and I am convinced that it is only while the full machinery is at his disposal, as it would not be if he were at Simla while the Departments were at Calcutta, or *vice versâ*, that the power is capable of being generated which is to result in vigilant and effective administration. These are the grounds for which, while I do not say that, were I presented with a clean slate, I should myself write upon it even the comely name of Simla over half the year, I yet come here without any sting of conscience, and with the most pleasurable anticipations, confident that Simla will give to my colleagues and myself the opportunity and the strength the better to discharge our duty in that great trust which has been laid upon our shoulders.

As regards the questions of municipal administration to which you have called my attention, I realise that the Supreme Government has a very close and personal concern in the sanitation and water-supply of the town ; and you may rely upon receiving from Lady Curzon and myself the same sympathetic interest in your local institutions, charities, and needs, as has been so uniformly displayed by our predecessors.

## RAILWAY CONFERENCE.

### 15th August, 1899.

[The first meeting of the Railway Conference in 1899, to consider Railway extensions in India, was held at Viceregal Lodge, Simla, on Tuesday, the 15th August, at 11 A.M. The following, who formed the Committee, as approved by the Viceroy, were present :—

*President:* His Excellency the Viceroy. *Members:* The Hon'ble Major-General Sir E. H. H. Collen, K.C.I.E., C.B.; the Hon'ble Mr. C. E. Dawkins; the Hon'ble Lieutenant-Colonel R. Gardiner, R.E.; F. R. Upcott, Esq., Secretary to the Government of India, Public Works Department; A. R. Becher, Esq., Accountant-General, Public Works Department. *Secretary:* Captain W. J. McElhinny, R.E.

The Viceroy, in opening the proceedings, spoke as follows :—]

In holding and in presiding over this Conference, I am following a practice which was instituted by my predecessor, Lord Elgin, who devoted himself with so much business-like energy, and with such beneficial results, to the development of Railways in India during his term of office. Under the practice established by him this Conference meets yearly at Simla. Every third year a programme of expenditure and construction is drawn up in the Public Works Department, by which the Government of India is more or less bound for the triennial period; and in the intervening years, the classification of prospective lines as originally adopted, according to their degree of urgency, has been examined and revised by the Conference, as a guide to the Department, in the light of later experience or of pressing need.

There are substantial advantages in this procedure. On the one hand, a comparison of the various proposals submitted to Government is conducted by an impartial Committee who make an honest endeavour to advise upon their selection, postponement, or rejection. On the other hand, a programme is drawn up for Government by which its proceedings are regulated, and which prevents a policy of drift or caprice. In other words, we are the gainers, firstly, by the possession of a system, secondly, by a reasonable prospect of some continuity in that system.

Nevertheless, I cannot say that I regard our proceedings as perfect, or as realising the maximum possible advantage, nor am I clear that this Conference, either in its character or in its results, corresponds with the intentions of those who originally suggested it. Their idea, I believe, was in some way to give a guarantee to promoters and to public opinion of the fair consideration of the various schemes submitted to the Government of India, and while not depriving the latter of its position as the final arbiter, to strengthen its decisions by the confidence attaching to an examination, whose proceedings or whose results should have the additional merit of publicity. Whatever the benefits of our annual Conference, I cannot claim for it that these objects have been fully attained. Indeed, I am somewhat doubtful as to whether it can legitimately be entitled a Conference at all. A Conference is a high-sounding title, which conveys the impression of a meeting and a discussion between the principal parties concerned, who are in this case the Government of India on the one side, and the Companies or promoters on the other. But a Conference in which one of the two parties is not represented, save by its manuscript statements or applications, seems to me to have an imperfect claim to the title ; and I should prefer to call our body what it is, namely, a Departmental Committee of officials of the Government of India, constituted to supplement the work of the Public Works Department, to apply to it the test of a wider examination, in which general considerations of policy shall play a part, and to recommend to the Government of India a systematic, and so far as possible, a scientific programme.

I have re-summoned the Conference this year, in order that I may have personal experience of the advantages or faults of the system before passing final judgment upon it, and because I propose, when our sittings are concluded, to take the public into our confidence to a greater degree than has previously been the case.

I propose to recommend to the Government of India that the conclusions at which we arrive with reference to the various lines, shall be formulated in an easily intelligible shape, and shall be published. In this way promoters will learn how their schemes stand in the estimation of Government, instead of having to be content as now with the official intimation of success, or the private inference of failure ; while the public will gain an idea both of the magnitude and complexity of the problem which we are called upon to discuss, and of the general principles upon which we attempt to decide it.

There remains to be considered the question whether it is possible to invest the proceedings of this so-called Conference with any of those features in which I have described it as lacking. Upon this point I have had the benefit of the opinion and advice of my present Public Works Colleague, Colonel Gardiner, who speaks with the double advantage of both official and commercial experience of Railways in India. There are many difficulties in the way. We cannot suddenly constitute a body resembling a Parliamentary Committee at home. We have not the materials ; the questions for decision are far more numerous and more complex ; the Government of India is much more intimately concerned than is the Government in Great Britain ; above all, India is a much bigger country than England, and Simla is not, like London, an easily accessible centre to all parts of the kingdom.

It has occurred to us, however, that there may be cases in which local interests are acutely involved, and in which local feeling is likely to be more fairly represented if it is heard upon the spot than by any official or semi-official representations either at Simla or Calcutta. It is, therefore, in my mind to constitute, should the case arise, a small peripatetic Commission, in which the Government should of course exercise the predominant influence, the Public Works Member in all probability taking the Chair, and which should, in the touring season, visit and conduct a public enquiry at any locality where such a problem called for decision, the Local Government or local commercial bodies being represented upon the Commission, so as to lend both impartiality and weight to its decisions, which should then be communicated in the form of a recommendation to the Government of India.

If we carry out this idea, the experiment will be a tentative one. If it is a failure, it can be dropped. Should it turn out a success, I conceive it as not impossible that the body so formed might constitute the germ or nucleus of a more permanent Commission, which should place Government in constant touch with the currents of public opinion, and which should also satisfy promoters as to the *bonâ fides* and thoroughness of the investigation to which their claims are submitted.

As regards the official programme prepared by the Public Works Department, there seems to me to be a disadvantage, so long as the triennial system is maintained, in not always keeping up that programme three years in advance. As matters now stand, it is drawn up in very third year. The first of these programmes, based upon the first Conference, was drawn up in 1896, when an expenditure of $29\frac{1}{2}$ crores was fixed for the three succeeding years. As is known, this total was, for various reasons, not worked up to, and only 25 crores were spent. Last year the second triennial programme was drawn up. Less ambitious ideas prevailed, and an expenditure of $20\frac{1}{4}$ crores, subsequently increased to $22\frac{1}{3}$ crores on account of lapses in expenditure on the grant for 1898-99, was estimated for during the years 1899-1900, 1900-1901, 1901-1902. Meanwhile, in the intervening years, the construction programme is annually examined and recast ; in the second year for the two remaining years of the triennial period, in the third year for the single remaining year. But it appears to me that we should do well to be always three years ahead with our financial working programme, and I, therefore, propose to recommend to the Government of India that Mr. Upcott should not limit himself to the two remaining years of the present term, but should include in his forecast the year

1902-1903, and should follow the same practice in succeeding years.

Concerning the general policy of Government towards Railways, it seems to me that, just as the Currency problem, which has agitated and perplexed the public mind for twenty years, has in part been solved by the steady compulsion of events, so also the same irresistible pressure is directing our Railway policy into more or less permanent grooves. It is easy to denounce the diversity and inconsistency of plans that has prevailed in the past ; easy either to laugh or to cry over the Homeric battle of the gauges. To me it seems more profitable to assist the adaptation of our policy to the lines which seem to be marked out before it both by past experience and by commonsense. The natural inclination is, in my judgment, in the direction, not of expanding, but of gradually restricting, Government agency. I must not be understood to deprecate in all cases State management or State construction. On the contrary, I see great advantages, both political and financial, in the maintenance of a Government staff. Still less would I impugn the advantage of State ownership, or the necessity of State control; I am myself a believer in the desirability of purchasing the few outstanding lines as they continue to fall in ; while State supervision is of the essence of State possession. Probably we shall, as times improve, and as better offers are made to us, gradually divest ourselves of the working of the majority, at any rate, of those lines which are still both owned and maintained by the Government. The terms under which we may be prepared to part with them appear to me to be a matter of financial expediency rather than of fixed principle. Our object should be to make the best bargain for the State. For my own part, I do not think that there is anything surprising in the fluctuations that have hitherto occurred in our policy. When Lord Dalhousie first introduced Railways into India, Government was unequal to the venture, and capital required to be attracted by easy and even generous . terms. Later on, when Government found that it had been financially a heavy loser by the arrangements so made, there was a sharp reaction, and the Railway policy of Lords Lawrence and Mayo was based upon strict Governmental and centralising lines. We who have now had a long experience of both systems, can discriminate between their virtues and vices, and can adopt a reasonable compromise. If that compromise tends towards the contraction of the area claimed by Government and an increasing expansion of the facilities afforded to Companies, it is because we do not want to overweight the shoulders of Government with a burden that they are unfitted to bear, because we want to reinforce our own power and resources with the assistance of capital, both British and Native—and I wish that there were more of the latter forthcoming, as well as of the former—and because in the spirit of healthy competition so engendered seems to be the best guarantee for the promotion of the public interest.

## PUNJAB LAND ALIENATION BILL.

*27th September*, 1899,

[At the meeting of the Governor-General's Legislative Council, held at Viceregal Lodge, Simla, on the 27th September 1899, the Hon'ble Mr. Rivaz moved for leave to introduce a Bill to amend the law relating to agricultural land in the Punjab. Mr. Rivaz having addressed the Council at some length on the subject, His Excellency the President spoke as follows :—]

The historical retrospect with which Mr. Rivaz commenced his interesting speech appeared to me to be of value in its general as well as in its particular application. He shewed that the question of agricultural indebtedness in many parts of India had attracted the attention of Government, and had elicited the opinions of expert authorities at intervals throughout the present century, but that, during the past 25 years, it has become genuinely pressing and acute. Minutes have been written, resolutions have been circulated, and laws have been passed, for the mitigation of the abuse. But all of these have dealt, so to speak, merely with the fringe of the subject ; and only to-day are we engaged for the first time in introducing a measure of first-class legislative importance to check this great and growing evil.

Does not this fact illustrate in a striking manner the method and deliberation with which we proceed? I am one of those, as may be known, who find that the machine of Government is apt to move somewhat slowly in this country, and to be a little ponderous and rusty in the revolution of its wheels. But for caution and slowness, in a matter affecting vast areas of territory, relating to the concrete rights of property, and touching the livelihood of hundreds of thousands, if not of millions, of the population, I have nothing but praise. Our studies and investigations can scarcely be too protracted ; our action must, on no account, be flustered or precipitate ; if our proposals are to be successful, full opportunity must be afforded to public opinion to digest and to accept them, provided, that is, that they are deserving of acceptance. It is very important that the mills of the *Sirkar* should grind slowly, because in the long run they are apt to grind exceeding small.

Let me apply these observations to the present case. Mr. Rivaz has just asked leave to introduce this Bill, which has, I may almost say, been for years in course of incubation. It represents the unanimous views of the Government of India. It has been accepted by the Secretary of State. It is supported, in the brief but powerful argument to which we have just listened, by the Lieutenant-Governor of the Province to which it is proposed to be applied. Yet so conscious are we of the importance of the precedent that we are setting, and of the far-reaching consequence of the solution that we propose, that we have resolved to give the amplest opportunity for the expression of the opinions, and even of the criticism, of those whose interests will be affected by this measure. In my opinion legislation in this Council, which is invested with the law-making prerogatives of the Government of India, should be deliberate in proportion to its facility. Laws that are made in haste are apt to be repented at leisure. For these reasons we now introduce this Bill, which public and expert opinion will have an ample opportunity of discussing during the next six months, and fortified, as we hope, by this outside assistance, we shall then take up the measure when we reassemble at Simla next year.

As regards the merits of the Bill itself, I would make these observations. The issues at stake are, in my judgment, as momentous as any that can attract the attention of the Government of India. There is no country in the world that is so dependent upon the prosperity of the agricultural classes as India. There is no Government in the world that is so personally interested in agriculture as the Indian Government. We are, in the strictest sense of the term, the largest landlords in creation. Our land revenues are the staple of our income; upon the contentment and solvency of the millions who live upon the soil is based the security of our rule. In the present case we have all the greater responsibility, from the fact that, in the Province of the Punjab with which we are now about to deal, we originated the present land-system which has had the unfortunate consequences that it is proposed to rectify, as well as the legal system which has given to the usurer his opportunity. A double responsibility, therefore, rests upon our shoulders. We cannot afford to see the yeoman farmers of the Punjab, the flower of the population, and the back-bone of our Native army, dwindle and become impoverished before our eyes. Neither can we acquiesce in the consummation of a social revolution which is in contradiction both of the traditions of Indian society, and of the cardinal precepts of British rule.

If it be asked why we have selected the Punjab as the field of this experiment, the answer is that there the problem is most serious, there the evil has reached, or is reaching, the most dangerous dimensions, and there it possesses a political and social as well as a purely agrarian complexion. But our vision is not centred upon the Punjab alone. This canker of agricultural indebtedness, which is eating into the vitals of India, and which is one of the twelve questions that, as I have remarked on a previous occasion, I have set before myself the humble intention to examine, and, if it may be, to attempt to solve, is not one of narrow or contracted application, though in particular parts it may be more grave in its incidence than in others. We shall, doubtless, require to handle it in different ways in different areas. We began some years ago after a tentative fashion in the Deccan. We are now proceeding with a bolder venture in the Punjab. Should we be successful in this enterprise, we shall be encouraged to proceed, and thus stone by stone, and layer by layer, to build up the fabric of economic and social stability for our rural population.

I do not shut my eyes to the fact that many objections can be, and probably will be, raised to this legislation. It will be said that we are taking away a right which we ourselves too generously conferred ; that we are depreciating

the values of land, which, in my opinion, have been unduly
inflated, or that we are affecting the credit of a section of
the population, to whom a mistaken system has given the
opportunity of borrowing up to the edge of their own ruin.
I have, in these few sentences, indicated what would be the
nature of my reply in each case. But I may add that, even
were these minor drawbacks to be realised,—and I do not
think that they will be to any appreciable extent,—they
must be weighed in the balance against the vastly superior
advantages to the land-owning and agricultural community
that we have in view ; and they must be measured by the
scale of the disaster, which, unless some drastic measures
be taken, will assuredly before long overwhelm the smaller
zemindar classes of our population. I trust that in the
public scrutiny to which we now commit this proposal,
these considerations of statesmanship may be borne in view,
and that it may be remembered that great and salutary ends
are not apt to be secured by timid and temporising means.

## BOMBAY IMPROVEMENT TRUST.

*9th November,* 1899.

[On the afternoon of Thursday, the 9th November, the Viceroy was present at the laying of the foundation-stone of the Bombay Improvement Trust Scheme at Agripada by Lord Sandhurst. Their Excellencies were received by Mr. Hughes, the Chairman, and the Members of the Board, and having taken their seats, Dr. Bhalchandra K. Bhatavadekar read an address epitomising the work of the Board. The Chairman, in a brief speech, in which he remarked on the auspicious presence of the Viceroy, invited Lord Sandhurst to perform the ceremony. His Excellency then laid the stone, and addressed the assembly in a speech of some length, in which he expressed gratification at the Viceroy's presence and gave a fore-cast of the work immediately to be done. The Viceroy then rose, and, after the cheers had subsided, spoke as follows :—]

*Your Excellency, Ladies and Gentlemen :*—When I landed in this city at the end of December last, I did not then anticipate that within less than 12 months I should again be a visitor in your midst. Still less could I have anticipated the circumstances under which I now come. Parts of India were then suffering, and Bombay in particular was suffering, from an epidemic which, although it appeared in some measure to have abated its force, was far from eradicated. Since then that epidemic has again burst out with renewed virulence both in Bombay and still more in other parts of this Presidency. Further, as if to intensify the affliction under which the people were weighed down, and to leave no source of misery unexplored, famine has fallen upon many districts in the northern part of this Presidency through which I have just been travelling, and, although most fortunately it does not affect this immediate part of the country or this city, it must yet be a source of great anxiety to your rulers, and must make them look for-ward with trepidation to the next period at which their annual accounts will have to be squared. If we were to accept the saying as of general application that " whom the Lord loveth He chasteneth, " we might draw the conclusion that the Bombay Presidency was very dear to Providence, such has been the range and the duration of its sufferings.

Throughout this period no impartial observer can fail to have been struck by two facts ; firstly, by the resigned and pathetic patience displayed by the mass of the people ; secondly, by the activity and zeal with which the Local Government, aided by the patriotic co-operation of representative citizens, has endeavoured to cope with its almost Herculean task. It is to indicate the sympathy of the Government of India with the woes of the people, and their admiration of the efforts which have been put forward for their amelioration, that I have come upon this informal visit to Bombay. To me, Gentlemen, it seems that the Government of India cannot and should not in the smallest degree wash its hands of interest in, and, in the ultimate resort, of responsibility for, that which passes in Presidencies and Provinces that may be remote from its immediate ken. The head of the Government of India should not, in my judgment, be a passing phantom that comes and goes amid the pageantry of processions and the firing of salutes. The interests of all India are his interests ; the salvation of all India is his duty ; there are none so humble or so remote, and for the matter of that none so powerful or so independent, as not to fall within the legitimate scope of his care.

And now as to the particular circumstances that have brought me here to-day. When I was planning out my amended tour to the centres of suffering in Northern and Central India, and when I offered myself to your Governor for a brief visit to Bombay and the Deccan, he was good enough to inform me of the projected gathering of this afternoon, and to invite me to play the principal part in it. I could not consent to deprive him of the leading position to which his long and keen interest in this scheme, conceived and now finally started during his term of office, entitled him, and which no other could possibly have filled in his place. But I readily arranged my plans so as to bring me to Bombay in time for this ceremony, and to enable me to support him in the discharge of his pleasant duty.

For, Gentlemen, what is the task upon which he and you are alike engaged, and one of the inaugural steps in which we are commemorating this afternoon? I take my description of it from the words that have fallen from Lord Sandhurst's lips just now. You are endeavouring to provide this great City of Bombay with the conditions which will make life here for the poorer classes sanitary, decent, and wholesome. You want to bring the fresh breezes of the sea into the congested lungs of Bombay, to destroy the microbes of fever and pestilence that prey almost unchecked upon the constitution of an overcrowded and enfeebled population. You wish to make your city not merely beautiful without, but healthy within. It is for these purposes that all these vast works of removal of old buildings and erection of new ones, of providing open spaces, of cutting wide and airy streets, of destruction, and re-construction, and reclamation, are designed. It is a scheme proportionate in conception to the magnitude of the problem. It may, I hope, prove to be proportionate in execution to the necessities of the case.

Lord Sandhurst will, I am sure, bear me out when I add that the Government of India has from the start, two years before I joined it, evinced a much more than Platonic interest in your scheme. We have supported you in your appeals to the Secretary of State ; we have surrendered a large area of valuable property for the purposes of the contemplated improvements; we have passed special legislation in order to assist the financial operations and to add to the credit of the Trust ; and we have lent the invaluable support of the credit of the Government of India to your Municipal loan. I feel, therefore, that I am only carrying out, with a certain hereditary fitness, an obligation which has been passed on to me by Lord Elgin's Government, in being present at the successful inception of a portion of that scheme which the support of himself and of his colleagues helped to launch into existence.

I said a little while back that it was a right and proper thing that Lord Sandhurst should play the leading part in the ceremony of to-day. It must gladden his heart, as he draws near to the close of his official connection with this Presidency, to feel that all the attention and labour and care that he has devoted to this city, and to these proposals, should begin to fructify in his time, and that, before he leaves these shores, the new Bombay will have started into being, a city not of palaces and towers, not of merchant princes or nobles, but of the toilers and sweaters who drink only of the dregs of the cup of human happiness, and to whom at least we should endeavour to secure that their scanty beverage is not bitter but sweet.

To few Governors, if to any, has it fallen to pass through such a fiery ordeal, such a seven times heated furnace of trouble and trial and affliction, as has attended Lord Sand-hurst during the past few years in Bombay. Such trials, if rightly met, broaden the sympathies at the same time that they steel the nerves of the man who is by temperament both humane and brave. I am sure that there is not an individual in the Bombay Presidency, European or Native, who does not know that in Lord Sandhurst he has had a Governor whose sympathies have always been with the suffering, whose courage has remained inflexible in the face of any calamity, however dire. He will leave behind him a record of arduous work honourably and conscientiously performed, and, what is not given to any but a few to enjoy, a place in the affectionate regard of the people.

I have the advantage of knowing, and of having worked for many years as a Colleague in Parliament of the new Governor who in a few months' time will take his place. The Parliamentary and public reputation of Sir Stafford Northcote, and the name of his father, who was one of the most liberal-minded and successful Secretaries of State whom India has ever had, would in any case have ensured to him a favourable reception in India. But the personal acquaintance that I have the honour to claim with Sir Stafford Northcote entitles me to assure the people of this Presidency that they will find in their next Governor a man of ripe experience and much sagacity, who will worthily sustain the traditions of his predecessors in respect of both sympathy with the people and sound judgment in administration. I hope that when next I visit Bombay I may find that the schemes which Lord Sandhurst has so energetically started may be far advanced on the way towards completion, and that I may see this fair city with smiles on her face and no longer with tears in her eyes. (*Loud cheers.*)

VOLUNTARY PLAGUE WORKERS, POONA.

*11th November,* 1899.

[At 4 P.M. on Saturday, the 11th November, the Viceroy attended a meeting of voluntary plague workers, numbering about 500 or 600, which was held in the Council Hall at Poona. His Excellency was received by Lord Sandhurst, who addressed the assembly, speaking in warm terms of the admirable service rendered by the voluntary workers, and remarking that a few words of approbation and encouragement from the Viceroy would be highly valued. Mr. Padamjee then read a brief address in which he thanked the Viceroy for his visit and his sympathy with the people in their distress.

His Excellency spoke as follows :—]

*Your Excellency, Ladies and Gentlemen :—*It is a source of great pleasure to me, in this beautiful hall, which I now see for the first time, to have received the words of sympathetic and appreciative welcome that have just fallen from the lips of Mr. Padamjee, who, I understand, has been for many years one of your most leading and representative citizens. In one respect I cordially endorse what he has said. I am glad to be able to congratulate you on this the occasion of my first visit to Poona, upon better times. There can be no doubt that you have suffered cruelly and long. Poona, during the past year, has, I am afraid, been like a city lying in the Valley of the Shadow of Death. The city has been largely deserted by its population, and fear and apprehension have naturally enough entered into the hearts of the people. Pestilence has not spared the home of the European any more than it has that of the Native, and in striking it, in cases which are known to us all, it has taken away the dearly beloved, the fair, and the young. There was another very pathetic case which I came across in my tour of inspection this morning, when I learned of the death of a worthy Mahomedan citizen of this place, Jaffir Yusuf, who contracted the plague in the very hospital which, largely by his own munificence and activity, had been called into being. And there have been other cases similar to these, such for instance as the one mentioned by Mr.

Padamjee in the remarks to which we have just listened.
At the same time, the extent to which the Native population
have suffered is shown by the fact that they have lost, I
believe, a total of more than 10,000 of their inhabitants in
this city. In these circumstances, Your Excellency and
Gentlemen, great credit is, I think, due to that brave band
who have never lost heart in the deepest hour of adversity,
but who, with unwavering courage, and with the purest self-
sacrifice, have continued to wage the battle against the foul
fiend that was encamped in your midst. It is to meet this
gallant band of fighters, and to congratulate them, now that
their victory may be said well nigh to have been won, that I
have come here this afternoon ; and warm, I can assure you,
are the feelings of respect with which, on behalf of the Government of India, I recognise their devotion ; and warm also
the thanks which I tender to them for the work that they have
done. As the Chairman of the Municipal Commissioners
himself indicated in his remarks, you have had an untiring
and chivalrous Commander in your Governor, and a double
compliment can perhaps not be better paid than by saying
that the soldiers have not been unworthy of their Captain.

It is quite certain that, but for voluntary effort—and I
understand from what you, Sir, tell me, that the majority of
those whom I am addressing are volunteer workers—the
state of Poona would have been much worse than it has been.
Of course the Government here as elsewhere has its own
organisation, and the officers of that organisation, both Civil
and Military, have distinguished themselves by their ubiqui-
tous and unsparing zeal. But there are strains which no
official mechanism in the world, however perfect, is adequate
to meet, without the supplement of some extraneous help.
Such a crisis does occur when you have a great epidemic
breaking out in a populous city. Then you require not
merely the trained energy of the official, but you also want
the quiet and more subtle influence and co-operation of
popular residents in the place, who will go to and fro, and in
and out, among the people, and who are none the worse off

if their local knowledge is also tinctured with a little of the enthusiasm of the amateur. You have had all these advantages in this place, and you have had further the assistance of a body of nurses as unselfish and devoted as in any country, or in any period of the world's history, have ever given themselves to the alleviation of the sorrows of their fellow creatures.

Your Excellency and Gentlemen, what the future of plague may be none of us can say : we can but struggle on and do our best. Whether a cure for the pestilence is ever likely to be discovered it would be rash for any one of us, and particularly for one like myself, who is a layman, to predict. At present, by taking each case as soon as you can, by removing the patient from an infected house or quarter into the nearest hospital, and by surrounding him there with the conditions under which he is certain of pure air, and sound treatment, and of stimulating sustenance, you endeavour, and I believe that in a constantly increasing percentage of cases you manage, to pull him through.

But there are many prophylactics against the plague, which can, and which in my opinion ought as widely as possible, to be employed. I say frankly on this occasion— and I do not care how widely my words may be spread— that in my judgment inoculation is by far the wisest system of prophylactics that you can adopt. I do not say so because I have the medical or the chemical knowledge which would enable me to pronounce with authority upon the constituent proportions, or upon the scientific results, of the serum. But I say so because, as a thinking human being, with the power of using my eyes and my ears, I cannot fail to be conscious of its demonstrable effects. If I find, as I do, that out of a hundred plague seizures among uninoculated persons, the average of those who die is something about 70 to 80 per cent., and if I find that in a corresponding number of seizures among inoculated persons the proportions are entirely reversed, and that it is 70 to 80 per cent., if not more, who are saved—and these are calculations which have been furnished to me from more than one responsible quarter—then I say that figures of that kind cannot but carry conviction to my mind : and I altogether fail to see how, in the face of them, it is possible for any one to argue that inoculation is not a wise and necessary precaution. It is all very well to say that it is not infallible. No one, so far as I know, claims that it is. Its effects are apt to be obliterated in the passage of time. It acts differently in different cases. There are some physical constitutions to which it is apparently entirely unsuited. Unless the serum is most carefully administered, as well as scrupulously prepared, there is some danger arising from contamination. These are the risks, but I think the small risks, attendant upon the introduction of a system for which no one that I know of claims absolute faultlessness. But that inoculation has saved thousands and thousands of lives that would otherwise have · been lost, that it gives to the patient a more than reasonable chance of recovery, that in spite of its theoretical conflict with the conservatism of Indian feeling, and with the traditions of Native medicine, the majority of the most distinguished Native medical practitioners in this country are already in its favour, and that more and more converts are being made from the remainder each day, these are propositions which I believe it to be impossible to dispute.

If you have any doubt about it take the case which was mentioned by His Excellency in his speech just now ; take the Cantonment which lies within the sight and knowledge of most of you in this room, and ask General Burnett, whose unfaltering devotion you know so well, what inoculation has done for him in the Poona Cantonment.

I do not say that you ought to force inoculation upon the people. I am entirely of the opposite opinion. It is difficult to force something upon a community which we ourselves who give it may be entirely convinced is for their good, but which, either from prejudice or from ignorance, they are equally convinced is for their harm. You can do it in the case of children because they are irresponsible. But it is not easy to do it in the case of a community of grown up men ; and still less easy is it in the case of an Asiatic country, where, as we all know, the feelings of conservatism are very strong, and where among the great mass of the population a knowledge of what we in European countries call medical science cannot be said to exist. But for the sake of those who know no better, in the interests not of science but of humanity—for that is the cause which I am pleading—and for the future welfare of thousands of human lives, let no effort be spared to spread the facts, to inculcate reason, and to win by persuasion that which you cannot extort by force.

But you may say to me (if I may turn an English proverb into terms that will be familiar to yourselves) that a seer of example is worth a maund of precept. I quite agree with that philosophy, and I may inform you that I have carried it out in my own person. Knowing that I was likely to spend many agreeable hours in visiting plague hospitals in this part of India, I practised my own precept, and I and my whole party were inoculated before we left Simla. I have had no cause to regret it ; and I cordially commend the example to others who may be placed in a similar position.

It now only remains for me to bid you farewell. My visits to Bombay and Poona have, I think, enabled me to realise better than the study of newspapers or the reading of official reports how genuine have been the sufferings of the people, and how heroic the efforts that have been made to alleviate them. I have also seen that, here at Poona, as elsewhere in the world, the dark cloud has its silver lining, and that the co-operation against human suffering and disease in which you have all been engaged has done a great deal to draw tighter the cords of harmony and fellow-feeling that should unite, and which I believe, at the present juncture more than at any previous time, do unite, all sections in this city. I shall go back to my work at headquarters encouraged and fortified by what I have seen, and I hope that the knowledge, little though it may be, that I have secured, will enable me the better to cope with any future emergency, should such arise. I will only add that, in such a case, I earnestly hope that the city of Poona may not again be one of the victims. (*Loud cheers.*)

## BANQUET AT GWALIOR.

*29th November*, 1899.

[The Viceregal Party arrived at Gwalior on the afternoon of the 28th November, His Highness Maharaja Sindhia with the principal officers of his State and the British officials at Gwalior receiving Their Excellencies at the Railway Station. On the following evening the Maharaja gave a banquet in honour of Their Excellencies in the Jai Bilas Palace (the East Wing of which was set apart by the Maharaja for the residence of the Viceroy and Lady Curzon) at which over 100 guests were present. After dinner the Maharaja entered and took a seat near the Viceroy. His Highness then rising proposed the health of the Queen-Empress, and after a short interval proposed that of Their Excellencies, reading the following speech :—

*Ladies and Gentlemen :—*I rise to propose the health of Their Excellencies Lord and Lady Curzon of Kedleston and to offer them a hearty welcome to Gwalior. (*Cheers.*) When I first had the pleasure of meeting Their Excellencies in Calcutta last January, I was received with such kindness and cordiality that I venture to trespass on Their Excellencies' attention, and on yours, Ladies and Gentlemen, for a short time, while I touch on some events which have occurred connected with the administration of my State.

And I will first mention those which may be described as calamities. While large portions of India were suffering from famine, it could not be expected that Gwalior would escape, and therefore, I have to record that in 1897 in the northern part of my State, there was much suffering among the people owing to the insufficiency of the rainfall. Various relief works were, however, opened, such as tanks, light railways and *kucha* wells, and advances were granted to cultivators for purchase of grain and cattle. By these means the distress was alleviated and the population to a great extent saved from deserting their homes. This year a similar misfortune has befallen the southern part of the State, but I trust that the measures projected for relief may serve to prevent acute distress. (*Cheers*) The plague which has been so great a scourge to many parts of India has, I am glad to say, hardly touched Gwalior, but about $2\frac{1}{2}$ years ago an outbreak occurred at a village in my territories, called Khandraoni, which I am sure is now a well known place. The epidemic, however, through the efficient arrangements of the Medical Department, was promptly stamped out and has never re-appeared. (*Cheers.*)

I am afraid, Ladies and Gentlemen, that the condition of the State currency may properly come under the head of calamities. This question called for serious consideration a few years ago on account of the great fall in the exchange value of the State coin and of the condition of the silver market. It was consequently found advisable to introduce the

British rupee into the State, and I am glad to say, that in the two Divisions of Gwalior and Isagarh, this is now the current coin. In the course of a year or two I hope the whole State will enjoy the same advantage. (*Hear, hear.*)

While the currency question was before me it became necessary to revise the revenue settlement of the various districts of the State This important and laborious task is now being expeditiously carried out by the Land Records Department on the basis of the Imperial rupee (*Cheers.*)

I have referred to the measures for suppressing the outbreak of plague, carried out by the Medical Department, but it is not my intention to enter into any further details regarding either this or the Educational Department at present, as His Excellency will have an opportunity of hearing more about them to-morrow, but I cannot help saying that much improvement has taken place in both. The relief of the sick is much more efficient, and with the greater accommodation for patients afforded by the opening of the Memorial Hospital, this will doubtless be increased. (*Cheers.*)

The Educational Department has also shown progress, and a new feature has been the opening of Girls' Schools, which I am most anxious to encourage. (*Cheers.*)

Under the head of Public Works, Their Excellencies will be able to judge of the progress made when they see the buildings recently erected in Gwalior, and I need only mention irrigation works and the improved communications by means of roads and of light railways. (*Hear, hear.*)

The most important duties of the State in connection with revenue administration have been entrusted to a Revenue Board which was formed soon after I took up the reins of Government It was composed of some of the sardars and high officials of the State, and it is a source of great pleasure to me to record that these duties have been loyally and efficiently executed.

An immense improvement has lately taken place in the condition of the Military Department since it was re-organised, and the greatest credit is due for this result to the Commander-in-Chief of my army, General Kashi Rao Surve, C.S.I. (*Cheers.*)

On two occasions it has been my pride and privilege to send a portion of my army across the frontier to serve with Her Majesty's forces in the field (*loud cheers*),—a pride tinged with regret that I myself have personally been unable to take part in these expeditions. (*Continued cheers.*) I need hardly say that the whole of the resources of my State, including my army, are at the disposal of Her Majesty (*loud cheers*), whenever and wherever they are required, for my greatest ambition would be to serve in person against the enemies of the Queen-Empress, if possible in the front line, or, failing that, I should gladly seize the opportunity of serving in any capacity or anywhere, even at the base of operations, with the armies of the Queen. (*Loud and continued cheers.*)

Closely connected as he has been for many years with the administration of the Gwalior State, I wish to place on record the able and efficient aid rendered to me by my Chief Secretary, Sir M. Filose, who has never spared himself in the discharge of the onerous duties of his office. (*Cheers.*)

On many previous occasions I have expressed my obligations to my friend Colonel Barr, for his ever ready help to me in the difficulties and perplexities which must occur to a young and inexperienced ruler, and I would repeat now my sense of the debt of gratitude I owe him. With Colonel Barr I would desire to connect the name of Colonel Pears, Resident at Gwalior, who has always lent me his assistance when I required it, and I would also beg to give my best thanks to those officers whose services have been lent to my State by the British Government. (*Cheers.*)

And this, Ladies and Gentlemen, brings me to that part of my speech which affords me the greatest gratification. Much as I am honoured by the visit of His Excellency to my capital, that honour is immeasurably enhanced by the fact that he is accompanied by Lady Curzon, whose gracious presence adds so largely to our enjoyment. (*Cheers.*) Ladies and Gentlemen, I now ask you to drink the health of Their Excellencies Lord and Lady Curzon of Kedleston.

The toast was very heartily received, and the Maharaja resumed his seat amid loud cheers.

His Excellency who was warmly received spoke as follows :—]

*Your Highness, Ladies and Gentlemen :*—In rising to thank His Highness for the agreeable manner in which he has proposed the health of Lady Curzon and myself, I feel that I am enjoying one of the happiest experiences of an Indian Viceroy in coming for the first time as a guest to the Ruler and the State of Gwalior. (*Cheers.*) There is in this place such a pleasing and uncommon blend of old-world interest with the liveliest spirit of modern progress, that one hardly knows whether the imaginative or the practical side of nature is more thrilled by all that one sees and hears. The official visits of Viceroys to Native States are sometimes deprecated on the score of the ceremonial, and perhaps costly formalities which they involve, and of their time-honoured attributes of pomp and display. I am not inclined to share these views. To me personally there is no more interesting part of my Indian work than the opportunities which are presented to me, on tour or elsewhere, of an introduction to the acquaintance, and, as I fondly hope, to the confidence of the Native princes and chiefs of India (*hear, hear and cheers*) ; and if these princes prefer, as I believe they do prefer, to receive the representative of the sovereign whom they all acknowledge, and for whom they entertain a profound and chivalrous devotion (*hear, hear*), with a dignity becoming both to his position and to their own rank, I think that he would be a captious and sour-minded critic who were to deny them an opportunity which I believe to be as highly appreciated by their subjects as it is valued by themselves.

The spectacle and the problem of the Native States of India are indeed a subject that never loses its fascination for my mind. Side by side with our own system, and some-times almost surrounded by British territory, there are found in this wonderful country the possessions, the adminis-tration, the proud authority, and the unchallenged traditions of the Native dynasties—a combination which, both in the picturesque variety of its contrast, and still more in the smooth harmony of its operation, is, I believe, without parallel in the history of the world. (*Cheers.*) The British Government, alone of Governments, has succeeded in the wise policy of building up the security and safeguarding the rights of its feudatory principalities ; and to this are due the stability of their organisation, and the loyalty of their rulers. I rejoice wherever I go to scrutinise the practical outcome of this policy, to observe the States consolidated, the Chiefs powerful, and their privileges unimpaired.

But I also do not hesitate to say, wherever I go, that a return is owing for these advantages, and that security cannot be repaid by license, or the guarantee of rights by the unchartered exercise of wrong. The Native Chief has become, by our policy, an integral factor in the Imperial organisation of India. (*Cheers.*) He is concerned not less than the Viceroy or the Lieutenant-Governor in the admin-istration of the country. (*Cheers.*) I claim him as my colleague and partner. (*Loud and continued cheers.*) He cannot remain *vis à vis* of the Empire a loyal subject of Her Majesty the Queen-Empress, and *vis à vis* of his own people, a frivolous or irresponsible despot. (*Hear, hear.*) He must justify and not abuse the authority committed to him; he must be the servant as well as the master of his people. (*Hear, hear and cheers.*) He must learn that his revenues are not secured to him for his own selfish gratification, but for the good of his subjects ; that his internal administration is only exempt from correction in proportion as it is honest ; and that his *gadi* is not intended to be a divan of indulgence but the stern seat of duty. (*Cheers.*) His figure should not merely be known on the polo-ground, or on the race-course, or in the European hotel. These may be his relaxations, and I do not say that they are not legitimate relaxations ; but his real work, his princely duty, lies among his own people. (*Loud cheers.*) By this standard shall I, at any rate, judge him. By this test will he in the long run, as a political institution, perish or survive. (*Cheers.*)

It is with the greater freedom that I venture upon these remarks on the present occasion because I do not know anywhere of a prince who better exemplifies their application, or who shows a more consistent tendency to act up to the ideal which I have sketched, than the young Maharaja whose splendid hospitality we are enjoying this evening. (*Loud and continued cheers.*) Before I arrived in India I had heard of his public spirit, his high sense of duty, his devotion to the interests of his country. During my first few days in Calcutta I had, as he has mentioned, the pleasure of making his acquaintance ; and now in his own State the opportunity is presented to me of improving it, which I very highly prize, and of seeing at first hand the excellent work which he is doing in almost every branch of administration.

The Maharaja appears to me, from all I have heard, to have realised that the secret of successful government is personality. (*Hear, hear.*) If he expects his officials to follow an example, he himself must set it. (*Hear, hear.*) If he desires to conquer torpor or apathy, he must exhibit enthusiasm. Everywhere he must be to his people the embodiment of sympathetic interest, of personal authority, of dispassionate zeal. There is no position to which a prince who fulfils this conception may not aspire in the affections of his countrymen (*hear, hear*), and there is scarcely any limit to his capacity of useful service to the State. (*Cheers*).

It is only five years ago since the Maharaja Sindhia was invested with full ruling powers ; but how much may be done within a short space of time by an exercise of the faculties and accomplishments which I have described may be gathered from the remarkable, but unassuming, record of administrative progress set forth in the speech which His Highness has just delivered. (*Cheers.*) It is a record which any ruler might be proud to point to, and any Viceroy gratified to receive. (*Cheers.*)

The Maharaja has mentioned the steps which he took, in 1896-97, to relieve the famine distress in those portions of his State which were then afflicted. But he has refrained from alluding to a measure then taken by him, which I regard as of at least equal importance in the evidence of public-spirited and practical sagacity which it supplied. He came to the rescue of some of the neighbouring States in their hour of need, and by a system of well-timed loans, in which the Government of India were only too happy to lend him the assistance of their guarantee, he enabled several of his brother Chiefs to tide over what would otherwise have been a serious crisis, at the same time that he obtained a reasonable interest upon his own outlay. The policy in fact was not merely one of opportune and generous relief, but also of sound and practical finance. (*Hear, hear and cheers.*) I hope that, should the occasion again arise, His Highness may be equally ready in protecting the interests of his own subjects ; while I rejoice to have heard, since my arrival in Gwalior that he has already volunteered to repeat his former action in lending a helping hand to some of his less wealthy and well-placed neighbours. (*Cheers.*)

The Maharaja has alluded to another measure, namely, the conversion of his Currency, in which we may find a further illustration of the same liberal ideas, combined with good business. (*Cheers.*) It is obvious that the existence of as many as five different coinages, of various and fluctuating value, in a State of this size, must have been fraught not merely with inconvenience, but with positive economic loss, to his subjects. Indeed the Maharaja himself has graphically described it as a public calamity. So it was: but it will not be so much longer ; for I entertain no doubt that the conversion, when it has been completely carried out, will result in a direct expansion of the revenue of the State, as well as in advantage to every class of the population, from the zemindar and cultivator of the soil to the merchant and bunia in the city bazárs. (*Cheers.*)

I must also express my acknowledgment of the excellent service that has been rendered, in a perhaps less showy but certainly not less important field of administration, by the revision of the revenue settlement in Gwalior, and by the operations of the Revenue Board, in both of which measures His Highness has had the invaluable and expert assistance of one of his ablest officials, Colonel Pitcher. (*Cheers.*)

And now I come to another department of the Maharaja's activity, in which he has shown a good deal of the spirit of the enthusiast, as well as of the aptitude of the statesman. I believe that His Highness may be said to have inherited his military instincts from his distinguished father, the late Maharaja (*cheers*), who was, as we all know, no mean soldier, and who was honoured by being made an Honorary General in Her Majesty's Army. (*Cheers.*) To-morrow morning I shall have the pleasure of inspecting both the Imperial Service Troops, which His Highness has furnished on so liberal a scale towards Lord Dufferin's great scheme of combined Imperial defence, and also his own military forces. I must not, therefore, praise that which I have not yet seen, except in the streets yesterday and to-day. But I am at liberty to appeal to notorious facts. The service which was rendered by the Gwalior Transport Corps in the Chitral and Tirah Campaigns is known to all ; and we also know how keenly their prince has interested himself in every detail of their equipment and discipline, and how earnest was his desire to be permitted to serve with them at the front. (*Cheers.*) His two regiments of Imperial Service Cavalry are, I am informed, equally fit for active service: and it must be a gratification to Sir Howard Melliss, and to his capable band of inspecting officers, to see how thoroughly the aid that they have given to the Maharaja in the organisation and training of these troops has been justified by results, the more so, as this is the last occasion upon which Sir Howard Melliss will inspect them before he retires from a service which has been of equal advantage to the Native States, whose Imperial Service regiments he has supervised, and to the Government of India, by whom he has for so many years been entrusted with the task. (*Cheers.*) As regards his own forces, the Maharaja's rule has been characterised by a similar advance in efficiency ; for whilst he has decreased the number of his troops, he has taken active steps, in which he has not been unassisted by the Government of India, to raise the standard and to improve the condition of the remainder. I am convinced that His Highness is speaking from the bottom of his heart when he declares that he has no higher ambition than to serve in person against the enemies of the Queen, in any capacity or place where the opportunity may be afforded to him (*loud cheers*), and I shall not fail to pass on to Her Majesty his loyal statements, and his manly and patriotic words. (*Continued cheers.*)

I was glad to note the generous and friendly tribute which was paid by the Maharaja to my Agent in Central India, Colonel Barr (*hear, hear*), as well as to the officer, Colonel Pears, who is at present filling the post of Resident in this State. I know from experience that Colonel Barr, who has been so long associated with His Highness, regards him with an affection that has in it almost a parental tinge (*cheers*) : and I rejoice to think that the many services which Colonel Barr has rendered to the Maharaja and to the State are not less frankly recognised in Gwalior than they are at the head-quarters of Government. (*Loud cheers.*)

Before I sit down I must not fail to thank His Highness for the singularly graceful terms in which he has included the name of Lady Curzon in this toast. We shall both look forward, while we are in India, to further opportunities of improving an acquaintance so happily begun, and so likely, as I hope, to deepen into a personal regard. I shall watch the future of His Highness with the keenest interest. I believe that he has before him a career that will be replete with advantage to his subjects and with honour to himself. I trust that he may be blessed with good health, that his spirits may remain eager, and his courage undimmed. (*Cheers.*) For my own part I can truthfully say that I never raised a glass to my lips with greater pleasure than on the present occasion, when I give to you all, Ladies and Gentlemen, the toast of ' His Highness the Maharaja Sindhia of Gwalior.' (*Loud and continued cheers.*)

[The Maharaja then rose and thanked the company for the kind manner in which they had received his health.]

ADDRESS FROM THE BRINDABAN MUNICIPALITY.

*5th December*, 1899.

[On Tuesday, the 5th December, the Viceroy with Lady Curzon and Staff spent the forenoon in driving to and visiting Brindaban and its temples. In a pavilion of one of these, the Seth Temple, the Viceroy received a deputation from the Municipal Board, who presented him with an address cordially welcoming him to their sacred city. This was the second occasion, they said, on which a Viceroy had so honoured them, Lord Ripon having visited Brindaban shortly after the local self-government scheme was extended to their Municipality. Though in point of population and income Brindaban was small compared with other Municipalities in the North-West Provinces, there was no other Municipality held in higher esteem, seeing it was closely connected with the life and deeds of their Lord Sri Krishna. It was this which gave Brindaban its sanctity, attracting to its shrines thousands of pilgrims from the remotest corners of India, many amongst them Hindus who, in order to attain salvation, were brought there to die. It was no easy task to make suitable sanitary arrangements for these, but the Municipality congratulated themselves on having satisfactorily done this. At one time plague was feared, but, thanks to Sir A. MacDonnell's precautions, this had been staved off, while the fairs and festivals continued with their usual pomp and splendour. Referring to the Famine which was already felt, their only consolation, they said, was that they had a wise statesman and able administrator in the Viceroy, and an experienced and sympathetic ruler in Sir Antony MacDonnell.

His Excellency the Viceroy replied as follows :—]

*Mr. Chairman and Members of the Municipal Board of Brindaban :*—I have learnt, with no small interest, from your address that I am only the second Viceroy who has visited the picturesque and sacred town of Brindaban. I once saw an album of photographs of the temples and shrines in this famous spot ; and I resolved that if ever again I found myself in the neighbourhood, Brindaban should at all hazards be included in my itinerary. A great and becoming reverence is paid by humanity to the birthplace of heroes and to the sanctuaries of nations. Whatever has attracted the enthusiasm or has inspired the devotion of large masses of mankind is deserving of more than a superficial attention ; since it is by such sentiments that men have as a rule been impelled to exceptional deeds. In Brindaban the piety of your devotees has adorned this locality with some of the most magnificent temples that have been erected in modern times—the majority of them, I may remark, under the secure and even-handed protection of British rule. But your most considerable ancient structure, the temple of Govind Deva, which I have seen described as the most impressive religious edifice erected by Hindu art in Northern India, also owes its restoration to the British Government, which 25 years ago allotted a sum of more than Rs. 30,000 to the task. I do not quote this fact so much as illustrating the considerate impartiality which the Supreme Power has consistently displayed in India towards the sectaries of rival creeds, as because it exemplifies what, in my opinion, is one of the primary duties of Government in this country. I regard the stately or beautiful or historic fabrics of a by-gone age, independently of the purpose for which they were set up, or the faith to which they were dedicated, as a priceless heirloom, to be tenderly and almost religiously guarded by succeeding generations; and during my administration of the Government of India no one shall find me niggardly or grudging in the practical realisation of this aim. We are not ordinarily so rich in originality ourselves as to afford to allow the memorials of an earlier and superior art or architecture to fall into ruin ; and I accept the conservation of the ancient monuments of India as an elementary obligation of Government.

When Lord Ripon came here in 1881, the Municipality, which his legislation had called into being, might have been described as still in its cradle. I am now confronted with a healthy adult which has since justified itself by its works. In keeping the town of Brindaban clean and healthy, in safeguarding the health of the thousands of pilgrims who annually crowd your festivals and fairs, and in warding off the pestilence from your doors, the Municipal Board has acquitted itself with credit in a delicate and onerous task. I am glad that you recognize the sagacious advice in this respect that you have received from your present Lieutenant-Governor, Sir Antony MacDonnell.

In the concluding words of your address you ask me to convey to Her Majesty the Queen-Empress the expression of your deep and earnest feelings of devotion. I am well aware that it is solely as her representative that I am accorded the friendly welcome that you have extended to me this morning ; and in conveying to Her Majesty your loyal message, I feel that I may truthfully assure her, in the opening words of your address, that she is regarded in this remote but not insignificant Indian town, not merely as the Sovereign, but as the Royal mother, of her faithful subjects.

## ADDRESS FROM THE AGRA MUNICIPALITY.

*5th December*, 1899.

[The Viceregal Party arrived at Agra from Muttra at 5 P.M. on Wednesday, the 5th December 1899, and half an hour later the Viceroy received in
Camp a numerous deputation from the Municipality, who presented an
address, which was read by Mr. Cobb, the Collector. In welcoming Lord
and Lady Curzon the Municipality expressed regret that their visit should
have been marred by the gloom of famine. They were, however, proud
that their city was destined to play no insignificant part in the alleviation
of distress. During the past four months no less than 19,000 tons of grain
and 13,000 tons of fodder had been thrown into the heart of the famine-
stricken area It had not yet been found necessary to inaugurate extensive
measures of relief. but they had opened a poor-house for the temporary
maintenance of starving refugees and the destitute in the city. It was unnecessary for them in the presence of so distinguished an Oriental traveller
as the Viceroy to make more than a passing allusion to the glorious inheritance of monuments bequeathed by great men of old to them, their unworthy
representatives. The address then went on to deal with education, hospitals, and sanitation, trade and water-supply.

His Excellency the Viceroy replied as follows :—]

*Mr. Chairman and Gentlemen:*—There was an old saying
in Europe according to which all roads were declared to
lead to Rome. This was a confession of the political and eccle-
siastical importance of the Imperial city. May we not
similarly say in India that all roads lead to Agra ? Hither
comes the traveller of every nationality and clime, intent
upon seeing the incomparable memorials of a by-gone age ;
hither comes the merchant, drawn to a locality which is
yearly becoming more and more an emporium of trade ;
and here in due course is to be seen each successive Viceroy,
alternately engaged in reverent contemplation of the marvellous relics of the past, and in a study of the new phenomena
which the restless energy and commotion of modern life are
perpetually introducing to his gaze.

There is a further sense in which Agra may be said to be
increasingly becoming a junction of the ways. Already
three railway systems meet in your city, which has become,
next to Delhi, the principal railway centre of Northern
India ; and which will attain an even greater importance

when the new line has been constructed which is to connect you *viâ* Muttra with the old capital of the Moghul Empire. To one before whose eyes the past and present are always mingling, as at Agra, in a mysterious haze of interwoven fancy and fact, there is something peculiarly dramatic in the emulous nineteenth century enterprise of these two great cities, which three hundred years ago looked out upon each other from their separate sites on the bank of the sacred river, with their rival coronets of domes and minarets and palace-towers.

You have reminded me in your address that you have been able to turn these advantages of position and communication to a very practical and remunerative service in the past few months. They have enabled Agra to figure as a great distributing-centre for the relief of the neighbouring states and districts that have been suffering from the aggravated scarcity that we all deplore. The North-West Provinces and Oudh have poured in their superfluous stores of grain into this city so rapidly, that the rolling-stock has sometimes proved inadequate to carry them ; while simultaneously, the country roads have been thronged with carts bringing in grass from the interior of the district. From Agra both of these supplies have been discharged again into the distressed States of Rajputana and even over a still wider area. If the sufferings of others have thus proved to your merchants a source of commercial gain, they need not damp your legitimate satisfaction at having found yourselves in a position to lend assistance to your neighbours : while I hope that you will have been careful not to deplete your own resources, in view of contingencies by which, should the winter rains fall short of their normal volume, you might yourselves be gravely affected in the future. For the present I am glad to learn that there is no prospect of such an emergency. The district appears to be well provided with wells and canals ; and in spite of the failure of the autumnal rainfall, the total outturn of the year's harvests will, I am told, exceed an 8-anna crop.

When the test works, to which allusion has been made, were started last month, they did not fill : and the City Poor-House still happily attracts but few inmates. These are favourable symptoms. But they do not exempt you from the duty of unremitting vigilance, since the experience of the past summer supplies but little ground for confidence either in the recurrence of normal conditions, or in the fulfilment of meteorological forecasts.

I am glad to learn, now that the affairs of your Corporation have been placed upon a sounder basis, that you are about to proceed with the final measures still required to ensure a full and adequate water-supply for the city, and also with new drainage works that are necessitated as a complement to the above scheme. Our standards in both respects are much more exacting even than those of the preceding generation ; and the Municipality that furnishes its citizens with decent homes, pure water and well-flushed drains, from a revenue raised by equitable taxation, and administered with honesty, is one that will find quite enough to fill its own hands, and that will deserve well of the public.

You have not erred in calling my attention even in a passing paragraph, to the glorious monuments of the past that have made the name of Agra a household word throughout the civilised world. I said in my reply to the Municipal Address that was presented to me at Brindaban this morning, that I regarded the conservation of national monuments as among the first duties of Government : and, if such be my views, you may imagine with what scrupulous and jealous care I shall apply this canon to the case of the priceless relics of the Moghul epoch at Agra. The British nation has, I hope, now purged itself of the spirit of stupid and unlettered vandalism which led it in earlier days, wherever possible, to turn a disused palace in India into a barrack, and to obliterate with a uniform whitewash the exquisite decorations of the classical age. An immense amount of care has been devoted in recent times to the examination, the illustration, the preservation, and the

repair of the principal monuments at Agra ; and at the present
date large sums are being annually expended upon the
up-keep of the Taj, of the Palace in the Fort, of the
Tomb of Akbar at Sikandra, and upon his deserted town
of Fatehpur Sikri.   I shall examine all these buildings,
which are already well known to me, with the most
minute care ; and shall not rest satisfied until, in each
case, the structure has been rendered secure against the
ravages of further decay and has received such attention as
may be feasible and desirable in faithful renovation, or
reproduction, of that which has been injured or destroyed.

With these memorials of a vanished epoch the modern
world, with its different objects and ideals, can never aspire
to compete.   In a more utilitarian age we expend the public
funds not upon forts and palaces and tombs but upon institutions of ascertained worth and of public value.   Hospitals,
Colleges, and Schools have taken the place of the regal
fabrics of the past.   I rejoice to hear that in this respect
Agra is not falling short of its ancient traditions ; and that
its monuments of the nineteenth century, if they are not
magnificent, are at any rate useful, and, instead of gratifying
the costly tastes of kings and princes, are devoted to the
unpretentious service of the community.

In thanking you, Gentlemen, for this address, may I add
one word of especial acknowledgment of the happy thought,
and the good taste, that have suggested to you the presentation to me, in place of the ordinary municipal casket, of
this beautiful specimen of the *pietra dura* handicraft for which
Agra has always been renowned.   It is a work which I have,
on previous occasions, not merely studied in the glorious
examples of seventeenth century art, but in the attempts of
modern artificers to reproduce it ; and from the cursory examination which I have so far been able to give to this table
I am led to think that your craftsmen retain a large measure
of the skill and ingenuity which rendered the architecture of
this place so famous a few centuries ago.   I should like myself that the specimens of this work should not merely be

known to the visitors who come to Agra during the cold weather, but that it should gain a wider field of publicity and popularity ; and I am convinced that my own possession of this table, for which I cordially thank you, will have that tendency, so far as it is seen by my friends, and will encourage many who do not come to Agra, as well as those who do, to give orders which are certain to be well executed.

## DARBAR AT LUCKNOW.

### 13th December, 1899.

[On Wednesday, the 13th December 1899, at 12-30 P.M., the Viceroy held a public Darbar at Lucknow, for the reception of the Talukdars and other Darbaris of Oudh. It was attended by the Lieutenant-Governor and all his principal officials, the district staff and military officers of Lucknow, the non-official European community, and a large number of ladies, including Her Excellency Lady Curzon and Lady MacDonnell ; the Talukdars and native gentlemen present, amongst whom were His Highness the Raja of Kapurthala, the Maharaja of Ajudhya, the Maharaja of Balrampur, Kanwar Sir Harnam Singh, and other leading men, numbering over 500. The scene was one of exceptional interest and brilliancy, the total number present being over 1,000. The proceedings took place in a large tent pitched in the Martinière Park. The Viceroy entering the Darbar Tent was attended by the Foreign Secretary, his Private and Military Secretaries and his Personal Staff. After taking his seat on the throne, the Darbar was declared open by His Excellency. The presentation of the Raja of Kapurthala, the Talukdars, and other Darbaris was then proceeded with, and at its conclusion His Excellency rose and delivered the following address :—]

*Talukdars and Darbaris of Oudh :*—In the concluding stages of a tour, which, while it has been one of hard work and of some strain, has yet taught me much and enabled me to see much that a Viceroy of India ought to know, it is with no small pleasure that I meet, in the dignified and time-honoured function of a Darbar, so famous and so loyal a body of Her Majesty's subjects as the Talukdars of Oudh. Already, upon my arrival at Calcutta, you have paid me the compliment of an address of welcome, presented to me by the hands of your President, the Maharaja of Ajudhya. And now, in the historic capital of your own Province, to which so many memories cling that are dear both to your race and mine, the opportunity is presented to me of returning the compliment, and of receiving you in a manner befitting the rank and traditions of the Talukdars of Oudh.

I regard a Darbar as an occasion of no ordinary significance ; not merely because of its picturesque and stately ceremonial, or of its harmony with the venerated traditions of an ancient polity, as because of the opportunity which it furnishes to a Viceroy to meet, in becoming surroundings, the leading men in the community, and to exchange with them those formal assurances which to my mind are invested with a much more than conventional courtesy, inasmuch as they are the real foundation stones of the stable fabric of Her Majesty's Indian Empire. Open speech and clear understanding between the Queen's representative and her trusted lieges are essential to the solidarity of a dominion which is built upon the co-operation of both ; and while I am honoured by holding my present office, I shall welcome, instead of shrinking from, any occasion for such an interchange of confidence and renewal of understanding. Indeed to me it seems that the times have passed by when rulers, or the deputies of rulers, can anywhere live with impunity amid the clouds of Olympus. They must descend from the hilltops and visit the haunts of men. They must speak to their fellows in their own tongue, and must be one in purpose and in heart with the people. Only so will they justify their high station : only so will their authority be free from challenge, because it will be founded upon trust.

It was in such a spirit that Lord Canning came to Lucknow in October 1859, to obliterate the scars of the Mutiny, and to inaugurate the new régime of generous clemency and benefaction to which the Talukdars of Oudh owe their status and their rights. In this assemblage to-day there are doubtless some who remember that historic occasion, and call to mind the assurance of Lord Canning that so long as the Talukdars remained loyal and faithful subjects, and just masters, their rights and dignities should be upheld by every representative of the Queen, and that no man should disturb them. It was in pursuit and in confirmation of Lord Canning's policy that Sir John Lawrence came here in 1867, to acknowledge the liberal manner in which the Talukdars had met his efforts to mitigate certain hardships which had resulted from the arrangements of 1858. It was in a similar spirit that, in 1882, Lord Ripon received the Talukdars upon the very spot where Lord Canning had presented to them their charter 23 years before. And while it is on the same site, it is also, I assure you, in an identical spirit, that after a further lapse of 17 years another Viceroy has come here to-day to renew to you the friendly assurances of the Sovereign power, and to mark yet another stage in the history of the undisturbed and happy relations that subsist between the Talukdars and the British Government. It was not till I had ascertained from enquiry that you yourselves were most anxious that this Darbar should be held, and that you recognized in it a compliment to your position as well as a confirmation of your privileges, that I arranged with Sir Antony MacDonnell for the ceremony of this afternoon.

I am not one of those persons who would venture to claim that the policy of the British Government in India has always or everywhere been distinguished by consistency, or foresight, or wisdom. We have made many experiments, and we have perpetrated some failures. I am not sure that Oudh has not been the scene of some of these experiments, and perhaps also the witness of some of these failures. We have sometimes poured new wine very hastily into old bottles, and have been surprised if they have burst in our hands. But whatever the errors or miscalculations of British Government in the past, we may I think claim with truth that we do not depart from our pledged word ; and that British honour is still the basis, as it is the safeguard, of British administration. It was once said by the most brilliant writer who has yet devoted his genius to the illumination of Anglo-Indian history, that " English valour and English intelligence have done less to extend and to preserve our Oriental Empire than English veracity." I agree with those words. Where the faith of Government has been pledged, there, even at loss to ourselves, at the sacrifice of our material interests, and sometimes even to our political detriment, we have, so far as my knowledge extends, uniformly held to our bond, and I hope shall continue to do so to the end. If ultimately we have profited by this conduct, no such considerations of expediency, believe me, have been our motive. We have pursued justice and truth, it may be sometimes with faltering steps, but for their own sake and for that alone.

Our relations with the Province of Oudh afford a not inapt illustration of steadfast adherence to this high standard of public honour. For 40 years our policy towards Oudh has never deviated from the ideal which, when the Mutiny was over, was deliberately accepted and promulgated by Lord Canning, and at a later date was ratified by Sir John Lawrence, *viz.*—that of maintaining the existence and privileges, guaranteed by binding engagements, of the landed aristocracy of this province. With this object have been devised the various measures of legislation that have from time to time been passed with reference to the Land Question in Oudh—the Oudh Estates Act of 1869, the Talukdars' Relief Act of 1870, the Oudh Rent Act of 1886. It is with the same object in view that your present Lieutenant-Governor, Sir Antony MacDonnell, has recently framed the Settled Estates Bill which, with a patience worthy of the statesman, and with the anxious desire to consider every point of view, and to conciliate all reasonable opposition, that has uniformly characterised his public career, he has successfully guided through the earlier stages of its inception and introduction.

It is unfortunately but too true that some members at any rate of your body have fallen upon evil times ; and that the pressure of financial embarrassment, due sometimes to extravagance and folly, but sometimes also to the force of circumstances beyond human control, has resulted in the increasing transfer and alienation, in other words, in the breaking up, of the estates which it has always been the desire of the British Government, equally with yourselves, to conserve. From these dangers, the unarrested progress of which would be fraught with mischief to the entire community, the Talukdars themselves petitioned the Government to find for them some relief ; and it is in deference to this request that the Bill of which I speak has been drawn up and brought in.

Gentlemen, it rests with yourselves whether, when this Bill has been passed into law, you take advantage of it or not. In deference to our engagements, in faithful execution of our pledged word, we cannot and we should not propose to dictate to you a curtailment of rights which, if acceptable to some, might be superfluous and obnoxious to others. We can but provide the means by which, without prejudice to the legitimate rights of creditors, those of you who desire to ensure the maintenance of their hereditary estates by direct settlement, may be able to do so. If the Court of Wards Bill, which has been introduced and passed by the Local Legislature with the same disinterested and conservative aim, be regarded by the Talukdars as the supplement of the Settled Estates Bill, to whose successful operation it should lend a great reinforcement of strength, I see no reason why you should not obtain speedy and permanent relief from the embarrassments of which you complain. But I repeat that, the Government having played their part, it is now for you to play yours, in the same temper of loyalty and good faith that has uniformly marked your relations with the Supreme Government since the present system began.

Gentlemen, everywhere throughout India I observe an increasing spirit of public activity, and an awakening to the conditions of modern life, which convince me that the conservatism of the most conservative of countries is not incompatible with a keen recognition of the necessities of an age of progress. The spread of railways, the increase of education, the diffusion of the Press, the construction of public works, the expansion of manufacturing and industrial undertakings, all of these bespeak, not the placid reveries of the recluse, who is absorbed in abstract thought, or in numb contemplation of the past, but the eager yearnings of a fresh and buoyant life. This spirit, as is natural, is most visible in the great centres of population, and in the districts which are traversed by main lines of rail. But it is also penetrating to unconsidered corners, and is slowly leavening the mighty mass. In this province, the natural richness of which has caused it to be designated the "garden of India," you have greatly profited by recent railway extensions, and you possess a railroad system which, running parallel in the main to the course of your great rivers, with frequent lateral connections, appears to be well adapted to the exploitation of your abundant resources. We hope, before any very long time has elapsed, to supply you with a further connecting link, in the shape of the Allahabad-Fyzabad line ; with a bridge across the Ganges. This important link, together with shorter communication with Lucknow, should be of great benefit to the Province.

The name of Lord Canning, to whom you owe so much, is perpetuated in the title of the College which exists in this City. It is not an unfitting tribute to his memory that the Talukdars should have lent so consistent a support to the Canning College, since its institution 35 years ago ; and I am glad also to be informed that you take an equal interest in the Colvin Institute, specially designed as it was for the education of your sons. While you thus show that you are not indifferent to the claims of higher education to which we owe in so large a measure the development of that growing energy and vitality of which I have already spoken, pray remember that among your tenants in the country villages and districts are many to whom higher education will never be anything more than a riddle, but to whom you owe it that their elementary education shall be something more than a name. In the ingenious glosses and paraphrases to which a Viceroy's utterances in India are not infrequently exposed, he is apt to find that praise of one thing is interpreted as involving unconscious disparagement of another. When I praise you, therefore, for your support of the higher education of your sons and families, I must not be understood to deprecate the claims of primary education among the masses of the people, and when I invite your attention to the great importance of the latter subject, I must not be supposed to be offering an affront to the former. Only, in proportion as the peasant population is poor, and backward, and helpless, so is the responsibility greater that is devolved upon their superiors to furnish them with the rudimentary means by which they may raise themselves in the world.

In Oudh may be observed a happy reproduction of a system with which we are very familiar in England, where the traditions and the spirit of territorial responsibility, resulting from the growth of centuries, are exceptionally strong. There we find the country gentleman sitting in gratuitous and voluntary discharge of the administration of justice among his neighbours, to their complete satisfaction, and with no small advantage, in the shape of increased knowledge and power of good, to himself. I am glad to think that this graft from an English stock, which after all is only an adaptation in Western forms of a custom familiar in the East, has found so congenial a climate in the Province of Oudh; and I should like to tender my thanks to those Native gentlemen who have thus assisted Government by acting as Honorary Magistrates. Every case which by a simple and straightforward decision they succeed in keeping out of the Law Courts, involves, in my judgment, not merely a saving of expense, friction, and heart-burning to the parties concerned, but also a positive service to the community.

Finally, Gentlemen, let me say with what satisfaction I have met to-day in this great assemblage and have had presented to me a number of Chiefs, some of them the sons or grandsons of those who stood by us in the great hour of trial 42 years ago, some of them—a dwindling number— the still surviving actors in those solemn and immortal scenes. I have noticed upon the breasts of others here present—a seamed and gallant band—the medals that tell me of participation in the defence of the Residency, of lives risked, and of blood shed in the cause of the British Government, with which was indissolubly bound up, in the agony of that fateful struggle, the cause of order as against anarchy, of civilisation as against chaos. Standing here at this distance of time, I who am of a later generation, and was not even born when these brave men performed the deeds at which the whole world has since gazed with admiring awe, count it as among my highest privileges that I should see the faces, and, as Her Majesty's representative, receive the homage, of these illustrious veterans. Still prouder and more inspiring is the thought that in this great Durbar, where are gathered in loyal harmony with our old allies the descendants of some who took another part, I may read the lesson of the Great Reconciliation, and may point the eternal moral that mercy is more powerful than vengeance.

[His Excellency's address had been previously translated into the vernacular and copies distributed to the Darbaris. After the distribution of *attar* and *pân* the ceremony came to a close.]

## FAMINE.

*19th January*, 1900.

[ In the Legislative Council held at Calcutta on Friday, the 19th January, the Hon'ble Mr. Ibbetson made a statement on the agricultural outlook and the measures in progress for the relief of distress. His Excellency, the President, addressed the Council as follows :— ]

Those Hon'ble Members who were present at the last meeting of this Council in the Simla Session on 20th October last, when statements were made upon the approaching famine by Mr. Rivaz and myself, will remember that even then the Government of India were seriously impressed with the gravity of the situation, and that our speeches were coloured with a profound anxiety as to what might yet be in store for us. Nothing that I saw in my ensuing tour, in the course of which I visited many of the suffering areas, in any way relieved that anxiety. On the contrary it was already evident, from the number of persons in receipt of relief or engaged upon relief works, from the stream of humanity pouring in upon them daily from all quarters of the country, and from the complete disappearance that was almost universally reported to me of the old-fashioned reluctance entertained by the Indian peasant to the acceptance, except in the last resort, of charitable relief, that we were likely, as time passed by, and if no rain were to fall in the winter months, to be confronted with a calamity as great as, if not greater than has ever befallen this country, so used, in consequence of the immense numbers of the population, to calamity on a large scale, so inured, from previous experience, to this particular aspect of human suffering.

The statement which has just been made on behalf of the Government of India by Mr. Ibbetson, will have shown you that these gloomy anticipations have been more than fulfilled ; that the area of visitation has expanded to a degree that has even surpassed our worst fears ; that, except in certain favoured provinces and localities, every condition of nature and climate appears during the past three months to have fought against us ; and that we are now face to face with a famine, of water, of food, of cattle, which in the particular areas affected is unprecedented in character and intensity. These are no rash words. From Bombay, from Rajputana, from the Central Provinces, in the reports that reach me, I continually come across the same idea, the same regretful confession, the same melancholy phrase. When, exactly three years ago, on January 14th, 1897, Lord Elgin presided over a great public meeting held in Calcutta to consider the then famine, he observed that $1\frac{1}{4}$ millions of persons were already on relief, and that the occasion had no parallel. In the present week of January 1900 there are nearly $3\frac{1}{2}$ millions of persons on relief, and the parallel has come and, alas! has been left far behind.

There is another respect in which the conditions are entirely different now. At that time the attention of England, and one might also say of Europe, was turned upon suffering India. Hundreds of thousands of pounds were contributed and sent out by generous hearts and eager hands. The whole external world seemed to share our sorrow, and in the different forms open to it contributed to the alleviation of Indian distress. Now we have to suffer and to struggle alone. It is not that England, or the British Empire, or humanity at large, has become less sympathetic or more niggardly. Our troubles, in so far as they are known in England, will excite just as genuine and poignant emotions as on the previous occasion. But, as we all know, the whole thoughts of England, and of almost every Englishman throughout the world, are fixed upon the war in South Africa, and upon that alone. Even in this country we feel the patriotic excitement and the nervous strain, whether we be Europeans or Natives ; and how much more must it be so in England, where the honour and prestige of the old country are felt to be at stake, and where almost every hearth has given some near or dear one to danger. And equally, if the war absorbs all interest, so does it exhaust the national generosity. I am afraid it is too much to expect

that England can again come to our rescue this time, as she
did so splendidly in 1897, or that, so far as can at present
be judged, we can anywhere outside of this country expect
a more than passive sympathy with our misfortunes.

It is clear then that we must fight our own battles with
our own means. Speaking for the officers of Government,
I am sure that the last thing that they desire is any public
advertisement ; whilst if we cannot look for financial help
from the outside, our own back must be broad enough to
bear the burden. With patience and fortitude we must
pursue our task, conscious that though we are not engaged
in stirring deeds which affect the fate of empires, we are yet
performing our duty, an English duty and an Indian duty,
and that we are trying to do what no war on the face of it
does, *viz.*, to save from death many millions of human lives.

Some notice has been excited by the fact that the
Government of India has recently issued a Circular letter to
the Local Governments, calling their attention to the exceptional circumstances of the present situation, and suggesting a greater stringency in the tests to be henceforward
applied. I have seen this circular described in the Native
press, of which I may say in passing that I am a not in-
attentive student, as disastrous and inhuman. Such a
criticism can surely not be based upon any knowledge of the
facts. I accept on behalf of the Government of India the
full responsibility for that letter. It expressed the deliberate opinions of my colleagues and myself. I am the last
person in the world to prefer the mere interests of economy
to those of humanity, and I acknowledge to the utmost the
obligation of Government to spend its last rupee in the
saving of human life and in the mitigation of extreme
human suffering. But the Government of India must
necessarily take a broader outlook, while it manifestly profits
by a wider knowledge, than its critics. We are acquainted
by the reports that we receive from our officers with what is
passing, not in one district alone, but in all parts of the
country. We are the custodians of the interests of the tax-

payers of India. We have to look to what may happen in future famines—and recent experience does not encourage us to regard famine as the rare and isolated phenomenon which it has hitherto been held to be. Above all, it is our duty jealously to watch and to conserve the character of the people. In my judgment any Government which imperilled the financial position of India in the interests of a prodigal philanthropy would be open to serious criticism. But any Government, which, by indiscriminate alms-giving, weakened the fibre, and demoralised the self-reliance of the population, would be guilty of a public crime.

Let me then mention a few of the considerations that led us to think that such dangers were not altogether remote. I lay it down as an initial proposition that the obligation upon Government in times of famine is to save human life and to prevent starvation, or extremity of suffering that may be dangerous to life. No Government can undertake, at such a time, any more than it does at other times, to prevent all suffering or to become a universal alms-giver to the poor. Indiscriminate private charity is mistaken, because it is as a rule misapplied, but indiscriminate Government charity is worse, because it saps the foundations of national character. What then did we find ? I have seen it stated that no one goes on to relief works who is not threatened with actual starvation. Such is most emphatically not the case. I have myself seen hundreds—I might say thousands—of persons upon relief works who were in no such state of necessity or destitution. I have heard of persons accepting relief whose credit would easily have tided them over to better times. know of cases in which men in receipt of famine relief have admitted that they have saved a portion of their famine wages, and in which families proceeding together on to the works have earned more than they would have done in the ordinary circumstances of life. Remember that by Rule 67 of the Famine Code no application for relief can be refused ; and that the criterion of acceptance has ceased therefore to be the judgment of the managing official, and has become the self-respect of the applicant. That the old standards in this respect are breaking down is evident from the information that reaches me from every direction. I hear in some quarters of village labourers going on to the works simply to fill the slack time until the cultivation of the fields begins in the spring. I hear in others of wages fixed under the Famine Commission scale which exceed the prevailing market rates. In the Khandesh District of the Bombay Presidency it had been found necessary, before our circular issued, to make a reduction of 25 per cent. in the minimum wage, because the great bulk of the people found no inducement to work at all, as long as the ordinary minimum was observed. In the Sholapur District of Bombay, a class of landowners has accepted relief, which has never previously done so ; 100,000 out of a population of 750,000 are already in receipt of relief, and if the present conditions continue until the summer, it is likely that 300,000 persons will be in receipt of alms, or 40 per cent. of the entire population—a proportion which I venture to say has never before been in receipt of Government relief, either in India or in any other country in the world. On the other hand, that our tests are not too severe is proved by the low rate of mortality and by the generally satisfactory condition of the · famine-stricken population. From all these considerations it must, I think, be obvious not merely that the present famine is abnormal in character, but that the need for close supervision and control on the part of Government is exceptionally great. I am not one of those who regard Famine Relief as an exact science. Reports of Commissions and Codes have a great value, in so far as they are the results of previous experience. But they are not immaculate. Neither are they laws of the Medes and Persians. Poor Law Administration in every country in the world, in England itself, is still in an experimental stage : no country and no Government has hit the ideal mean between philanthropy and justice, between necessary relief and pauperisation. I contend that in India we are still engaged in the same process of working out our own salvation, and that each fresh crisis must be met by its own rules. Let those rules be based upon previous experience, and let them not err—if they do err at all—on the side of severity. But never let them ignore the obligatory relations upon which society is based—the duty of the landlord to the tenant, of the tenant to the labourer, of the community to its items, of the father to his family, of a man to himself. If for all these relations, at any period of emergency, you hastily substitute the duty of the State to its subjects, you extinguish all sense of personal responsibility and you destroy the economic basis of agrarian society.

I have only two further remarks to make. I should like to recognize the generosity with which Native States—and I am alluding more particularly to some of the States of Rajputana and Central India—have accepted from the Government of India an interpretation of their obligations in respect of scarcity and famine more liberal and more exacting than has ever before, at any rate in those States, been applied. We have done our best to help them by the loan of officers, and by the offer of expert advice. But the Chiefs or Darbars have also helped themselves, and have worthily proved their right to the affection of their people. Secondly, and lastly, I should like to ask the public and the press of this country to remember, when they are in a critical mood, that to relieve the Indian poor from starvation and to save their lives, British Officers freely sacrifice their own. When I was at Jubbulpore, and again at Nagpur, I saw the modest tombstones of English officers who had perished in the last famine of 1896-97. These men did not die on the battlefield. No decoration shone upon their breasts, no fanfare proclaimed their departure. They simply and silently laid down their lives, broken to pieces in the service of the poor and the suffering among the Indian people ; and not in this world but in another will they have their reward. Only last week there was admitted to a Calcutta Hospital an English officer, shattered in health and paralysed in his limbs, who had done nothing but wear himself out in famine work in the Central Provinces. I do not desire to exaggerate these sacrifices. Englishmen are ready to perform them everywhere and unflinchingly, and the Government of India is not behind its subordinates in its alacrity and zeal. But let not our efforts be weakened by any ungenerous or discordant note. The crisis is one which, not less than an Imperial War, demands the loyal and enthusiastic co-operation of all who love India. To that co-operation in the months of trial that lie before us, on behalf of the Government of India, I unhesitatingly appeal.

## ANCIENT MONUMENTS IN INDIA.

*7th February,* 1900.

[The annual meeting of the Asiatic Society of Bengal was held at the Society's rooms in Park Street, Calcutta, on Wednesday evening, the 7th February, Mr. H. H. Risley, C.I.E., President of the Society, presiding. There was a very large attendance of members and friends, a number of ladies being present. Their Excellencies the Viceroy and Lady Curzon arrived shortly after ten o'clock and were received by Mr. Risley, Major Alcock and other officials of the Society The election of officers took place, His Honor Sir John Woodburn becoming President for the ensuing year, and Mr. Risley being elected a Vice-President.

Mr. Risley then delivered the Presidential address, at the conclusion of which His Excellency the Viceroy, who was received with applause, spoke as follows :—]

*Ladies and Gentlemen :*—I hope that there is nothing inappropriate in my addressing to this Society a few observations upon the duty of Government in respect of Ancient Buildings in India. The Asiatic Society of Bengal still, I trust, even in these days when men are said to find no time for scholarship, and when independent study or research seems to have faded out of Indian fashion, retains that interest in archæology which is so often testified to in its earlier publications, and was promoted by so many of its most illustrious names. Surely here, if anywhere, in this house which enshrines the memorials, and has frequently listened to the wisdom, of great scholars and renowned students, it is permissible to recall the recollection of the present generation to a subject that so deeply engaged the attention of your early pioneers, and that must still, even in a breathless age, appeal to the interest of every thoughful man.

In the course of my recent tour, during which I visited some of the most famous sites and beautiful or historic buildings in India, I more than once remarked, in reply to Municipal addresses, that I regarded the conservation of ancient monuments as one of the primary obligations of Government. We have a duty to our forerunners, as well as to our contemporaries and to our descendants,—nay, our duty to the two latter classes in itself demands the recogni-

tion of an obligation to the former, since we are the custodians
for our own age of that which has been bequeathed to us
by an earlier, and since posterity will rightly blame us if,
owing to our neglect, they fail to reap the same advantages
that we have been privileged to enjoy. Moreover, how
can we expect at the hands of futurity any consideration
for the productions of our own time—if indeed any are
worthy of such—unless we have ourselves shown a like
respect to the handiwork of our predecessors? This
obligation, which I assert and accept on behalf of
Government, is one of an even more binding character in
India than in many European countries. There abundant
private wealth is available for the acquisition or the conservation of that which is frequently private property. Corporations, societies, endowments, trusts, provide a vast
machinery that relieves the Government of a large portion
of its obligation. The historic buildings, the magnificent
temples, the inestimable works of art, are invested with a
publicity that to some exten saves them from the risk of
desecration or the encroachments of decay. Here all is
different. India is covered with the visible records of vanished dynasties, of forgotten monarchs, of persecuted and
sometimes dishonoured creeds. These monuments are, for
the most part, though there are notable exceptions, in British
territory, and on soil belonging to Government. Many of
them are in out-of-the-way places, and are liable to the
combined ravages of a tropical climate, an exuberant flora,
and very often a local and ignorant population, who see
only in an ancient building the means of inexpensively
raising a modern one for their own convenience. All these
circumstances explain the peculiar responsibility that rests
upon Government in India. If there be any one who says
to me that there is no duty devolving upon a Christian
Government to preserve the monuments of a pagan art, or
the sanctuaries of an alien faith, I cannot pause to argue
with such a man. Art, and beauty, and the reverence that
is owing to all that has evoked human genius, or has inspir-

ed human faith, are independent of creeds, and, in so far as they touch the sphere of religion, are embraced by the common religion of all mankind. Viewed from this standpoint, the rock temple of the Brahmans stands on precisely the same footing as the Buddhist Vihara, and the Mahomedan Musjid as the Christian Cathedral. There is no principle of artistic discrimination between the mausoleum of the despot and the sepulchre of the saint. What is beautiful, what is historic, what tears the mask off the face of the past, and helps us to read its riddles, and to look it in the eyes—these, and not the dogmas of a combative theology, are the principal criteria to which we must look. Much of ancient history, even in an age of great discoveries, still remains mere guess work. It is only slowly being pieced together by the efforts of scholars and by the outcome of research. But the clues are lying everywhere at our hand, in buried cities, in undeciphered inscriptions, in casual coins, in crumbling pillars, and pencilled slabs of stone. They supply the data by which we may reconstruct the annals of the past, and recall to life the morality, the literature, the politics, the art of a perished age.

Compared with the antiquity of Assyrian or Egyptian, or even of early European monuments, the age of the majority of Indian monuments is not great. I speak subject to correction, but my impression is that the oldest sculptured monument in India is the Sanchi Tope, the great railing of which cannot possibly be placed before the middle of the 3rd century before Christ, although the tope itself may be earlier. At that time the palaces of Chaldœa and Nineveh, the Pyramids and the rock tombs of Egypt, were already thousands of years old. We have no building in India as old as the Parthenon at Athens; the large majority are young compared with the Coliseum at Rome. All the Norman and the majority of the Gothic Cathedrals of England and of Western Europe were already erected before the great era of Moslem architecture in India had begun. The Kutub Minar at Delhi, which is the finest early Mahomedan

structure in this country, was built within a century of
Westminster Hall in London, which we are far from
regarding as an ancient monument. As for the later glories
of Arabian architecture at Delhi, at Agra, and at Lahore,
the Colleges of Oxford and Cambridge, which we regard
in England as the last product of a dying architectural
epoch, were already grey when they sprang, white and
spotless, from the hands of the masons of Akbar and Shah
Jehan ; while the Taj Mahal was only one generation older
than Wren's Renaissance fabric of modern St. Paul's.

There is another remarkable feature of the majority
of Indian antiquities—of those at any rate that belong to
the Mussulman epoch—that they do not represent an
indigenous genius or an Indian style. They are exotics,
imported into this country in the train of conquerors, who
had learnt their architectural lessons in Persia, in Central
Asia, in Arabia, in Afghanistan. More than a thousand
years earlier a foreign influence had exercised a scarcely
less marked, though more transient, influence upon certain
forms of Indian architecture. I allude to the Greek types
which were derived from the Grœco-Bactrian kingdoms,
that were founded upon the remains of Alexander's conquest, and which in the centuries immediately preceding
the Christian era profoundly affected the art and sculpture
of North-West India and the Punjab. Indian sculptures
or Indian buildings, however, because they reflect a foreign
influence, or betray a foreign origin, are not the less, but
perhaps the more interesting to ourselves, who were borne
to India upon the crest of a later but similar wave, and
who may find in their non-Indian characteristics a remini-
scence of forms which we already know in Europe, and of
a process of assimilation with which our own archæological
history has rendered us familiar. Indeed a race like our
own, who are themselves foreigners, are in a sense better
fitted to guard, with a dispassionate and impartial zeal, the
relics of different ages, and of sometimes antagonistic
beliefs, than might be the descendants of the warring races

or the votaries of the rival creeds. To us the relics of Hindu, and Mahomedan, of Buddhist, Brahmin, and Jain are, from the antiquarian, the historical, and the artistic point of view, equally interesting and equally sacred. One does not excite a more vivid, and the other a weaker emotion. Each represents the glories or the faith of a branch of the human family. Each fills a chapter in Indian history. Each is a part of the heritage which Providence has committed to the custody of the ruling power.

If, however, the majority of the structural monuments of India, the topes, and temples, the palaces, and fortresses, and tombs, be of no exceeding antiquity in the chronology of architecture, and even if the greater number of those at any rate which are well known and visited, are not indigenous in origin, it remains true, on the other hand, that it is in the exploration and study of purely Indian remains, in the probing of archaic mounds, in the excavation of old Indian cities, and in the copying and reading of ancient inscriptions, that a good deal of the exploratory work of the archæologist in India will in future lie. The later pages of Indian history are known to us, and can be read by all. But a curtain of dark and romantic mystery hangs over the earlier chapters, of which we are only slowly beginning to lift the corners. This also is not less an obligation of Government. Epigraphy should not be set behind research any more than research should be set behind conservation. All are ordered parts of any scientific scheme of antiquarian work. I am not one of those who think that Government can afford to patronise the one and ignore the other. It is, in my judgment, equally our duty to dig and discover, to classify, reproduce, and describe, to copy and decipher, and to cherish and conserve. Of restoration I cannot, on the present occasion, undertake to speak, since the principles of legitimate and artistic restoration require a more detailed analysis than I have time to bestow upon them this evening. But it will be seen from what I have said that my view of the obligations of Government is not

grudging, and that my estimate of the work to be done
is ample.

If then the question be asked, how has the British Government hitherto discharged, and how is it now discharging
its task, what is the answer that must be returned ? I may
say in preface that were the answer unfavourable—and I will
presently examine that point—we should merely be forging
a fresh link in an unbroken historic chain. Every, or nearly
every, successive religion that has permeated or overswept
this country has vindicated its own fervour at the expense
of the rival whom it had dethroned. When the Brahmans
went to Ellora, they hacked away the features of all the
seated Buddhas in the rock-chapels and halls. When
Kutub-ud-din commenced, and Altamsh continued, the
majestic mosque that flanks the Kutub Minar, it was with the
spoil of Hindu temples that they reared the fabric, carefully
defacing or besmearing the sculptured Jain images, as they
consecrated them to their novel purpose. What part of
India did not bear witness to the ruthless vandalism of the
great iconoclast Aurungzeb? When we admire his great
mosque with its tapering minarets, which are the chief
feature of the river front at Benares, how many of us remember that he tore down the holy Hindu temple of Vishveshwar
to furnish the material and to supply the site? Nadir Shah
during his short Indian inroad effected a greater spoliation
than has probably ever been achieved in so brief a space of
time. When the Mahratta conquerors overran Northern
India, they pitilessly mutilated and wantonly destroyed.
When Ranjit Singh built the Golden Temple at Amritsar, he
ostentatiously rifled Mahomedan buildings and mosques.
Nay, dynasties did not spare their own members, nor religions
their own shrines. If a capital or fort or sanctuary was not
completed in the life-time of the builder, there was small
chance of its being finished, there was a very fair chance of
its being despoiled, by his successor and heir. The environs
of Delhi are a wilderness of deserted cities and devastated
tombs. Each fresh conqueror, Hindu, or Moghul, or Pathan,

marched, so to speak, to his own immortality over his predecessor's grave. The great Akbar in a more peaceful age first removed the seat of Government from Delhi to Agra, and then built Fatehpur Sikri as a new capital, only to be abandoned by his successor. Jehangir alternated between Delhi and Agra, but preferred Lahore to either. Shah Jehan beautified Agra and then contemplated a final return to Delhi. Aurungzeb marched away to the south and founded still another capital, and was himself buried in territories that now belong to Hyderabad. These successive changes, while they may have reflected little more than a despot's caprice, were yet inimical both to the completion and to the continuous existence of architectural fabrics. The British Government are fortunately exempt from any such promptings, either of religious fanaticism, of restless vanity, or of dynastic and personal pride. But in proportion as they have been unassailed by such temptations, so is their responsibility the greater for inaugurating a new era and for displaying that tolerant and enlightened respect to the treasures of all, which is one of the main lessons that the returning West has been able to teach to the East.

In the domain of archæology as elsewhere, the original example of duty has been set to the Government of India by individual effort and by private enthusiasm; and only by slow degrees has Government, which is at all times and seasons a tardy learner, warmed to its task. The early archæological researches, conducted by the founders and pioneers of this Society, by Jones, Colebrooke, Wilson, and Prinsep, and by many another *clarum et venerabile nomen*, were in the main literary in character. They consisted in the reconstruction of alphabets, the translation of manuscripts, and the decipherment of inscriptions. Sanscrit scholarship was the academic. cult of the hour. How these men laboured is illustrated by the fact that Prinsep and Kittoe both died of overwork at the age of 40. Then followed an era of research in buildings and monuments; the pen was supplemented by the spade; and in succession, descriptions, drawings, paintings, engravings, and in later days photographs and casts, gradually revealed to European eyes the precious contents of the unrifled quarries of Hindustan. In this generation of explorers and writers, special honour must be paid to two names ; to James Fergusson, whose earliest work was published in 1845, and who was the first to place the examination of Indian architecture upon a scholarly basis, and to General Sir A. Cunningham, who only a few years later was engaged in the first scientific excavation of the Bhilsa topes. These and other toilers in the same field laboured with a diligence beyond praise ; but the work was too great for individual exertion, and much of it remained desultory, fragmentary, and incomplete.

Meanwhile the Government of India was concerned with laying the foundations and extending the borders of a new Empire, and thought little of the relics of old ones. From time to time a Governor-General, in an access of exceptional enlightenment or generosity, spared a little money for the fitful repair of ancient monuments. Lord Minto appointed a Committee to conduct repairs at the Taj. Lord Hastings ordered works at Fatehpur Sikri and Sikandra. Lord Amherst attempted some restoration of the Kutub Minar. Lord Hardinge persuaded the Court of Directors to sanction arrangements for the examination, delineation, and record of some of the chief Indian antiquities. But these spasmodic efforts resulted in little more than the collection of a few drawings, and the execution of a few local and perfunctory repairs. How little the leaven had permeated the lump, and how strongly the barbarian still dominated the aesthetic in the official mind, may be shown by incidents that from time to time occurred.

In the days of Lord William Bentinck the Taj was on the point of being destroyed for the value of its marbles. The same Governor-General sold by auction the marble bath in Shah Jehan's Palace at Agra, which had been torn up by Lord Hastings for a gift to George IV, but had somehow never been despatched. In the same régime a proposal was

made to lease the gardens at Sikandra to the Executive
Engineer at Agra for the purposes of speculative cultivation.
In 1857, after the Mutiny, it was solemnly proposed to raze
to the ground the Jumma Musjid at Delhi, the noblest ceremonial mosque in the world, and it was only spared at the
instance of Sir John Lawrence. As late as 1868 the removal
of the great gateways of the Sanchi Tope was successfully prevented by the same statesman. I have read of a
great Mahomedan pillar, over 600 years old, which was
demolished at Aligarh, to make room for certain municipal
improvements and for the erection of some *bunias'* shops,
which, when built, were never let. Some of the sculptured
columns of the exquisite Hindu-Mussulman mosque at
Ajmere were pulled down by a zealous officer to construct
a triumphal arch under which the Viceroy of the day was to
pass. James Fergusson's books sound one unending note of
passionate protest against the barrack-builder, and the military engineer. I must confess that I think these individuals
have been, and, within the more restricted scope now left
to them, still are inveterate sinners. Climb the hilltop at
Gwalior and see the barracks of the British soldier, and the
relics, not yet entirely obliterated, of his occupation of the
Palace in the Fort. Read in the Delhi Guide-books of the
horrors that have been perpetrated in the interests of regimental barracks and messes and canteens in the fairy-like
pavilions and courts and gardens of Shah Jehan. It is not
yet 30 years since the Government of India were invited
by a number of army doctors to cut off the battlements of
the Fort at Delhi, in order to improve the health of the
troops, and only desisted from doing so when a rival band
of medical doctrinaires appeared upon the scene to urge
the retention of the very same battlements, in order to prevent malarial fever from creeping in. At an earlier date
when picnic-parties were held in the garden of the Taj, it
was not an uncommon thing for the revellers to arm themselves with hammer and chisel, with which they wiled
away the afternoon by chipping out fragments of agate and

cornelian from the cenotaphs of the Emperor and his lamented Queen. Indeed when I was at Agra the other day, I found that the marble tomb of Shah Jehan in the lower vault, beneath which his body actually lies, was still destitute of much of its original inlay, of which I ordered the restoration.

That the era of vandalism is not yet completely at an end is evident from recent experiences, among which I may include my own. When Fergusson wrote his book, the Diwan-i-Am, or Public Hall of Audience, in the Palace at Delhi was a military arsenal, the outer colonnades of which had been built up with brick arches lighted by English windows. All this was afterwards removed. But when the Prince of Wales came to India in 1876, and held a Durbar in this building, the opportunity was too good to be lost ; and a fresh coat of whitewash was plentifully bespattered over the red sandstone pillars and plinths of the Durbar-hall of Aurungzeb. This too I hope to get removed. When His Royal Highness was at Agra, and the various pavilions of Shah Jehan's palace were connected together for the purposes of an evening party and ball, local talent was called in to reproduce the faded paintings on marble and plaster of the Moghul artists two and a half centuries before. The result of their labours is still an eyesore and a regret. When I was at Lahore in April last I found the exquisite little Moti Musjid, or Pearl Mosque, in the Fort, which was erected by Jehangir exactly three hundred years ago, still used for the profane purpose to which it had been converted by Ranjit Singh, *viz.*, as a Government Treasury. The arches were built up with brick-work, and below the marble floor had been excavated as a cellar for the reception of iron bound chests of rupees. I pleaded for the restoration to its original state of this beautiful little building, which I suppose not one visitor in a hundred to Lahore has ever seen. Ranjit Singh cared nothing for the taste or the trophies of his Mahomedan predecessors, and half a century of British military occupation, with its universal paintpot, and the exigencies of the Public Works Engineer, has assisted the melancholy decline. Fortunately in recent years something has been done to rescue the main buildings of the Moghul Palace from these two insatiable enemies. At Ahmedabad I found the mosque of Sidi Sayid, the pierced stone lattice-work of whose demi-lune windows is one of the glories of India, used as a tehsildar's kutcherry, and disfigured with plaster partitions, and the omnivorous whitewash. I hope to effect the re-conversion of this building. After the conquest of Upper Burma in 1885, the Palace of the Kings at Mandalay, which, although built for the most part of wood, is yet a noble specimen of Burmese art, was converted by our conquering battalions into a Club House, a Government Office, and a Church. By degrees I am engaged in removing these superfluous denizens, with the idea of preserving the building as the monument, not of a dynasty that has vanished never to return, but of an art that, subject to the vicissitudes of fire, earthquake, and decay, is capable of being a joy for ever. There are other sites and fabrics in India upon which I also have my eye, which I shall visit, if possible, during my time and which I shall hope to rescue from a kindred or a worse fate.

These are the gloomy or regrettable features of the picture. On the other hand, there has been, during the last 40 years, some sort of sustained effort on the part of Government to recognize its responsibilities and to purge itself of a well-merited reproach. This attempt has been accompanied, and sometimes delayed, by disputes as to the rival claims of research and of conservation, and by discussion over the legitimate spheres of action of the Central and the Local Governments. There have been periods of supineness as well as of activity. There have been moments when it has been argued that the State had exhausted its duty or that it possessed no duty at all. There have been persons who thought that when all the chief monuments were indexed and classified, we might sit down with folded hands and allow them slowly and gracefully to crumble into ruin.

There have been others who argued that railways and irrigation did not leave even a modest ½ lakh of rupees per annum for the requisite establishment to supervise the most glorious galaxy of monuments in the world. Nevertheless, with these interruptions and exceptions, which I hope may never again recur, the progress has been positive, and, on the whole, continuons. It was Lord Canning who first invested archæological work in this country with permanent Government patronage by constituting, in 1860, the Archæological Survey of Northern India, and by appointing General Cunningham in 1862 to be Archæological Surveyor to Government. From that period date the publications of the Archæological Survey of India, which have at times assumed different forms, and which represent varying degrees of scholarship and merit, but which constitute, on the whole, a noble mine of information, in which the student has but to delve in order to discover an abundant spoil. For over 20 years General Cunningham continued his labours, of which these publications are the memorial. Meanwhile orders were issued for the registration and preservation of historical monuments throughout India, local surveys were started in some of the subordinate Governments, the Bombay Survey being placed in the capable hands of Mr. Burgess, who was a worthy follower in the footsteps of Cunningham, and who ultimately succeeded him as Director-General of the Archæological Survey. Some of the Native States followed the example thus set to them, and either applied for the services of the Government archæologists, or established small departments of their own.

In the provinces much depended upon the individual tastes or proclivities of the Governor or Lieutenant-Governor, just as at headquarters the strength of the impetus varied with the attitude of successive Viceroys. Lord Northbrook, who was always a generous patron of the arts, issued orders in 1873 as to the duties of Local Governments; and in his Viceroyalty, Sir John Strachey was the first Lieutenant-Governor to undertake a really noble work of renovation and repair at Agra—a service which is fitly commemorated by a marble slab in the Palace of Shah Jehan. The poetic and imaginative temperament of Lord Lytton could not be deaf to a similar appeal. Holding that no claim upon the initiative and resources of the Supreme Government was more essentially Imperial than the preservation of national antiquities, he contributed in 1879 a sum of 3¾ lakhs to the restoration of buildings in the North-West Provinces ; and proposed the appointment of a special officer, to be entitled the Curator of Ancient Monuments, which, while it did not receive sanction in his time, was left to be carried out by his successor, Lord Ripon. During the three years that Major Cole held this post, from 1880 to 1883, much excellent work in respect both of reports and classification was done ; and large sums of money were given by the Government of India, *inter alia*, for repairs in the Gwalior Fort and at Sanchi Tope. But at the end of this time succeeded a period of some reaction, in which it appeared to be thought that the task of the Central Government, in the preparation of surveys and lists, was drawing to a close, and that Local Governments might, in future, be safely entrusted with the more modest, but, I may add, not less critical, duty of conservation. More recently, under Lord Elgin's auspices, the archæological work of Government has been placed upon a more definite basis. The entire country has been divided into a number of circles, each with a surveyor of its own, and while the establishment is regarded as an Imperial charge, the work is placed under local control and receives such financial backing as the resources of the Local Governments or the sympathies of individual Governors may be able to give it. In the North-West Provinces, where I was recently touring, I found Sir A. MacDonnell worthily sustaining, in point of generous and discriminating sympathy, the traditions that were created by Sir John Strachey.

For my part I feel far from clear that Government might not do a good deal more than it is now doing, or than it has hitherto consented to do.  I certainly cannot look forward to a time at which either the obligations of the State will have become exhausted, or at which archæological research and conservation in this country can dispense with Government direction and control.  I see fruitful fields of labour still unexplored, bad blunders still to be corrected, gaping omissions to be supplied, plentiful opportunities for patient renovation and scholarly research.  In my opinion, the tax-payers of this country are in the last degree unlikely to resent a somewhat higher expenditure—and, after all, a few thousand rupees go a long way in archæological work, and the total outlay is exceedingly small—upon objects in which I believe them to be as keenly interested as we are ourselves.  I hope to assert more definitely during my time the Imperial responsibility of Government in respect of Indian antiquities, to inaugurate or to persuade a more liberal attitude on the part of those with whom it rests to provide the means, and to be a faithful guardian of the priceless treasure-house of art and learning that has, for a few years at any rate, been committed to my charge. (*Loud and continued applause.*)

## FAMINE RELIEF.

*16th February*, 1900.

[On Friday, the 16th February, a public meeting, convened by the Sheriff of Calcutta, was held at the Town Hall, Calcutta, at 4-30 P.M., for the purpose of organizing a Charitable Relief Fund for the relief of distress in the famine-stricken districts in India. There was an immense gathering, all sections of the community being well represented. On the Viceroy reaching the daïs the Sheriff (Prince Mahomed Bakhtiyar Shah) declared the meeting open. Maharaja Bahadur Sir Jotendro Mohun Tagore, K C. S. I.. then moved that His Excellency be requested to accept the office of President of the meeting The Hon'ble Mr. T. W. Spink having seconded the motion, the Viceroy rose to address the meeting and was very warmly received.

His Excellency spoke as follows :— ].

It is a source of much distress to me that the first occasion upon which I should have been invited to take the chair at a great meeting of the citizens of Calcutta, convened by the Sheriff in deference to a requisition from the leading members both of the European and Native communities, should be of the present character. It is a sorrowful task to stand up and to speak of the sufferings of millions of our fellow creatures who, while we are living in comfort and affluence, are enduring severe hardships and privations, and are practically only being saved from the clutches of death by the direct action of the State. And yet, on the other hand, I can imagine no occasion more loudly calling for a meeting such as this, or for the presence of the Viceroy in the chair, than one in which he should, as the head of the Government of India, as the official spokesman of society, and as the representative of Her Majesty the Queen, address that appeal to the Indian world which he is probably only anticipating its natural instincts in making, but which nevertheless will derive force and concentration from the circumstances under which it is delivered.

You are all aware, Ladies and Gentlemen, that we are confronted in India by a famine of unparalleled magnitude. Of each famine as it comes these words are apt to be used ;

and I am conscious of the dangers of exaggeration. At the same time, from the figures and facts submitted to me, from the totals already on relief, and from the estimates of the probable duration and extent of the suffering that have been sent up, I entertain little doubt that, in the territories that are seriously affected, the description is literally true. I might emphasize the tragedy and the pathos of the situation by adding that in some parts of India plague co-exists with famine, and that, for instance, in Bombay City, more people are now dying in each week from plague than has ever been the case before, at the same moment that in other parts of the Bombay Presidency more people are only being saved from death from famine by Government relief. On the present occasion, however, I prefer to say nothing further about plague. Sufficient for the day is the evil thereof. The picture is already sombre enough without any darkening of the colours, and it is to the situation as created by famine alone that I invite your attention this afternoon.

I have during the past few days received accounts specially sent to me at my request from every affected province or part of India, which enable me to give you the most recent tidings. When I spoke in Council exactly four weeks ago from to-day, the numbers throughout India in receipt of relief exceeded $3\frac{1}{4}$ millions. To-day, in spite of the closer stringency of tests which has been applied, and which I may say in passing has been unanimously welcomed by the Local Governments and officers as both timely and necessary, the total exceeds $3\frac{3}{4}$ millions. No such number of persons has ever before been simultaneously relieved by any Government in the world. But I am constrained to admit that, in spite of every legitimate precaution that may be taken, these totals are not likely to prove the maximum, but that in the spring and summer months that lie before us, they will be substantially increased.

Bombay reports to us a distress that is attacking classes and strata of society hitherto exempt. The Punjab says that the loss of crops in that province has been the greatest on record, and that whereas in 1897 the numbers on relief steadily declined from the month of February onwards, in the present year they will as surely mount up. In the Central Provinces $1\frac{1}{2}$ millions of persons are already on relief, and the Chief Commissioner contemplates that before June this total may have swollen to 2 millions. The Central Provinces were the dark spot of the famine of 1896-97. But the intensity and extent of the drought are greater now, and must leave a blight upon that unhappy province for many a long year to come. In Central India, even fertile Malwa, which has always been an asylum for famine-stricken wanderers from other parts, has itself been stripped bare, and hundreds of thousands of poor fugitives who crowded over the border in the early days of scarcity, have drifted back again, to pick up a meagre subsistence wherever they can. Famine conditions of the worst type prevail in Western Rajputana, where Jodhpur has lost as much as 90 per cent. of its stock of cattle ; other States little less ; and they are spreading towards the eastern parts of that region.

All these circumstances will show you that there is no exaggeration in describing the present as an unprecedented emergency, and that it is with as forcible and overpower_ing a ground of appeal as any pleader for charity ever possessed, that I appear before you this afternoon. I think I may say with truth that except in some Native States which either did not possess the requisite organisation, or which began rather late in the day, mortality from famine has so far been almost completely, if not absolutely, repressed. Such deaths as have occurred here or there have been of a character normal in any period of distress, owing to lowered physique. At such times some of the invalids and weaklings of the village inevitably die. But there has been a conspicuous absence on the present occasion of the poor emaciated wastrels, the living skeletons, whose pitiful likenesses nearly broke our hearts when they appeared in the illustrated papers three years ago. When I remember that the great Duke of Wellington, who had to fight a big famine in the Deccan while in command there at the beginning of the present century, wrote in one of his Despatches that at Ahmednagar alone 50 persons died of starvation each day, and when I contemplate the enormous numbers with which we are now dealing, without any loss of life, I do feel some glow of honourable pride. To any who may think that the recent rains which have fallen in some parts of India, and the fringe of which has even reached us in Calcutta, may sensibly alleviate the position, I must regretfully point out that while they have been of some assistance in parts of the Punjab, even there they have produced no check upon the upward rise of the relief figures, while elsewhere in the afflicted parts of Bombay, Rajputana, Central India, and the Central Provinces, there has been no rain at all. There the ground is like an oven, which as the spring grows into summer will become hotter and still more burning.

Ladies and Gentlemen, a month ago I hardly contemplated that, great and increasing as our sufferings were, we could expect very much practical assistance from England. Sympathy from all, help from the particular friends of India, contributions from a few, I felt certain that we should receive. But that in the midst of all its anxieties and troubles the British nation should open wide its purse to us seemed to me to be unlikely and even not to be expected. I scarcely thought that the expression of my doubt would be transmitted home. But never was I more pleased than when I ascertained that I had underrated the degree of interest which many of my countrymen in England take in India, however great their absorption in other concerns, and when the Lord Mayor of London came forward and offered to place the prestige and help of the Mansion House at our disposal. I felt then, and the Secretary of State shared my opinion, that to all in England who were willing to give the opportunity should not be denied ; that whether the offerings were great or small, they would be acceptable; and that though the old country could not do for us again what it did in 1896-97, something of value might be expected from its generosity. It is in these circumstances that a branch of the Fund, which we are about to inaugurate this afternoon, is being opened to-day in London by the Lord Mayor, to which the subscriptions of our English friends and sympathisers will be sent.

Meanwhile we had already decided to open an Indian Famine Fund here, and to make our appeal to the entire country. My first step in the constitution of the requisite machinery was to ask Her Majesty the Queen-Empress if she would again consent, as in 1897, to be Patron of the Fund. Along with her gracious acceptance of this post, Her Majesty generously announced a contribution of £1,000 towards the fund, only one among many examples of her noble fellow-feeling for her Indian people.

In India, I have already found that a similar interest and a like generosity prevail. Before this meeting or this fund were made known, the Maharaja of Darbhanga came to me, and in that spirit of open-handed and large-hearted munificence which we have learned in a comparatively short time to associate permanently with his name, he offered to inaugurate any such fund by a donation—a truly princely donation—of $1\frac{1}{2}$ lakh, or £10,000. Other generous offers and promises have since followed, and already I think I may say that the ship that we are launching this afternoon is fairly under way.

I may mention the following additional donations :—

|  | R |
| --- | --- |
| Maharani of Hattwa | 1,00,000 |
| British India Steam Navigation Co. and Messrs. Mackinnon, Mackenzie & Co. | 80,000 |
| Nawab of Dacca | 50,000 |
| Maharaja of Burdwan | 10,000 |
| Messrs. Ralli Brothers (in addition to R20,000 given to Bombay, R30,000 in all) | 10,000 |
| „ Apcar & Co. | 10,000 |

| | R |
|---|---|
| Messrs. Cooper Allen & Co. | 10,000 |
| „  Gillanders, Arbuthnot & Co. | 5,000 |
| „  Graham & Co. (and R5,000 promised to Bombay—R10,000 in all) | 5,000 |
| „  Thomas Duff & Co. | 5,000 |
| „  Birkmyre Brothers | 5,000 |
| „  Schröder Smidt & Co. | 5,000 |
| „  Whiteaway, Laidlaw & Co.   ... | 5,000 |
| India General Steam Navigation Co. and Kilburn & Co.   ... | 5,000 |
| Barry & Co. | 5,000 |
| Jardine, Skinner & Co.   .. | 5,000 |
| Or in all   ... | R4,65,000 |

I may add that I have been fortunate enough to persuade Sir F. Maclean, the Chief Justice of Bengal, who was Chairman of the Committee in 1897, to give us the advantage of his experience and authority in the same capacity now ; and also to enlist the energies of Mr. Donald Smeaton as Secretary.

And now, Ladies and Gentlemen, you may expect a few words from me as to the conditions under which we appeal to your charity, and the objects to which it will be applied. I am not inclined to draw any pedantic distinctions between the spheres of Government duty and of private benevolence. Wide as is the scope of the former, inasmuch as it includes the whole duty of saving human life, it is not so ample as to leave no margin for outside assistance. We are not asking you to relieve Government of its due burden, or to save us from one penny of expenditure that ought properly to fall upon our shoulders. Whatever you give us will make no difference in the extent and character of our outlay. That is fixed for us by the high conception that we entertain of our public duty. But, for all that, there is an ample field for private generosity, both in supplement to that which the State can do and must do, and often in pursuit of that which the State cannot do at all. It is our task to keep the people alive, and to see them safely through the period of their sufferings. But no expert knowledge is required to recognize that there are a hundred ways in which the condition of their sufferings may be alleviated while they still last, and a fresh start in the world be given to the sufferers when the worst is over. The legitimate objects of private charity have indeed been carefully analysed and scientifically laid down both by Government during the last famine, and by the Famine Commission afterwards. We ask your money to provide warm raiment, clothes, and blankets, for the poor workers who spend their nights out of doors either in the open air or under flimsy mats of straw. In the Punjab, as you know, it is still very cold at nights. Later on, when the rains come, the same covering will be required to ward off the chills that bring fever and dysentery in their train. Think again of the good that may be done by the distribution of small comforts, of milk and arrowroot and cornflower, and other medicinal sustenance, to the aged and infirm, to invalids, and above all to children. My one happy experience in connection with the whole famine is my recollection of having saved the lives of two poor little children in Kathiawar, who were very nearly gone, but for whom I ordered milk to be supplied until they were quite recovered, as I have since heard with satisfactory results. A third object to which the funds subscribed by charity are devoted is the relief of orphans, although I hope that our timely measures and vast outlay may prevent there being many of this class upon the present occasion. Then there is a class who appeal peculiarly for private assistance, since they deliberately, though for the most honourable of motives, elect to stand outside of State Relief. I allude to the *purda-nashin* women whom our system does not touch, and to the destitute but respectable persons and classes who are too proud to apply for Government help, who find it derogatory to labour, and who would sooner die than beg. In Native States these are likely to be provided for. But there is many a silent sufferer of these classes in British India for whom I would plead. Finally there remains the great object upon which the bulk of the money that was subscribed in 1897 was spent, *viz.*, the provision of cattle, of grain, of fodder, of implements, to enable the sufferers to make a start again in life when the time of adversity is past. Government does what it can in such cases by *takavi* advances, by remissions of rent, and otherwise ; but it is beyond our power to cover the whole field that is open : and there is not a donor, however humble, in India or in England, of even a rupee, or a shilling, to our cause, who may not be honestly confident that that petty sum will bring a ray of light, a dawning of hope, into the heart of some unhappy peasant who for months will not have known what light or hope were.

These then are the objects upon which will be expended such funds, whether from England or from India, as the public may be willing to give us. Let me add that, on the present occasion, we propose to make no discrimination between the claim of Native States and of British India. In the famine of 1897 organized relief was only in an experimental stage in Native territory ; relief fund committees had not been created ; the agency for distribution did not exist, and the fund was primarily raised for British India. This year, however, famine is much more pronounced in the Native States : the distress in many of them is very acute ; their recuperative power will be small ; the Chiefs and Durbars have, under the initiative of Government, accepted a responsibility quite new to them, and have organized a system which has, in many cases, placed a severe strain upon their resources. We owe them a return for their gallant efforts, and their people deserve the public bounty just as much as do our own. In some of these Native States private charity has already come to the assistance of the Durbars. The Seths of Bikanir and Bundelkhund have been loyally and generously assisting the Chiefs. Private committees exist in Jaipur, Ajmere, Abu, and other places. As we have read in the newspapers, public committees and funds were started some time ago both in Bombay and in the Punjab. While Native generosity is thus forthcoming in many parts, though not, I regret to say, equally in all, it is a pleasure to me to add that I know of many cases in which English Officers personally engaged in the famine fight, are setting aside no small portion cf their own salaries to supplement the relief which they are already administer-ing on behalf of Government. Similarly, many a native official is labouring manfully in the common cause.

In conclusion, Ladies and Gentlemen, though I do not suppose that there is any one in this hall who would ask why Bengal and Calcutta should be asked to contribute when they are not suffering, yet should such a thought occur to any man, I would say to him that this is the very reason why I invite him all the more to subscribe. Not merely is Indian suffering an Indian interest, irrespective of province, or district, or city, but there is in the circum-stances of the present case a peculiar reason for a generous response in this part of the country. While no rain has fallen elsewhere, Bengal has enjoyed a full share. The suffering of others has even proved your gain : for the Bengal cultivators have realised for their surplus crops a price that, in ordinary times, they would not have touched. Apart from this, however, was there ever a case in which the rich man out of his abundance should more freely give to the poor man in his misery ? If any rich man in this city is in any doubt as to whether he should subscribe, I would gladly give him a railway ticket to a famine district and take what he chose to give me on his return. He might go with a hard heart ; but he would come back with a broken one. Nor need any poor man desist from offering his mite. A mite to him may be almost a fortune to the starving. To each of us, therefore, the call should come ; to every one, European or Native, official, merchant, or professional man, it may equally appeal. In yielding to it, we shall be obeying a summons that lies at the root of all religion and is the consecration of our common humanity. (*Loud and continued applause.*)

[The first Resolution was then moved by the Hon'ble Maharaja Rameshwara Singh Bahadur of Darbhunga (President of the British Indian Association), and was as follows :—

That the Meeting recognizes the fact that the time has come when a charitable fund should be formed for the relief of distress in the famine-stricken districts of India : that the need of relief is more urgent than it was in 1897 ; such relief being supplementary of the operations of Government and designed to meet cases not clearly or adequately covered by those operations ; and that to this end subscriptions should be invited from the well-to-do throughout this country, and contributions from abroad be thankfully received.

The Resolution was seconded by the Hon'ble Mr. Allan Arthur (President of the Chamber of Commerce), and supported by His Honour the Lieutenant-Governor of Bengal, the Hon'ble Nawab Bahadur Sir Khwaja Ahsanulla, K.C.I.E , of Dacca, and the Hon'ble Mr. P. M. Mehta, C.I.E.

The second Resolution was proposed by the Hou'ble Sir Francis Maclean, K.C.I.E., Q C , Chief Justice of Bengal, and was as follows : —

That this Meeting accepts the statement of the objects to which private subscriptions may be legitimately devoted as set forth by the Government in the *Gazette of India* of the 9th January 1897 (copy extract circulated), and the organization there suggested for the collection and administration of subscriptions to the Fund ; and resolves that a General Committee composed of the following gentlemen be appointed, with power to add to their number and to appoint an Executive Committee to administer the Fund.

The Resolution was seconded by Maharaja Bahadur Sir Narendra Krishna, K.C I E., and supported by The Most Reverend the Lord Bishop of Calcutta and the Hon'ble Rai Bahadur B. K. Bose, C.I.E.

All these gentlemen addressed the Meeting in turn.

The Most Revd. Archbishop Göethals then moved, and Raja Ban Behari Kapur of Burdwan seconded a vote of thanks to His Excellency the Viceroy for presiding and for accepting the official Presidentship of the General Committee.

The Viceroy briefly acknowledged the vote of thanks and said that he was glad to be able to announce further subscriptions of Rs. 10,000 from Maharaja Sir Jotendro Mohan Tagore, Rs. 5,000 from the Maharaja of Mymensingh. and Rs 2,000 from Raja Runjeet Singh. His Excellency invited all present to show their practical interest in the famine fund by subscribing before leaving the Hall.]

## CONVOCATION OF THE CALCUTTA UNIVERSITY.

*17th February,* 1900.

[The Annual Convocation of the Calcutta University for the purpose of Conferring Degrees was held in the Senate House of the University on Saturday afternoon, the 17th February 1900, at 3 P.M. The Viceroy as Chancellor of the University presided, and was received at the Entrance Hall by the Vice-Chancellor (Sir Francis Maclean) and the Fellows and Members of the Senate, including the Lieutenant-Governor of Bengal and the Lord Bishop of Calcutta, who occupied seats on the daïs to the right of the Chancellor and the left of the Vice-Chancellor respectively. A considerable number of ladies and gentlemen were present, including Her Excellency Lady Curzon, and the hall was well filled with students. His Excellency was attired in the new robe recently presented by himself to the University for the use of future Chancellors, and made on the model of the robe worn by the Chancellor of the Oxford University. After the candidates had been presented with their diplomas by the Vice-Chancellor, His Excellency addressed the Convocation as follows:—]

*Mr. Vice-Chancellor and Graduates of the Calcutta University:*—Believe me that it is with no small pleasure that I have for the second time taken my seat in this hall to-day at your annual Convocation as Chancellor of the Calcutta University. With each succeeding year my interest in my Indian work tends to increase rather than to diminish ; and the recurrence of this annual anniversary brings me back with renewed ardour to the contemplation, not merely of your own academic history during the past twelve months, but of the progress of that great educational undertaking of which this University is the exemplar and head.

There have just passed before me a number of young men who have this afternoon received the degrees which the Calcutta University bestows upon those who have successfully surmounted its tests. I wonder if any of these young men have paused to ask themselves what is the object of the examination that they have so recently passed, and of the teaching that has enabled them to pass it. I hope that they do not look at the matter exclusively from the utilitarian point of view. On the face of it, it may appear that they have been acquiring knowledge which has a definite and realisable value, because it will help them to obtain a career for themselves, and sustenance for their families and belongings. It is quite a legitimate and even an honourable object to acquire such knowledge, and use it in order to obtain such employment. But it would be an insult to knowledge, to regard knowledge as a means only, or employment as the only end. The ultimate justification of our educational system, culminating as it does in the degrees of the Indian Universities, is that the character of the individual student shall thereby be moulded into a higher moral and intellectual type. If this ideal be reached, he becomes not only a better pleader, or clerk, or journalist, or official in the Government service, or whatever his future career may be, but he becomes a finer specimen of a man. He exercises a healthy influence on his environment. He inspires others with his example. He elevates and purifies the tone of the society to which he belongs, or the administration of which he forms a part.

Gentlemen, this aspect of University education is invested in India with an interest greater, I think, than in any other country. In an English University, and in European Universities generally, we teach our young men to a large extent, it is true, in foreign and even in dead languages, and to some extent in subjects which are of value rather as a mental discipline than as a practical accomplishment. For instance, many a young man learns to write Greek Iambics, of which he will assuredly never compose another in his life ; or he studies Euclid, though in a few years' time he will have ceased to remember a single proposition. But with all this variety and transience of subject-matter, it remains true that the thoughts, the precepts, the ideas, the framework in fact of knowledge which is there communicated to his mind are,—whatever the language in which they were originally expressed, or the age to which they belong— not essentially different from those of the modern world of which he is a component part. We imbibe, for instance, much the same conceptions of liberty and patriotism from an oration of Demosthenes as we do from a speech of Burke. The philosophy of history is as profound in the pages of

Thucydides as it is in those of Gibbon. The same problems of mental and moral science, though expressed in different formulas, are examined by Plato and Aristotle as by Berkeley and Spencer. A Greek tragedy does not set forth a paler image of the moral forces that govern the world, though it be the product of a pagan imagination, than does a Milton or a Wordsworth.

But here all is different. We teach you in your Indian Colleges, and we examine you in the Indian Universities upon subjects not merely conveyed to you in a foreign language, but representing foreign ideas and modes of thought. They are like an ærolite discharged into space from a distant planet, or like exotic plants imported from some antipodean clime. They are the outcome of an alien school of science, of philosophy, of logic, of literature, of art. Well may an intelligent observer look to see what is the issue of so remarkable an experiment, and well may he wonder whether the result of this daring alchemy will be fusion or discord. Above all, he will ask—and that is the question that I also ask, and that I want you to put to yourselves— what is the effect that is produced upon individual character, and upon that aggregate of individual characters that makes up the national character of the East, by a curriculum almost exclusively borrowed from the West? When these two intellectual streams meet, the positive, the synthetic, the practical,—and the imaginative, the metaphysical, and the analytic—do they run side by side in the same channel, as we have sometimes seen rivers do after their confluence, one clear and bright, and the other stained and dark from the soil through which it has flowed ; or do they mix their waters in a fresh and homogeneous current, with an identity and a colour of its own ?

Gentlemen, I have no doubt that much might be said on both sides of this question. There will be those who urge that the speculative side of the human intellect with difficulty assimilates the positive method, and that reflectiveness is incompatible with action. They will argue that a veneer of

Western learning and culture upon an Oriental substratum furnishes a flimsy and unstable fabric ; that you cannot amalgamate the subtlety and acumen of the East with the more robust and masculine standards of the West ; and that the more complete the illusory and ephemeral success of the experiment, the more violent will be the recoil, and the more disastrous the consequences. There is some truth in this pessimism. But it is far from being the whole truth. We are all of us familiar with the half-denationalised type of humanity who has lost the virtues of his own system, while only assimilating the vices of another. He is a sorrowful creature, whether he be a European or an Asiatic. We know the man who cloaks the shallowness of his intellectual equipment in a cloud of vague generalisation, or who has acquired the phraseology of a foreign literature without so much as touching the hem of its thought. We know the student who sells his European text-books the moment he has passed his University examinations, because literature has ceased to be for him a mercantile asset. There is the popular story of the man whose pecuniary value in the native marriage market is enhanced by the possession of a degree (*laughter*), and who is said to study in order to become an eligible suitor. For all I know, there may be too many of all these types in this country, although I hope there are none of them here (*laughter*) ; and I have no doubt that analogous types are to be found in Western Universities, and that if you brought European students over here and set them down to study Indian metaphysics, you would presently develop some specimens equally incongruous, equally superficial, and equally absurd. But because we all know these freaks, and smile at them, when they cross our path, do not let us run away with the idea that they are universal phenomena, or that they are the normal and inevitable product of the amalgamation of East and West.

My own feelings are of an exactly opposite character. I am surprised, not at the egregiousness of the failures, but at the quality and number of the successes. I am struck by the extent to which, within less than 50 years, the science and the learning of the Western world have entered into and penetrated the Oriental mind, teaching it independence of judgment and liberty of thought, and familiarising it with conceptions of politics, and law, and society, to which it had for centuries been a complete stranger. I say within less than 50 years, because I date the birth of Higher Education in India from the celebrated Education Despatch of the Court of Directors in 1854. Before that time there was not a University in India, not an Educational Department in any province, not a single training college for teachers in the whole country, no inspection of Government colleges and schools, while the grant-in-aid system hardly existed. During the half century that has since elapsed, the progress achieved seems to me to have been not slow but startling. Of course it may be said that the topmost layer alone is affected ; and that beneath the surface crust are to be found the same primordial elements, the old unregenerate man. But how can you expect anything else within so short a space of time ? The process thus commenced can only be downward, not upwards. It is one of infiltration, and of soaking in ; and the surface must be saturated with the dew before its moisture can percolate to the lower sociological strata.

Anyhow, whether my views be right or wrong, and some may think me too sanguine, I see clearly that the die is cast, and that there is no going back. When Lord Macaulay wrote his famous Minute, and the British Government resolved that your Higher Education should be a European education, whether they acted wisely or unwisely, they took an irrevocable decision, and a decision from which it would not in my judgment be politic, even if it were possible, to recede. (*Applause.*) A week ago I read in the newspapers a telegraphic message that could only have emanated from China, that home of the paradoxical and outworn. This is what the Reuter's message said : " Edict been issued Peking, ordering return to learning of Confucius, and rejection of depraved modern ideas." (*Laughter.*) Gentlemen, the depraved modern ideas, which are anathema to the Chinese mandarin, have come to India, not to be abolished, but to stay. No Englishman is likely to propose a return to the excellent but obsolete ordinances of Manu ; and I doubt, if he did, whether any Hindu pundit would be prepared unreservedly to follow.

No, I prefer to think, not merely that the choice has been made, but that it has been justified. When one of the most illustrious of my predecessors, Lord Wellesley, opened his short-lived College at Fort William, and placed over its portal the inscription—

*Nunc redit a nobis Aurora diemque reducit,*

which, for any of you who do not know Latin, I may translate thus—" The dayspring has returned from us, and has brought back the light to you"—I believe that he furnished a true and just motto for the cause of Higher Education in India ; and I hold that, substantially, that is the service which we have rendered, and are still endeavouring to render, to you. (*Applause.*)

But, again let me say that the defence of my confidence does not lie in the intrinsic merits of the education itself, nor even in the eternal value of its truths. It consists in the effect that it is capable of producing, and that it has already produced upon character and upon morals, upon the standards of honour, of honesty, of justice, of duty, of upright dealing between man and man. I see faults in the present system. They are manifest to all. I see abuses against which we must be on our guard. Chief among them is the tendency, inevitable, I think, wherever independence of reason is first inculcated in a community that has long been a stranger thereto, to chafe against the restraints, to question the motives, and to impugn the prestige of authority. This is a dangerous tendency, against which Young India requires particularly to be on its guard. For the admission of independence is a very different thing from the denial of authority. On the contrary, the truest independence exists where authority is least assailed ; and almost the first symptom of enlightenment is the recognition of discipline. The ignorance of these conditions is a malady with which a society, still in a comparatively early stage of intellectual emancipation, is liable to be afflicted. It is a sort of measles in the body politic, of which the patient will purge himself as time goes on. It may give us cause for anxiety ; but it need not, if carefully prescribed for, excite alarm. It should not close our eyes to the vastly superior range of benefits that is produced by Higher Education in the fields of which I have been speaking, and to the tolerably healthy condition of the learner as a whole. For my own part, if I did not think that Higher Education were producing satisfactory result in India, I should be ready to proscribe your examinations, to burn your diplomas, and to carry away in some old hulk all your teaching and professorial staff, your Syndicate, your Senate, your Vice-Chancellor, and even your Chancellor himself, and to scuttle it in the Bay of Bengal. (*Laughter.*) It would be better to revert to the old Adam, than to inculcate a hybrid morality or to nourish a bastard civilisation.

There is another aspect of Higher Education about which I have not time to say more than a word this afternoon, and which indeed is hardly connected with the courses of an examining University such as this. I have been speaking of the objects of Higher Education as being in the main those of intellectual and moral discipline, and as affecting the character of the·individual to start with, and the community in the long run. But Higher Education has other and not less noble fields of action open to it ; among which I would rank none superior to the obligations of extending the range of human knowledge by original study, by experiment, and by research. A new and splendid opportunity for the gratification of these ambitions is likely before long to be afforded by the enlightened munificence of a Bombay gentleman, Mr. Tata, of whom you have all heard. (*Applause.*) It has given me the greatest pleasure to accept his offer on the part of the

Government of India and to assist in the deliberations that
it is to be hoped will result in giving to his generous ideas
a practical form.   You have, I believe, in your own midst, a
society which, on a humble scale, because it is only possessed of humble means, attempts to diffuse scientific knowledge among the educated population of Bengal.   I allude
to the Indian Association for the Cultivation of Science,
to which Dr. Sircar has, I know, devoted nearly a quarter
of a century of unremitting, and only partially recognized,
labour. (*Applause.*)  I often wonder why the wealthy
patrons of science and culture with whom Bengal abounds,
do not lend a more strenuous helping hand to so worthy and
indigenous an institution.   I was rejoiced, however, to read
in the papers only two days ago that the Bengal Government
has recently instituted three postgraduate scholarships for
original research. (*Applause.*)

Gentlemen, when I addressed this Convocation for the
first time last year, I indicated that, in my opinion, much
remained to be done in the co-ordination of our educational
system in India, in the correction of admitted backslidings
and abuses, and in the more vigilant discharge by the
Supreme Government of the responsibilities with which it
is endowed.  You may be sure that the matter has not
slipped from my mind since ; even though in the overwhelming pre-occupations of official life, and of the scores
of great questions that seem perpetually to be calling for
investigation and reform, I have not yet been able to carry
into full effect the views which I then sketched in intentionally vague outline.  There are two considerations by
which any sensible man must be affected who attempts to
handle the educational problem in India, more especially if
he be, by virtue of his position and antecedents, an outsider
and, to some extent, an amateur.  The first of these is the
desirability of ascertaining by consultation with those who
have devoted their lives to the task, and who may fairly be
called experts, what is the trend of authoritative opinion
upon the subject.  The reformer must carry this with him ;.

otherwise he is impotent or, if not that, he will certainly find this work abortive. The second desideratum is a recognition of the familiar axiom about going slow. The prudent General reconnoitres his country before he delivers the assault. He ponders the respective advantage of flanking movements and of a frontal attack. Above all, he desires to clear the ground of any obstacles that may retard his advance or jeopardise his success. It is for this reason— if I may borrow a metaphor from that South African campaign that absorbs so much of our interest just now— that I have, during the past year, been testing the various drifts or fords in the rivers that lie between me and the enemy, and have been delivering a series of attacks upon the smaller positions that separate me from that beleaguered garrison which I desire to relieve. Various Government Resolutions that have seen the public light will have afforded you some indication of what I mean. Though I have paid my tribute to the cause of Higher Education this afternoon, and have indicated my opinion of its essential permanence in our system, I am no friend of those who argue that Primary Education can, therefore, be neglected. On the contrary, I am one of those who think that, as time passes by, Secondary and Higher Education should become more and more a field for private effort, and should make a decreasing demand upon Government intervention and control. On the other hand, Primary Education can never lose its priority of claim upon the interest and support of the State. For that Government would but imperfectly discharge its duties which, while it provided for the relatively intelligent and literate minority, ignored its obligation to the vast amorphous and unlettered mass of the population, and left it to lie in contented ignorance. We have recently called the attention of the Local Governments to their duty in this respect, which appears, in some cases, to have been disregarded. Again, there have seemed to us to be many flaws in the system under which text-books are at present prescribed, both for the lower schools and for the higher classes of affiliated schools and colleges. Long lists of books are drawn up that are apt to encourage cramming ; the catalogues are not always carefully compiled, and unsuitable works creep in. The Local Governments, and in some cases the Universities, have not very strictly interpreted their great responsibility in the matter ; and Government assistance is given to the promotion of studies for which no Government authority has been invoked or supplied. I have observed traces of a similar laxity in the process of affiliation of colleges and schools, and a tendency sometimes to increase the number of the affiliated without due regard to the character of the teachers, the quality of the training, or the degree of discipline. In all these matters it appears to me that closer supervision is required, and a more effective control. Do not imagine for a moment that I am departing from that which has always been the mainspring of the educational policy of the Government of India ever since Sir Charles Wood's celebrated Despatch in 1854, *viz.*, the substitution, where possible, of Government aid for Government management, and the encouragement of private initiative and effort. I do not want to take back the pupil and to shut him up in a Government nursery. I am no friend of leading strings, particularly when they are made of red-tape. But I do say emphatically that the grant-in-aid system from the start involved as its corollary a due measure of State inspection and control, and that to call upon the State to pay for education out of the public funds, but to divest itself of responsibility for their proper allocation to the purposes which the State had in view in giving them, is to ignore the elementary obligations for which the State itself exists. My desire, therefore, is to revindicate on behalf of the State and its various provincial agents that responsibi_ lity which there has been a tendency to abdicate, and to show to the world that our educational system in India, liberal and elastic as I would have it remain, is yet not free to assume any promiscuous shape that accident or intention may force upon it, but must conform to a scientific and orderly scheme, for which in the last resort the Supreme Government should be held accountable, whether it be for praise or for blame. In later years I may be able to say something more to you of the realisation of these ambitions.

Gentlemen, the Vice-Chancellor is waiting to address the students who have this afternoon received their degrees from him, and who are about to go forth to the world with the *imprimatur* of the Calcutta University upon them, and with their future in their hands. I will only stand between him and them for the additional moment that is required to impress upon them the reflection that with the receipt of a degree, their education is not exhausted but is only just beginning, and to urge them to continue the pursuit of knowledge for its own sake in the life, be it official, or professional, or private, that lies before them.

I will now call on the Vice-Chancellor to address the Convocation. (*Loud and continued applause.*)

### ADDRESS FROM THE PLANTERS OF DIBRUGARH.

*7th March,* 1900.

[On Friday night, the 2nd March, the Viceroy left Calcutta for a fortnight's tour in Assam. He was accompanied by Her Excellency Lady Curzon, Sir W. Cuningham, Foreign Secretary, Mr. W. R. Lawrence, Private Secretary, Major the Hon'ble E. Baring, Military Secretary, and other members of the staff. Mr. Cotton, Chief Commissioner of Assam, joined at Gauhati. On Wednesday morning the 7th, the party arrived at the Rehabari Station, where the Planters of Dibrugarh presented an address to His Excellency. The address, which was read by Mr. Alston, after cordially welcoming the Viceroy, expressed appreciation of the sympathetic attitude hitherto adopted by the Government of India in regard to the Emigration and Labour Laws of Assam, and confidence that the Viceroy would be supported by the experience gained in his visit in maintaining the policy of his predecessors in this direction. The importance of retaining the safeguards afforded by legislation was dwelt upon. Reference was made to the gradual reclamation of Assam by the tea industry, and some disappointment was expressed at the temporary stoppage of all work on the upper section of the Assam-Bengal Railway. The address concluded by commending for consideration the necessity of an exhaustive mineral survey of the surrounding hill tracts, by expressing a hope that the Viceroy's visit to the province would be repeated, and by cordially welcoming Her Excellency to Assam.

His Excellency the Viceroy replied as follows :—]

*Gentlemen :*—It cannot fail to be a source of much gratification to me on this the first occasion of a visit not merely by myself but by any Viceroy of India, to the extreme borders of Assam, to receive so warm a welcome at the hands of the pioneer body whose energy and outlay have been responsible for the reclamation of this remote, but flourishing, corner of Her Majesty's Indian dominions. Most of my travels hitherto have been connected with the north-western outposts of the Indian Empire, where questions of high politics and of imperial strategy absorb the attention of the student. But because those momentous issues are here in the main replaced by problems of internal development and industrial exploitation, that is no reason why a Governor-General of India should take any the less interest in your enterprise or fortunes. Indeed, my own conception of the high office that he is privileged to fill is that, during his time, he should, as far as opportunity and health may permit, visit all quarters of the vast dependency temporarily committed to his charge, and should endeavour by personal contact with places and men to form a correct appreciation of local as well as of imperial concerns. In this spirit, Gentlemen, I have come, albeit on a hasty visit, to Assam, and in my replies to the addresses with which here and elsewhere, I am favoured, I shall discuss, with a frankness similar to that with which you have honoured me, the subjects that are of common interest to us both.

I am glad to note that you record your sincere recognition of the wisdom and sympathy of the attitude consistently adopted by the Government of India with regard to the Emigration and Labour Laws of this Province. I agree with you in thinking that the time has not yet come when the protection and control, by special statute agency, of the industry in which you are engaged can safely be dispensed with, and the Bill that has lately been introduced into the Legislative Council is proof conclusive of my agreement. A day will probably come in the future when exceptional Labour Laws will not be required for the tea plantations of Assam, any more than they are in the Duars and Terai of Bengal, and when for the present artificial system will be substituted the natural operation of the laws of demand and supply. That is the ideal to which successive Viceroys and Secretaries of State, and I imagine also successive generations of Planters all look forward ; but the means of access to these parts of Assam must be greatly improved, and the conditions of employment must be ameliorated and rendered more secure, before a natural stream of cheap and free labour can be expected to flow up and down the Brahmaputra Valley. In the meantime, it is our duty to prepare the way for that consummation, by regularising and purifying from abuse of reproach the existing contract system. I am pleased to think that our present effort to do so has, in its main outlines, met with the frank and cordial acceptance of the Planters, who reprobate not less than do the Government of India both the processes and the results of an unlicensed and illicit system of professional recruiting falsely masquerading under the designation "free." The temporary postponement of the measure will give us further opportunities of considering the views both of the planting industry and of the executive officers of the Province upon the points concerning which agreement has not yet been attained. I was much gratified at being able to persuade Mr. Buckingham, in whom in your address you have signified your entire confidence, to give to the Government of India the benefit of his co-operation in our Legislative Council, and although, for the reason that I have named, we have not as yet been able to take full advantage of his services, I shall hope to be fortunate enough to have established a lien upon them for the session of next year, when we shall resume the discussion of the bill.

While avowing your belief, which I share, that upon the development of communications, both by water and land, the future prosperity of the Province largely depends, you add an expression of disappointment at the temporary suspension of work upon the upper section of the Assam-Bengal Railway. I am as well aware as any of you can be of the unfortunate consequences of any such stoppage, but may I point out to you that the Government of India are no more able to certify in advance the complete execution, still less a generous expansion, of their railway programme than you are able to guarantee a first class crop from your tea gardens? Both of us are dependent upon conditions outside of human control. The external world seems sometimes to imagine that the Government of India enjoy unlimited resources for building railways, and that only some malevolent bureaucratic streak in our composition stands in the way of the prompt realisation of the works which we have already commenced, and the even prompter acceptance of whatever fresh proposals may be placed before us. These of course are not the facts. Our railway programme must be strictly co-ordinated to our financial resources, and to the triennial outlay that is sanctioned by the Secretary of State. A year of bad weather, of high mortality, of low prices, will disorganise the whole of the calculations of the tea planter, and will compel him to curtail all the pet schemes of extension that he may have planned for the ensuing season. In the same way, the terrible famine, from which parts of India are now suffering, reacts upon the whole of our administrative and financial programme. We cannot, at the same time, produce 4 or 5 crores for famine relief, and yet spend them on railways. Governments, in fact, have their lean years as well as companies, and syndicates, and individuals, and we have to do what every private person would do in the same circumstances, *viz.*, cut down our expenses and economise all round. Now let me apply these reflections to the case of the Assam-Bengal Railway. I am as anxious to push it through as any man ; but the immediate demands are beyond our means. In the present year we were asked for 124 lakhs, and we have, with the utmost difficulty, given 96 lakhs ; next year we are asked for 127 lakhs, but, owing to famine and other causes, we cannot, from our own resources, provide one-half of that sum, nor, I am afraid, will the popular, though Utopian, argument that it cannot be sound policy to postpone or to delay the execution of a remunerative scheme apply in the present case. So difficult is the country which this railroad traverses that the total average cost per mile of the 740 miles of metre gauge line is likely to be 1½ lakh, or £10,000 a mile, a total only reached by the heaviest broad gauge lines in Upper India. I doubt if the most sanguine of the believers in the future of Assam, whom I am now addressing, will assure me of returns within a measurable period of time, that will even infinitesimally recoup this enormous outlay, or will convert the Assam-Bengal Railway, for many a year to come, into anything but a heavy annual drain upon the pocket of Government.

Gentlemen, the suggestion that you have made of a geological survey of the hilly tracts of this district by a Government expert is new to me, but it is one to which, if it comes up to Government, with the approval of the Chief Commissioner, I shall be glad to give the most favourable consideration. The Government should certainly lose no opportunity of opening the door, by such assistance as it can legitimately afford, to the enterprise of its citizens, particularly in a neighbourhood where their activity and initiative have already effected so much.

You have been kind enough, in the concluding paragraphs of your address, to make special mention of the fact that Lady Curzon has accompanied me upon this journey, and to hint that this can only have been accomplished at the cost of some discomfort and fatigue. You must, I think, have temporarily forgotten that it is in one of the superb steamers of the India General Steam Navigation Company that we have made the trip—an act of generous assistance on the part of the Company, without which I am afraid that we should never have succeeded in reaching Dibrugarh in the brief time at our disposal : while the contrast of a day on board the *Buzzard* with any average 24 hours while I am in Calcutta tempts me to think that there is less fatigue in penetrating to the remotest corner of Assam than there is in never moving from my own writing table at Government House. Neither Lady Curzon nor myself will easily forget the hearty and loyal reception which you have extended to us. During the next two days we shall be busily engaged in inspecting the industries of this most interesting neighbourhood. I have previously been down coal mines both in England and in Tonking ; I have inspected spouting oil-wells and refineries on the shores of the Caspian ; and I have examined tea plantations both in Ceylon and Japan. But I understand that you propose to spare me any similar travels in the future by showing me all these curiosities within the space of a few miles, and in less than 30 hours. I am sure that I shall profit by what I see, and that Lady Curzon and I will carry away with us a happy recollection of our excursion to this busy scene alike of British enterprise and British hospitality.

## ADDRESS FROM THE PLANTERS OF TEZPUR.

*9th March*, 1900.

[The Viceregal party arrived at Tezpur, Assam, on the afternoon of Friday, the 9th March, and were received by Mr P. G. Melitus, Commissioner of the Assam Valley Districts, the Hon'ble Mr. J. Buckingham, C.I.E, and a large assembly, including the leading planters of the district and many ladies. In the evening Their Excellencies were entertained at a banquet given in their honour by the principal planters of Tezpur and the surrounding district, at which about 120 people were present. After dinner Mr. Buckingham read an address on behalf of the planters, offering to the Viceroy, the first who had visited the Brahmaputra Valley, and to Lady Curzon, a cordial welcome. Assam, it was pointed out, was perhaps the one Province in India which is most in need of Government sympathy and assistance. Its early history furnished a record of conflict and disorder and the scanty cultivation and sparse population bore witness to those misfortunes. It required all the energy of the British planters, backed by British capital, to utilise the resources of the Province. Scarcity of labour was a serious difficulty, the indigenous population being wholly insufficient to develop the Province. Imported labour was consequently necessary, and year after year the cost of this had increased while the supply had diminished. Land transport was a heavy charge; the cost of metalled roads had proved to be prohibitive; and the only alternative was the construction of light railways, to which His Excellency's attention was specially invited. The connection of Gauhati with the railway system to Bengal was also urged in the interests of the passenger and labour traffic. It was represented that in the Brahmaputra Valley there were large tracts of culturable waste lands admirably suited for the production of cereals and food grains, which, if brought under cultivation, would afford protection from scarcity and famine. Reference was made to the Chenab Canal Colony, and to His Excellency's expressed approval to bring the waste lands of Upper India under cultivation; a similar encouragement was solicited for Assam, and as there was no prospect of bringing the waste lands under cultivation by an overflow of labour from the tea gardens, it was suggested that this labour should be specially imported. In conclusion a desire was expressed that the Local Boards of each district should not only have the benefit of the advice of the Civil Engineers of the Public Works Department, but should be able to look to those officers to carry out the works.

His Excellency the Viceroy replied as follows :—]

*Gentlemen:*—I have already, at Dibrugarh, expressed the pleasure which it gives me, as head of the Government of India, to visit this important Province, and, if it be the fact that I am the first visitor in that capacity to this

part of the Brahmaputra Valley, I concur with you in thinking that there is every reason why I should not be the
last. I also accept the proposition that Assam is a Province demanding in a peculiar degree the sympathy and
assistance of Government; but if that statement be held
to imply that such sympathy and such assistance have not
yet been forthcoming, I must, in justice to the Government over which I preside, deprecate what would, I think,
be an unjust imputation. I have sometimes in the Press
observed an inclination to represent Assam as a sort of
abandoned Garden of Eden, watered by great rivers, and
furnished with the fruit of the Tree of Life, which, but
for the frowns of an angry Providence, represented in this
case by the Government of India, would long ago have
recovered its pristine richness and beauty. Such a picture
would, in my opinion, be both over-coloured and over-
drawn. The Province of Assam is indeed in a backward
condition, compared with some other and more highly-
favoured localities, but its backwardness is no more due to
any indifference on the part of the Government of India,
than it has been to any lack of initiative on the part of the
British pioneers who have come hither, and with so much
courage and perseverance have sunk their capital and
expended their energies in its exploitation. On the contrary, the services of these pioneers have constituted a claim
for unusual consideration at the hands of Government,
which, for a long series of years, has authorised an expenditure upon Assam that the revenues of the latter have
hitherto failed to balance. At the present time a larger
proportion of the gross receipts of this Province is expended
upon administration and development than in any other
Province in India. In the last recorded financial year, viz.,
1898-99, the gross income—Imperial, Provincial, and Local
—amounted to 147 lakhs, the gross expenditure chargeable
to revenue was 123 lakhs, which, with an additional 120
lakhs representing capital outlay on the Assam-Bengal
Railway, constituted a total disbursement of 243 lakhs,

or an excess of expenditure over revenue of nearly one crore of rupees. Again, so far from the railways in Assam being remunerative, there was, in the same year, a loss of 10 lakhs on their working expenses, exclusive of the interest charges on the Railway Capital Account. It is clear, therefore, from these calculations that Assam is at present contributing nothing to the military and other general charges of the Indian Empire, but that she is actually absorbing a good deal of Imperial capital. We are in fact engaged in the development of an asset which may one day recoup our outlay, but, for the present, the balance is on the wrong side of the ledger.

Gentlemen, in your address you speak of the conditions by which the efforts of the British planter have been handicapped and retarded. You point correctly to a long previous history of rapine and misgovernment in the Brahmaputra Valley, to a scanty indigenous population, to the paucity of labour entailing reinforcement from the outside, to the increasing cost of that importation, and to the external competition which your industry has to face. To these sources of difficulty with which Government has, to the best of its ability, helped you to cope, by means of special labour laws under which your contracts are enforceable by the Criminal Courts, and by railway extensions both in Assam and in Bengal, which have been planned in the interests of this Province, should be added that which, in my opinion, is the main explanation both of the backwardness of the Province and of the anxieties by which you are oppressed. I allude to the climate of Assam. Lord Beaconsfield, when Mr. Disraeli, once said that the true secret of the woes of Ireland consisted in the fact that she lies under weeping skies, and is surrounded by a melancholy ocean. A similar diagnosis gives the real clue to the impediments of this Province. A humid and malarial atmosphere, injurious to the indigenous population, which steadily recedes in numbers, and fatal to the immigrants from the drier plains of Behar and Bengal, an atmosphere

which is still further poisoned by exhalations from the
recently upturned soil, and which carries mysterious and
deadly diseases in its train,—this is the real enemy of Assam,
with which private enterprise and Government patronage
alike find it hard to contend. When the provincial death-
rate, is always greatly in excess of the birth-rate, and when a
labouring population of over half a million persons requires
to be imported from the outside, and to be perpetually
replenished, the conditions are such that expansion can
scarcely pursue a natural course, and, however encouraged,
is liable to the fluctuations that are inseparable from that
which is not an organic but an artificial growth.

Gentlemen, in your address you invite my special attention to the increased cost of labour importation. This is a
subject to which, in connection with the legislation now
before the Government of India, I have necessarily given
close study. The very rapid rise in the cost, which is
said to have nearly doubled in ten years, is no doubt partly
to be attributed to the keen rivalry and to the familiar
wiles of the many middlemen, to whose fingers some
money sticks at each stage on the passage of the coolie
from India to Assam. In so far as the evil is to be attributed to the system of recruitment practised by these
unlicensed traffickers, it will be arrested by our Bill. The
increasing demand for labour here, owing to the opening
of new tea gardens, is a further explanation of the enhancement of cost. But, Gentlemen, we should both of us
be shutting our eyes to the facts did we not realise that
the main cause, which no legislation can greatly affect,
or altogether remove, is the increasing industrial competition that prevails in the Indian labour market itself. You
desire for the work of your plantations the hardy aboriginal tribesman or *jungli* of Chota Nagpur. But he is also
wanted for the coal mines of Bengal, for work on railways,
and for the tea gardens of the Duars and the Terai. Now
in those employments be it remembered that he earns a
higher wage than you are able to give him, that he is

engaged for a shorter term, that he is nearer to his own home, and that he can frequently return thither within the year. You have to consider whether, with your lower monthly wage, your four-year contract, and your great distance from the source of recruitment, you can permanently, and successfully, compete with your rival employers. In the long run, a problem of this sort will not be settled by Labour Commissions, or by Government Bills ; it will be decided by the immutable laws that regulate demand and supply. You cannot make water run up-hill, and you cannot provide labour for an industry below its market price. The wage question itself I need not now discuss, since the postponement of the Bill till next year will afford ample time for its re-examination.

The subject of feeder lines of railway, and of a Government guarantee, which figured next in your remarks, I will reserve for treatment in my reply at Gauhati, where I understand that it also occupies a prominent place in the address to which I shall be called upon to respond.

I pass to the question of the waste lands of Assam and of the measures that may properly be taken for their reclamation and cultivation. Your contention is that these lands, amounting, as you say, to no less than $6\frac{1}{2}$ million acres, are suitable for the production of rice, jute, corn, and other cereals, and that, as they cannot be cultivated by the overflow of time-expired labour from the tea gardens, labour must be specially imported from elsewhere for the purpose. This is a subject upon which, as you know, the Government of India have, for long, been in correspondence with the Chief Commissioner, and upon which, as the question is largely hypothetical in character, differences of opinion may be expected to exist. This is not the only country which presents the spectacle of sparsely populated and unreclaimed tracts lying at no insuperable distance from congested centres of population. Nothing is easier for the doctrinaire than to say—' Why not bring the people from the district where there are too many to the district where there are too few ?'—but there are a good many intervening fences to be cleared, of which the doctrinaire is apt to take insufficient account. There is the unhealthiness of the climate, upon which I have previously touched, the reluctance of the immigrant, and the novelty of the conditions. You call my attention to the Chenab Canal Colony, which I visited last April. There the circumstances are entirely different ; the movement is merely from one part of the Punjab to another ; the place is extremely healthy ; there is no jungle to be cut down, and no clearing to be made ; the Government have brought the water, and nature may be trusted to do the rest ; finally, the applicants, instead of requiring to be coaxed by alluring offers, or imported at considerable cost, jostle each other in their anxiety to be taken on. In the present case it is no doubt true that, in any scheme of Government colonisation, we must look in the main to external sources of recruitment. The time-expired tea coolies, I daresay, make the best settlers, because they are already acclimatised, and I should think that it would be to the interest of the planter himself to settle his coolies upon neighbouring plots of land, so as to retain a call upon their services after the expiration of the contract ; but I agree that the labour supply of the gardens, and the labour supply of the Province, are subjects which should not be confused and which should be treated independently of each other. As regards the particular question whether a *ryotwari* or a big *zemindari* form of tenure is more suitable to the development of a backward Province, I will not here recapitulate an argument which has already covered a perhaps sufficient amount of paper. Two desiderata are unquestionably wanting, namely, first, the man, or men, to initiate the experiment ; second, the colonists to undertake the reclamation. If Mr. Cotton can produce any of the former, I do not think that he will find the Government of India grudging or obstinate in insistence upon terms, provided always that these do not contemplate a mere commercial speculation in land, and that they include some effective guarantee that the estates will be brought under cultivation within a reasonable period of time. In my opinion, the main question at issue is not the size of the grant—that is a relatively small matter—but the capacity, the stability, and the aptitude of the grantee. Perhaps, later on, when we get the connection completed between Gauhati and the main line of the Assam-Bengal Railway, we may be able to try some colonisation scheme which will appeal to the land hunger of the many, even more than to the public spirit or enterprise of the few.

Gentlemen, in one of your later paragraphs you express a desire that the Local Boards in Assam should call upon the Civil Engineers of the Public Works Department, not merely for advice, but for the execution of public works in the Province. We have already in the former respect conceded all that your Chief Commissioner asked and have, indeed, insisted upon even more; since we have required that the opinions of the Inspectors of Works shall not only be sought, but shall not be disregarded by the Local Boards or their servants, the District Engineers. The further proposal that the Public Works Department should also be responsible for the execution of the works, is one that is approved neither by Mr. Cotton nor by the Government of India. The question has also arisen in Bengal, and we agree with the Lieutenant-Governor of that Province in thinking that the adoption of the change would stifle the legitimate energies and independence of local self-government; since it would transfer to an official department the authority and responsibility in respect of public works that ought properly to remain with the Boards.

In conclusion, Gentlemen, let me assure you that the candid interchange of opinions between us which the present and other occasions during the past week have afforded, cannot fail to be of much benefit to me in my future administration ; that I shall always feel that I know the planters and understand their aspirations better from having met them in the homes which they have created and on the lands which their industry has reclaimed ; and that Lady Curzon and myself will carry away the most agreeable recollections of this beautiful valley and its adventurous and public-spirited pioneers.

## ADDRESS FROM THE PEOPLE OF ASSAM.

### *13th March*, 1900.

[On Tuesday morning the 13th March, the Viceroy received an address from the People of Assam at Gauhati. Here the members of the Reception Committee, appointed in public meeting, assembled, and on behalf of themselves and of the people presented the address, which opened with cordial expressions of welcome to Their Excellencies, of loyalty to the Queen-Empress. and of gratification at the Viceroy's visit to the Province. It referred to the delay which had taken place in the construction of the Assam-Bengal Railway, and a hope was expressed that the Viceroy's visit would result in its speedy completion, and in the commencement of the projected railway along the north bank of the Brahmaputra—the connecting link between the Assam-Bengal and Eastern Bengal systems. A system of light feeder lines from the main trunk lines to open up outlying areas of culture and population was also urged. The desirability of Assam being permanently represented in the Viceroy's Legislative Council was pointed out ; as also the necessity, in the matter of land tenures, for long term settlements (in place of the present short terms) with the right of sub-letting intact without any further enhancement of land revenue. The address concluded with a eulogistic reference to the services of Mr. Cotton, the Chief Commissioner.

His Excellency the Viceroy replied as follows :—]

*Gentlemen:*—The configuration and physical features of the administrative area of the Province of Assam are such that it is almost impossible for a Viceroy, within the limited space of time at his disposal, to visit the entire Province or to see more than conspicuous illustrations of its industry and life. Lord Northbrook, in the famine year of 1874, visited the Surma Valley, and came over the hills to Gauhati, the only previous Viceroy who has set foot in any part of Assam. My own tour on the present occasion has been confined to that which in Assam itself you regard, I believe, as Assam Proper, *viz.*, the valley of this magnificent river, second to scarcely any in Asia in the volume of its water and in the productive quality of its alluvion. That a full fortnight will have been required, travelling at a very high rate of speed by water and only spending five days on land, to ascend and descend this mighty current, between the confines of Bengal and a

point short of that at which it pierces the Himalayan
barrier and enters the plains of India, is an indication of
the wide extent of your Province and of the degree to
which the Brahmaputra and its tributaries are the vital artery
of Assam.

That the people of Assam, from whom I am now receiving an address, are a courageous and high-spirited race may
I think be inferred from the fact that, although it is not yet
three years since you were visited by the most appalling
natural calamity that has ever befallen this part of India—I
speak of the great earthquake of June 1897, which wrought
wide-spread havoc to property and was attended with
serious loss of life—there has nevertheless not been a single
mention of this disaster in any of the three addresses which
have been presented to me while journeying in this
Province, or in any of the subsidiary speeches to which it
has been my good fortune to listen. The Government of
India helped to the best of their ability in the heavy outlay
that was entailed upon you. But the main brunt of the
burden has fallen upon your own shoulders ; and I congratulate you upon the patience and recuperative power that
have been displayed.

Gentlemen, your address contains some observations
upon the railway question in Assam. You note the long
period over which the construction of the Assam-Bengal
Railway has been spread, and you urge the commencement
of the projected line to connect this place along the
northern bank of the Brahmaputra with Eastern Bengal. I
have already remarked at Dibrugarh that the Assam-
Bengal Railway is the most expensive line that we have
constructed for many years. I wish I could add that
I think it will be one of the most promising. For many
years to come I am afraid that it will be a millstone round
the neck of the Government of India ; although if our loss
were to be your gain, I for one should not protest against
the burden. Since I spoke at Dibrugarh on the matter, I
am happy to be able to state that the difficulty which I there

confessed as to the provision of funds for the railway during the ensuing year has been removed by permission being accorded to the Company to raise debentures to the extent of 75 lakhs ; so that its financial requirements for the forthcoming twelvemonth have now been fully met, and there is no fear of that suspension of work which was apprehended in an earlier address. As regards railway connection with Bengal, with this splendid waterway at your doors, and with an efficient steamer service, I think you can afford to wait for a while ; although, with such means as we possess, the line is being steadily pushed on from the west, the Teesta and Dhurla rivers are being bridged, and the line to Mogul Hat is being converted from the 2 feet 6-inch to the metre gauge, and is being extended in the direction of Dhubri. Later on, whenever the railhead reaches the opposite shores of the Brahmaputra confronting this place, you will be able to congratulate yourselves upon offering to the scientific engineer an opportune island in the middle of the stream, which I am sure will inspire him with dreams of an unprecedented mechanical triumph in the shape of a Brahmaputra Bridge.

You proceed to urge upon me, as also did the community by whom I had the honour to be addressed at Tezpur, the advantages of a system of light feeder lines in Assam, ramifying from the main system, and bringing into connection therewith outlying areas of culture or population. It is further represented that, whilst the capital for many of these railways or tramways is forthcoming—an assertion about which I do not feel in every case quite confident— they can only be successfully financed if a guarantee or subsidy be given by the Government. Other conditions that are asked for, concerning the use of lands, roads and timber, I need not enter into at the present moment ; since it is not about these that I personally should ever wish to be stiff, or that, on ordinary occasions, any difficulty is apt to arise.

Now as regards the general merit of these feeder lines I am in substantial agreement with yourselves, and I believe that, if more widely extended, they would be the most effective forerunner of the prosperous future that we all hope awaits Assam. But different views may legitimately be held about the best methods of financing their construction ; and when I have to consider the question of an Imperial guarantee, it is clear that I cannot look at the matter exclusively through Assamese spectacles ; but that I am obliged to correlate it with the demands of other localities not less deserving, and with the inexorable limitations of our annual programme.

There does not seem to me to be any distinction in practical finance between a Provincial guarantee and an Imperial guarantee. Of course if the Local Government can provide the money from its own resources without raising its demands upon the Imperial Exchequer, and without abandoning or neglecting other public works, a strong case is made out. But that is not the situation with which we are as a rule confronted : and when the proposal is made to guarantee provincially, and then to revise the Provincial Contract at the expense of the Imperial Government, I can see no difference between such a procedure and an Imperial guarantee pure and simple. Now, if the guarantee be Imperial, the capital must be entered, under the financial system to which we are bound by the Secretary of State, upon the annual programme. That is a strictly limited programme, which, for the ensuing year, amounts to $6\frac{1}{2}$ crores. All expenditure upon railways within that sum is carefully worked out by the Government of India upon an examination of the conflicting demands and needs of the entire country. No expenditure beyond it is possible except in a year when the revenue justifies an outlay more ambitious than the original forecast. In a year such as the present, with enormous calls for famine weighing us down, any such excess is absolutely impossible. If an archangel from heaven were to come and offer me a scheme, certain to be ultimately remunerative, but involving an immediate entry upon the programme of capital outlay, I should be obliged to refuse him. You may call the system inelastic and exasperating if you please ; and, in many respects, I agree with you, and am struggling to effect a reformation. But do not quarrel with the Government of India for doing that which it has no other present alternative than to do. Once a year, at budget time, we cut our coat ; and it is a big coat. But, like other tailors, we cannot make it bigger than the cloth provided to us admits of, and hence it results that there are frequently parts of the body which remain for a while indifferently clad.

If, however, the Local Government is unable to accept the risk of a guarantee within its existing contract, and if the Imperial Government is crippled by plague and famine, what, it may be asked, are you to do? Now it does not seem to me that the financial possibilities are by any means exhausted if in any particular case neither a Provincial nor an Imperial guarantee can be given. I own that I do not myself quite understand the position of those promoters who represent to the Government of India as pleas for an Imperial guarantee that the chances of its being called upon are so remote, the prospects of the concession for which they ask so radiant, and the capital outlay involved so small, that the Government of India will not incur the faintest risk in giving the pledge, but who nevertheless are unable themselves either to produce the money or to persuade others to do so, without it. But even supposing their position to be explicable and sound, I would point out that other methods are still open. I was travelling only three days ago on the Tezpur-Bali-para Railway, a 2 ft. 6-in. line running for 20 miles from Tezpur on the north bank of the river into the interior, and serving several important tea gardens *en route*. This little line was constructed for a capital expenditure, including interest during construction, of only 4 lakhs, or £26,000. In the fourth year of its existence it is already earning $5\frac{1}{2}$ per cent. upon the capital outlay up to date. This itself appears to me to be a very remarkable and encouraging precedent. But the reason for which I especially notice it is that the only form of outside assistance which the promoters received was not a guarantee, either from the Imperial or the Provincial Government, nor any direct financial help from the latter, but a small subsidy from the District Board of Tezpur. I do not know if this subsidy was required to raise the capital for construction. But whether it operated in that direction or not, does it not suggest an example worthy of imitation? In the South of India I can quote to you a precedent of an even more adventurous and stimulating character. There the District Board of Tanjore has set aside a special additional cess of three pies per rupee in its taxes to constitute a fund against which capital can be raised. With the money so acquired, it has succeeded in building many miles of metre-gauge line upon which it is now earning substantial dividends, being joint proprietor of the lines with the Madras Government. I cannot say whether the circumstances are such as to admit of a similar plan being adopted here, but at least it is worthy of examination.

Your next petition is that a permanent seat in the Legislative Council may be allotted to Assam. I quite appreciate the naturalness of this request. But it is one that has also to be considered from the wider standpoint of Indian interests at large. When the Council was expanded by the Act of 1892, there was not found to be within this Province that substantial community of interests which would render any one delegate truly representative of the whole. A tea planter would faithfully represent the tea-planting industry; and when measures affecting that industry are under discussion, we are usually able to rely upon the services of some gentleman, such as Mr. Buckingham at the present juncture, who does ample justice to his clients. But in the Native population of Assam, so widely scattered and representing no such solidarity of opinion or counsel, whilst it might be possible, though it would be difficult, to find some one who would duly represent such divergent elements, I doubt whether it would be possible to find any one who could represent the interests of the entire Province, European and planting as well as Native. The constituency is, in fact, too composite to admit of a permanent single mouth-piece. Moreover, there are wider considerations to be borne in mind. Exclusive of the five non-official Members who are returned to the Legislative Council of the Governor-General by the non-official Members of the Councils of Bombay, Madras, the North-West Provinces and Bengal, and by the Calcutta Chamber of Commerce, we only have five seats at our disposal for the whole of the rest of India. If I were to undertake permanently to allot one of these seats to Assam, I should be adopting a course that would be resented as unfair by the rest of India, and that would not necessarily conduce to the representative character of the Council itself. You may rely upon me, and I doubt not upon my successors after me, to give you provisional representation, from whatever section of the community, when called for by the legislative programme of Government. But the request for a permanent seat in the Council is one which, in the present stage of development of the Province, which you have yourselves described as backward, it is not possible to concede.

Your remarks upon the system of land tenure in Assam, and upon the desirability of a longer term, will be carefully considered when the new settlements are made, at no great distance from the present time. Sooner or later there can be little doubt that a longer settlement will come. It is a mark in every community of advancing agricultural development. But I would ask you to remember that the short term and the *ryotwari* tenure now prevailing were devised in strict relation to the conditions both of agriculture and population in the Brahmaputra Valley. You have here a nomadic population which reclaims the land from the waste, cultivates it for a few years, and then, when the soil begins to be impoverished, moves on. In every year, for $\frac{1}{4}$ million of acres brought into cultivation, another $\frac{1}{4}$ million are thrown out, the total temporarily-settled area of $1\frac{1}{2}$ million acres remaining comparatively stationary. It is to accommodate this tendency that annual leases have been permitted; and how faithfully they have responded to the needs of the time is shown by the fact that, though any ryot who chooses to take a ten years' lease acquires thereby that proprietary interest in the land which you appear to advocate, only the scantiest advantage has hitherto been taken of this provision. The main reason for which cultivation does not extend in this Province is that the indigenous population is stationary; and the main reason for which the indigenous population is stationary is not the system of land tenure but the nature of the climate. The question of sub-letting will be taken up when the new settlement is made. As to the question of the land revenue rates, no answer can be given upon that point until the reports of the Settlement Officers are received. But the Government of India will assuredly approach the matter with no *a priori* conclusions or prepossessions in their mind.

Gentlemen, I have been pleased to listen to the spontaneous testimony that you have borne to the labours of your Chief Commissioner. No one, connected or unconnected with the Government of India, can fail to recognise that his heart has been in his work, and that he has done his best to push the interests of this Province with the zeal of a parent, and with an enthusiasm proportionate to the magnitude of the undertaking. In the discharge of his task, to which he has applied great vigour as well as high abilities, I believe that he has earned the confidence of all sections, Native as well as European, of a singularly diversified community.

There is only one observation in your address which I would at all deprecate, and that is the sentence in which you modestly disparage the character of the welcome that you have given to Lady Curzon and myself. No such reflection has even dimly occurred to our minds. The loyalty of a people and the warmth of their feelings are capable of being testified in a score of other fashions than by magnificent preparations and costly displays. In Gauhati, however, we have been particularly struck by the good taste and spontaneity of your welcome. Here, as elsewhere in this Province, we feel that we have met with a reception that has sprung from the hearts of those who have offered it; and in tendering to you, one and all, our thanks, let me assure you that in turning our back upon the Brahmaputra Valley, its noble waterway, its expanding industries, and its friendly people, we shall not banish Assam from our affections, but shall keep a tender spot therein for this enterprising and hopeful corner of the British Empire.

## TELEGRAPHIC PRESS MESSAGES BILL.

*16th March,* 1900.

[At the meeting of the Governor-General's Legislative Council, held at Government House, Calcutta, on Friday, the 16th March, the principal business was the consideration of the Bill to provide for the protection of certain Telegraphic Press Messages. The Hon'ble Mr. Ibbetson was down on the List of Business to move that the Report of the Select Committee on the Bill be taken into consideration, and following this motion were 20 other motions by various members for 20 different amendments of the Bill. Before the motion for the consideration of the Select Committee's Report was made, however, His Excellency the President addressed Council as follows :—]

The Government of India have decided to withdraw this Bill during the present Session and to postpone its consideration until a later date. The reasons which have impelled us to take this step are as follows:—

The groundwork of the proposed legislation was, firstly, a desire to protect a large number of newspapers in this country from the theft of their foreign telegrams by those who had not paid for them, but who, in respect of local publication, were enabled not merely to pirate, but even, when at a distance from the place of issue, to anticipate the original purveyor of the news ; and, secondly, to lend a desirable stimulus to the expansion of the foreign news service provided in India.

Now, the first condition of such legislation, if it is to attain its object, should clearly be the unanimity of those in whose legitimate interest the protection is offered and the Bill introduced. The correspondence which has been published with Local Governments and other parties, shows that even at an earlier stage dissentient voices of no small weight were raised. These objections it was hoped by my Hon'ble friend who has been in charge of the Bill, to minimise, if not to remove, by the changes which he persuaded the Select Committee to introduce into the Bill. But it would appear that these changes, though satisfactory to some, have alienated the support, or, at any rate, not excited the approval, of the majority ; while the state of the Agenda paper reveals a considerable and contradictory variety of opinion on the part of the various sections and interests represented in this Council that leads me to doubt whether, in the present condition of affairs, there is a sufficient consensus of authority and approval behind the Bill to justify the Government or India in passing it at the present moment into law. There are circumstances in which the Government, convinced of the urgency of a case, or of the indispensable necessity of a proposed remedy, is justified in overriding opposition, and in using its full powers to place a measure upon the Statute Book. But this case scarcely appears to fall within that category. I am about the last person to use previous delay in settling a matter as a plea for further procrastination. At the same time, a case cannot truthfully be represented as urgent which has been continuously discussed and invariably postponed for a period of 30 years ; whilst even the advocates of this Bill will, I think, admit that, strong as, in their opinion, is the case for reform, the case would be much stronger if they were all agreed as to the particular shape which that reform should take, and if it could be said with truth that the protection of legitimate interests was not likely to be attended with some injury to the interests of others. That we have not succeeded in reaching a stage of even general or substantial concurrence is demonstrated by the fact that, whereas the original Bill, and those Local Governments and parties who advocated it, contemplated a protection of 36 hours all round, the Select Committee was so much impressed by the arguments directed against that position, that they substituted a double period of protection, 36 hours in one case, and 18 in another ; whereupon a large number of papers which had supported the original Bill withdrew their adherence, denounced the compromise effected by the Select Committee, and appealed for a single term of 24 hours, with the remarkable reservation in one case that the signatory party would prefer to substitute 18 hours, and in another that he would prefer to substitute 36. Meanwhile, the Native Press have, as we all know, maintained an attitude of uncompromising, and not unintelligible, hostility from the start. In these circumstances, I fail to find any sufficient cohesion of opinion, or argument, to justify the Government of India in pressing through the Bill. If the supporters of the measure had been able to present a united front, I think that they would have been in a better position. As it is, their individual disagreements have weakened their collective force.

But there are two other reasons that induce me to think that postponement is desirable. The first of these, to which I attach minor importance, is this. I am revealing no secret when I say that the main ground which has hitherto dissuaded the Government of India from undertaking legislation of this description has been the desire to have the benefit of English experience and guidance in the matter. I am far from laying down the general proposition that we should, in all cases, or even in the majority of cases, take our cue from the Imperial Parliament at Westminster. But where legislation of a somewhat experimental character is involved, entailing the acceptance of principles not hitherto universally accepted, and affecting a form of enterprise which, so far from being Indian in character or conception, is of Western origin, and was introduced in the first place into India from England, then I think that the example of the British Parliament is of value, and may with advantage be followed; whilst an English precedent is manifestly of superior value and authority to a Colonial precedent, upon which alone we can at present rely. Whether legislation for the protection of copyright in foreign telegrams is likely to be undertaken at an early date in England I have no means of knowing. But at least we do know that since this Bill was introduced here, a Committee of the House of Lords which was examining into the subject has reported, and has recommended legislation upon definite lines. Now I do not say that we are bound to sit still here and twiddle our thumbs until some Government at home acts upon the recommendation of that Committee ; but at least there seems to be good ground for suspending action here for a while in order to see what view is taken of the matter by the British Government and the British Parliament, which, on the whole, are better able to set an example to us than we are to them. Should they fail to do so, it will, at any time, be possible for us to exercise our own initiative and to resume the discussion of the matter without waiting for their lead.

The second reason, to which I attach even greater weight, is the following. One of the main grounds for which this Bill has been advocated is the stimulus that its passing into law will give to newspaper enterprise in this country. I am not sure that I attach to this argument the full value that its supporters do ; for I am a little sceptical of the extent to which newspapers in India are at present retarded from extending their foreign telegraphic correspondence, because the telegrams are liable to be filched as soon as they arrive. The same drawback in England does not appear to crush enterprise, or to frighten off competition ; and I suspect that in any country the paper which in the long run will secure the best market is the paper that will give the best news and doubtless pay the most for doing so, whether that news is, or is not, liable to be lifted by the predatory energies of rival organs. However that may be, I agree with those who hold that a surer encouragement to journalistic enterprise in India is likely to be found in a substantial diminution in the rates for telegraphic transmission from Europe than in the protection of already existing enterprise out here. Nearly a year ago, in the Budget Debate, I indicated the strong opinion that I entertained about the reasonableness, and even necessity, of such a reduction. A despatch was sent home by the Government of India as far back as last May stating our

views, and arguing our case with such force as we could
command. Since then there has been a good deal of discussion on the matter ; and it is likely that before long
definite negotiations with the Companies will be undertaken. That they will result in a very material reduction
of rates I cannot for a moment doubt ; and that such a
reduction will throw into entirely different perspective the
question of Press telegrams and foreign intelligence in
this country seems to me highly probable. Enterprise
and expenditure, instead of being confined to a few, will
become the characteristic of the many, and I will even go
further and anticipate a time at which the number of those
requiring protection may be so largely increased that
instead of the demand being presented, as now, by one
class of paper, and resented by another class, it may come
with approximate unanimity from the great majority of
high class journals in India, both Native and European.

I would sooner wait to give legislative protection until
the great mass of opinion is united in our favour than I
would proceed with public opinion divided as at present,
some for and some against, and those who are for and
those who are against arguing on different and mutually
destructive grounds ; and I would sooner pause to see what
consequences a reduced telegraphic tariff will produce
than legislate under conditions which are doomed at no
distant date to disappear.

These are the reasons for which the Government of
India have decided not, at the present moment, to proceed
further with this Bill.

## ANGLO-INDIAN ASSOCIATION.

*23rd March,* 1900.

[A Deputation of the Anglo-Indian Association (representing the domiciled Anglo-Indian and Eurasian Community throughout India), headed by Mr. L. P. Pugh, waited on the Viceroy at Government House, Calcutta, at 4·30 P.M. on Friday, the 23rd March, and were received by His Excellency in the Council Chamber. The object of the Deputation was to represent to the Viceroy the grievances and dis. advantages under which the Community labours. Statements were made by Mr Pugh, and two other members of the Deputation, specifying the particular grievances complained of and suggesting how they might be remedied

His Excellency the Viceroy replied as follows :—]

*Gentlemen,*—Since I received an address from your Association more than a year ago, shortly after I had taken up my present office, I can truthfully say that the appeals and claims and prospects of the community which you represent have occupied a good deal of my attention. I never fail to read, or to study. anything that bears upon the subject, or to converse with those who are qualified to give me useful information. These efforts on my part to arrive at the truth, and to analyse the difficult problem of your future, rest upon the double basis of personal sympathy—since no man with a heart can fail to be touched by the misfortunes of a community, partly, if not mainly, of his own race, who appear to have fallen upon hard times—and of political interest—since no Viceroy of India can be indifferent to the fortunes of a section of the population, increasing in numbers, but apparently not increasing *pari passu* in wealth, contentment, or opportunity. Every Viceroy from Lord Canning downwards has gazed at the problem, and has been left sympathetic but puzzled. Some, like Lord Lytton, have tried to do something positive. Others have felt the difficulty of State intervention. That I am receiving you to-day is, I hope, an evidence that I am not anxious to be included in the passive category, or to bow you out with a compliment and a smile. Nothing would have been easier for me

than to acknowledge your representations, and to have
returned the civil but stereotyped reply that they will
receive the .careful consideration of Government. Of
that reception they are in any case certain. But if I go
beyond, and consent, as I have consented, to meet you
here to-day, and to listen to a statement of your troubles
from the lips of your accredited spokesmen, and if I
refrain from the language of mere perfunctory politeness in
reply, then I must claim the liberty to speak to you with
perfect candour, conscious that you will not resent anything
that is said to you in good faith and with sincerely
friendly intentions, and that it is bad policy for the Government of India and the community which you represent
to go on misunderstanding each other for ever, as they
will continue to do if both parties evade the real issues,
and show no inclination to grapple with the facts.

Now I observe that the Society which you represent has
recently acquired a new name, and is designated the
Imperial Anglo-Indian Association. The choice of this
name is the latest phase in a long contention over the
question of the nomenclature that it would be best and
wisest for you to adopt. In the various stages of this
discussion, I find that the names Eurasians, East Indians,
Indo-Britons, Statutory Natives of India, Domiciled British
and Europeans, have all at one time or another been, and
to some extent still are, employed. Though I myself
think that controversies over nomenclature are the most
barren of all human disputes—since in the long run the
world judges men not by what they call themselves, but
by what they are—yet it would appear that this has been
regarded as a most vital question by many of your number,
and that almost as much energy has been expended upon
it as upon the practical discussion of the future. I may
be short-sighted ; but I do not myself see why there should
be any deep and insidious sting—these are the words
which I have found in the utterances or writings of more
than one of your spokesmen—in the name Eurasian as

applied to persons of mixed blood or descent—though I am far from contending that I have any right to expect my views to be shared by any one else—nor do I understand the great and wide-spread anxiety to discover a new label. Above all, Gentlemen, I am compelled to say that if I were to judge by the natural meaning of words, I should have no idea of what the Imperial Anglo-Indian Association could mean. Anglo-Indian is a phrase which is applied in popular acceptance to a particular individual and society, British as a rule in origin, which spends its life, official, professional, or otherwise, in India, and as a rule finally goes home. Thus when we speak of Anglo-Indian officials, judges, clubs, newspapers, opinion, and so on, everybody understands exactly what is meant. You have a perfect right to take the same name if you please, and to some extent it covers the component elements of your Society. But I am not certain that you do not rather confuse some of your friends and well-wishers by adopting a designation that in popular parlance means something else, whilst the title certainly does not become any the more, on the contrary, I think that it becomes the less, intelligible by having the epithet Imperial prefixed to it. True and loyal and devoted sons of the Empire we know you, and your history has shown you, to be. But so are we all ; and why your Society should especially require the adjective Imperial to describe it I have never seen explained. But there is another result of the expression of your designation and composition which is of more practical consequence. I believe that you desire in the main to call attention to the claims and to focus the aspirations of what has hitherto been called the Eurasian community, although there is also the case of many English or European families domiciled, perhaps born and bred, in the country, whose blood has never been commingled with a native strain, but whose interests you desire equally to promote. But the result of this very elastic classification appears to me to be not clearness but confusion ; since, when you make your demands, that which applies to your constituents at one pole, bears little or no relation to those who are at the other. The arguments from race do not, for instance, apply to the domiciled Europeans: and the interests, and employment, and prospects of the latter depend upon conditions wholly apart from those that retard the advance of the man of mixed descent. Your Society in fact, as at present constituted, rests upon two bases which have *a priori* little in common with each other, *viz.,* domicile and race ; and the considerations that are apposite in the one case, are often irrelevant in the other. Whilst, therefore, by casting your net so wide, you no doubt envelop a larger haul of fish, I am less confident that you advance the general interests of your clients, which is, after all, the main object for which you exist.

I have only one other word of advice to give before I pass on to an examination of your specific claims. If I were one of your Directors, I almost think that in the interests of your cause I should move a motion for a withdrawal of the pamphlet in which you bring your case before the public. The case has so much to recommend it in its intrinsic features that it seems a pity that it should be weakened by exaggeration and by declamation, since such an attitude cannot but prejudice your chances. To suggest that the Government of India and the India Office are engaged in a deep and malignant conspiracy to deprive you of your birthright, that they desire, or that any one else desires, to stamp upon you the brand of inferiority or subordination, or that as a community you are hunted down and proscribed—phrases which very fairly represent the spirit of some of your publications—is, in my judgment, very ill-judged and quite untrue. Such statements are sufficient to set people against you. Your object should be to attract, not to alienate, public support ; and you will do this by sober reasoning, and not by angry rhetoric. There are pages of the pamphlet in which your claims are fairly and moderately stated. This seems to be the case when you are engaged upon a Deputation, as you have been this afternoon. But when you are talking among yourselves, you seem, if I may say so without offence, to boil over in a rather superfluous fashion ; and on such occasions things are said which I am afraid would hardly stand the test of a critical examination.

There is another suggestion that I would make in passing. Who are your clients and what are their numbers ? I observe that in the pamphlet they are represented by one of the speakers, whose words are reported, as being over a million strong. On the other hand, in an able essay that I read the other day upon the Eurasian question by a Mr. Nundy, which I would commend to the careful attention of every one here present, I find that the total of that community was estimated by the writer as 120,000. There is a wide margin between these two extremes. Of whom does this margin consist ? When you call yourselves Anglo-Indians, do you include Englishmen who are not permanently domiciled in India ? Do you include domiciled foreigners of other races, and, if so, how can they be termed Anglo-Indians ? And do you embrace Eurasians of, for instance, Portuguese descent, and, if so, how can they fall into the Anglo-Indian category ? Would it not be well to let the public know who, and of what numerical strength, are the various classes for whom you plead, and who are included under the common heading which you have decided to adopt?

And now I pass from these preliminary observations, which, if they have been critical in character, have assuredly not been unfriendly in intention, to an examination of the specific proposals which have, from time to time, been put forward by your spokesmen, and the majority of which have been repeated in the statements to which I have just listened.

The first of these is the proposal to employ Eurasians on a larger scale in the Indian Army by the constitution of a special regiment or regiments enlisted from that class.

Of course, as it is, Eurasians are frequently accepted as recruits, a point as to which it would be well if your spokesmen in the pamphlet agreed with each other ; for, whereas one of them states that thousands have been so admitted, another declares that this admission on sufferance, which he implies to be rarely exercised, is an insult to your people. Now, in this context, I frequently see mention made of the loyalty and bravery shown by Eurasians during the Mutiny--and of this fact there cannot be a shadow of a doubt -- and by the Eurasian Corps that were raised in that time. But it does not follow therefrom that the Corps were a success ; and, as a matter of fact, they were all disbanded between 1860 and 1870, on the grounds that they were as costly as a British force, that the same confidence was not reposed in them, and that there were not sufficient recruits forthcoming (I think this a very remarkable and dispiriting reflection) to maintain a total strength of only 700 men. Nevertheless, at intervals ever since the proposal has been made or revived that the experiment in some form or another should be repeated ; for there have never been wanting friends of your cause in the Government of India, who have been anxious to find what opportunity they could for the employment of a class that has so large a claim upon our sympathy. The formation of a regiment is, however, I need hardly say, in the main, a military question ; and when I add that the last five Commanders-in-Chief of the Army in India without exception—and I believe that the series extends unbroken to an even more distant period —have been opposed to the experiment, you will perhaps understand how it is that it has not greatly prospered. It was proposed at one time that a company of garrison artillery should be raised from Eurasians ; but the first artillery soldier in India of the day, who happened to be in high office, declined to support the scheme on the ground that it would be more expensive and less efficient than a corresponding European force. When I arrived in India, these topics were still under discussion, and I am happy to have been instrumental in sending with the assistance of some of my Colleagues who shared my desire to help you, a despatch to the Secretary of State last year, in which we proposed the experimental raising of a Eurasian regiment in India. This is the first time, I believe, that such a proposal has ever gone home with the assent of a majority of the Government of India. The Secretary of State, who has quite recently replied, has been unable to accept our proposal ; and I see no reason why you should not be acquainted with the main reasons. The initial cost of such a regiment would be $2\frac{1}{2}$ lakhs, the annual recurring cost $5\frac{1}{2}$ lakhs ; and it has been felt unfair to place this increase of burden upon the Indian taxpayer, unless a responsible assurance could be given that there would be a commensurate increase in our military strength. So far this assurance has not been forthcoming. There were also subsidiary difficulties about the scale of pay, not merely in the Military, but also, as a probable consequence, in the Civil services, and about the necessity for legislation, since Europeans in India cannot be enlisted for local service without the passing of a bill through the British Parliament, a fence which even friendly Secretaries of State sometimes find it difficult to surmount. Such has been the fate that has attended our proposal. I am sorry that it has not fared better. But you will do well to look facts in the face, and to realise that Governments are compelled to regard this question to a large extent from the utilitarian point of view ; and that, until you can convince them that a Eurasian regiment, which would cost quite as much as, if not more than, a British regiment, will be at least as efficient for military purposes, they are hardly likely to give it to you for the sake of sentiment, or even of political expediency alone. As regards the subsidiary suggestion which you have submitted this afternoon for the formation of a Eurasian Army Hospital Corps, the same difficulties apply. Eurasians could never serve for the rates of pay that are now given to the native equivalent ; nor could the subordinate duties, such as those of *bhistis*, bearers, and

sweepers, be carried out by a Eurasian Corps. The long
and short of it is that, for the present at any rate, the objections to Eurasian enlistment in the regular army are held
at home to outweigh the advantages. I would gladly
reverse this current of opinion if I could. But it rests,
believe me, not upon any prejudice or hostility—there is not
a trace of that—but upon expert advice which it is difficult
to contest, or to overturn. At the same time, if you were
to submit your proposals as to an Army Hospital Corps in a
definite and intelligible shape, I shall be prepared to place
them before the Military Authorities, though I can give you
no assurance as to the reception that they may meet with.

I pass to the question of the employment of Anglo-
Indians and Eurasians upon Railways. Last year, I caused
a letter to be addressed to the Presidents of the various
associations throughout India that represent your cause,
drawing their attention to the great opening that appears to
be present to your community for employment, notably in
the Traffic, Locomotive, and Engineering Departments, and
to the meagre advantage that has so far been taken of
these facilities. The figures show that out of a total of
308,000 persons employed upon Railways in India, only
7,000 are Eurasians, or less than $2\frac{1}{2}$ per cent. I am glad to
have heard this afternoon that you have taken serious notice
of this suggestion, and I hope that you will not let the
matter drop. I doubt, however, if you are sufficiently aware
of the possibilities. In the three Departments that I have
named, there are some 1,150 posts on every thousand miles of
line in India, the pay ranging from Rs. 30 to Rs. 400 a month,
or 25,000 posts in all, for which Anglo-Indians and
Eurasians are free and qualified to compete. Why do you
not enter for these appointments? Why, on the contrary,
do you allow the European and Native employés to increase
at the rate, during the past year, of $3\frac{3}{4}$ and $4\frac{1}{2}$ per cent.
respectively, while your numbers have only increased at the
rate of less than $\frac{3}{4}$ per cent.? You are mistaken if you
suppose that the Railway administration can ever give you

a fixed proportion of these appointments for which you can qualify at leisure. Railways are commercial undertakings, and they are apt to be somewhat indifferent to sentiment. I can but point out to you the broad, and not unremunerative, avenue that is here afforded to your energies, and invite you to profit by it more materially than you appear hitherto to have done.

And now I turn to your claims as regards appointments in the Civil Service. I understand you to complain that you no longer have the share that you once enjoyed in the higher ranks of the Public Service, and that in respect of the lower ranks you are handicapped by competition with Natives of this country. You claim accordingly that a certain proportion of appointments in all ranks of the Public Service should be reserved for you, provided that you can satisfy the requisite intellectual tests. Now I might remind you that the days to which you refer were times when the number of Eurasians was much less than it is at present, when the competition was smaller, and when the connection between European and Eurasian was more immediate and direct. I might also point to the case of Eurasian Engineers who are even now enjoying very high appointments and pay. But it is sufficient to note that your appeal ignores *in toto* two landmarks in recent history, which I am afraid that no amount of special pleading—I use the term in no invidious sense—can avail to submerge. The first of these was the report of the Public Service Commission, upon which the Eurasian community was represented, and which deliberately laid it down as a broad principle, subsequently accepted by the Secretary of State, and since acted upon by the Government of India, that there should be two classes of the Public Service, the Imperial Service, recruited in England, though not necessarily from Englishmen, and the Provincial and Subordinate Services, recruited in India. If Indians desire to join the former service, they have to go to England, and to pass the examinations there in order to do so. The same opportunities are open to yourselves. It is simply impossible to throw over the findings of the Commission, and to ignore the entire principle upon which the Public Service is recruited by creating a special exemption in your or in any other case.

The second landmark is the principle laid down by the Secretary of State in 1893 about Simultaneous Examinations. Under that ruling, you enjoy precisely the same opportunities, as regards the competitive test, as do any other communities in this country. You are equally eligible to employment with them. Nay, the Government have gone further, and have in practice in many of the Subordinate Departments reserved a special proportion of places for yourselves. In the Subordinate Accounts Department, in the Provincial Branch of the Survey of India, in the Salt Department, in the Customs Department, in the Opium Department, I find that a large proportion of the appointments is either reserved to domiciled Europeans and Eurasians, or is open to them. Nor do these facilities always pass without protest, or meet with the prompt justification that might be desired. In the Opium Department, where $\frac{3}{4}$ths of the appointments are opened to your community, the Government of India have twice in the last 10 years received protests from the Bengal Government in favour of recruitment from England, on the ground that sufficiently qualified candidates were not forthcoming out here. For a similar reason a few years ago the Government of India were obliged to ask that a larger proportion of appointments not reserved for the Indian Civil Service in the Finance Department, in the Accounts Branch of the Public Works Department, and in the Traffic Branch of the Railways, should be recruited from home. Now it is no good to represent these proceedings as an evidence of spite or unfairness on the part of Government. They are nothing of the sort. We are more than anxious to employ you. But how is it possible to create special privileges in your favour when you do not even take advantage of those which are already open to you? I am ready to select any branch of the Public Service, and to scrutinise its composition, with an eye that is friendly and even partial to your aspirations. There are some quarters in which I may be able to help you; but if I am to do so, I must at least demand some justification from those whom I am invited to favour.

The question of Education is the next upon which I will say a word. Upon this point your pamphlet, to which you have referred me, contains a number of statements which strike me as being very rash, and which I, for my part, cannot endorse. You actually say that no experienced statesman in India will deny that the time has long since arrived when the Government should abolish the Education Department and all State Colleges in India, and should devote to Primary Education the vast sums squandered on High Education, and leave private enterprise to carry it on. I may compromise my own reputation with the author of this astonishing paragraph; but I am afraid that I cannot accept his conclusions. Indeed, I understand that you do not altogether accept them yourselves, since you have elsewhere invited my support for Hill Schools for Anglo-Indian boys, who, I suppose, would hardly be content if I were only to provide them there with a primary standard of education. You say that Government treats your schools with a parsimony that is almost scandalous. When I read these words, I referred to Mr. Cotton's last Quinquennial Review of Indian Education, which was issued last year, and I found that the pupils in those schools were steadily increasing, and that the grants to them both from Provincial Revenues and from Government were largely on the increase also. More recently I have heard a complaint as to the unsuitability of the High School and Calcutta University Examination for Anglo-Indian boys, and as to the desirability of introducing the Cambridge University Local Examinations in this country. Before pronouncing upon this suggestion, one would have to co-ordinate the value of such an examination with the examinations already established in India. The suggestion has, I think, some merit ; and it is undoubtedly desirable to afford to your children the chance of passing an examination that possesses a common standard of value. But if you have a system of Universities in a country, I see some difficulty in giving them the go-by altogether, and in regulating your education by the standards of a foreign institution.

When you speak about Technical Education, you employ a phrase which is on everybody's lips, but which not everybody takes the trouble to understand. I am quite in favour of a training which will fit a young man for industrial employment, but I do not feel at all clear that the best method of attaining that end is by introducing the teaching of special trades into the curriculum of our schools. I think that technical instruction should follow at a later stage ; and, whilst we are quite willing to give State aid to encourage any such enterprise, I think that local administrations and private initiative may be expected to help Government in a matter in which we have not the means to take a big plunge ourselves. I understand from your statement to-day that you do not substantially disagree with these views, and that you are taking steps for the establishment of allied Technical institutions.

As regards the Hill Schools for colonisation, I do not know what part of the world you propose to colonise, or what sort of education you would suggest. I believe that a Eurasian agricultural colony was tried in Southern India a few years ago and proved a failure. I do not draw from this any inference as to other or larger schemes : and I am glad to hear that you propose to renew the experiment. It seems to me that Eurasians might be very useful in the peopling of many blank spaces on the map of the British Empire outside of India—say in South Africa ; and that the idea is worthy of careful examination. But it is hardly in a shape to be submitted to Government until it has attained a much more definite form.

I have now dealt, Gentlemen, with all of the suggestions that you have put before me. There are many other suggestions, I daresay neither novel nor exciting, which, if I had time, I might be willing to place before yourselves. There are many forms of handicraft in India, mechanical and otherwise, for which your community seems to me to be well adapted, but all the talk about which generally ends in smoke. Why a speaker at a public meeting in Calcutta should find the greatest difficulty in getting his speech accurately reported because there are so few competent short-hand writers, why mill-owners should have to import mechanics from the British Isles, why band-masters and bandsmen should have to be imported from Europe, why the supervisors of Native labour in workshops and factories should be often of similar origin, why the higher classes of domestic servants are so commonly drawn from communities other than your own—are all problems which puzzle me considerably, but which your community might, I think, assist to solve. The fact is, I suspect, that its numbers are being gradually bisected into two classes, those who are so near to the European standard, that they have not the slightest difficulty in obtaining lucrative employment, and who, therefore, do not protest ; and those who are gradually drifting away from it, and wish to preserve a superiority which they are scarcely competent to maintain. I know that there is no more unpopular philosophy to preach to any community than Self-Help ; and if such a doctrine were to imply in the present case that the Government are resolved to remain apathetic while you prosecute your own fortunes, I would not for a moment endorse it. On the contrary, I am anxious to do you every good turn that I properly and legitimately can, and my action in respect of Regiments and Railways has suffici-ently vindicated my intentions. But if I am to have any success, I must call upon you to formulate your programme with definiteness and precision, to eschew fallacious rhetoric, to view your position in its true perspective, and to convince the Government of India that in aiding you they are aiding a community to whom they are not merely bound by ties of race or sentiment, but who are qualified to bear their full share in the work-a-day competition of modern life.

I should like to add that, if you, Mr. Pugh, or the Society over which you preside, care to address any representations to me upon any of the points that I have raised in my reply, I shall be most happy to consider them.

[Mr. Pugh thanked His Excellency warmly for the kind manner in which he had received the deputation, remarking that. notwithstanding His Excellency's criticism, which had been in many respects scathing, they were assured of his friendly feelings towards them. They would be glad to accept His Excellency's offer to make further representations. not with a view of answering his criticisms, but of showing how far they could see their way' to take advantage of the suggestions His Excellency had offered.]

DINNER TO Mr. & Mrs. DAWKINS.

*26th March,* 1900.

[On Monday evening, the 26th March, Their Excellencies the Viceroy and Lady Curzon entertained the Hon'ble Mr. and Mrs. Dawkins at a farewell dinner at Government House prior to their departure from India. A large number of guests were invited to meet them. After the health of the Queen had been drunk, the Viceroy rose and proposed the health of Mr. and Mrs. Dawkins in the following terms : —]

*Ladies and Gentlemen,*—I have invited you here this evening to join me in bidding farewell to Mr. and Mrs. Dawkins. I doubt if any previous Viceroy has been placed in the unhappy position of having to say good-bye to two Finance Ministers within the space of 15 months after his first arrival in this country. It is almost exactly a year ago since we gathered at this board to offer our parting wishes and regrets to Sir James Westland. To-night we are engaged in the same function in the case of his successor. I do hope that Sir Edward Law will break the chain of continuity, and will spare me the painful honour of bowing out a third Finance Minister during my time. (*Laughter.*) I doubt if the Government of India could survive the shock of a third bereavement, or whether I could possibly bring myself to compose another funeral oration. (*Laughter.*)

Now, Ladies and Gentlemen, on these occasions it is usual to give a short biographical sketch, dating from the earliest period, of the guest of the evening. I am sorry to be unable to conform to this respectable practice on the present occasion, because the earlier stages of Mr. Dawkins' career are buried, so far as my knowledge is concerned, in a complete, though no doubt honourable, obscurity, until the time when I was fortunate enough to be a fellow-student with him at Balliol College, Oxford. For all I know he may have been in childhood and youth a second Babbage, or calculating prodigy, a pride to his family and a terror to his neighbours (*laughter*) ; or the halo of future distinction may have hovered at an early period over his brow, unobserved by anybody, including himself. (*Laughter.*) Whichever of these two hypotheses be correct, my knowledge of Mr. Dawkins dates only from the auspicious moment when we both took our seats at the feet of our dear old Master, Jowett, and both drained to the dregs the joyous vintage of undergraduate life at the University of Oxford.

The Master, as he was universally called, took, as is now well known from his published letters and Life, a keen interest in India, to whose Government the College over which he presided has now contributed three Viceroys in unbroken succession. He encouraged young men who were destined for the Indian Civil Service to go to Balliol and to complete their studies there; and, were he now living, nothing would, I am sure, have given him greater satisfaction than the knowledge that three of his pupils, and contemporaries of each other, had come out simultaneously to India as Viceroy, Finance Member, and last but not least, as Private Secretary. I cannot say, however, that Jowett was responsible for turning my thoughts in the direction of India, nor, so far as I know, did he exert a similar influence on my friend, Mr. Dawkins.

Nevertheless, in the dim background the image of India was all the while summoning Mr. Dawkins with inexorable finger. At one time he contemplated entering the Indian Civil Service. After passing into the Home Civil Service, almost the first post that he occupied was that of Private Secretary to Lord Cross, at that time Secretary of State for India; and although for a time the siren-voices of other departments and occupations sang in his ears, and lured him away, his ultimate destiny was all the while secure. In the interval of which I am speaking, Mr. Dawkins was initiating himself in the study and in the practice of high finance. He excogitated taxes and he manipulated budgets. (*Laughter.*) He and Sir Alfred Milner, another common Balliol friend of ours, were the young lions of the Treasury of that day. (*Laughter.*) They were the two champions who upheld the arms of Mr. Goschen, in his annual struggle with the Amalekites in Budget debates. (*Applause.*)

And now came a break in Mr. Dawkins' career, in which he was for the first time called upon to display his abilities on a wider and more cosmopolitan field. We all know of the pattern individual who surveyed mankind from China to Peru. (*Laughter.*) Mr. Dawkins with an originality that did him infinite credit, reversed the order, and decided to commence with Peru. Egypt and India were the next stages on his eastward march, and though he is now turning his steps homewards, I should never be surprised if he were one day to complete the parallel and were to be heard of as a great financial mandarin in the Celestial Kingdom, clad in a yellow jacket, a peacock feather, and a red button. (*Laughter.*) As representative of the bondholders in Peru, Mr. Dawkins had the satisfaction of placing their interests on a sound basis, and of establishing a reputation that insured his being called to Egypt by Lord Cromer when Sir Alfred Milner left that country. Assuredly there could be no better training for a future Finance Minister of India. His school was the intricate labyrinth of an Oriental administration, rendered all the more tortuous by the devices of international intrigue, but on to which the clear light of day had been shed by a short generation of British finance. His master was Lord Cromer, himself an old Indian Finance Minister, and the most distinguished living public servant of England outside of her shores. It was fresh from this invaluable experience that a year ago Mr. Dawkins came out to India to take the financial tiller from the capable hands of Sir James Westland.

I will not now enter into the circumstances which have been responsible for the shortness of Mr. Dawkins' stay among us. I will only say this, that brilliant as were the prospects that were offered to him elsewhere, and that are now taking him home, prospects as brilliant as any that were ever offered to a man of his age in the world of finance, Mr. Dawkins was yet willing to sacrifice them all in the interests of the country whose service he had entered when he accepted the post of Finance Member of the Governor-General's Council in India. Bitterly as we regretted it, and we regarded it as a public as well as a private misfortune. neither the Secretary of State nor I felt that this was a sacrifice which we had any right to allow our guest of this evening to make. But it was at our instance that he consented to remain in India for a year in order to give to myself in particular, and to the Government of India in general, the benefit of the profound study that he had made of the question of Indian Currency, of his wide knowledge and experience, and of his high authority in finance. (*Cheers.*)

How India at large and the Departments of the Government of India have profited by one short, though busy, year of Mr. Dawkins' initiative and advice is known to all, or nearly all of those who are seated at this table.

It is as yet too early to pronounce the verdict of history upon the Currency Policy of the present administration. The full measure of credit, if it be earned, will not be given till later on when the new system has had a fair trial, and when its stability has been conclusively established by the test of time. Meanwhile, it will be conceded by all that Mr. Dawkins has launched the ship with conspicuous skill, and that it rides proudly and triumphantly on the waves. (*Applause.*) A stable exchange, a currency responding to the needs of Indian business and finance, but standing in a fixed and permanent relation to the currency of the Empire, and, lastly, an intimate connection between the financial systems and resources of Great Britain and India—these were the objects which Mr. Dawkins set before himself, and which, in the brief space of 12 months, he has done much to achieve. He bequeaths to his successor a task not free from anxiety, and a responsibility not diminished by initial success. But the foundations have been well and truly laid, and the superstructure ought to stand. (*Cheers.*)

There are two other respects in which Mr. Dawkins has won in an exceptional degree the confidence of those with

whom he has been brought into official connection. The
first of these has been his freedom from bureaucratic prejudices, his accessibility to all, and his manifest desire not
merely to conduct the business of his Department, but to
encourage the trade, to develop the resources, and to set
free from artificial trammels the enterprise of the Empire.
His attitude with regard to the financial transactions of the
Presidency Banks, the taxation of imports, and telegraphic
transfers, has been one of genuine and practical sympathy
with the mercantile community in India ; while in the long
discussion that has attended the question of the Banks he
has shown a readiness to meet criticism and an anxiety only
to win his point by carrying conviction that is not always
found behind an official waistcoat. (*Applause.*)

The second respect in which Mr. Dawkins has deserved
the thanks of the public, and perhaps more especially of
myself, has been his conduct of the business of his Department, and the share he has borne in the work of the
Government of India.   The machinery by which this country
is ruled is a wonderful piece of mechanism.   It is the result
of a century of scientific elaboration, and it is worked by
the most upright and highly trained body of engineers in
the world. (*Cheers.*)   But I may be pardoned for saying
that it has so many wheels that they sometimes retard each
other's progress, so vast a weight that the elasticity of the
parts is apt to be lost in the ponderousness of the whole, so
many written rules for observance that the spirit is sometimes
sacrificed to the letter, so fixed a groove of operation that it
may almost be said to start and swerve at any novel departure.
Now, I am one of those who hold that the man should be
master of the machine, not the machine the master of the
man. (*Applause.*)   Administration should be cautious and
reasoned, but that is no ground why it should not be firm
and prompt.   We are a Government who write much, but
that is no reason why we should do nothing but write.
(*Laughter.*)   Lord Wellesley remarked of the Secretaries of
the Government of India that they combined the industry of

clerks with the talents of statesmen. Yes ; but I should like
to eliminate the clerk, and to exalt the statesman. (*Cheers.*)
*Non est scribendum sed gubernandum* is the motto that I
should like to fix over the doors of every Government Office.
If the choice lies between settling a matter in six weeks or
in six months, I would sooner take the six weeks, if between
six months and six years, I would prefer not to take the six
years. I cannot see why dilatoriness should be regarded as
an equal virtue with despatch, or why the Departments of
Government should practise a different economy from that
which prevails in the farmyard, and should sit contentedly
upon eggs that have long since been addled. (*Laughter and
applause.*)

I mention these views, Ladies and Gentlemen, because in
putting them into practice I have had the unfailing sympathy
and co-operation of Mr. Dawkins. He has brought to the
task of Indian Government a mind keen and alert, an intelligence trained in the best of schools, a natural capacity for
business, a dislike, equal to my own, of procrastination and
shams, and a keen desire, in the short space that has been
available to him, to be up and doing. I can hardly say how
much I shall miss such a Colleague, or to what extent virtue
will have gone out of the Government of India by his departure.

There is perhaps a third respect, which I should not omit
to mention, in which Mr. Dawkins has, during the year that
he has been among us, won the regard of all, and in which
he has been largely assisted by the lady who sits by my side.
(*Applause.*) I allude to the zest with which he and she have
entered into all the interests and pursuits of life at Simla and
at Calcutta, and have endeared themselves, by many acts of
kindness and hospitality, to a wide circle of friends. From
all these many quarters will come equal regrets at their impending departure, and equal hopes for their success and
happiness in the life that lies before them. What the fates
may have in store for Mr. Dawkins I cannot tell. He may
live to sway the counsels of a Senate, and to control the

finances of a larger Empire even than that of India. However that may be, I hope that in his new occupations he may sometimes turn a thought to the country which he has served so faithfully for a year, to the colleagues who mourn his departure, and to that vast charge of Empire—the noblest burden that can be laid upon the shoulders of any Englishman—to which he has, for a short period, lent so strenuous a helping hand. (*Loud cheers.*)

Ladies and Gentlemen, I ask you to charge your glasses and to drink to the long life, success, and prosperity of Mr. and Mrs. Dawkins. (*Loud cheers.*)

[Mr. Dawkins then rose and returned thanks on behalf of himself and Mrs. Dawkins.]

### DEBATE ON THE BUDGET.

*28th March*, 1900

[The annual debate on the Budget took place in the Legislative Council at Calcutta, on Wednesday, the 28th March 1900, and lasted from 11 A.M. till a quarter past four, being a shorter time than usual, the result of a suggestion by His Excellency the President that written speeches of unusual length should be taken as read and laid upon the table, a summary being given of them if necessary. The great majority of the Members present took part in the debate, which was closed by His Excellency with the following speech :—]

I should like to thank Hon'ble Members for the readiness which they have shown to act upon the suggestion which I ventured to make at the beginning of this sitting, namely, that such parts of their proposed speeches as dealt with matters of a technical character, or were likely to extend to unusual length, should be taken as read, and should be laid upon the table for subsequent publication in the Gazette.

In closing this last debate of the present Session of Council, I am constrained to admit that it has not been a Session very prolific in legislation. It has not, for that reason, been, in my opinion, any the worse. On the contrary, I think that we opened the Session with too full a wallet. Our Session is, owing to the conditions of our life at Calcutta, necessarily limited in duration. All the stages of legislation, after the preliminary enquiries and introduction of the various Bills, have practically to be got through in the space of three months. In the case of small or uncontentious measures this is enough, and more than enough. In the case of an important measure, which has been long debated, and has probably only reached the stage of legislation after years of previous discussion, it may also be sufficient. But I doubt if it is sufficient in cases where several important measures may be simultaneously on the Agenda paper, and where, in the course of the examination of the Bills themselves, acute difference of opinion may be developed, or alterations may be made in a Bill in Select Committee or elsewhere that radically affect its original character. In such cases I would sooner be charged with undue caution than with extravagant haste. We are free in India from the particular temptation that impels Government to legislate at all hazards in the British Parliament, namely, the desire either to fulfil the promises sometimes rashly given upon platforms at a previous election, or to establish a better record than their political opponents for the purposes of the ensuing one. Being free from these temptations, and having no standard of action beyond our own sense of responsibility, and of the public needs, I think that it behoves us to legislate sparingly, to look very closely to the quality, and not too much to the quantity, of our output, and, while very jealously guarding the duty of Government, which is to lead public opinion and in no way to abrogate the supreme authority vested in us, at the same time not to push our measures through with undue precipitation, above all, not to give to any party or interest the idea that its views have been imperfectly considered, or contemptuously brushed aside.

For these reasons we have, during the present Session, postponed the Assam Labour Bill, upon which we did not receive, until too late a date, all the replies that we had asked for ; and the Coal Mines Bill, in which amendments so substantial were introduced in Select Committee, that we felt it desirable again to consult the Local Governments, before proceeding further with the Bill. It was on similar grounds that I announced the withdrawal of the Press Messages Bill ten days ago. Now there may be some people who may make this series of postponements a source of reproach, and may interpret them as a sign of weak or distracted counsels. I do not think that, at any rate in the present case, there would be the slightest justification for such a reproach. Speaking for the rest of my colleagues as well as myself, I can truthfully say that we have acted only after careful deliberation and in the public interest, and I believe that our decision has been ratified by public opinion, and has been acceptable to the majority of

Hon'ble Members who sit upon this Council. For my own part, I say unhesitatingly that, in proportion as our Legislative machinery in India is prompt and powerful in its action, and is free from many of the clogs that impede legislation in England, so should it only be employed with much forethought and deliberation. That does not mean for a moment that Government must never pass unpopular Bills. All legislation is unpopular with somebody; and I have seen enough of Parliamentary life to have heard the most salutary measures denounced as iniquitous at the time of their introduction, and to have seen Statesmen and Governments savagely abused for the passing of Acts which were after-wards extolled as their principal title to fame. I daresay, therefore, that this Council in my time will pass some Bills that will be stoutly resisted and roundly assailed. All I hope is that we shall not be guilty of the particular vice of legislation in a hurry.

Passing from these general considerations to the discussion in which we are at present engaged, it will, I am sure, be the opinion of all who heard the Hon'ble Mr. Dawkins last Wednesday, that he placed before us a clear and even luminous statement, dealing with a large variety of subjects, and a great mass of figures, with the easy confidence that betrays the hand of the master, and wins the confidence of the pupil. I am sure that we all of us regret that we shall not listen to many more such statements from his lips, and that the Government of India will not profit in future years by Mr. Dawkins' wide experience and expert counsel. He is unfortunately leaving us, after a too brief period of Indian service. During that time he has had to contend with circumstances representing a transitional phase in our financial history; and he has further seen all prospect of a notable Budget, of a large surplus, of great schemes, of a sensible relief of taxation—in fact all the legitimate aspirations of a financier—stolen from him by the sad famine against which we are now struggling. One by one, there-fore, his Spanish castles have been dissolved in thin air, and he has been compelled to present a curtailed programme and a stern business statement, in which, if there is nothing startling or sensational, it is yet a matter of sincere congratulation, not merely that equilibrium is maintained, but that a slight surplus is even estimated for the forthcoming year. Nevertheless, in his year of office Mr. Dawkins has not failed to leave his mark, and it will be found to be a durable mark, upon our financial history and system. He has successfully inaugurated the new era under which the sovereign has become legal tender in India, and stability in exchange has assumed what we hope may be a stereotyped form. This great change has been introduced in defiance of the vaticinations of all the prophets of evil, and more especially of the particular prophecy that we could not get gold to come to India, that we could not keep it in our hands if we got it here, but that it would slip so quickly through our fingers that we should even have to borrow to maintain the necessary supply. As a matter of fact, we are almost in the position of the mythological king, who prayed that all he touched might be turned into gold, and was then rather painfully surprised when he found that his food had been converted into the same somewhat indigestible material. So much gold, indeed, have we got, that we are now giving gold for rupees as well as rupees for gold, that is, we are really in the enjoyment of complete convertibility—a state of affairs which would have been derided as impossible by the experts a year ago. Mr. Dawkins has further introduced several useful reforms in the method of stating our accounts. That delusive column that appeared to represent Loss by Exchange has vanished. The dreadful and bewildering symbol of Rx. has been politely bowed out of existence. I remember last year, when still a newcomer from England, and before I had become accustomed to the multiplicity of Indian financial symbols, being considerably puzzled at the occurrence in the same statement of no less than five different methods of computation, namely, Rupees, Tens of Rupees, Pounds Sterling, Lakhs, and Crores. Now, I have never myself understood why finance, because it is complex, need also be made obscure. But Mr. Dawkins is one of the few financiers whom I have found willing to subscribe to that elementary proposition. A useful step has also been taken by him, by which the only public works that will in future be charged against the Annual Famine Grant, or as it is sometimes called Famine Insurance Fund, of $1\frac{1}{2}$ crores—will be works that are designed and executed exclusively as a protection against famine. This does not mean that such works can be brought up to the full margin of the grant, for protective public works are necessarilly limited in number. What it does mean is that the allocation of the grant for such famine protective purposes as are available will be more easily traceable, the unappropriated balance being devoted as now to avoidance of debt. Perhaps in this respect we may be able to carry correct definition even further in the future. During his term of office Mr. Dawkins has further adopted a liberal policy in his attitude towards banking and other enterprise in this country : and if he has not been here long enough to carry to a final conclusion the important question of banking amalgamation or reform, he has appreciably expedited the solution of the problem, and has facilitated the labours of his successor by the free and fearless discussion which he has inaugurated, both in private conference and in public despatch, upon this momentous issue. Finally, in the reply to which we have just listened, Mr. Dawkins has shown an ability to meet the criticisms which have been passed upon his budget in the course of this debate which renders it a cause of additional regret that this is the last occasion on which we shall listen to a similar performance from him.

Such are some at any rate of the services which have been rendered by our retiring Finance Member. I now pass to an examination of certain features in the Budget, and of the observations that have fallen from some of my Hon'ble Colleagues this afternoon.

It has been made abundantly clear that the main source of disturbance in the calculations, both of the past and the ensuing financial year, has been famine. But for famine Mr. Dawkins would have had a great surplus, and might have introduced what is generally known as a popular Budget. Let me endeavour to give you an idea of the extent to which this cyclonic disturbance has affected, and is still affecting, India. I put on one side for the moment the fact, which is known to you all from the weekly *Gazette*, that we are now engaged in relieving, in one form or another, nearly 5,000,000 persons, more than the entire population of many not inconsiderable States. Such a thing has never been heard of before in the history of India, or indeed of any other famine. How greatly this famine transcends in importance its predecessor may be illustrated by the fact that in the Central Provinces, the centre of the deepest scarcity both in the famine of 1897 and now, whereas at the height of the 1897 famine, that is, at the close of the month of May, less than 700,000 persons were in receipt of relief, on the present occasion, $1\frac{1}{2}$ million of persons are already receiving relief at the end of March. In one district alone, that of Raipur, over 30 per cent. of the whole population are upon relief, that is, 500,000 persons out of a total of 1,600,000 are being supported by the State. In four districts of Bombay between 20 and 30 per cent. of the entire population, in three districts of Berar, 20 per cent., and in the Ajmere-Merwara Division 20 per cent., are on relief.

But let me represent the severity of the affliction to you from another point of view. I see it sometimes stated, and the critics of British rule in India are very fond of this argument, that the real causes of recurring famine are not the failure of rain, the exhaustion of the soil, or the loss of crops, but the pressure of land taxation and the drain upon the resources of the people. Now I cannot pause to-day to discuss the question of land assessments. We

have listened to some interesting observations on the subject
from Mr. Bose, the Maharaja of Darbhanga, and Mr.
Mehta. What they have said will have the earnest attention
of Government. But I may point out, in terms of pounds,
shillings, and pence, exactly what a great Indian drought
does involve in the destruction of agricultural wealth ; and
those who hear the figures may then judge how far any
revision or modification of our revenue system, putting
aside the question whether it be or be not desirable or
feasible, would of itself alone enable an agricultural population to stand the shock of a calamity at once so sudden and
so devastating.

The wheat crop of India averages 6 million tons, worth
at least £24,000,000. This year the estimates received from
the provinces point to a crop of about 3,000,000 tons. Even
if we allow that the money value of these 3,000,000 tons
in a famine year is greater than in an ordinary year, we yet
cannot put the losses of the Indian agriculturist on this one
crop alone at less than from £8,000,000 to £10,000,000.
Take another great staple crop—cotton. The Indian cotton
crop averages in value £12,000,000 sterling. This year its
outside value does not exceed £5,000,000, or a loss of
£7,000,000 sterling. A third great crop is oilseed, namely,
linseed and rapeseed. It ordinarily covers 18 millions of
acres. In the present year this crop is practically non-
existent outside of Bengal, the North-Western Provinces
and Oudh.

These losses, great as they are in relation to the annual
produce of India as a whole, are still greater in relation to
the produce of the famine region, to which they are practically confined. I will take the case of a single province.
A very careful return of this year's harvests of food-grains
has just been received from Bombay. On a very moderate
computation, the loss to the cultivators in that Presidency,
as compared with the value of the harvests in preceding
years, has been £15,000,000. They have also lost about
£4,000,000 on their cotton crop. What they have further

lost in the matter of cattle it is impossible to conjecture, but the figures must be enormous.

These facts appear to me to be sufficient of themselves to explain how it is that the present famine is so terrible and the distress so great; and how impossible it would be for any Government to anticipate the consequences of a visitation of nature on so gigantic and ruinous a scale.

Now let me turn to the financial aspect of the famine. The cost of famine to the Government of India is incurred in a number of different ways: in direct famine grants to the Local Governments, in the decrease of revenue arising from suspensions and remissions, in indirect expenditure, and in increase of prices. Summarising these heads, I find that the cost of the present famine, partly estimated, partly already incurred, will be somewhat as follows. Famine Relief in the past year, $308\frac{1}{4}$ lakhs, in the ensuing year, $500\frac{1}{4}$ lakhs; loss of revenue in the past year, 236 lakhs, in the ensuing year, 121 lakhs; compensation for dearness of provisions and increase in cost of food-supplies in the past year, 37 lakhs, in the ensuing year, 71 lakhs; or a grand total of over $12\frac{3}{4}$ crores, or nearly $8\frac{1}{2}$ millions sterling. To this should be added the temporary cost of other direct charges, such as loans to Native States, amounting in the past year to 48 lakhs, in the ensuing year, to 75 lakhs, and agricultural advances amounting to $37\frac{3}{4}$ and 20 lakhs in the two years respectively.

So much for the financial aspect of famine. Perhaps the figures of cost, when viewed alongside of those of the numbers of persons affected, and the loss of crops involved, may give to the public some sort of idea what a great famine in India means. That to some extent its magnitude has already been realised in England is, I think, clear from the liberal contributions that are now pouring in upon us from British sources. I am confident that I shall not err if I take advantage of the present opportunity to express our united acknowledgments to the Lord Mayor of London, in particular, and to the Lord Mayors and Mayors of other great towns in Great Britain and Ireland, for the patriotic readiness with which they have inaugurated the various relief funds, and also to the generous British public for the splendid manner in which, in the midst of all their distractions, they have remembered our sorrows, and are, weekly and daily, giving of their substance for India's relief. We have done our best for them in respect of their war ; and they are nobly repaying the obligation in respect of our famine. Nor must we fail to include in our thanks those British Colonies in both hemispheres who are once again showing a most practical sympathy with our misfortunes ; and whose union with the mother country, and with her great Asiatic dependency, whether it be for the purpose of conducting a war, or for that of alleviating the suffering of the masses, strikes a harmonious and resounding note at the dawn of a new century, which will re-echo throughout the world.

When in the month of December last a warning Circular was issued by the Government of India concerning relief tests and relief distribution, apprehension was expressed in some quarters that its purport might be misunderstood by the Local Governments who might thereby be led to restrict relief to a dangerous degree, and to read into the cautious utterances of the Supreme Government, a hint that relief *must* be contracted, and expenditure curtailed, however urgent the requirements of the people. The Circular has now been in operation for three months. The numbers upon relief are in themselves sufficient to show how little ground there was for the apprehensions which I have quoted. On the other hand, we know from the replies of Local Governments that our insistence on the proper application of test and precautions, and on the limitation of relief to the strict necessities of the case, was greatly needed ; and that our warning has led to very desirable reforms. We are satisfied from the reports as to the health and general condition of the people in the distressed tracts which we constantly receive that sufficient relief is being given, and

we also have the best of reasons for beliving that, had not
the conditions of relief been made more stringent, and had not
additional precautions been applied, the State would now
be engaged in the support of many who were by no means
at the end of their resources.

There remains one more test which I should like to
apply to our famine-relief system. I refer to the test of
the death-rate. I have called for the figures, and I have been
astonished at the number of famine-stricken provinces and
districts in which the mortality is scarcely at all in excess
of the normal. In the Central Provinces, there is only
a single district in which the excess is so marked as to attract
attention. I saw a letter a day or two ago from a visitor
to the worst area in that province, and he reported that
there was little to distinguish the persons upon relief-works
from labourers engaged upon Government work in ordinary
times. I understand the same impression to be borne out
by the personal experience of Mr. Rees. Contrast these
facts with the shocking mortality in the last famine. In
some of the districts of Bombay, in Berar, and in Ajmere,
where the death-rate has risen, the chief cause of the deaths
attributed to privation is the enormous influx of destitute
refugees from the neighbouring Native States, where the
same perfection of relief-works, and the same care for the
life of the people, do not exist. I am afraid that in many
of these States deaths from starvation are numerous. Jaipur
is managing its own relief generously and well, but in
January 1,250 deaths from starvation were reported, mostly
wanderers from Marwar. In the same month, 250 starvation
deaths were reported from Kotah. In Udaipur, which has
been very backward, there were 1,100 starvation deaths in
January, and 3,250 in February. I might quote other and
similar cases. The problem in Native States is a difficult one,
arising from the want of experience of the Durbars, the
complete novelty to many of their number of the principle
itself of State-relief, the lack of organisation, and the wild
character of some of the hill tribes. Many of the Native

princes have shown wonderful energy and public spirit. But the real efficacy of the system adopted by the Government of India is best shown by contrasting it with that which prevails in adjoining tracts not directly under British administration. The experience of such a famine as this is enough to extinguish for ever the fallacy that these visitations are less severe in their incidence, or less calamitous in their result, in Native territory than they are in British India. The figures and facts prove irrefutably an entirely opposite condition of affairs.

Now in connection with famine, there are two classes of remedial or preventive measures frequently suggested to us, about which I should like, at this stage, to say a word. The employers of labour in India are in the habit of saying, ‘ Here we are in great straits for want of labour in our mines, our factories, or our mills. On the other hand, only a few hundred miles away are thousands of able-bodied persons, who are only being saved from starvation by the intervention, and at the cost, of Government. Why does not Government spare its own pocket, and at the same time help us, by moving these people from where they are not wanted to where they are ?’ Nothing, indeed, can sound more simple on paper. But nothing is more difficult in practice. In the first place, human labour, and particularly native labour, is not like a cartload of bricks, or gravel, or stones, which can be taken up here and dumped down there, wherever you please. In the second place, we and our officers have too much to do in time of famine to be able to convert Government into a sort of vast Emigration Bureau. For such a purpose is wanted a close enquiry into the conditions of labour, the organization of transport, protection of the labour when transported, and so on. If we undertake to move these large batches of men, we shall also, if the experiment proves a failure, be held responsible, and shall have to bring them back again. In all likelihood very many of them would die on the way. Now that is not primarily our business. It is emphatically a case in which capital should help itself, and

should not shift its own responsibility on to Government.
It is the business of Government to lend every assistance in
its power, and that I would most gladly do. But I should
like to see the employers of labour a little more willing to
help themselves. I know that, if I were one of their number,
and were in need of labour, I would have my agents out at
once, travelling here, there, and everywhere, and picking
out the stuff that I wanted in suitable provinces and localities.

The second suggestion that is frequently made to me, I
admit as a rule from the outside of India, where I am afraid
that a good deal of ignorance of the actual position prevails,
is that the obvious method to stop famines is to introduce
irrigation. Some of these writers seem to plume themselves upon the originality of the idea, and to be unaware
that such a thing as irrigation has ever been heard of
in India, or has been so much as attemped here. They
do not seem to realise that irrigation has been going on
in India for quite a considerable number of years, that about
19 millions of acres in India are already under irrigation,
and that upon the works so undertaken has been spent a
capital outlay of no less than $25\frac{1}{2}$ millions sterling. Worthy
people write me letters, based upon the hypothesis that
any Indian river which ultimately discharges its waters
into the sea is really so much agricultural wealth gone
astray, which somehow or other the Government of India
ought to have got hold of at an earlier stage, and turned
into crops and gardens. Now I have had a very careful
estimate made out for me of the extent of *fresh* ground in
the whole of India which we are likely to be able to bring
under cultivation, either by new irrigation projects, or
by extensions of existing systems. Under the head of Productive works, that is, works which may be expected to yield
a net revenue that will more than cover the interest on
the capital outlay, the estimated increment is about $3\frac{1}{2}$
million acres, and the estimated outlay between 8 and 9
millions sterling. Under the head of Protective works, that
is works which will not pay, and which, inasmuch as they

constitute a permanent financial burden on the State, can only be undertaken in exceptional cases, and then as a rule do very little towards the prevention of famine, we contemplate spending about 10 lakhs a year, and shall probably in this way about double the area of 300,000 acres which is covered by that character of work at the present time. It seems, therefore, that the total practicable increase to the irrigable area of India under both heads will not amount to much more than 4,000,000 acres. This increase will, of course, be of value in its addition to the total food-supply of the country, in the employment of labour thereby given, and in its effect upon prices in time of famine. But I am afraid that it cannot be expected to secure immunity from drought to districts now liable to famine, or to help directly their suffering inhabitants. Indeed, when a desert tract is brought under cultivation, a stimulus is given to the growth of population, and more mouths have in time to be fed. The fact remains that the majority of the irrigation works that were most feasible, or most urgently required as protective measures against famine, have now been carried out, and that there is not in irrigation that prospect of quite indefinite expansion with which the popular idea sometimes credits it. At the same time, I am so much in agreement with the general proposition, which has received a good deal of support from many quarters in the course of the present debate, that irrigation should be encouraged, both because of the extension thereby given to the growth of food-supplies in this country, and because, in the case of what are known as productive works, of the extraordinarily remunerative character of the capital outlay, that I have inaugurated, since I came to India, a definite and, as I hope a permanent extension (so long as we can find the works to undertake) of our Irrigation programme. In my predecessor's time, the annual Irrigation grant amounted to 75 lakhs. Last year I persuaded Sir James Westland to increase this ; and in the financial year just expired we have spent 90 lakhs, some of it being directly applied to the provision of labour in famine districts ; while, during the forth-coming year, in spite of the general curtailment of our programme owing to famine, I have prevailed upon Mr. Dawkins to fix the Irrigation grant at 100 lakhs, or 1 crore of rupees. I am hopeful that generosity in this respect will not be a misplaced virtue, either in the direct returns that it will bring in, or in its general effect upon the prosperity of the country. For the reasons that I have named, I doubt whether irrigation can continue to do as much in the future as it has done in the past, owing to the gradual exhaustion of the majority of the big schemes. Still, even if our sphere of action is less grandiose and spacious than in bygone days, I believe that, for a long time to come, and certainly during my day, we shall find more than enough to occupy our funds with smaller and less ambitous designs.

I pass to the question of military expenditure. The principal military incident of the past year has of course been the campaign in South Africa, to which we have lent a force of rather over 8,000 British officers and men from India, as well as some 3,000 Natives for non-combatant services. Now, I myself should have been glad if the British Govern-ment had seen their way to employ some of our gallant Native regiments, infantry, and, perhaps still more, cavalry, as well ; and at an early stage in the war, I made the offer, on behalf of the Government of India, to send a large force. I should have been willing to send 10,000 men. I believe that, had the offer been accepted, it would have provoked an outburst of the heartiest satisfaction in this country, where the manifestations of loyalty have been so wide-spread, and, in my opinion, so conspicuously genuine. You must not imagine for a moment that the Home Government were indifferent to the offer, or were unconscious of the great display of patriotism in India that would have more than justified its acceptance. They were as well aware of these facts, and as grateful for the spirit displayed, as has been Her Majesty the Queen-Empress, who, throughout the war, has not ceased to press upon me her desire that I should lose

no opportunity of testifying her admiration for the devoted
loyalty of the Indian princes, the Indian army, and the
Indian people. Nor did the refusal of the offer involve the
slightest slur upon the Native army. It was refused for more
reasons than one. It was though undesirable to import any
racial element into the contest. The British on one side were
engaged in fighting the Boers on the other; and, had other
combatants been engaged, it might not have stopped at Indian
forces. There was the further consideration that, had Great
Britain transferred a portion of her Indian army to fight
her battles in South Africa, an impression might have
been produced that her own strength in white men was not
sufficient for the strain of a second class campaign; an
impression which might have had unfortunate consequences
in its effect upon a local population perpetually hovering
on the verge of revolt. For these reasons the offer was
declined.

Now, it cannot be expected for one moment that a war
so momentous—revolutionising all our ideas, and not
ours alone, but those of the entire world, upon questions
of armament, of tactics, and of the whole science and practice of warfare--should pass by without leaving a direct
impress upon the military policy of India, as it will do
upon that of every military power in the globe. A storm
has taken place in the great ocean, the commotion caused
by which will be felt thousands of miles away on every
beach and shore. Here, as elsewhere, we shall require
to set our own house in order, to overhaul our military
machine, and to profit by the lessons learned. We have already set to work to do it. Do not imagine that this
sort of reforms can anywhere be undertaken without an
additional outlay. The first result of the Transvaal war
will, I firmly believe, be an increase to the budget of every
military nation in the world. If two small republics, however rich in money and in guns, could stand up for many
months against the main strength of the British army,
and could put the British nation to an expenditure which,

before the entire bill is paid, may be nearer to 100 millions than 50, are we to stint the annual expenditure that may be required to protect this vast Empire of India, as large as the whole of Europe without Russia, against the infinitely more formidable dangers by which it may one day be threatened ? I venture to say that no sterner critic, and no more uncompromising foe of extravagance, or of levity in military expenditure, has ever entered the offices of the Government of India than myself. But, at the same time, as head of that Government, I know my responsibilities, and, if my colleagues and I are convinced that the military protection of India against the perils by which she may be menaced absolutely require that this or that expenditure should be incurred, we shall not flinch from undertaking it. My greatest ambition is to have a peaceful time in India, and to devote all my energies to the work of administrative and material development, in which there are so many reforms that cry aloud to be undertaken. I see no present reason why those aspirations should be interrupted or destroyed. But I do not wish or mean to place myself in a position in which later on, should the peril come, public opinion shall be able to turn round upon me and say, ' We trusted you ; we would have given you what you asked for the legitimate defence of India. But you neither foresaw the future, nor gauged the present ; and yours is the responsibility of failure, if failure there be.'

I say then that I see no chance of a reduction in the military estimates for some time to come. There are many respects in which we can save, or in which expenditure can be overhauled, scrutinised, and cut down. In the present and following year, we shall make a very considerable saving in consequence of the Frontier Policy which has been inaugurated during the past 12 months, and in the withdrawal of regular troops serving beyond our administrative frontier. There are many such fields of possible reduction. But the sum total of these economies is small in relation to the heavy items of expenditure that cannot possibly be escaped. Take re-armament alone. Sir E. Collen has told us in his Memorandum that the cost of re-arming the Native army and Volunteers in India with a magazine rifle will amount to $1\frac{1}{2}$ crores by itself, and yet who would urge for a moment that the expenditure should not be undertaken, or should be unduly delayed? If we are spending over 12 crores in two years, as I have remarked in an earlier part of my speech, in saving 50 millions of people from the peril of death by starvation, shall we grudge the crores that may be required to save 300 millions of people from the perils— almost worse than death—of disorder, and anarchy, and chaos, that might ensue were the British arms on or beyond the frontiers of India at any time to experience a serious disaster? Let not any one carry away the idea that because for a few months, or even for a year, we have been able to spare 8,000 of our British troops for Africa, the British garrison in India can be permanently reduced by that amount. There can be no more complete or foolish illusion. Because a man lends for a night the watchdog that guards his house to a neighbour who is being attacked by robbers, does it, therefore, follow that his own house will be able to get on in future without protection? There is always some risk in denuding India of any considerable portion of her garrison. That risk is greater or less according to the conditions of the time, and the attitude of neighbouring powers. It was present upon the present occasion, and the late Commander-in-Chief and I, in deciding to lend to Her Majesty's Government a certain number of troops for South Africa—and here let me remark in passing that the papers have been wrong in speaking of the demands or orders of Her Majesty's Government, seeing that the latter have never done, and could not do, more than ask us to lend what we might be willing to spare —took upon ourselves to run that risk. But because we are likely to surmount it successfully on this occasion, would it be statesmanship to make the risk permanent?

I wonder if those persons who employ this curious argument would have said that, if we had been able to accept the offers of the various Native Princes who so loyally proffered their personal services to the campaign, it was a proof that India could get on permanently without those Chiefs; or supposing we had sent 10,000 or 20,000 Native troops to South Africa, that the Native army ought, therefore, in future, to be reduced by that number. Let no one, therefore, be taken in by this sort of argument. These are not days when the military strength of any empire is likely to be reduced. They are not days when the military strength of the Indian Empire can with safety be reduced. If Lord Dufferin could hold 14 years ago that the present armed strength of India, which was raised by him to its present total, was necessary for the preservation of order in this great country, for the fulfilment of our engagements, and for the protection of our boundaries, will any sensible man be found to tell me that anything has occurred since, whether it be in the experience of warfare in South Africa, or in the events that we hear of from day to day in Central Asia, and on the borders of Afghanistan, to prove that we can now fulfil our obligations with less ? No, there are two great duties of Imperial statesmanship in India. The first is to make all these millions of people, if possible, happier, more contented, more prosperous. The second is to keep them and their property safe. We are not going, for the sake of the one duty, to neglect the other. We would prefer to discharge our responsibility,—and it is no light one—in respect of both. With these remarks I will bring the present debate to a close, and will now adjourn this Council *sine die.*

ADDRESS FROM THE AMRITSAR MUNICIPALITY.

*9th April*, 1900.

[The Viceroy accompanied by Lady Curzon and the members of His Excellency's staff left Calcutta for a visit to Quetta and the frontier, on Wednesday night, the 28th March. Halting *en route* at Lalkua for a few days for some shooting, Their Excellencies proceeded to Amritsar where they arrived on the 8th April and were received by the Lieutenant-Governor of the Punjab, his Staff and the local officials. In the morning a visit was made to the Golden Temple, and in the afternoon at the Town Hall, in the presence of a large assembly of Europeans and Natives, the members of the Municipality presented an address of welcome to the Viceroy. After expressions of loyalty the address remarked that though Amritsar could not boast any great antiquity, yet with the Golden Temple in its midst, it had ever been the centre of the Sikh race, with all its traditions of loyalty and gallantry in the field. Nowhere had the recent successes of the British arms been hailed with greater rejoicing than at Amritsar. Its long standing commercial prosperity showed no decline, and no opportunity had been lost of extending and encouraging the trade and enterprise of the city. They thanked the Viceroy for the concession to construct a railway from Amritsar to Taran-Taran and Sinhali. Reference was made to education, sanitation, etc., and particularly to the fact that Amritsar had been spared from plague and famine. Thousands of Bikaniris who had flocked to the city were being housed, and liberal subscriptions had already been given to the famine fund.

The Viceroy replied as follows :—]

*Gentlemen of the Municipal Committee of Amritsar :*— Years ago, when I was travelling in India, I came to Amritsar, and took my place in the obscure crowd of pilgrims of all nationalities who elbowed their way along the stone causeway that leads to your Holy Temple, the shrine and centre of the Sikh faith. Now that I come back again as Viceroy of India, I regard this city and its picturesque and historic associations with a not diminished interest, while I am almost able to act the part of a cicerone to Lady Curzon, who visits Amritsar for the first time, and whom you have gracefully included in your address of welcome.

Every traveller, and still more every Viceroy, must be aware of the loyalty and the valour of the noble race of Sikhs. These virtues are independent of locality, or climate, or conditions of service. I have seen masculine

Sikh Policemen in Shanghai, managing with perfect ease a noisy crowd of Celestial ragamuffins. I have seen a stalwart Sikh regiment upon the parade ground at Hong-Kong. As Under-Secretary for Foreign Affairs in England I was brought into contact with the brave deeds of Sikh soldiers in the heart of East Africa, and at the sources of the Nile. Wherever they go, courageous and manly and true, loyal to the sovereign whom they serve, faithful to the regiment whose badge they wear, devoted to the officers whom they follow, and fearless even unto death—such are the Sikh soldiers, the pith of our Indian army. As I move about India, I see at remote frontier outposts, no less than at the sites of historic sieges or engagements, the scenes of their heroism and self-sacrifice ; and I come across tablets and monuments that perpetuate the record of their daring. Your allegiance, therefore, requires no assertion in words, since it has been so amply vindicated by deeds. At the same time it has been a source of the greatest satisfaction to myself as head of the Government of India, and still more if it be possible, to that venerable Sovereign, who loves India so well, that, in the recent troubles with which her Empire has been assailed in South Africa, there has come from the whole of India, and not least from this province of the Punjab, so spontaneous an outburst of fidelity while the skies were still overcast, and so loud and unanimous a note of rejoicing when the clouds rolled away. You have followed this war with intense interest, because many of yourselves, or of your fellow citizens, have served with the British officers who have been engaged, perhaps under the Commander-in-Chief, Lord Roberts, himself ; and because you know from your own experience that the victory of British arms does not carry with it extermination or hardship to the vanquished race, but is the starting point of a new era of peace and prosperity and good-will between the conquerors and the conquered.

But I must turn from the contemplation of your history and your loyalty to the concrete facts of everyday life, which a busy mercantile city like Amritsar is not so modest or so foolish as to hide from the eyes of a passing Viceroy. Your city has, I know, for many years past, been building up a solid commercial and industrial reputation, and is as anxious, and apparently as capable, to do business, as it is to produce soldiers. I am always glad when I hear the hum and see the smoke of factories in India. Not that I think either of them beautiful. Both indeed, from the aesthetic point of view, are detestable. But I rejoice because I know that they mean good wages and steady occupation to hundreds, often to thousands, of Indian artisans, and that in the lamentable decline of native handicrafts, they provide a substitute which is practical and remunerative, even if it be not delectable. I am only anxious about one thing. When you employ European mechanical appliances to assist you in producing manufactures of Asiatic type or origin, pray do not at the same time borrow European designs. They are commonly base, and inartistic, and vulgar. I was visiting this morning your principal carpet factory, where the carpets are still, I am glad to see, woven by hand. But I thought that I detected in some of the patterns an admixture of foreign taste. Pray do not be beguiled into this error. Adhere to your old Indian and Persian models, which were the product of a race of natural artists, and upon which the modern world will never improve. Above all, I would say to the Native princes and noblemen, when you order a carpet for your palaces or mansions, do not think of going to Europe and of patronising the hideous designs of Kidderminster or of Brussels. Buy your carpets in your own country, and make it a condition that they are of Indian colouring and Indian pattern. There is a tendency among rich men in India to think that the latest European fabrication is the most fashionable, and therefore the best. There is no inherent connection between fashion and merit ; and the latest pattern is often the worst art.

You speak in your address of a Technical School supported by the Municipality. Whether it be for the revival of Oriental arts and industries, or for the study of Western methods and appliances, I hope that this school is conducted on business-like lines. If Technical Education is to be a success in India, it must enable a man to become, not a great scholar, but a good workman. You must train him not so much in principles as in practice.

A very fair test of the work done by Municipal Committees is supplied by the state of sanitation in the city or town whose revenues they administer. It is gratifying to learn that you have so far escaped both plague and famine, although both are visitations to which a place that is so great a centre of pilgrimage must, from the nature of things, be particularly exposed. I am also pleased to learn of the useful purposes to which you have devoted, and are proposing to devote, your Municipal credit. I would only suggest that you complete the drainage system before you undertake the water-supply ; a consideration which must, I think, be present to your own minds, seeing that in your address you have admitted that without a complete drainage system the benefit of a pure and wholesome water-supply would be gravely impaired.

You conclude by reminding me that your own immunity from famine has not rendered you blind to the sufferings, or deaf to the appeals, of others, and that you have recently held a public meeting in Amritsar to organise local contributions to the Famine Relief Fund. India can in no way better vindicate its solidarity of feeling and its claim to a national existence than by recognizing a common interest in public misfortune. Adversity is very capricious and partial in its visitations. It spares here while it strikes there. But the favoured of to-day may be the victim of to-morrow ; and in relieving the troubles of others, you are also earning a similar relief, should you ever stand in need of it yourselves in days to come.

. Allow me to thank you, Gentlemen, most cordially for your address, and for the handsome casket in which it is enclosed.

## DARBAR AT QUETTA.

### 12th April, 1900.

[At 4-45 P.M., on Thursday, the 12th April 1900, His Excellency the Viceroy held a public Darbar in the Sandeman Memorial Hall, Quetta, for the reception of the Chiefs, Sirdars, and other Native gentlemen of Balu- chistan. The Darbar was attended by His Highness the Khan of Kalat, the Jam of Las Beyla, and about 300 Khans and Sirdars, and by all the princi- pal civil and military officials in Quetta, including the Agent to the Governor-General for Baluchistan, the Lieutenant-General Commanding the Forces, Bombay, the Brigadier-General Commanding the District, and by a large number of Political Officers and many ladies, including Her Excellency Lady Curzon and Mrs. Barnes. The Viceroy having, with due ceremony, arrived at the Hall and taken his seat on the daïs, the formal presentation to His Excellency of the Khan of Kalat and his attendants, the Jam of Las Beyla and his attendants, the Sarawan and Jhallawan Sirdars, the notables of Kalat and the principal Sirdars and Darbaris of their districts, was proceeded with. At its conclusion Mr. Barnes, addressing the Viceroy, gave a brief account of the Jirga Hall which has been built in memory of the late Sir Robert Sandeman. He referred to the remarkable results achieved in the Baluchistan Agency by Sir Robert Sandeman during the 15 years in which he held the Agency. These results, he remarked, were mainly due to Sir Robert Sande- man's energy, resolution, and conciliatory policy. The uniform success attending his policy had exercised a profound and far-reaching effect on the policy of the Government of India elsewhere on the north-west frontier. The Memorial Hall was the outcome of a spontaneous movement on the part of the Baluch and Brahui Sirdars, whose example was followed by the Khan of Kalat and others. Its total cost was Rs. 1,16, 305 which included a subscription by the Imperial Government of Rs 17,661. At the same time Sir Robert Sandeman's European friends raised a considerable sum which was devoted to perpetuating his memory in Quetta. The Hall building will be maintained by Government, the surrounding gardens being made public. Mr. Barnes concluded by expressing pleasure that the first cere- mony in the Hall should be a Viceregal Darbar, and that it should be their good fortune to have it declared open by a Viceroy with His Excellency's intimate knowledge of the frontier, and with his well known sympathy with, and interest in, its people, and in the career of the great administra- tor in whose memory the building is erected.

His Excellency then rose and addressed the Darbar as follows :—]

*Your Highness, Sirdars, and Khans :*—I am sorry not to be able to speak to you in your own language. But my words will presently be translated and will thus reach your ears, However, though I cannot myself address you in a form that you will understand, I feel that I may claim to know something of your history, your customs, and your country. For many years, before I was appointed by Her Majesty the Queen to be her representative in India, I had spent much of my time in travelling upon the Indian frontier, and in neighbouring countries. I have met most of the tribes, and I know the principal chieftains along 1,000 miles of that frontier from the Pamirs to Quetta ; and I take a warm interest in these people and am attached to their rulers. Years ago, I devoted some time to travelling through Persia, a country with which many of you have close relations. On another occasion I stayed in Chitral with Mehtar Nizam-ul-Mulk, just before he was murdered by his brother, who is now a prisoner in British India ; and on the last occasion that I was in Quetta, more than five years ago, I had ridden down to Chaman by Ghuzni and Kandahar from Kabul, where I had been for a fortnight as the guest of the Amir. Seven years before that time I was also here with Sir Robert Sandeman when the Khojak tunnel had not even been commenced ; and we rode over the mountains to Chaman by the old road. All these experiences have taught me to know and to love the frontier, and to take no common interest in the Baluch and the Pathan. The reason for which I have been drawn to these regions, and have acquired this attachment is a simple one. I admire the manly spirit and the courage of the border tribesmen. I dislike war with them and desire to maintain an honourable peace. In many cases, as for instance formerly in Baluchistan, they are constantly quarrelling with each other, and are accordingly weak and disunited. I want them to unite with the British *Raj* in the settlement of their feuds and in the defence of their own country. Anyone who attacks it should be regarded as a common foe. I want them to become, as many of them do, the trusted soldiers and the loyal feudatories of the Great Queen ; and to realise that, while there is no use in fighting us, because we are so strong as always to defeat them in the end, their religion, their traditions, even their independence, are most safe when they enter into friendly relations with the British Government, and receive from us those guarantees which we are always ready to give in return for faithful service and good behaviour. I believe in speaking the truth boldly to the men of the frontier, as to all other men ; and in telling them frankly where, in their own interests, they will do well and where they will do ill. The Sirdars of Baluchistan have learned this lesson from a long and successful experience ; and the history of this country for the past 20 years, with its change from perpetual anarchy to peace, its steady progress, and its growth in population, wealth, and contentment, is an evidence of the truth of my saying.

I am addressing to-day in this Darbar different classes of Chiefs and persons, to each of whom I will say a few words. There are present here His Highness the Khan of Kalat and the Jam of Las Beyla. They possess ancient titles, and they rule over famous or interesting territories. Among the ancestors of His Highness the Khan was Nasir Khan the First, who was beloved as a just and upright ruler. The example of great ancestors should never be forgotten by their descendants. If a State declines in interest or importance it is the ruler who is rightly held to blame. Rulers are invested with a supreme responsibility to their subjects. This may be difficult to exercise when their own position is insecure, and when they are exposed to political danger or to personal risk. But what excuse can there be for their not taking an active interest in the walfare of their people, and shewing liberality and enlightenment in administration, when they are secured against any external danger by the protection of the British Power? The *Sirkar* gives with generous hand, but he also expects in return, and this obligation must be paid.

Secondly, I see present here the Sirdars of the Baluch confederacy. Sirdars, you owe to the British Government the reconciliation of your old· disputes, and the general tranquillity which you now enjoy. I know your traditional loyalty. I remember the help that you rendered in the Afghan war. But, Sirdars, it is not only in times of crisis that you have a duty to Government. We rely upon your swords when fighting begins. But peace has its service not less than war ; and I call upon you to perform this service. I have been shocked to hear of the too frequent outrages against Government in recent years in which Marris and Brahuis have been engaged. They are a disgrace to the tribes and a discredit to the Chiefs. I believe that it is possible for the Sirdars, if they are resolute and united, to prevent these outrages. I am certain that, in many cases, it is possible for them to capture and to punish the criminals. I say to you, therefore, Sirdars, that the Government does not give to you your pay and service for nothing : and that I expect you to put a stop to these lawless proceedings, and to purge your tribal honour from this tarnish. When I see good service rendered, I am quick to recognise it ; and it is with pleasure, therefore, that I have learned from my Agent, Mr. Barnes, that in giving warning of a robber gang, Khan Sahib Baha-ud-din Bazai, and in attacking and dis‑ persing a body of raiders, the Rustamzai Levies of Nushki, have recently rendered valuable help to Government. I am pleased to acknowledge the conduct of these men, and I hold it up as an example.

Thirdly, there are here present the Sirdars and Khans of districts under British Administration. You also, Sirdars and Khans, are mostly in receipt of pay or *muafi* allowances from Government ; and you also have your corresponding duties to perform. There have recently taken place in British Baluchistan a number of murderous attacks upon Englishmen and Europeans, which are sometimes called, or miscalled, *Ghaza*. Believe me, Sirdars, that the idea that any one can earn the favour of Almighty God by killing some one else against whom he bears no grudge, and who has done him no wrong, simply because he follows another religion—which is only another way of worshipping the same God—is one of the stupidest notions that ever entered into the brain of a human being.  If we could lift the *purdah* of the future world and see what fate has attended these wretched murderers, I do not think that there would be many future *Ghazis* on the Pathan border, or in Baluchistan.  However it is enough for me to deal with the attitude of Government ; and about this I wish you to cherish no illusions.  I am determined, so far as lies in the power of Government, to put a stop to these abominable crimes.  I shall shrink from no punishment however severe ; I shall prohibit the carrying of all arms if I find that to be necessary ; and I shall hold those responsible who are to blame.  The leaders of the people can cooperate with Government in two ways.  They can throw the whole weight of their influence and authority against the perpetrators of these vile outrages ; and they can assist Government to capture the offenders.  I shall not be slow to reward those who render good and faithful service.  But I also shall not be quick to pardon those who are satisfied with doing nothing, and who openly neglect their duty.

Sirdars and Khans, as you are aware, a great famine is prevailing in many parts of India.  How great it is, and with what efforts the Government of India is endeavouring to cope with it, is shown by the fact that nearly 50 lakhs of persons are being kept alive by the powerful hand of the *Sirkar.*  We wish none of the people to die : and we spend the money of Government in giving them work and in saving them from starvation.  In Baluchistan you never have a famine so terrible as this.  But I know that, for three years past, there has been a deficient rainfall and considerable distress in certain parts of this country, particularly in the Marri and Bugti Hills, and a great mortality of cattle.  Here too the *Sirkar* has not been behindhand in relief.  A grant of one and a half lakhs has been made for the construction of roads by those who are in need ; a quarter of a lakh is being spent in the distribution

of grain among the Marris and Bugtis ; and the Famine
Relief Fund has recently made to Baluchistan a special
grant of R10,000. I hope that these efforts may tide
over the remaining period of scarcity, and that you will
have good rains in the forthcoming summer.

And now, Your Highness and Sirdars, let me say, in
conclusion, what a pleasure it is to me to inaugurate with
this important Darbar the Memorial Hall to my old friend,
Sir Robert Sandeman, in which I am now speaking.
"Sinneman Sahib," as you all called and knew him, has
now been dead for eight years. But his name is not forgotten, and his work will go on living, as I hope, for ever.

For what was Sandeman's work for which we honour
and remember his name ? It was the building up of the
powerful and peaceful frontier-province of Baluchistan with
the good-will and acquiescence of its ruler, its Sirdars, and
its people. When he first came to Kalat in 1875, the
Baluchistan State was a prey to civil war, the tribes were
disorganised and fighting, Peshin and Sibi were under
Afghan Governors, there was no British Administration in
the country, and the passes were either closed to trade,
or were infested by marauding gangs. Contrast the present position, when we see a Baluchistan that is pacified
and prosperous from the Arabian Sea to the Registan
Desert, and from the Persian border to the Suleimans and
the Gomul. I do not say that there are never troubles, or
disorders, or disputes. But there is no civil war. There
is a growing trade ; justice is dispensed ; property is increasingly safe ; the population is multiplying ; every man
who does right knows that he is certain of the protection
of the British *Raj.* This is Sir Robert Sandeman's work,
and for this he will always be remembered.

It also seems to me a right thing that his memorial
should be a Jirga Hall. For above all else he carried
through his policy by his use of tribal methods, of which
the Jirga is the foremost, by his knowledge of tribal character, and by his conciliation of tribal feelings. He was

a strong and independent man. But he never coerced by force where he could lead by free will. He had the power of character to dictate, but he also had the tact and good humour to persuade. It was for this that he was trusted by all men and was beloved by the people. I am proud to come here to-day as Viceroy of India, and to open this Memorial Hall to one who was not merely my friend but a strong and withal kindly ruler of men and a noble-minded son of Great Britain. Since I was here with him, his successor with whom I stayed later on, Sir James Browne, has also passed away. He, too, had a wonderful influence with the tribes and was trusted by every Pathan on the border. The Frontier is a hard master. It is greedy of the life-blood of its servants ; and both these brave and able men died at their posts. No more competent successor to them could have been found than my present Agent, Mr. Barnes. He learned his lessons in the school of Sandeman, and with energy, and ability, and a high sense of duty, he has pursued the same path, and carried on the same work. I rejoice to think that Baluchistan, the apple of the Frontier's eye, has been so well guarded by a series of such devoted and capable officers of the Queen : and in such hands may it long continue to prosper. (*Applause.*)

[A translation of His Excellency's address was then read in Pashtu by a native officer of the Agency, the Chiefs and Sirdars listening to it with the closest attention and being evidently greatly impressed with it. Lithographed copies of the address were also distributed to the Chiefs and Sirdars present.]

## STATEMENT ON FAMINE.

*19th October,* 1900.

[ A meeting of the Legislative Council of the Governor-General of India took place at Viceregal Lodge, Simla, on the 19th October, 1900. Before proceeding with the business of the Council His Excellency the President made the following statement regarding the administration of the recent famine in India :— ]

Exactly a year ago to-day I made a speech in this Council upon the then impending famine. Throughout the twelve months that have intervened, this famine, which within the range of its incidence has been the severest that India has ever known, has been the main preoccupation of Government. It has engrossed our whole attention, has placed a terrible strain both upon our resources and our officials, has disorganised our finances, and has addressed a perpetual and irresistible appeal to our individual humanity. Now that it is drawing to a close, it may not be inappropriate that I should attempt to sum up the results of the past year's experience ; so that the public may realise within a short compass what the Great Famine of 1899-1900 has meant, how we have endeavoured to meet it, what a mark it has left, or will leave, upon the history of the country, and what is the teaching that may be derived from a study of its features.

We cannot, I think, be accused of having failed to anticipate or to provide for this great drought. Our anxiety as to the prospects dated from as far back as July 1899. In the early autumn the Local Governments and ourselves were busily occupied in making preparations for the possible failure of the monsoon. When I spoke in October, relief operations had already commenced, and half a million persons were on relief. The numbers rapidly rose month by month, till, in July last, they touched the unprecedented total of considerably more than six millions of persons. Even now over two millions are still in receipt of relief ; though we hope that, in the course of next month, the necessity may disappear, and that the whole of this number may before long go away to their homes.

The main statistical features of the famine are already sufficiently well known and may be briefly dismissed. It has affected an area of over 400,000 square miles, and a population of about 60 millions, of whom 25 millions, belong to British India and the remainder to Native States. Within this area the famine conditions have, during the greater part of the year, been intense. Outside it they have extended, with a gradually dwindling radius, over wide districts which have suffered much from loss of crops and cattle, if not from actual scarcity. In a greater or less degree nearly one-fourth of the entire population of the Indian continent have come within the range of relief operations. It is difficult to express in figures, with any close degree of accuracy, the loss occasioned by so widespread and severe a visitation. But it may be roughly put in this way. The annual agricultural production of India and Burma averages in value between 300 and 400 crores of rupees. On a very cautious estimate the production in 1899-1900 must have been at least one-quarter, if not one-third, below the average. At normal prices the loss was at least 75 crores, or fifty millions sterling. In this estimate India is treated as a whole. But in reality the loss fell on a portion only of the continent, and ranged from almost total failure of crop in Guzerat, Berar, Chhattisgarh, and Hissar, and in many of the Rajputana States, to 20 and 30 per cent. in districts of the North-Western Provinces and Madras, which were not reckoned as falling within the famine tract. If to this be added the value of some millions of cattle, some conception may be formed of the destruction of property which a great drought occasions. There have been many great droughts in India, but there has been no other of which such figures could be predicated as these.

It must further be remembered that, unlike previous famines, that of 1900 was separated by the short space of only two years from a drought not greatly inferior to it in extent and scarcity. Some tracts which suffered in 1896-97 have been fortunate enough to escape in 1899-1900. But the most calamitous feature of the recent famine has been that there were others which not only suffered again, but suffered in a worse degree. This was the case in the Central Provinces, and in portions of Rajputana, Central India, the South-East Punjab, and the Bombay Deccan. Apart from this area of two-fold distress, the centre of gravity tended, on the present occasion, to shift towards the west. The cluster of Native States lying between the Nerbudda, the Jumna, and the Sutlej, were swept into the area of scarcity. Finally, the fertile provinces of Guzerat and Kathiawar, whose rainfall is generally so abundant and so steady that they have been styled the Garden of India, were attacked ; and there, in proportion as the immunity hitherto enjoyed has been the longest, so was the suffering the most widespread and enduring.

This was the situation with which we were confronted a year ago, and which has gradually developed since. It was not merely a crop failure, but a fodder famine on an enormous scale, followed in many parts by a positive devastation of cattle—both plough cattle, buffaloes, and milch kine. In other words it affected, and may almost be said to have annihilated, the working capital of the agricultural classes. It struck some of them when they were still down from the effects of the recent shock. It struck others, who had never before known what calamity was, and who were crushed and shattered by the suddenness and directness of the blow. It attacked Natives States to whose Durbars had never previously been brought home the obligation of famine relief on an extended scale, and whose dearth of administrative staff was enhanced by the poverty of their financial resources. It laid its hand upon primitive hill men unused to discipline or restraint, implusive, improvident, lazy, living in an almost barbarous state in wild and inaccessible jungles. It sharpened the lurking nomadic instinct of wandering tribes, and sent them aimlessly drifting about the country, a terror to the famine officer, and an incubus to the camps. For a year it never left hold of its victims

and one-half of the year had not elapsed before famine had
brought its familiar attendant Furies in its train ; and
cholera, dysentery, and fever had fallen upon an already
exhausted and enfeebled population. This is the picture
of suffering that India has presented during the past year.
Let us now examine the steps that have been taken to
ameliorate it.

In such diverse circumstances the methods of relief, the
difficulties encountered, and the degree of success attained,
have varied greatly. The preceding famine had bequeathed experiences and lessons of the utmost value, which
were carefully gathered up by the Commission of 1898, and
which have profoundly affected the policy of the present
famine. The stress laid by the Commission on the
necessity for starting relief before the people have run
down ; their advocacy of more extensive gratuitous relief,
especially in the form of kitchen relief ; their recommendations concerning the special treatment of aboriginal and
forest tribes ; their approval of small or village relief works
in special circumstances in preference to large works :
these and other injunctions will be found to have influenced
our measures and shaped our course throughout the famine.
The Commission's recommendations were generally in the
direction of greater flexibility in relief methods and greater
liberality of relief. The dangers of ill-regulated profusion
are obvious ; and, apart from all considerations of cost, it
would be a national misfortune if relief were ever made so
facile or so pleasant as to destroy the self-respect and self-
reliance of the people. But the Commission were not
unmindful of this danger ; and their findings amounted to
this that they recognised that, in the last famine, we had
not succeeded in preventing great mortality and suffering,
and that they thought better results might be attainable
by a larger expenditure of money and a somewhat greater
regard to the circumstances of special localities and classes.
They said in effect that if it was good policy to combat a
famine, it was good policy to combat it effectively. It is

possible that in certain directions their recommendations erred on the side of over-liberality. Their wage-scale is an instance. It was tried in all provinces at the commencement of the present famine, but was speedily reduced by the independent consent of all Local Governments. Again, their advocacy of gratuitous relief may be said by some to have led, in the present famine, to a scale of alms-giving unprecedented in magnitude, and likely to embarrass future famine administration. This question I will discuss in a moment. I merely mention the matter now to show that, in the present famine, we have broken new ground, and, acting upon the lessons of its predecessor, have accepted a higher standard of moral and financial obligation than has ever before been recognised or acted upon in this or any country.

If, indeed, a special characteristic should be attributed to our campaign of famine relief in the first year, it has been its unprecedented liberality. There is no parallel in the history of India, or in that of any country in the world, to the total of over six million persons who, in British India and the Native States, have for weeks on end been dependent upon the charity of Government. Let me compare these figures with those of the preceding famine. In 1897 the high water mark of relief was reached in the second fortnight of May, when there were nearly 4 million persons on relief in British India. Taking the affected population at 40 millions, the ratio of relief was 10 per cent. In one district of Madras, and in two districts of the North-Western Provinces, the ratio for some months was about 30 per cent.; but these were exceptional cases. In the most distressed districts of the Central Provinces, 15 or 16 per cent. was regarded in 1896-97 as a very high standard of relief. Now take the figures of the present year. For some weeks in June and July upwards of $4\frac{1}{2}$ million persons were on relief in British India. Reckoned on a population of, say 25 millions, the ratio of relief was 18 per cent. as compared with 10 per cent. in 1897. In many districts the proportion exceeded 20 per cent. In several it exceeded 30 per cent. In two districts it exceeded 40 per cent. In the small district of Merwara, where famine has been present for two years, 75 per cent. of the population has been on relief. Nothing that I might say can intensify the simple eloquence of these figures.

The next test that I apply is that of the number of officers whom we have lent both to British districts and to Native States to reinforce the overworked, and in many cases undermanned, local establishments. From the Army 84 Staff Corps Officers, 17 Native Officers, 10 British Non-Commissioned Officers and Privates, and 228 Native Non-Commissioned Officers and Privates, have been deputed for periods of various length to famine duty in British India and Native States. They have done excellent work. Including the above, the total number of public officials deputed from civil and military employ to famine duty has amounted to 637. Among these were 35 Assistant Surgeons, and 141 Hospital Assistants, 44 Civil Engineers, 10 Royal Engineers, and 24 Public Works subordinates. Large as these numbers were, we would gladly have sent more, had the men been forthcoming. Since the famine began, I cannot recall ever having refused an application, if it was possible to grant it. We literally scoured the remaining provinces of India for the loan of men, and with great generosity, wherever practicable, their Governments responded to the appeal. After my return from Guzerat, we collected and sent down a large number of additional Hospital Assistants, of whom I had noted a regrettable paucity, to Bombay. Similarly in the Native States, as the Chiefs and Durbars have repeatedly acknowledged, it has only been owing to the administrative knowledge, the unflagging energy, and the devotion of the British Officers whom we have lent to them, that they have escaped a disastrous breakdown.

My third test is that of financial outlay. The direct expenditure on famine relief in British India and in Berar, from the commencement of relief operations up to the end of August, has been 54 lakhs of rupees. We estimate a further expenditure of about 150 lakhs up to the 31st March next, making in all, in round numbers, about 10 crores of rupees. In loans and advances to landholders and cultivators, we have expended R238 lakhs. We have made advances for plough cattle and for agricultural operations this autumn free of interest, and on very easy terms as to eventual repayment; and our expectation is that not more than one-half will be recovered. In the matter of land revenue, our latest estimate is that, of a demand of R392 lakhs in the Central Provinces and Bombay, R164 lakhs will be uncollected during the year. In the distressed districts of the Punjab, suspensions aggregating R41 lakhs are anticipated. With these figures I compare those for the famine of 1896-97, calling attention, however, to the fact that, in 1896-97, the area and population in British India affected by famine were considerably larger than in the present year. The total direct expenditure on famine relief was 727 lakhs of rupees; 130 lakhs were advanced as *takavi;* and land revenue to the amount of about 2 crores was suspended. In this comparison, our further outlay in connection with relief in Native States has been omitted, for the reason that, in 1896-97, the calls upon us in that respect were insignificant. In the present famine, our loans to Native States in Rajputana have amounted to 69 lakhs of rupees: to Native States in the Bombay Presidency we have lent 78 lakhs of rupees, besides guaranteeing the repayment of loans to the amount of 105 lakhs of rupees borrowed by other States in the market. We have also come to the assistance of the Nizam of Hyderabad whose extensive dominions have suffered from severe drought. In all, our actual loans to Native rulers in connection with the present famine amount, in the aggregate, to over 3½ crores. This is exclusive of the guaranteed loans. Without this assistance it may be safely said that the States would have been wholly unequal to the task of relieving their subjects, and even, in some cases, of carrying on the ordinary administration of their territories.

I now pass to an examination of the methods of Famine relief which we have adopted. In one respect they have differed materially from those of the preceding famine. Profiting by its lessons, we have learned to apply a much more flexible system. Thus, in 1897, the effective relief of the aboriginal races in the Central Provinces was regarded as an insoluble problem. They suffered and perished in their jungles. This year congenial work and extensive gratuitous relief were provided for them in the forests, and the Gonds and Baigas have survived with no exceptional mortality. Again, whereas in 1897 there was a terrible mortality in the Central Provinces when the rains set in, owing to the abrupt closing of relief works without a simultaneous expansion of home or village relief, in the present year we have scattered broadcast over the country an extensive system of kitchen relief upon which, while no one disputes its general necessity or its success, the only criticism that has been passed is that it has erred on the side of liberality, and has been abused by able-bodied persons who preferred to be fed for nothing in the kitchen to earning their own livelihood in the fields. In 1897 the complaint was one of parsimony and lack of preparation. If we have now, in some cases, gone too far in the opposite direction, some allowance must be made for the natural recoil from earlier mistakes.

Guzerat supplies another instance of the degree in which we have accentuated and added to the flexibility of the Famine Code. When the great outbreak of cholera had disorganized the large relief works, and had driven the terrified workers away to their homes, and when extraordinarily high death-rates revealed the existence of very widespread destitution and suffering, the Government of India did not hesitate to advise the Bombay Government to meet the situation by enlarging the customary bounds of gratuitous relief, and by opening petty village works to take the place of the deserted Public Works relief camps. The effect of this policy was that, whereas in the middle of May the number of persons on gratuitous relief in the five districts of Guzerat was little more than 50,000, at the end of June it had risen to 50,000: at the end of July to 308,000: and by the middle of August to 385,000, the last figure representing more than 12 per cent. of the entire population of those districts. Before the present famine, such a percentage would have been regarded as a flagrant abuse of famine relief. We were, however, satisfied that a strict adherence to the labour test principle would, in June and July last, have failed to meet the very special set of circumstances created by the cholera outbreak in Guzerat, and I have no doubt that the satisfactory decline in the death-rate was largely due to the policy adopted.

In drawing attention, however, to the greater liberality of relief that has been practised, the question may be asked whether it was after all only due to the superior intensity of this year's famine, or whether it has denoted greater efficiency and perfection of method, or has perhaps only been the result of promiscuous and thoughtless charity. Some part of it must no doubt be attributed to the greater severity of the recent distress which I have already demonstrated. Upon the second head we may safely claim to have profited by experience in the improvement of our relief arrangements, and in their more accurate adaptation to the special circumstances of different districts, the special requirements of different classes, and the different seasons of the year. No critic would dispute this proposition. As regards the third point it is not without a smile that, while I now read in some quarters that the conditions of relief, notably in respect of kitchen relief in the Central Provinces, have been relaxed to a dangerous and demoralising degree, I remember that, nine months ago, the Government of India were being assailed for the alleged stringency and harshness of the warnings that they had given in the Circular of December 1899. Looking back upon our entire experience, I

have now no hesitation in saying that our warning note was
well-timed and was wisely issued. Our enquiry was followed by a very salutary re-organizaticn of relief works in the
Central Provinces and elsewhere, by large additions in all
provinces to the superior famine staff, and by considerable
improvements in the supervision and conduct of relief
measures. One of its results was the exposure of the inade-
quacy of the superior staff, and of the dangers which were
certain to ensue if this were not rectified. It was in consequence of this discovery that we offered the substantial help,
in respect of Staff Corps Officers, Medical Officers, officers
drafted from the Postal, Salt, and Police Departments, and
Engineers, of which I have already spoken.

I should like to add that, in my opinion, there was no
inconsistency between the position taken up by the Government of India in the first months of the famine, and their
subsequent attitude in permitting a vast expansion of gratuitous relief during the rains in the Central Provinces, and in
counselling the Government of Bombay to relax the conditions
of relief in Guzerat, when cholera had disorganized the large
works. Conditions are radically different at the beginning
and at the height of a famine : and a degree of firmness
at the outset is essential which would, at a later stage, be
altogether out of place. If this be borne in mind, our policy
will on examination prove to have been consistent throughout. On the one hand we have set our face against indiscriminate and pauperising charity, and have endeavoured to
insist on relief being administered with the care and method
which we owe to the tax-payer and to the exchequer. On
the other hand we have been prepared to accept any expenditure of which it could be shown that it was required to
save life, or to mitigate genuine distress. The only intelligent, and the only possible, policy is based on these two
principles. There is no contradiction between them. No
famine has ever been, or ever will be, successfully administered, that does not exhibit, according to the point from
which it is scrutinised, the opposite characteristics of

strictness and leniency, or that is not open to the charge
—if charges are to be brought—of being at different
moments profuse and grudging.

Nevertheless, we may still be asked whether we are quite
satisfied that the abnormal mortality in Guzerat, the widespread misery described by competent observers, and the
temporary breakdown of the relief machinery in that part,
were not due to any fault in our initial instructions. That
the mortality was very great cannot be denied. In Broach
the monthly death-rate rose from 2·96 *per mille* in October
1899, to 24·83 in May 1900. In the Panch Mahals, the
death-rate for the same month of May was 46·60 *per mille ;*
in Kaira 21·07 ; in Ahmedabad 24. These rates include
deaths from cholera, a most virulent wave of which swept
over Guzerat in April ; although it is impossible to distinguish accurately between the mortality for which cholera
was directly responsible, and that which was due to other
diseases, to debility, to privations, and to the temporary dis-
organization of the camps. I have seen the report of a
special enquiry which has just been conducted into the
Guzerat mortality by the Sanitary Commissioner to the
Bombay Government. He specifies no fewer than eight
causes for the excessive death-rate in that district. They
were—insufficient and unwholesome food ; resort to Rangoon
rice and other unaccustomed grains ; bad cooking and bad
water ; the physical softness of a people who had never
previously experienced famine ; the unwillingness of certain
classes, such as the Bhils and herdsmen, to apply for relief ;
and the vagabond instincts of large sections of the population. Some of these causes were preventible or reducible ;
the majority were not. If a perfect relief system is anywhere attainable, it is obvious that it is more likely to be
realised in a district where the people are already acquainted
with the principles of relief, and where they feel no natural
reluctance to avail themselves of it. Neither of those
conditions was present in Guzerat. The rapidity and
completeness of the calamity took the people by surprise ;

the weakness and incapacity for resistance of the people took the Local Government by surprise. Had there been greater previous experience in either respect, the results might have been modified. The failure was certainly not due to any antecedent orders on the part of Government, or to any parsimony in the scheme of relief. On the contrary, the actual cost of relief per head in Bombay exceeded the cost-rate in other parts of India. While, therefore, I feel that the excessive mortality in Guzerat is a phenomenon, of which it is difficult to give a full explanation, and which may still call for further enquiry, I think that a good deal of weight should be attached, in a comparison, for instance, between Guzerat and the Central Provinces, to the different temperament of the afflicted populations, and to their relative familiarity or unfamiliarity with relief methods.

If we examine the death-rate elsewhere, we shall find that, in the Central Provinces, it remained satisfactorily low until the concluding months of the famine. Excluding epidemic disease, the provincial rate for April was only 3·25 *per mille*, and for May 3·42 *per mille*. These were the worst months in Guzerat. In June, the rate (excluding cholera and small-pox, which carried off 23,000 persons) rose to 4 *per mille*, and in some parts was higher. In July it rose to 5·35 *per mille*, while some districts showed a local rate of from 7 to 10 *per mille*. In August, the death-rate in one district rose to no less than 15·21 *per mille*. It is a curious fact, however, that this high mortality was not accompanied by any exterior evidence of starvation or even of emaciation. The people in fact did not die of want of food, but from the sudden change in climatic conditions, which occurs during and after the rains.

In the Punjab the mortality statistics exhibit much the same features as in the Central Provinces, though in a slightly less degree. In Hissar, where the death-rate has been highest, it has never exceeded 8 *per mille*, excluding cholera. The result of my examination has been to show that relief has been fully and sufficiently given in the

Punjab, and that there has been no mortality from starvation, or even from direct privation, save in the case of wanderers from Native States, who arrived in too dehilitated a condition to be saved.

In Berar the death-rate has been generally moderate, except in two districts adjoining the Nizam's Dominions, where there was much pauper emigration across the border. In the last weeks of the hot weather, the mortality rose everywhere, especially in those two districts ; but no one has been found to suggest that it was due to any deficiency of relief.

I do not speak of the mortality in the Native States, which has in many cases been shocking, because the Government of India cannot be held responsible for a system which it does not control, and because my sole desire has been, while stating the best, and admitting the worst, that can be said about our own methods, to ascertain how far the latter have justified themselves, or are capable of amendment. Broadly speaking, it may be said that no endeavours which it is in the power of the most philanthropic or generous of Governments to put forward will avail to prevent an increase of mortality during a severe famine.. No relief system in the world will counteract the effects of reduced food supply, cessation of wages, high prices, and break up of home, among millions of people, or will prevent famine from being attended by its twin sister, pestilence.

When, however, I read the records of earlier famines, and compare their results with this, I do feel some cause for satisfaction. We are sometimes told of the wonderful things that happened in India before the days of British rule, and are invited, in most unhistorical fashion, to regard it as a Saturnian age. I have looked up the statistics of the last great famine that occurred in Bengal, while that province was still under Native administration. This was in the year 1770. I speak of local administration, because, although the Diwani of Bengal had been assumed by the

Company a few years before, the latter had not yet taken over the civil administration, which remained in the hands of the former Native officers of the Delhi Government. Throughout the summer of that year it is on record that the husbandmen sold their cattle ; they sold their implements of agriculture ; they sold their sons and daughters, till at length no buyer of children could be found ; they ate the leaves of trees, and the grass of the field : and, when the height of the summer was reached, the living were feeding on the dead. The streets of the cities were blocked up with promiscuous heaps of the dead and dying ; even the dogs and jackals could not accomplish their revolting work. Disease attacked the starving and shelterless survivors, and swept them off by hundreds of thousands. Before the end of May 1770, one-third of the population was officially calculated to have disappeared ; in June the deaths were returned as 6 is to 16 of the whole inhabitants : and it was estimated that one-half of the cultivators must perish. Two years later Warren Hastings, who had assumed the Government of Bengal on behalf of the British Power, stated the entire loss as at least one-third of the inhabitants, and subsequent calculations revealed that the failure of this single crop, in the single province of Bengal, had carried off, within nine months, no fewer than ten out of less than thirty millions of human beings.

After this appalling record of what famine meant in India a century ago, it was almost with a sense of relief that I read the other day in a manifesto issued by an English M. P. to his constituents, whom I may observe in passing that he no longer represents, that " Lord George Hamilton and Lord Curzon have looked helplessly on, while two millions of human beings have perished of starvation and disease in India." Had this statement been true, however damaging to the Secretary of State or to myself, it would yet have pointed an extraordinary contrast between the methods and results of 1900, and those of the 18th Century. But that it is not true is known to every intelligent person in England

and in this country. Every man, woman, and child, who has perished in India in the present famine has been a burden upon my heart, and upon that of Government. Their sufferings have never been absent from our thoughts. It cannot truthfully be said, even by the most envenomed of opponents, that we have looked helplessly on. On the contrary, I fearlessly claim, and I challenge contradiction, that there has never been a famine when the general mortality has been less, when the distress has been more amply or swiftly relieved, or when Government and its officers have given themselves with a more whole-hearted devotion to the saving of life and the service of the people.

What the actual mortality may have been it is impossible to tell with complete accuracy. At a later date the forthcoming census will throw useful light upon the problem. At the same time, from a comparison of the normal deathrate of the famine-stricken districts in British India, with which alone, of course, I am competent to deal, with the death-rate throughout the twelve months' duration of the drought, we can ascertain that there has been an excess mortality of 750,000, or three-quarters of a million persons. But, out of this total, we also know that cholera and smallpox have accounted for a recorded mortality of 230,000, figures which are admitted to be below the mark. Making this deduction, therefore, we arrive at an excess mortality of half a million in British India, more or less attributable to the famine conditions of the year. To say that the greater part of these have died of starvation, or even of destitution, would be an unjustifiable exaggeration ; since we know that many other contributary causes have been at work, while the figures include the deaths of immigrants from Native States, for which our administration cannot be held responsible. When further it is remembered that this total is not more than 2 per cent. of the entire population in the tracts to which it applies, it will be obvious that no very remarkable depopulation has occurred, and it will be recognized that it is with ample justification that I give the assurance that, in the entire history of Indian famines, while none has been more intense, in none have the deaths been so few.

So far my remarks have been confined almost exclusively to what has been done in the recent famine in British India. I must add a few words about the Native States, many of which have been affected in a scarcely inferior degree to our own territories. As I indicated a year ago, while we have sedulously refrained from assuming the direct responsibility for famine relief in those areas, and have shrunk from any unsolicited interference with Native administration, we have yet, in the discharge of our duty as the paramount power, and in the interests of the States themselves, tendered them constant advice, have lent them competent officers, have made them liberal loans, and have supplied co-ordination and system to their methods of relief. On the whole, we may congratulate ourselves upon the success that has attended these efforts. In a few States the duty of succouring their subjects has been so neglected by the Durbars as to need strong interference ; and in others the good intentions of rulers have been frustrated by the dishonesty and peculation of subordinate officials, who could not resist turning even the starvation of their fellow-creatures to their own profit. But, in the majority of cases, the Chiefs have shown a most laudable disposition to accept our methods of relief, in so far as their resources and the agency at their command permitted. In some of the Rajputana States, especially in Jaipur, Jodhpur, Bikanir, and Kishengarh, the arrangements have been admirably planned and carried out by the rulers themselves, and have aroused the admiration of persons familiar with the famine system of British Provinces. Surveying the Native States as a whole, we may say that there has been an awakening to the call of philanthropic duty, which has been most gratifying.

Nevertheless, the difference of the standards in vogue may be judged from a comparison of the figures on relief in the two areas. In Bikanir and Jodhpur, for instance, the numbers relieved in any month never exceeded 6 per cent. of the nominal population, while in the British districts of Ajmer-Merwara, 25 per cent. of the population were for months on relief. Even in the States under the Bombay Government, in which for various reasons the initiative and supervision of the Political Officers were more in evidence than in Central India and Rajputana, the scale of relief was very different from that in Guzerat. In Kathiawar, the numbers on relief never exceeded 13 per cent. of the population. In Palanpur they reached, but did not exceed, 15 per cent. in one month alone. In the same month (July 1900), one-third of the aggregate population of the four distressed districts of Guzerat was on relief. The two great States of Baroda and Hyderabad flank the Bombay territory on the north and east. In Hyderabad and Baroda the numbers on relief never rose to 5 per cent. of the nominal population ; and yet both States were visited by drought and famine not less severely than the adjoining districts of the Bombay Presidency. Meanwhile, the difference in the standards of relief was further testified by the eagerness with which thousands of fugitives streamed across the border from Native States into British territory, where they passed themselves off as British subjects, in the hope of enjoying the superior wages and comforts of our relief works, our poor-houses, and our hospitals.

I do not dwell on this point in order to disparage the efforts, in many cases most praiseworthy, made by Native States to relieve their people ; but simply because the difference between the standard of relief, at which we have by degrees arrived, and the standard of relief recognised as liberal in the best managed Native State, is one of the elementary facts of famine experience. We may gladly admit that more has been done for their people by the Chiefs and rulers of Rajputana on this occasion than in any other historic famine. There are many bright examples of benevolence and humanity. The Maharaja of Jaipur has extended his princely munificence not only to his own people, but to India at large. There is the instance of the late Maharaja of Kishengarh, who, though suffering from a mortal illness, took the keenest interest in the relief arrangements of his State, and never once alluded to his own ill-health. There is also the case of the wife of Maharaja Pertab Singh of Jodhpur, who, not content with opening an orphanage, resided there herself in order to superintend it. These instances, and their number might easily be increased, show the spirit with which the famine has been faced in Rajputana by some, at least, of its rulers. As for the people, they have borne their trials, as the Indian people always do, with exemplary fortitude and resignation.

I now pass to the subject of the charitable help which has been rendered to us in our long struggle, from so many quarters, in so many parts of the world. An impression appears to prevail that, on the present occasion, this assistance has been scant and disappointing. I do not share these views. Looking to the circumstances under which our appeal has been made, and even accepting the test of comparison with the famine of 1896-97, I still hold that the amount contributed has been munificent, while its utility can scarcely be overrated. In 1896-97 the total collections amounted to 170 lakhs, of which 10 lakhs remained over at the beginning of the recent famine. In the present year, the Central Relief Committee has received a sum of close upon 140 lakhs, or not far short of one million sterling.

Analysing the subscriptions, I find that India has contributed about the same amount to the Fund as in 1896-97 ; that is to say, about 32 lakhs. If the contributions from the European community are deducted, India may be considered to have contributed at the outside less than one-fifth of the total collections of 140 lakhs. More might have been expected from the Native community as a whole, notwithstanding individual examples of remarkable generosity. The little Colony of the Straits Settlements, for instance,

which has no connection with India beyond that of sentiment, has given more than the whole of the Punjab. A
careful observation of the figures and proceedings in each
province compels me to say that, in my opinion, Native
India has not yet reached as high a standard of practical
philanthropy or charity as might reasonably be expected.
Though private wealth in India is not widely distributed,
its total volume is considerable. If Englishmen in all parts
of the world can be found, as they have been found, twice
in three years, willing to contribute enormous sums for the
relief of India, on the sole ground that its people are the
suffering fellow-subjects of the same Queen, it surely behoves the more affluent of the Native community not to lag
behind in the succour of those who are of their own race
and creed.

The collections from abroad have amounted to 108 lakhs,
as against 137 lakhs in 1896-97. The United Kingdom's
contribution of 88½ lakhs, compares indifferently with its
contribution of 123 lakhs in 1896-97, but, in the circumstances of the year, it is a noble gift. The City of Glasgow
has been especially generous, with a donation of 8¼ lakhs,
and Liverpool with 4½, in addition to nearly 16 lakhs from
the rest of Lancashire. Australasia has given nearly 8 lakhs,
in place of the 2 lakhs sent in 1896-97. The Straits Settlements, Ceylon, and Hong Kong, have also been extremely
generous. Even Chinese Native Officials have collected
handsome sums on behalf of the Fund. The liberal donation of Germany, at the instigation of the Emperor, has
already been publicly acknowledged. Finally, the United
States of America, both through direct contributions to the
Fund, and by means of privately distributed gifts of money
and grain, have once more shown their vivid sympathy with
England's mission, and with India's need.

I pass to the mode in which the Famine Fund has been
distributed. The formation of the Fund was accompanied
by two announcements ; the one, that in the distribution
of the money the four objects of relief recognised in 1896-97

would be adhered to : the other that the claims of Native
States would be fully considered. These principles have
been faithfully adhered to by the Central Committee. Until
the detailed expenditure accounts of the Local Committees
are received, we cannot accurately state the distribution
under the several headings. But we know approximately
that, of 137 lakhs allotted by the Central Committee, 111
lakhs have been for cattle and seed and subsistence to cultivators. The allotments to Native States aggregate nearly
50 lakhs of rupees. The allotments to Rajputana alone
amount to 22 lakhs. Measured by the population of the
distressed areas, Rajputana has thus been not less generously
treated than the Central Provinces. In the case of wealthy
States like Gwalior, Hyderabad, and Baroda, the Central
Committee have restricted their grants to such amounts as
the Political Officers have thought it expedient to ask for.
Speaking generally, the grants made in Native territory have
far exceeded the expectations of the rulers or their subjects.
The gratitude of the latter has been expressed in homely
and touching phrase. " If the English had not sent us this
money, the thread of our lives would have been broken."
" These are not rupees which have come over the sea, they
are the water of life." " We have *heard* of the generosity
of Hatim Bai, but we have *tasted* that of the Great Queen."
How timely was the arrival of this charity, and how much
it meant, is seen in scores of affecting incidents. " Now I
have got through to the other side," said a poor cultivator,
with tears in his eyes, to the English officer who had given
him a few rupees to buy fodder for his famished bullocks.
There is ample evidence that this gratitude is of an enduring
nature. Some of the happiest memories of famine officers
are those of unexpected visits from men who had been
helped back to their old life by grants of seed and bullocks,
and who returned after many days to again acknowledge
the value of the gift. Nor should the self-respect which
in not a few cases stood between a needy person and the
proffered gift, or the scrupulous regard which led to its

return because it might be misapplied, be overlooked. From Rajputana comes an old-world tale of a Rajput Chief, dwelling in his bare house among his destitute tenants, who distributed among the latter the grant allotted to his village, but refused any gift for himself—" I am a Rahtor. I could not take charity,"—and who with difficulty was induced to take a small loan. From Rajputana also comes the story of the man who was given a little money to convey his family and himself to a relief work because he said that he had no means of feeding them on the way, but who came back and returned the gift because, as he said, he had not spoken the truth, since he had five goats which he could kill, one each day, eating part of the flesh, and selling the remainder. It is these incidents which lead one to hope that this great national charity has not been misplaced, but has been received in the spirit in which it has been offered.

In a famine campaign which has lasted for so long, and has provided so many opportunities for chivalry and self-sacrifice, it would not be difficult, but it might be invidious, to select any names for special mention. Numerous cases of devotion amounting to the loftiest heroism, have been brought under my notice. I have heard of Englishmen dying at their posts without a murmur. I have seen cases where the entire organisation of a vast area, and the lives of thousands of human beings, rested upon the shoulders of a single individual labouring on in silence and solitude, while his bodily strength was fast ebbing away. I have known of Natives who, inspired by his example, have thrown themselves with equal ardour into the struggle, and have uncomplainingly laid down their lives for their countrymen. Particularly must I mention the noble efforts of the Missionary Agencies of various Christian denominations. If ever there was an occasion in which their local knowledge and influence were likely to be of value, and in which it was open to them to vindicate the highest standards of their beneficent calling, it was here; and strenuously and faithfully have they performed the task.

From this record of the past I will now turn for a few
moments to the future. After the sombre picture that I
have been compelled to draw, it is with no small relief that
we may contemplate the existing situation and outlook.
The monsoon was late in coming, but it has lingered long ;
and except in the Eastern parts of the Bombay Deccan,
where I hear of crops withering from the premature cessation
of the rains, of a poor *kharif,* and of anxious prospects,
the outlook is everywhere promising. The early autumn
crops are already being harvested, and prices are steadily
falling back to their accustomed level. A good cotton crop
is on the ground, and as the cotton crop of India is worth
thirteen millions sterling in an average year, its importance
to the agriculturist will be readily understood. Preparations
for the winter crops are being actively made, and there is
every expectation that the sowings in many parts will be
unusually large, and will be made in the most favourable
circumstances. A good winter harvest means cash to the
farmer, as a good autumn harvest means cheap and abundant
food to the poorest classes. If we have the good fortune
to see our anticipations realised, next year should witness
the export trade in agricultural produce again revive, and
the import trade expand with the improvement in the
purchasing power of the people.

That the famine-smitten tracts will at once or speedily
lose the marks of the ordeal through which they have passed,
is not to be expected. The rapidity of the recovery will
depend upon many circumstances—upon the vitality and
stout-heartedness of the tillers of the soil, upon the
degree of their indebtedness, upon the goodness or badness
of the next few seasons, upon the extent to which their
cattle have perished, and not least upon the liberality,
in respect of revenue remission, of the Government. As
regards the loss of stock, our latest reports are more
encouraging than at one time we could have foreseen, and
justify us in the belief that, if the seasons be propitious,
recuperation will be more rapid than might at first sight

be deemed likely. In olden times, after a famine such as we have experienced, the districts would have been depopulated, and the land would have lain waste for a generation, for lack of hands to till it. There may be isolated tracts in the jungles and mountain fastnesses of Central India and Rajputana, where the approaching Census will reveal a melancholy decrease of population. But, treating India as a whole, neither in Native States nor in British territory is the wholesale and lasting desolation which followed the footsteps of a famine a hundred years ago any longer within the bounds of possibility. The standard of humanity has risen with the means of combating the peril; and in proportion as the struggle has been arduous, so are its after-effects mitigated.

I have alluded to the attitude of Government. In so far as generosity in respect of advances, of loans, of suspensions, and most of all of remissions, is concerned, the figures that I have previously given will have shown that on our part there has been no hanging back. Our first object has hitherto been to pull the sufferers through. Our first object now is to start them again with reasonable chances in the world. Behind these two objects lies the further and binding duty of profiting by the lessons that the famine has taught. It will not do for us to sit still until the next famine comes, and then bewail the mysteries of Providence. A famine is a natural visitation in its origin; but it is, or should be, a very business-like proceeding when once it has started. There are many subjects into which we shall require to make careful enquiry, and an investigation into which we have already suggested to the Secretary of State. We shall want to compare the various relief systems and their results as practised in the different provinces; to see in what respects our Codes are faulty, where they are too rigid, and where they are too lax; to still further investigate the vexed question of large works as against small works, and of relief concentration as against relief dispersion. We shall have to examine the

rival merits of relief establishments, and of unconditional
gratuitous relief when the rains break. We must consider
how far sudden and excesssive mortality is to be explained
or prevented. We must ascertain the best means of bringing home relief, in the form of revenue remissions and
suspensions, with the greatest promptitude and directness
to the people. We must investigate and report upon the
various public works that have been undertaken in the
course of the recent famine, and must provide for the execution of a continuous programme of preventive works in
the future.

In this connection I would remind my hearers that the
last Famine Commission in their report devoted much
attention to the matter. Unfortunately the recent famine
came upon us before their recommendations had had time
to bear fruit; and in the rush and hurry of the overwhelming calamity of the past year, works had often to be im-
provised so to speak in a moment, to meet the demands of
a particular area, whether the work was or was not likely to
be of permanent value. Against this danger we shall require to guard by insisting upon the methodical preparation
of district programmes, and upon the formation of provincial branches, to be charged with this special duty. Railway earthwork has been pretty well exhausted for the
present. More roads exist than can be properly kept up.
But there are few parts of the country where works for the
storage of water are not practicable. They may not, probably will not, be directly remunerative. But if such a
work will conduce to greater security of the crops, and if it
can be maintained at a moderate cost, it is just the sort of
work which should be taken up or kept in hand for an
emergency. No direct programme of relief should be considered complete until every possible irrigation or water
storage scheme in the district has been examined, until a
definite opinion has been come to as to its practicability
and utility, and until detailed plans and estimates have been
prepared for every accepted scheme. Such works will not

fall within the category of the vast productive irrigation projects such as have been executed in many parts of India. These are only possible amid certain physical surroundings, in the alluvial plains of the Punjab and the North-Western Provinces, in the deltaic tracts of Madras and Sind, and within the dry zone of Burma. All the possible schemes of this character are well known, and are gradually being undertaken. Tank storage again is not everywhere practicable. It is often found impossible to construct new tanks without injuring those already in existence ; there is risk of water-logging the soil, and the water-supply is apt to fail altogether, and to run dry at the very moment when it is most wanted, namely, in time of famine. Nor are the average results of works of this description that have already been carried out very favourable. It is possible to reclaim land for cultivation at a cost that is too heavy. On the other hand, it would seem that the underground storage of water might be more widely and systematically undertaken, and that a more generous policy might be adopted towards the con-struction of wells. All these are matters which we should investigate and set on foot before the next famine comes. The annual rainfall of India we can neither regulate nor forecast. The social habits of the people we cannot alter in a decade, or in a generation. But if we can neither prevent nor cure, at least we can do a good deal by way of precaution.

There is one recommendation that was made by the last Famine Commission which should, I think, be of value to us in our policy of preparation, inasmuch as it has since received the sanction of the Secretary of State. This was the proposal that the cost of investigating and preparing new projects falling into the class of protective works should form a charge against the annual Famine Grant. Hitherto such preliminary outlay has been chargeable to the ordinary Public Works head of the provincial budget, and this has no doubt deterred the provincial Governments in the past from expending money in investigating projects for canals and irrigation reservoirs, which might prove, on examination, to be impracticable, and which, even if practicable, would have to stand over indefinitely until required for purposes of famine relief. There are other respects in which I think that the Famine Grant might be turned to better account in carrying out its original object than is at present the case; but I have not time to deal with them now.

I must apologise to Council for having detained them so long. But a famine such as we have lately experienced is not an every day or an every year occurrence. It cannot be met with a sigh, or dismissed with a shudder. It is a terrible incident, an abiding landmark, in the history of the Indian people. As such, its management and its study impose a heavy responsibility upon those of us who are charged with the government of this great dependency. It is with the object of demonstrating to the Indian public that in the administration of the recent famine, we have not been unworthy of our trust, and that this year of strain and suffering will not have passed by without our profiting by its lessons, that I have made this speech.

## PUNJAB LAND ALIENATION BILL.

### 19th October, 1900.

[At a meeting of the Legislative Council of the Governor-General of India at Simla, on the 19th October 1900, a lengthened debate took place on the Punjab Land Alienation Bill on the motion that the Reports of the Select Committee on the Bill be taken into consideration. Four amendments, brought forward by the Hon'ble Kunwar Sir Harnam Singh, were subsequently discussed, and negatived. On the motion that the Bill be passed (which was agreed to by the Council) His Excellency the President spoke as follows :—]

When the Government of India utilises its legislative power to pass what is certainly a drastic, and has been described in the course of these debates as a revolutionary, measure, affecting any subject, but more particularly affecting the land, there are two questions as to which it should, in my opinion, satisfy itself. The first is—Has the existence of an evil, calling for legislative interference, been established? The second is—Is the particular legislation proposed the right remedy?

The first of these questions we had answered to our own satisfaction a year ago. A careful study of the reports and returns, extending over a period of more than 30 years, had convinced the Government of India that the alienation of land in the Punjab, practically initiated by the British power after annexation, is progressing with increased and alarming rapidity ; that in consequence of this progress land is passing away from the hands of the agricultural classes whom it is our policy to maintain upon it, and into the hands of classes or persons who, whatever the part that they may play in the economy of agrarian life, are not, in our judgment, either necessary or desirable as landholders ; and that consequently a grave political as well as economic danger threatens the province, which it is the bounden duty of Government to avert. Nothing that has occurred in the interim has tended to shake our confidence in the substantial justice of this conviction. On the contrary, I think that it has been strengthened by the evidence that has since poured in. We have been told, it is true, that there can be no political danger in leaving things as they are, because the discontent of the Punjab peasantry is never likely to take the form of active rebellion. I should be sorry to think that our political objections to a continuance of the *status quo* were supposed to be based upon such fears as these. It is not a disloyal peasantry that we apprehend. It is a despondent, debt-ridden, expropriated, and impoverished land-owning class, particularly a class recruited from the stable and conservative elements so forcibly described by the Hon'ble Mr. Tupper, which would be both a source of weakness to the province, and of alarm to the State. Again, it has been said to-day that the *sowkar* is a very useful and even indispensable factor in rural life, who is quite content if he secures his reasonable profits, and has no *à priori* appetite for land. So far as I can see, the model money-lender whom I have described, and whose utility I do not dispute, will not be at all injured by this Bill. The *zemindar* will still require money, and the *bunia* will continue to provide it. But it is the Shylock, who insists upon his pound of flesh, and who, under the existing system, is in the habit of taking it in land, because it is the one security which his debtor can furnish, at whom we aim. A money-lending class I fully believe to be essential to the existing organisation of agrarian life in India; but we do not desire to see them converted into land grabbers, either voluntary or involuntary, at the expense of the hereditary occupants of the soil.

I do not, therefore, feel any doubt as to the seriousness of the malady which we have been called upon to diagnose, and for which, if we value our responsibility, it is our duty to prescribe. But there arises the second question, whether we have, or have not, adopted the right prescription.

Now there is one objection that has been raised to our Bill, which would equally apply to any Bill. It has been said that social customs and institutions cannot be changed by arbitrary dispositions, either of law or executive authority; that they should be allowed to work out their own salvation;

and that, in the process of what is described as evolution, but is in reality only blind and irresponsible abnegation of control, the desired reform will some day come. With me this argument carries no weight; for it is the argument, both of the optimist, in so far as it cheerily but thoughtlessly assumes that things, if left to themselves, will come right in the end, which I may observe in nine cases out of ten is not the case; and of the pessimist, in so far as it contends that Governments ought not to attempt to solve problems, because their solution is hard; while it is also in direct violation of historical facts. If successive British Governments had contentedly accepted the proposition that social and agrarian evils are not to be rectified by legislation, where, I wonder, would the boasted advance of the 19th Century have been? How would the men in our coal mines, the women and children in our factories, ever have secured the full protection which they now enjoy? Would Labour have emancipated itself from the all powerful control of Capital? Had they not been guaranteed by Legislative enactments, where would the valued privileges of compensation for improvements, compensation for accidents, compensation for disturbance, have been? Even in India itself how should we have built up the fabric of social and agrarian rights without the instrumentality of the law? Finally, as regards this particular case of land in the Punjab, I do not see how there can be anything immoral or revolutionary in taking away or modifying a privilege which it is proved beyond possibility of doubt was for the most part one of our own arbitrary creation. If it is an improper thing to diminish or destroy proprietary rights in land because it involves an interference with the course of nature, equally was it an improper thing to create them as we did 50 years ago, when they did not already exist. You cannot apply the argument at one end of the scale, without admitting it at the other. This is the answer to the plea of inviolable promises and inviolable rights that was put forward to-day by Sir Harnam Singh. The objections in principle to legislation of this description may, therefore, I think, be disregarded.

There remains the question whether this particular Bill and the methods to which it proposes to give the sanctity of law, are the best remedy that could ¡have been devised. I have been a good deal struck in the discussion both in Council and in print, by the absence of any alternative prescription. Inaction, I may point out, is not an alternative. It is only an evasion of responsibility. It does not, of course, follow, because no other suitable or likely remedy has been pointed out, that ours is the sole or the right one. Such a contention would be both illogical and foolish. But given an evil which all admit, if the method of cure or rather of prevention which is suggested by the responsible physician is questioned, either by the patient or by the public, the onus, I think, lies upon the latter of indicating a better plan. The fact that in the present case no such rival panacea has been forthcoming leads me to claim that the Government proposal, whether it be sound or unsound, at any rate holds the field.

I now turn for a few moments to the Bill itself. It will not be denied that we have proceeded with the various stages of its growth and enactment, with singular care and deliberation. The Bill in its original shape was the outcome of years of patient study. In the form which it has now finally assumed, it also bears the impress of repeated reference, of diligent reconsideration, and of an anxious desire to meet, in no dogmatic frame of mind, the criticisms whether of expert authority or of public opinion. We should, I think, have been very obstinate and unwise had we adhered to every clause, or even to every leading feature of the Bill, as introduced last year. It was emphatically a case in which a responsible spirit was called for, and in which some concession was required to the arguments of opponents, not for the mere sake of compromise, but in order to bring the measure into closer harmony both with the feelings of the community and with the needs of the case. It is in such a spirit that the Bill has been conducted through Committee by the Hon'ble Mr. Rivaz, on whose behalf it will, I am sure, be admitted by all of his colleagues that, if he has been clear as to where to stand firm, he has also known exactly how to conciliate and where to yield. As a result of the labours of the Select Committee, for which I must, on behalf of the Government of India, thank all its Members, the Bill now emerges a more efficient, a more elastic, and therefore a more workable measure. In the old Bill, for instance, the Revenue Officer's authority for every permanent alienation of land was made obligatory even in cases of merely formal sanction to alienation between non-agriculturists. Now this sanction has been wisely dispensed with. Next, we have extended the maximum period of mortgage, when made by a member of an agricultural tribe outside his tribe or group of tribes, from 15 to 20 years; we have added another form of mortgage which is likely to prove both serviceable and popular; and we have given power to the Local Government to prescribe, in case of necessity, yet other variations. These are only a few among the many changes, and, as I think, improvements, which have been introduced into the Bill. I do not say that they have converted it into a perfect measure. I have seen enough of agrarian legislation in the British Parliament to know that it never attains perfection, that it often fails in what are thought in advance to be its most certain effects, and that strange and unforeseen consequences ensue. No doubt our Bill will not differ from English or Irish Land Bills in this respect. Some of its provisions will not do what is expected of them. Others will meet with a surprising and unexpected vogue. That is the fate of all experimental legislation; and that we are making a great experiment I for one have never denied. Given the desirability of making it, which I have already argued, the utmost that we can do is, as far as possible, to anticipate every likely consequence, and to graft upon it the wisdom of the most expert intelligence.

There are some features in the Bill upon which I admit that the arguments are very evenly balanced. It has been said, for instance, that we have drawn the restrictions too tight, that the phrase "agriculturist" is too narrow and inelastic a term, and that there should be no restriction upon dealings between members of that class. I am not insensible of the danger of unduly narrowing the market for the compulsory vendor, or again of excluding as a purchaser the *bonâ fide* cultivator who may not happen to fall within the agriculturist definition. But, on the whole, I think that, in these respects, we have gone as far as prudence and the main principles of our legislation allow. The embarrassed land-owner should find a sufficiently wide market within the limits of his tribal group ; while the category of agriculturists is, as has been shown, neither so rigid nor so exclusive as has sometimes been assumed. Money-lenders are inside as well as outside it ; nor need the credit of the debtor be permanently impaired for lack of a partner to the desired transaction.

As regards the future of this legislation, I will not be so rash as to prophesy. I should be treading upon too uncertain ground. One thing only I will predict, namely, that the gloomy forebodings of its opponents will not be realised. The case for the Opposition, as I may call it, has been stated upon a previous occasion in this Council, and again to-day, as well as in a printed Minute of Dissent, by the Hon'ble Sir Harnam Singh. If we are to believe the opinions which he has expressed or recorded at different stages, and I quote his actual words, the majority of the peasant proprietors of the Punjab are to be reduced by this Bill to a state of serfdom worse than that of the Middle Ages ; it is to be followed by the impoverishment of millions of men living upon the soil ; it is to doom the people to perpetual misery, and to destroy their happiness and contentment ; British prestige will be rudely shaken ; agricultural credit will be destroyed ; and the progress of the province will be retarded for at least 50 years.

Every age and every epoch has had its Cassandra ; and I do not complain of my hon'ble friend for donning the familiar garb. I venture, however, to think that if his superlatives had been fewer his invective would have been more convincing, and that his vaticinations will be found to have been a good deal exaggerated. If this be so, I am confident that no one will be better pleased than the Hon'ble Member himself. I will not rush to the opposite extreme. I have no intention of claiming that universal peace, or prosperity, or affluence will settle down upon the land in consequence of this Bill. Far from it. There are many questions as to the future to which I should hesitate to give a confident reply. Will this measure really secure to the agricultural tribes of the province the full possession of their ancestral lands ? Will it restrain them from reckless borrowing ? Will it save them from the mesh of the usurer ? Or, while protecting them from usurers of other castes, will it hand over the feebler and less thrifty units in the class to the richer and more powerful members of the tribe ? Or, again, will it effectually divorce the money bags of the province from the one form of investment which has always been dear to successful speculation ? It would require a keener insight than mine to answer such questions with any certainty. It may be permissible, however, to anticipate that while all of these consequences will to some extent ensue, no one will follow to the exclusion of the others. The monied classes, the *nouveaux riches*, will still have their opportunity of obtaining land, but not on such easy terms as in the past. The agricultural tribesmen will not all in a moment be converted to frugal or provident habits ; but the opportunities and the temptations of borrowing will, it is hoped, be less. The weakling and the spendthrift will still go under, and his possessions will pass to his stronger brethren. But the transfer will be more frequently to men of his own tribe or tribal group, and less frequently to outsiders who are not connected either with the traditions or with the traditional occupation of the province. The transition will not be abrupt or sensational. It will be enough if, though gradual, it is sure. I shall myself watch the venture with the warmest sympathy and interest, not merely because I have been head of the Government of India at the time when this Bill has passed into law, not because I know it to have been framed with the most conscientious regard for the public interest ; but because it is the first serious step in a movement which is designed to free the agricultural classes in this country— the bone and sinew of our strength—from an incubus which is slowly but steadily wearing them down.

## RAJKUMAR COLLEGE, RAJKOT.

*5th November,* 1900.

[On Monday afternoon, the 5th November 1900, the Viceroy, accompanied by Lady Curzon and His Excellency's Staff, distributed the prizes to the students of the Rajkumar College. A large gathering assembled for the occasion, including the Ruling Chiefs of Kathiawar, while the young students, or Kumars, numbering 48, were dressed in the costumes of the different States and families to which they belonged.

In opening the proceedings, Mr. Waddington, the Principal, gave an interesting account of the history of the college, in the course of which he said that, originally established for the sons of Kathiawar Chiefs, it had extended its influence beyond the limits of the province, and nearly one-third of those on the rolls were recruited from Guzerat. Lately they had had additions from the Deccan and Dharwar. He thought His Excellency's intimate knowledge of the life of the great public schools and universities of England would give added weight, if such were needed, to his counsel, for His Excellency would be able to appreciate the difficulty of the endeavour to transplant and foster what was best in the traditions of the English public schools and colleges among young India, without impairing that affection for their home and country which must always be the spring of useful citizenship.

At the conclusion of the address the Kumars went through an excellent programme of songs and recitations, after which His Excellency distributed the prizes, and then addressed the assembly as follows :—]

*Your Highnesses, Chiefs, Ladies, and Gentlemen :—* Between two and three years ago, before I came out to India as Viceroy, there was placed in my hands a book containing the addresses that had been delivered by an English Principal to his pupils in an Indian College. The College was the Rajkumar College at Rajkot, in which I am now speaking ; the author of the addresses was the late Mr. Chester Macnaghten. I had not till that time been aware either of the existence of the College, or of the name of the Principal. But from what I read I formed the opinion that here was an institution which, in spite of some discouragement at the start, and amid many drawbacks and obstacles, was doing a noble work for the rising generation of the princely and aristocratic families of Kathiawar and Guzerat ; and that it had in its first Principal a man of high character, of lofty ideals, and with a peculiar gift for exciting enthu-

siasm. Mr. Macnaghten has since died, after a service of
26 years as the head of this College, with which his name
will always be associated, where now before the entrance
his statue stands, and which his ideals may I hope for long
continue to inspire. But he has found a worthy successor
in Mr. Waddington, to whose interesting address we have
just listened, and who carries on the work of the College
upon the same liberal and progressive lines. In such hands
its future should be as secure as its past has already been
fruitful.

Gentlemen, a year ago when I was at Rajkot I visited
this place and was shown over the buildings by Mr.
Waddington. Unfortunately the College was then in vaca-
tion, and only a few of the Kumars were in residence. Still
I was enabled to understand the internal economy of the
College, and to grasp the principles which regulate both the
physical and the mental tuition of the boys. You may
judge what a pleasure it is to me, who am an old public
school boy and college man myself, to see you all here
to-day, upon the occasion of your annual Prize Distribution
or Commemoration Day, to have listened to your recitations which seemed to me to be most excellently done, to
be invited to hand the prizes to the successful competitors
of the past year, and to say a few words to the assembled
Kumars. One feature of these functions I will, however,
spare you. I do not propose to tell the boys who have not
won prizes on the present occasion that they are just as
clever and as good as the boys who have, though this is the
customary form of encouragement to administer, because
it is obviously not the case. Neither will I tell you that
your education, when you leave this college, is not ended,
but is only just beginning ; because I assume that you are
sufficiently intelligent to know that already. Nor will I say
that you should henceforward act in a manner worthy of
the traditions of the College, because if this institution has
existed for 30 years without producing in its students the
*esprit de corps* of which I speak, nothing that I can say

would now inculcate it, while it would be doubtful whether in such a case the place itself was worthy to exist at all. I prefer to make a few observations to you connected both with the present position of the College, and with the future that lies before those who have passed through its courses.

To me it is quite clear that the Rajkumar College demands, just as I think that it also deserves, the continued support and confidence of the Chiefs. It was by their contributions and princely endowments that this institution was started. By their donations were built the lecture rooms, and living quarters, and halls. They have given the prizes and medals which it has been my good fortune to distribute to-day. No assistance was rendered by Government either in the construction or in the maintenance of these buildings. The Political Agent in Kathiawar is, I believe, the Chairman of the Governing Council; and undoubtedly the advice which an experienced officer like Colonel Hunter is in a position to give you must be invaluable. Indeed but for the exertions of one of his predecessors, Colonel Keatinge, in all probability the College would never have sprung into being; while later incumbents of the post, such as that capable and sympathetic administrator, Sir James Peile, have sedulously watched and encouraged, its growth. On the other hand, while you cannot dispense with this form of aid and guidance, it is upon the continuous interest and liberality of the Chiefs themselves that the future of the College must in the main depend. If they continue to give their support it will flourish. If they are apathetic, or indifferent, or hostile, it will dwindle and pine. From this point of view I was very pleased to hear of the wise step by which a number of the Ruling Chiefs, most of whom have themselves been educated in the College, have lately been associated with its government, by being placed upon the Council. They are bound to its interests by the double tie of old fellowship and of responsibility as members of the ruling order; and in their hands, if they do their duty, its future should be safe.

At the present moment I believe that no fewer than 12 out of the 32 Ruling Chiefs of Kathiawar have been educated at Rajkumar ; and I am not paying either them or the College any undue compliment when I add that they are among the most enlightened and capable of their class. (*Applause.*) Of course we cannot compel every Chief or Thakor to send his sons or the cadets of his family here. There were a large number who resented the apparent wrench to social habits and Native traditions at the beginning. Some have never yet quite relinquished this suspicion. There will also always be a certain number of parents who will prefer private tuition for their sons, or education at the hand of Native teachers, or a course of study abroad. I would not interfere with their discretion : each parent has his own ideas about the bringing up of his boys ; and I can conceive nothing worse than to force all fathers or all sons into the same mould. You would get a very dismal and flattened-out type of character as the result. Nevertheless, broadly speaking, I would appeal to the ruling families of Guzerat and Kathiawar, and indeed of the Bombay Presidency as a whole, to continue their support to this institution, and to send their sons and grandsons here ; both because I think that the system itself is sufficiently elastic to escape the dangers of stereotyping a particular form or cast of character of which I have spoken, and because I do not entertain a doubt that the general influence of the College has been, and is, of inestimable value in its influence upon the well-being and good government of the province.

And now a few words to the young men and boys whom I see before me. Mr. Waddington used what seemed to me to be wise words when he spoke of the difficulty of transplanting the best in Western thought and tradition without impairing the Indian's love for his home and his country. That is, and has been, and will continue to be, the difficulty all along. There can be no greater mistake than to suppose that because in this, and the other Chiefs' Colleges in Northern and Central India, the boys are given the nearest equivalent of which India admits to an English public school education, the aim is, therefore, to turn them outright into English boys. If this College were to emancipate its students from old-fashioned prejudices or superstitions at the cost of denationalisation, I for one should think the price too heavy. The Anglicised Indian is not a more attractive spectacle in my eyes than the Indianised Englishman. Both are hybrids of an unnatural type. No, we want the young Chiefs who are educated here to learn the English language, and to become sufficiently familiar with English customs, literature, science, modes of thought, standards of truth and honour, and I may add with manly English sports and games, to be able to hold their own in the world in which their lot will be cast, without appearing to be dullards or clowns, and to give to their people, if they subsequently become rulers, the benefit of enlightened and pure administration. Beyond that we do not press them to go. After all, those Kumars who become Chiefs are called upon to rule, not an English but an Indian people ; and as a prince who is to have any influence and to justify his own existence, must be one with his own subjects, it is clear that it is not by English models alone, but by an adaptation of Eastern prescriptions to the Western standard that he can hope to succeed. Chiefs are not, as is sometimes imagined, a privileged body of persons. Gol Almighty has not presented them with a *sunnud* to do nothing in perpetuity. The State is not their private property ; its revenues are not their privy purse. They are intended by Providence to be the working bees and not the drones of the hive. They exist for the benefit of their people ; their people do not exist for them. They are intended to be types, and leaders, and examples. A Chief at whom any one of his subjects can point the finger of scorn is not fit to be a Chief. If these views are correct, it is clear that this College has a great and responsible work devolved upon it, since it ought to be, not merely a school of men, but a nursery of statesmen ; and that the worst way of discharging its trust would be to rob its pupils of their surest claim to the confidence of their countrymen—which is this, that, though educated in a Western curriculum, they should still remain Indians, true to their own beliefs, their own traditions, and their own people.

Therefore, Chiefs and pupils of the Rajkumar College, I say this to you—and it is my parting word—be loyal to this College ; spread its name abroad, and see to it that in your own persons it is justified before men. While you are proud to acquire the accomplishments of English gentlemen, do not forget that you are Indian nobles, or Indian princes. Let the land of your birth have a superior claim upon you to the language of your adoption, and recollect that you will be remembered in history, if you earn remembrance, not because you copied the habits of an alien country, but because you benefited the inhabitants of your own. If I could feel that my poor words were likely to waken in any of the young men whom I am addressing, and who may be destined to high responsibility in the future, a keener and fresher sense of duty than has perhaps hitherto occurred to his mind, the pleasure which I have experienced in coming here to-day, which is already great, would be tenfold, nay a hundredfold, greater. (*Loud and prolonged applause.*)

## DURBAR AT RAJKOT.

### *6th November*, 1900.

[ At 10 A.M. on Tuesday, the 6th November 1900, His Excellency the Viceroy held a public Durbar in the Connaught Hall at Rajkot for the reception of the Ruling Chiefs and Sardars of Kathiawar. A large number of British officers, Civil and Military, and many ladies were present, including Her Excellency Lady Curzon, and Mrs. Hunter. The Kumars of the Rajkumar College, with their Principal, were also present and occupied seats on the daïs. The Viceroy having been received with the usual ceremonies at the Durbar Hall and having taken his seat on the daïs, the formal presentation of the Chiefs to His Excellency was proceeded with. When the introductions were completed His Excellency rose and addressed the Durbar as follows : —]

*Chiefs and Durbaris of Kathiawar:*—Since I have been in India nothing has surprised me more than that none of my predecessors has ever found the time or the interest to visit Kathiawar. When I came here last year for the first time to show my sympathy with the Chiefs and people in their misfortunes, and to acquire some personal know-ledge of the manner in which they were combating the great famine, I was much struck with the peculiar charac-teristics of this Province. It seemed to me to present in an unusual and attractive combination the features of an old territorial nobility, standing midway between the para-mount power and their own subjects, and bound by solemn obligations to both, with abundant evidences of modern enlightenment and civilization. It is a country that pos-sesses sites of ancient and historic sanctity which are yearly visited by thousands of pilgrims. It contains a number of small but flourishing cities and ports. It is intersected by a network of railways, having indeed nearly as many miles of railroad as it has of first-class roads. It is well endowed with hospitals, schools, dispensaries, and the latest symptoms of progress ; and it can boast of some of the most cultivated Chiefs on the western side of India. My visit last year was a short one ; but I resolved that I would take the first opportunity of returning, in order to improve my acquaintance with Kathiawar at a more favourable moment in its fortunes.

That is the object, Chiefs and Durbaris, with which I have invited you here to-day. I desire to convince you that, though you live in a somewhat unfrequented corner of the Indian continent, which is away from the principal lines of movement and of travel, your welfare and your concerns are very dear to the Government of India (*applause*), and that the head of that Government takes a personal interest in your well-being. (*Applause.*) It is an object of ambition to me to meet, and to make the acquaintance of, as many of the Chiefs and Nobles of India as may be possible during my time. I like to know them, in order to realize their position, its advantages, and its difficulties—for it is attended by both—and to appreciate their work. For this reason I make longer tours and wider diversions from the beaten track than some of my predecessors have done. I have spoken of the benefits that result to myself, in the shape of increased knowledge, of greater sympathy, and of a more intelligent discrimination. I trust it is not vain to hope that they may be, in some measure, reciprocal.

To many of the Chiefs and Thakors residing in out-of-the-way parts, and only brought into contact with the agents of the Local Government, the Government of India in all likelihood appears a dim and mysterious force, that is seldom materialised into positive existence. To all such I should like to invest it with greater nearness and actuality. I wish them all to realize that the Viceroy is not merely the figure-head of Imperial authority, but is also their counsellor and friend. (*Applause.*) If he comes and sees them, and speaks to them in their own homes, they may realize that they are not overlooked or forgotten ; but that they play their part—and it is no mean part—in the collective administration of the Empire.

Chiefs, the feature in Kathiawar that struck me most last year was the recognition among you—in spite of minute subdivisions of territory and jurisdiction, and of many possible causes of disunion—of common interests and a corporate life. The Chiefs of this Province reminded me in fact of a sort of mediæval Guild constituted for purposes of co-operation in matters where the interests of all coincide, or can best be advanced by common action. You have your annual meeting of Karbharis, a species of Local Diet or Parliament, to discuss the administration of the corporate funds. You have the fund known as the States General Fund contributed in fixed proportions by all. You have a system of railways owned by the different States and managed by a body upon which the various proprietors are represented. Recently a convention has been concluded to facilitate the administration of justice between the several States, each enjoying a separate jurisdiction of its own. At Rajkot this corporate existence is typified by the existence of a number of admirable buildings or institutions, designed for the welfare, not of one State only but of all. There is the Rajkumar College where I spoke yesterday ; there is a Training College for school teachers ; there is a Hospital for women ; and a Chemical Laboratory. These institutions have been founded by the liberality of individual Chiefs or donors, and they are administered out of the joint funds. I had the advantage of visiting the majority of them last November.

During the past year you have had presented to you an opportunity of displaying both collective energy and individual zeal in your encounter with the most serious famine that has afflicted Kathiawar since the famous visitation of 1812-13. Two days ago, I was inspecting the celebrated inscriptions of the Emperor Asoka on the great rock that lies at the foot of the holy hill of Girnar. In those edicts were enjoined upon the people of the Emperor's vast dominions the lessons of charity, and piety, and the sparing of animal life. It is gratifying to me to think that these precepts were not forgotten in the recent distress by the Chieftains of Kathiawar. They have, with rare exceptions, risen to and fulfilled their obligations.

Under the able leadership, and subject to the constant advice of Colonel Hunter (*applause*) in whom the Kathiawar States are about to lose a firm friend, and the Government of India a most valued officer, all the machinery of famine works, and famine relief, with which we are now so sorrowfully familiar, has been forthcoming in this Province. Works, and poor-houses, and hospitals, have everywhere been open throughout the past twelve months; the infirm and destitute have been cared for; and a means of livelihood has been offered to every man, woman, and child, who had the hands with which to work. Advances have been made to help the ruined cultivators to start again in the world; and in the generous interpretation of their obligations several of the Durbars have not shrunk from incurring heavy debt.

Here, as elsewhere, the famine has taught us lessons which should be valuable for the future. It is sometimes disputed whether railways or irrigation are of greater service in the prevention of drought. This is a very barren and senseless controversy, since it may fairly be said that neither is a preventive at all. On the present occasion the famine struck a great many areas in India where there were excellent railway communications and abundance of tanks. But the water dried up in the tanks just when it was most wanted; while the railways, though they could bring grain to the famished peasant, could not make it germinate in the parched and moistureless soil. But I venture to say that if there is a part of India where both railways and tanks efficiently demonstrated their value in time of famine, it was here. The railways poured in grain from the distant markets with a regularity that kept prices at a point consistently lower than in the dearth of 1897; and if there was any Chief in Kathiawar who was diffident about a forward railway policy, I think that his doubts must have been removed during the past summer. He has only to look up the records of the great famine of 1813, when Kathiawar parents sold their children, and men killed and devoured each other, to realize the full meaning and value of a constant and cheap supply of grain. As regards irrigation the experience of the past year should also have taught you the necessity of storing rain water in irrigation tanks wherever the contours of the land are favourable. Such works will not obviate famine, but they will greatly mitigate its intensity.

There is another lesson which I hope that the famine has taught you, and that is the positive necessity of laying by a portion of your incomes in every year as an emergency fund to meet these sudden and terrible strains. The fascination of living up to one's income is well known in all classes and countries ; that of living in excess of it is also not without its votaries among the Native Chiefs. But, when famine ensues, a rude awakening comes, for the exhausted treasury is powerless to meet the demands that fall thick and fast upon it, and the State is thereupon burdened with a debt that may hamper its development for years to come. On the present occasion there has necessarily been a considerable recourse to loans. The finances of some of the States, greatly to their credit, were able to weather the storm without any recourse to outside assistance. But they were in the minority. In these circumstances the Government of India has rendered you every possible assistance in its power. I have myself kept a most careful watch upon the requisitions of the Native States in all parts of India where there has been famine ; and I think it will be conceded without demur that, whilst avoiding prodigality or slackness, we have neither grudged nor stinted our help. (*Applause.*) Apart from the loans made by local funds in the Kathiawar Agency, which amounted to nearly 11 lakhs, and to the private loans guaranteed by the Agency, which amounted to 40½ lakhs more, the Imperial Exchequer has lent to the Kathiawar Chiefs sums of money which, excluding such loans as have already been repaid, represent a still outstanding debt of nearly 50 lakhs of rupees. I think, therefore, it may truly be said that we have all pulled, heartily together—Imperial Government, Local Government, Chiefs and people—in order to tide the Province over its dark hour of misfortune ; and in this loyal co-operation in the cause of suffering humanity, I find solace in contemplating the trials of the past year, as well as a hopeful augury for the future.

Chiefs of Kathiawar, I should not come here as Viceroy of India were I not confident that my message to you was one of sympathy and encouragement. (*Applause.*) You are the representatives in this part of India of a system of which no one is a more convinced supporter than myself. (*Applause.*) I am a firm believer in the policy which has guaranteed the integrity, has ensured the succession, and has built up the fortunes of the Native States. (*Applause.*) I regard the advantage accruing from the secure existence of those States as mutual. In the case of the Chiefs and the States it is obvious, since old families and traditions are thereby preserved, a link is maintained with the past that is greatly cherished by the people, and an opening is given for the employment of native talent which the British system does not always or equally provide. But to us also the gain is indubitable ; since the strain of Government is thereby lessened, full scope is provided for the exercise of energies that might otherwise be lost to Government, the perils of excessive uniformity and undue centralization are avoided, and greater administrative flexibility ensues. So long as these views are held—and I doubt if any of my successors will ever repudiate them—the Native States should find in the consciousness of their security a stimulus to energy and to well doing. They should fortify the sympathies of Government by deserving them. To weaken this support would be to commit a suicidal crime.

If the Native States, however, are to accept this standard, it is obvious that they must keep pace with the age. They cannot dawdle behind, and act as a drag upon an inevitable progress. They are links in the chain of Imperial administration. It would never do for the British links to be strong and the native links weak, or *vice versâ*. As the chain goes on lengthening and the strain put upon every part of it increases, so is uniformity of quality and fibre essential. Otherwise the unsound links will snap. I, therefore, think, and I lose no opportunity of impressing upon the Indian Chiefs, that a very clear and positive duty devolves upon them. It is not limited to the perpetuation of their dynasties or the maintenance of their *raj*. They must not rest content with keeping things going in their time. Their duty is one, not of passive acceptance of an established place in the Imperial system, but of active and vigorous co-operation in the discharge of its onerous responsibilities. When wrong things go on in British India the light of public criticism beats fiercely upon the offending person or spot. Native States have no right to claim any immunity from the same process. It is no defence to say that the standards there are lower, and that, as censors, we must be less exacting. That would be an admission of the inferiority of the part played by the States in the Imperial scheme, whereas the whole of my contention rests upon its equality, and the whole of my desire is to make it endure. In Kathiawar it is gratifying to me to think that these propositions, which I regard as the fundamental principles of Indian statecraft, are generally accepted, and that the majority of the Chiefs and Thakors whom I am addressing are already engaged in putting them into operation.

Holding the views that I do, I welcome nothing more than the opportunity of giving such encouragement as lies in my power, as the head of the Government, to those who have it in their power so greatly to help and encourage me. I hope that I have not been remiss in this direction. There has never been a year in Indian history when the loyalty of the Indian princes and people has been more triumphantly vindicated. Aroused by the stirring events that were passing in foreign lands, and thrilled by the sense of partnership in the British Empire they have freely offered their troops, their resources, and their own swords, for the service of the

Queen both in Africa and in Asia. It has not been possible to accept all these offers, and indeed in South Africa it was not possible to accept any. But the war in China has presented me with an opportunity of showing how greatly Her Majesty, and Her Majesty's Government, have valued these demonstrations of loyalty, which I was not slow to seize. It will always remain a source of pride to me to have been instrumental in persuading them for the first time to send the Imperial Service Troops outside of these shores. I frankly admit that it is not the purpose for which those contingents were originally raised. They were offered by the Chiefs, and accepted by the Government, to take part in the defence of India. But the opportunities that we can furnish for their employment in India, or upon the Indian frontiers, are few and far between ; and when the Chiefs came forward and begged to be allowed to share the larger responsibilities of Empire, and to vindicate their loyalty upon a wider field (*applause*), he would, I think, have been a cold and narrow-minded pedant who, on such an occasion, would have damped their enthusiasm or waived aside the offer. It was, therefore, with peculiar pleasure that I urged Her Majesty's Government to accept the offers, so spontaneously and generously made, and that I have since superintended the despatch to China of picked contingents from the Imperial Service Forces. Kathiawar did not take part in this particular contribution. But, in the South African war, her Chiefs had already shown the spirit by which they were animated. From the relatively small forces of Imperial Service Cavalry that are maintained by the Chiefs of this Province, Junagadh gave 15 horses for South Africa, Bhavnagar contributed 100 horses, as well as 50 to Lumsden's Horse, and the Indian Government borrowed 35 horses from Jamnagar. You have, therefore, not been left outside of the great movement that has, throughout the past year, swept, like a mighty tide, from one end of the British Empire to the other. You have contributed your share to its volume and its strength. I am now arranging for the despatch to

Australia of a selected contingent of 100 officers and non-commissioned officers of the Native Army and the Imperial Service Troops, who have been invited by the Colonial Authorities as the guests of the new Federal Government of Australia to assist on the 1st January at the inauguration of the new Commonwealth. It will be a fitting thing that on a day when a new off-shoot of the British Empire is to start into official being, the festival should be graced by the presence of those who will symbolise the part that has been played in the consolidation of the parent fabric by Indian swords and by India's sons. (*Applause.*) It is, therefore, in a memorable year, Chiefs and nobles of Kathiawar, that I have come hither to address you ; a year that has been one of anxiety and suffering ; but that has also been one of noble devotion, and the recognition of a higher aim. If it has been a sorrow to me to observe the pain and the anguish, it has also been a comfort to note the spirit which they have engendered, and to have touched the instrument whose chords have thrilled to so sublime a tune. I take this opportunity, therefore, through you, of thanking the Chiefs of India for the part that they have played in a year that fitly marks the passing away of an old century and the opening of a new. A hundred years hence, may it be in the power of some successor of mine to speak to the Indian princes and people in language of similar good cheer and congratulation. (*Loud applause.*)

### ADDRESS FROM THE BOMBAY MUNICIPAL CORPORATION.

*8th November,* 1900.

[The Viceroy arrived in Bombay on the evening of the 7th November and, on the following day, His Excellency, accompanied by Lady Curzon, Lord Northcote, and the members of Their Excellencies' Staffs, drove in State from Malabar Hill to the Town Hall, to receive an address of welcome from the members of the Bombay Municipal Corporation. The Hall, which was beautifully decorated, was thronged with an enthusiastic audience, who rose as Their Excellencies entered and greeted them with loud and prolonged cheering.

The Corporation in their address said that seldom had the heart of the country been so stirred on the advent of any Viceroy as it had been on the advent of Lord Curzon. The kindling words in which His Excellency announced the noble and statesmanlike policy he had determined to pursue, the moral earnestness which seemed to pervade his lofty determination, his uncommon intellectual equipments, matured by varied experience, and informed by personal acquaintance with and knowledge of the country, as well as many other countries of the East, above all the generous and cultured love which seemed to animate his breast, loving " India, its people, its history, its government, the absorbing mysteries of its civilisation and life," all combined to give the people assurance that it was their good fortune to secure in His Lordship a statesman and an administrator to whom the destinies of the Indian Empire could confidently be entrusted at a time when it was passing through many and great troubles. The address went on to refer to the severity of the visitations of famine and plague which had afflicted the Presidency, and the splendid way in which His Excellency had redeemed the pledges he had given when first he took upon himself the duties of Viceroy. No acts of his Lordship's administration had, however, been more appreciated than those directed to secure an impartial administration of justice. The sum of the impressions created by His Excellency in the short period of two years might be expressed by saying that he had won their hearts, captured their imaginations, and extorted the respect and admiration of the whole country. Referring to matters of local import, they begged His Lordship to consider whether it would not be right and expedient, considering the financial difficulties of the city, to make the whole plague expenditure a charge on the financial resources of the country as a whole. The imperial character of the plague expenditure could scarcely be denied, and it would be only just that the whole country should help in providing against an emergency of so special a character. Reference was made to the effort made for the re-sanitation of the city, and confidence was expressed that advice and help would be given by the Government of India in securing the completion of the scheme. The Corporation eulogised Lord Northcote for the interest he had shown in the work. The address concluded by offering a sincere welcome to the

Viceroy and Her Excellency Lady Curzon. The Viceroy on rising to reply was received with a fresh outburst of cheering. When it had subsided His Excellency spoke as follows :—]

*Your Excellency, Members of the Municipal Corporation, Ladies and Gentlemen:*—When I landed at the Apollo Bunder, in December 1898, I little thought that, within less than two years' time, I should twice again visit this great city. Still less could I have anticipated that within so short a period of my assuming office, I should be deemed worthy of the honour of such a ceremony as that of this morning. It is, as you know, the trials and the sufferings through which Bombay has been passing that have brought me back into this Presidency upon the two occasions to which I have referred. It is your gracious recognition of the motive that actuated these visits—a recognition very characteristic of the warm-hearted Indian people *(cheers)*—that has brought me to this Town Hall to-day, and has made me the recipient of the exquisite and sumptuous gift in which the address that has just been read from the Bombay Corporation will henceforward be enclosed.

You have said with truth in this address that the troubles by which India in general, and this Presidency, perhaps, more particularly, have been afflicted, have gone on increasing and multiplying during the past two years. Lord Elgin thought that he had coped with the worst famine of the century : we have now gone through a worse. It was hoped that Plague would soon be extirpated from your midst; but it has grown into an annual visitor, whom, in spite of all our efforts, we can neither altogether elude nor defeat. True, there is one calamity which we have been fortunate enough to escape during our time of trial, and that is warfare in our own territory or upon our frontiers. Indeed, the most striking incident in recent Indian History, the most conclusive testimony to the loyalty of her princes and people, and the most absolute demonstration of the reality of the peace that we have enjoyed,—is the fact that

we have spared between 20,000 and 30,000 soldiers from
the Indian Army for the wars being waged elsewhere by
the forces of the Queen, and have thus not unhandsomely
borne our share in that great outburst of Imperial sentiment
that has marked the disappearance of the old century and
the opening of the new. (*Cheers.*)

You have been good enough to speak in terms of praise
of the manner in which we have met our misfortunes. I
do not take this praise to myself. For instance, in our
struggle with Plague and Famine, the Captain can do little
but frame his orders, see closely to their execution, keep
an eye upon every part of the field, and encourage his men.
When, therefore, I see or hear the head of the Government
praised for the efficiency or liberality of the measures that
have been taken, or given the credit for their success, I feel
almost a sense of shame.

For I think of all the accumulated advice and experience
that have been freely placed at his disposal by those who
know so much more than he ; and I remember the brave
men who, with no reward to hope for, and no public
applause to urge them on, have for month after month,
whether in the scorching heat, or through the soaking rains,
spent of their energy and life-blood and strength in fighting
the real battle, wherever the enemy threatened, or the
worst danger lay. Theirs is the true credit ; and it is only
on their behalf, and as their official head, that I can
accept with contentment what I could not, without injustice,
appropriate to myself. (*Cheers.*)

Gentlemen, before I pass on to the larger aspects of
British policy and rule, upon which you have touched, I
will refer to the local questions which you have submitted
to my notice. They have taken the customary form of an
appeal to the Government of India for more funds.
(*Laughter.*) Indeed, I sometimes wonder if a Viceroy, as he
goes round on tour, were, at each place at which he halts,
and is addressed by an impoverished and importunate
Municipality (*laughter*), to accede to only one-half of the

petitions for financial assistance that he receives, what sort
of welcome he could meet with from his colleagues in the
Government when he got back to Calcutta. (*Laughter.*)
The first event, I take it, would be the arrival of a letter
from his Finance Minister handing in his resignation.
(*Laughter.*) The second would be the receipt of a telegram
from the Secretary of State to say that a Royal Commission
was about to sail from England to investigate the straits to
which the Government of India had been reduced by a
too blind philanthropy on the part of its Chief. (*Laughter.*)
Inasmuch as I desire to escape both these forms of rebuke,
and, as you, Gentlemen, having expressed your interest in
the continuance of my administration, cannot possibly wish
that I should incur them, you will understand how it is
that even the most tender-hearted of Viceroys on tour is
perhaps more often compelled to refuse petitions than he is
able to grant them.

The first of the particular requests that you have placed
before me on the present occasion is that the whole of the
Plague expenditure, direct and indirect, of the City of
Bombay—and I presume that the same argument would
apply to Poona, Belgaum, Dharwar, and any other spot
that is similarly afflicted—shall be taken over by the Imperial Government. I think that this proposition has only
to be frankly stated for it to be seen that, under no system
of finance and with no succession of surpluses that it is
possible to conceive, could such an obligation be accepted
in advance by the Supreme Government. When a terrible
calamity, such as plague, befalls, drying up resources and
arresting progress all round, it is emphatically a case for
generous and open-handed treatment, but it is not necessarily a case for wholesale exemption. Such generosity,
I venture to assert, the Bombay Government received
from the Government of India, when we made up our last
budget, to a greater extent than has ever before been shown
by the Government of India to a Local Government. We
took over the whole of the direct Plague expenditure of

L.C.S.                                             23

the Bombay Presidency for the past financial year and we framed our estimates for taking over the whole again in this, the charge in the two years amounting to over 25 lakhs of rupees. In addition, we assumed the whole charge for the research laboratory at Parel, amounting to $2\frac{1}{2}$ lakhs in the two years. More than this, we made up to the Bombay Government the entire excess of all provincial expenditure over the provincial balance. Why, when we had our debate at Calcutta the Bombay representatives, and my friend, the Hon'ble Mr. Mehta, was one of them, were almost clamorous in our praises. (*Laughter.*) We were the most liberal Government of the century. (*Laughter.*) But now I come here and I find that the grateful children of the Government of India are already beginning to ask for more : and that they are not above squeezing the parent who has shown such overwhelming proofs of her affection. (*Laughter.*) Gentlemen, your request is one with which I most cordially sympathise, but which it is out of my power to concede.

The next respect in which you hint, not obscurely, at assistance from the Government of India is the contemplated purchase of the Tramways of Bombay by the Municipality. This is a subject with which I do not feel competent to deal adequately. But it occurs to me that, before the point is reached at which it may be necessary to discuss the question of borrowing powers or the methods of a loan, there are a number of questions to which it is desirable that a reply should first be given. They are, firstly, whether the purchase is desirable in the interests of the City and its inhabitants ; secondly, if so, what would be the probable cost ; thirdly, whether the borrowing powers enjoyed by the Corporation would be best exercised for such an object ; fourthly, whether the citizens of Bombay would be prepared to submit to additional taxation for the pleasure of owning their Tramways ; and, fifthly, whether the administration of these lines would be most efficiently and economically conducted by the Corporation. (*Cheers.*)

When an answer has been given to these questions we shall all be in a better position to discuss the financial expedients that may be required.

There is a third matter of local interest for which you bespeak my attention without, as I understand, at the present juncture formulating any request. This is the carrying out of your great scheme for the improvement of the city, in which I take the deepest interest, both from what I heard of it from Lord Sandhurst, when I was here a year ago, and from the part that I was permitted to play in the inaugural function at Agripada last year. I was not myself aware, until I received your address, that the Act was taken in hand at a time of panic or was passed into law in a hurry. On the contrary, I thought that few measures had been longer on the anvil, or had been more anxiously considered both by the Local Government, and by the Government of India. I do not, of course, know in what direction amendment may be required. But it will be the natural inclination of the Local Government to minimise all chances of friction between the Municipality and the Trust; while Municipal interests are already so largely represented upon the latter that they should not fail to secure becoming attention. In any case, the solution of such matters may safely be left in the hands of your present Governor (*cheers*), to whom you have paid so high and deserved a tribute in your address (*cheers*), and who, in a marvellously short time, has established an enduring hold upon the esteem and affection of all classes in the Presidency. (*Loud cheers.*)

This, Gentlemen, exhausts the list of local topics to which you have called my attention. I now pass to the wider field of thought that has been opened by the terms of your address. You have spoken of the impartial administration of justice, not so much in the Law Courts, since they are independent of official control, as in the exercise of executive and administrative authority, as having been the guiding principle which I have borne in view. It is true that I have tried never to lose sight of the motto, which I set

before myself when I landed here, namely, to hold the scales
even. (*Cheers.*) Experience has shown me that it is not
always an easy task ; but experience has also convinced me
that it is always the right one. (*Cheers.*) If a man is to
succeed in carrying it out, he must expect sometimes to be
abused, and frequently to be misunderstood. By one party
he will be suspected of disloyalty to the rights of his countrymen ; by the other of imperfect sympathy with its aspirations or its aims. Every one appreciates the advantages of
an umpire. But there are always some players of the game
who think that the main duty of that functionary is to give
their own side in. I sometimes note symptoms of this tendency in India. One side interprets an act of justice as a
concession to clamour ; the other laments that it does not
straight away secure all the articles of an impossible charter.
These little drawbacks may sometimes worry and sometimes impede ; but they do not for one moment affect the
conviction with which I started two years ago, and which I
now hold, if possible, more strongly still (*cheers*), that it is,
by native confidence in British justice that the loyalty of
the Indian peoples is assured. (*Cheers.*) Any man who,
either by force or by fraud, shakes that confidence, is
dealing a blow at the British dominion in India. (*Loud
cheers.*) If to justice we can add that form of mercy
which is best expressed by the word consideration, and
which is capable of showing itself in almost every act and
incident of life, we have, I think, a key that will open most
Indian hearts. A century ago there was a very intelligent
and observant French priest, the Abbé Dubois, who spent
thirty years of his life in India, and who wrote a most
admirable book upon the manners and customs and feelings
of the people. I quote him because, as a foreigner and a
Catholic missionary, he could not be suspected of any undue
partiality to the British Government, and because as a
Frenchman, with the memory of the French dominion in
India, of which the British arms had only recently robbed his
countrymen, fresh in his mind, he could hardly be expected

to bless the conquerors. This was what he wrote :—
"The justice and prudence which the present rulers display
in endeavouring to make these people less unhappy than
they have hitherto been, the anxiety which they manifest in
increasing their material comfort ; above all, the inviolable
respect which they constantly show for the customs and
religious beliefs of the country ; and, lastly, the protection
which they afford to the weak as well as to the strong—all
these have contributed more to the consolidation of their
power than even their victories and conquests." ( *Cheers.*)
Gentlemen, the era of victories and conquests is now over,
but the other and more abiding source of strength remains ;
and an English Viceroy may safely repeat at the dawn of
the 20th century what the French Abbé said at the opening
of the 19th as to the character and motives of British rule
in this country.

I was asked the other day whether, after two years' Indian
experience, I had at all changed the views to which I have
often given expression regarding the importance of the part
that is played by India in the structure of the British Empire.
My answer was that they have not been changed, but confirmed.   In the writings of a political philosopher I recently
came across the astounding utterance that "there is more
true greatness within a two miles' radius of the British
Museum than in the whole of Asia." In my judgment this
was a very arrogant and a very foolish remark.   It is a proposition to which history is every day giving the lie.   It is
the Eastern and not the Western problems that continue to
agitate the world, and Asia has still to be disposed of before
the intellect of the West can exclusively concentrate itself
upon Western concerns.   The past year has, moreover,
been one which has conspicuously demonstrated the part
that is played by India in the Imperial system.   It was the
prompt despatch of a contingent of the Indian Army a year
ago that saved the Colony of Natal. (*Cheers.*) They were
Indian regiments who accomplished the rescue of the Lega-
tions at Pekin. (*Cheers.*) We have rendered this service

to the Empire in a year when we have been distracted by famine and plague, and weighed down by our own troubles. (*Cheers.*) If our arm reaches as far as China in the East, and South Africa in the West, who can doubt the range of our influence, or the share of India in Imperial destinies? (*Cheers.*)

I have also been asked, since I came to India, whether I was at all disillusioned with my work, and whether my love for the country had at all diminished. Again my answer has been in the negative. The work to be done seems to me just as important; the opportunities for doing it to be even more numerous. More than a century ago the orator Burke remarked that the British Empire in India was an awful thing. He had not seen it; he had only studied it from a distance of 10,000 miles; and the Empire of which he spoke was but a fraction of that which now acknowledges the sway of the British Crown. If it was awful a hundred years ago, what is it now? Is not the custody of the lives and fortunes of 300 millions of human beings—between one-fourth and one-fifth of the entire human race—a responsibility that might daunt the boldest energy, and sober the flightiest imagination? Moreover, they are not members of one race, or even of a few races, but of a swarm of races. As I go about on tour and see the people in the streets, the difference to the outward eye is enormous. A street crowd in Lahore does not present the smallest resemblance to one in Bombay. Bombay is utterly unlike Calcutta. And what is this external difference compared with that within, the difference of feature compared with that of character and creed? And again, what are any of these differences compared with those that separate the huge Indian majority from the microscopic British minority to whom their rule has been committed? These are the common-place, every-day, reflections that are borne in upon me every hour that I spend in this country. How can a man be anything but absorbed, anything but enthusiastic about such a work? Every day some fresh thing seems to require doing, some new subject demands to be taken up. There is, I know, a school who say, "Leave well alone. You are in the unchanging East. Don't worry yourself unduly about reform. No one ever wanted to be reformed in Asia." Gentlemen, do you remember the answer of the economist Turgot, in the reign of Louis XVI of France? He was always pushing fresh reforms. Perhaps if he had pushed even more, there would have been no French Revolution. When his friends came to him and said that he was going ahead too quickly, he replied— "You forget that in my family we do not live beyond fifty." If this was the defence of the French statesman, may not a Viceroy of India reply to a similar charge, "You forget that I only have five years (*cheers and laughter*)—five years within which to affect the movement, or to influence the outturn, of this mighty machine?" For such a task every year seems a minute, every minute a second,—one might almost say that there is hardly time to begin.

There is one respect in which it has been my constant endeavour to infuse an element of the modern spirit into Indian administration. I can see no reason why, in India as elsewhere, the official hierarchy should not benefit by public opinion. (*Cheers.*) Official wisdom is not so transcendant as. to be superior to this form of stimulus and guidance. (*Cheers.*) Indeed, my inclination where Government is attacked is not to assume that the critic must inevitably be wrong, but that it is quite conceivable that he may be right. In any case I enquire. Of course, it is easy to disparage public opinion in a continent like India ; to say that it is either the opinion of the merchants, or the Civil Service, or the Army, or of amateurs in general ; or, if it be native public opinion, that it only represents the views of the infinitesimal fraction who are educated. No doubt this is true. But all these are the various sections upon whose intelligent co-operation the Government depends. (*Cheers.*) To the masses we can give little more than security and material comfort in their humble lives. They have not reached a pitch of development at which they can lend us anything more than a passive support. But the opinion of the educated classes is one that it is not statesmanship to ignore or to despise. (*Cheers.*) I do not say that one should always defer to it. If a ruler of India were to adopt all the wild suggestions that are made to him by the various organs of public opinion, he would bring the fabric of Indian Government toppling down in a month. (*Laughter.*) Neither must he carry deference to the pitch of subordination ; for I can conceive nothing more unfortunate, or more calamitous, than that Government should abrogate one jot or tittle of its own responsibility. A benevolent despotism that yielded to agitation would find that, in sacrificing its despotism, it had also lost its benevolence. All these are truisms which no one will dispute. But there remain a multitude of ways in which Government may endeavour, and in my opinion should endeavour, to enlist public opinion upon its side. It can harken to both sides of a case ; it can take the public into its confidence by explaining what to the official mind seems simple enough, but to the outside public may appear quite obscure ; in framing its legislation it can profit by external advice, instead of relying solely upon the arcana of official wisdom. It can look sympathetically into grievances instead of arbitrarily snuffing them out. These, at any rate, are the principles upon which I have tried, during the past two years, to conduct the administration of India, and they seem to have been so far successful as to win approval at your hands. (*Cheers.*)

Gentlemen, let me add, in conclusion, that it is in the power of public opinion in this country to repay the compliment. It can very materially strengthen the hands, and lighten the task, of the head of the Government. If he is so fortunate as to possess its support, there are many things which he can undertake, which otherwise he would be tempted to leave on one side. A Prime Minister in England is strong in proportion to the Parliamentary strength of his party. A Member of Parliament is strong in his constituency in proportion to the size of his majority. In this country, if the analogy may be pursued, all India are the constituents of the Viceroy, and his strength is proportionate to their allegiance. (*Cheers.*) I gladly welcome this opportunity of conveying my thanks to those who have so ungrudgingly given me their confidence during the short time that I have held my present post; and I hope that it may be continued to me, easing my burden and invigorating my spirits, until the end. (*Loud and prolonged applause.*)

## BANQUET AT TREVANDRUM.

### 21st *November*, 1900.

[The Viceregal party left Cochin on the afternoon of the 19th
November, and, after spending the next day at Quilon, travelled all
the following night in house boats by a canal, which connects the
lagoons along the coast, to Trevandrum, which was reached on Wednesday
morning, the 21st November. Here their Excellencies met with a
very cordial reception from the Maharaja of Travancore, and from the
people of Trevandrum, the streets of which for several miles to the
Residency were densely thronged and brilliantly decorated. In the
evening the Maharaja gave a banquet at the Durbar Hall in honour
of Their Excellencies, to which over 60 guests were invited. At the
conclusion of dinner His Highness proposed the health of the Queen-
Empress, after which he proposed the health of Their Excellencies in the
following terms :—

" *Ladies and Gentlemen*,—It is now my most pleasing duty to propose
the health of my noble and illustrious guests, Their Excellencies Lord and
Lady Curzon.

Travancore has never before had the proud distinction of welcoming the highest representative of our august Sovereign. I feel most
deeply the privilege and the honour which His Excellency has accorded
to me and my loyal people, by his very kind acceptance of my invitation to this remote corner of India, at so much personal inconvenience and discomfort ; and my gratification is immeasurably enhanced
by the gracious presence of Her Excellency. I offer their Excellencies,
with every feeling of respect, my warmest and heartiest welcome.

In His Excellency, we have not only the most trusted councillor
of the great Queen-Empress, but also a distinguished member of one
of the historic families of England, an intrepid explorer, a profound
scholar, an accomplished author, a brilliant orator, and an acute and large-
hearted statesman.

His Excellency came out to India equipped with considerable
knowledge of the country and inspired by a genuine love for ' its people, its
history, its Government ; the absorbing mystery of its civilisation and
life.' With what conspicuous ability, courage and success he has grap-
pled with the complex problems that confronted him at the outset
of his Viceroyalty ; what genuine sympathy he has displayed by his
own munificence and evoked by his personal influence for the sufferers
from the dire visitations which have afflicted several parts of India ;
how cheerfully and bravely he has borne the burden and heat of
the day, in his anxiety to safeguard human life and alleviate human
suffering ; what striking proof he has given of firmness and justice,
and of regard for the aspirations, feelings, and even the scruples of the
people—are matters of contemporary history, and could not have failed

to impress the countless millions under His Excellency's rule with the conviction that their welfare is his supreme end and aim.

His Excellency is still in the full flower of manhood, and we may confidently hope that the past, which is an unbroken record of brilliant achievements, is but an earnest of the future, and that the Viceroyalty, which itself is considered 'the crowning reward of a life's ambition,' would prove but a stepping-stone to a still brighter and more glorious career.

I regard the honour of this visit as a practical proof of His Excellency's great personal kindness and of his gracious recognition of the unswerving loyalty and attachment of this ancient State to the British Crown. Many are the marks of kindness and consideration which my State, my House, and myself have received from the paramount Power. While gratefully referring to two of the recent acts of such kindness, the sanction accorded for the extension of the South Indian Railway to Quilon, and the increase of my personal salute, I beg to tender my special thanks to His Excellency for the ready recognition of the step taken to perpetuate my House.

I count myself especially fortunate that I have the opportunity of coupling with the toast of His Excellency the name of a lady whose gracefulness, amiability, and boundless hospitality, have won for her universal esteem and admiration.

Ladies and Gentlemen, I ask you to pledge, with enthusiasm and all honours, a bumper to the health of Lord and Lady Curzon."

The toast was very heartily received. In responding to it the Viceroy spoke as follows :—]

*Your Highness, Ladies and Gentlemen,—*Since I have been in India I have had a great desire to visit the State of Travancore. I have for many years heard so much of its exuberant natural beauties, its old-world simplicity, and its Arcadian charm. Who would not be fascinated by such a spectacle? Here Nature has spent upon the land her richest bounties ; the sun fails not by day, the rain falls in due season, drought is practically unknown, and an eternal summer gilds the scene. Where the land is capable of culture, there is no denser population : where it is occupied by jungle, or backwater, or lagoon, there is no more fairy landscape. Planted amid these idyllic scenes is a community that has retained longer than any other equally civilised part of the Indian continent its archaic mould ; that embraces a larger Christian population than any other Native State ; and that is ruled by a line of indigenous princes

who are one in origin and sentiment with the people whom
they govern. Well may a Viceroy of India find pleasure
in turning hither his wandering footsteps ; good reason
has he for complimenting such a ruler and such a State.
(*Applause.*)

His Highness the Maharaja has proposed my health in
a speech that contained so much of personal eulogy that
it is difficult if not impossible for me to reply. Perhaps,
however, as he is so familiar with my good points, such as
they are, he will allow me to say that I am not less aware
of his. (*Laughter and applause.*) I know His Highness by
repute as a kindly and sympathetic and diligent ruler,
whose merits have been tested, and for whom the affection
of his people has been continuously enhanced, by fifteen
years of prosperous administration. I know him to com-
bine the most conservative instincts with the most enlightened views. Has not the Government of India itself signified in the most conspicuous manner its recognition of his
statesmanship and his services by the addition to his salute
to which His Highness just now alluded ? (*Applause.*)

There are two matters of domestic concern which I
should not like to pass by without mention on the present
occasion. If one of them brings a note of sadness into my
speech, the effect may, I trust, be compensated by the satisfaction which the other may reasonably evoke. The
sorrowful incident is the recent death of the First Prince
of Travancore, an amiable and accomplished prince, a man
of culture, of travel, and of learning, the first graduate I
believe among all the Indian Princes, who seemed destined
to cast a fresh lustre upon the name of the famous ancestor
which he bore. I deeply sympathise with His Highness,
and with his people, upon the premature death of this
gifted member of the Royal House. On the other hand, I
must be allowed to congratulate him upon the steps that
have recently been taken, by renewed adoption, for the
perpetuation of the ruling line. In due time I trust that
the expectations which have been aroused by this interest-

ing event may meet with fulfilment, and that there may never be wanting in the Travancore State a succession of princes, royally born, well nurtured, and qualified by instinct and training to carry on its ancient and honourable traditions. (*Applause.*)

His Highness has alluded in his speech to the contemplated extension of the South Indian Railway to Quilon. I am glad to think that he has encouraged this most important step, which I believe will be fraught with great advantage to his dominions, by an advance of 17 lakhs from the State funds ; and also to congratulate him upon the possession of a large and carefully accumulated balance in the Treasury, which his enlightened zeal will doubtless suggest to him fresh opportunities of utilising for the material development of the country. I am a believer, not in the talent that is laid up in a napkin, but in the talent that is turned to productive employment, and that brings other and more and more talents after it. (*Applause.*)

In one respect His Highness enjoys a position of peculiar responsibility ; for he is the ruler of a community that is stamped by wide racial differences, and represents a curious motley of religions. In such a case a prince can have no higher ambition than to show consideration to the low, and equity, and tolerance to all. In the history of States no rulers are more esteemed by posterity than those who have risen superior to the trammels of bigotry or exclusiveness, and have dealt equal mercy and equal justice to all classes, including the humblest, of their people.

In this category of princes His Highness, who has given so many proofs of liberality of sentiment, may attain a conspicuous place, and may leave a name that will long be cherished by later generations.

Ladies and Gentlemen, I have only, in conclusion, to thank His Highness for the very graceful allusion that he has made to Lady Curzon, who is just as enchanted with all that she has seen in Travancore as I am ; and to ask you all to signify our gratitude for the lavish hospitality extended

to us, our interest in this fascinating spot, and our regard
and admiration for its illustrious ruler, by pledging a full
toast to the health and happiness of His Highness the Maharaja of Travancore.

[The toast was very cordially received.]

## THE MAHARAJA'S COLLEGE, TREVANDRUM.

*23rd November*, 1900.

[On Friday morning, the 23rd November, the Viceroy and Lady Curzon drove to the Jubilee Hall, Trevandrum, where were assembled the students of the Maharaja's College, who presented His Excellency with an address of welcome. Their Excellencies were received by the Maharaja and the College authorities, and, amid the hearty cheers of the students, were conducted to seats on the daïs. The address, which was read by one of the students, opened with expressions of welcome and loyalty, gave some details of the history and working of the College, and concluded with the remark that when it might please Her Majesty to call the Viceroy to a still higher position, it would be an abiding memory with them that they once stood face to face with a statesman whose name would live in history. The Dewan of the State then announced that, to commemorate Lord Curzon's visit to Trevandrum, the Maharaja had decided to endow an annual prize of Rs. 500 for an original essay on a scientific subject to be called "The Maharaja of Travancore's Curzon Prize." The announcement was received with much applause.

The Viceroy then addressed the assembly as follows :—]

*Your Highness and Students, past and present, of this College,*—I am sure that we have all heard with the utmost pleasure the announcement that has just been made by the Dewan of the gracious and liberal manner in which His Highness desires to commemorate my visit to this place. (*Cheers.*) It is very characteristic of the enlightenment and generosity of His Highness (*cheers*), and the opening which will thus be afforded to the accomplishments and abilities of the young men who have studied in this College, even though it does not serve to remind them in the future of the occasion of the foundation of the prize, will at any rate be a valuable incentive to their own studies.

Nothing gives me greater pleasure in my tours through India than to visit those institutions where the young men are being educated who in the next generation will have the fortunes of the country to so large an extent in their hands. Whether the College be one that is training up young Chiefs and Nobles who will one day be called upon to manage estates or to govern peoples, or whether it is qualifying young men who, although not of such exalted birth, will yet supply the officials, and administrators, and public servants of the future, the spectacle is equally interesting, and equally inspiring. When we are at school or college ourselves we hardly appreciate what a work is going on among us. We are absorbed in the friendly rivalry of passing examinations, or winning prizes, or excel-ling in games. Our horizon seems somewhat limited because it is so full. But all the while every minute of the time that we spend in the school or the college is leaving its mark on our character. We are being influenced from day to day by the boys we associate with, by the masters, who teach us, by the books that we read, by the half unconscious effect of our surroundings ; and almost before we have realised it, we are turned out into the world with a stamp fixed upon us which remains with us for life, and models all our conduct and actions, much as the face of a monarch is minted for all time upon the surface of a coin. I think it is a good thing, therefore, now and then, for boys and young men while at school to pause, and to question themselves as to the die that is being stamped upon them, and as to the sort of currency, whether of gold or silver or copper, or some less pure alloy, of which they are going to be turned out.

Pupils of this College, if there is one word of advice that I might offer to you, it would be this : Do not all fall into the same mould. Do not passively accept the same metal. Take as a stimulus to your imaginations the singular variety and interest of the State to which you belong. I do not suppose that in the whole of India there is a State with greater fertility of resources, with more picturesque sur-roundings, with ampler opportunities for work, with richer prospects of development. (Cheers.) It is also a very patriotic State. (Cheers.) Every good Travancorean thinks that there is no place like Travancore, no college like Trevandrum College, no prince like His Highness the the Maharaja. (Loud cheers.) Well, with this fund of patriotism to start with, which should supply you with the initial impetus, I say : Look about you while you are still young, test your own aptitudes, and make up your mind as to the manner in which, when your academic education is over, you are going to serve the State. Do not follow each other like a flock of sheep, who always go through the same hole in a hedge. The hedge of public duty is capable of being pierced in a great many places, and the man who wants to get·to the other side will waste a lot of precious time if he waits for his turn in the crowd that is trying to scramble through a single aperture.

Think therefore of the number of openings that lie before you in this interesting country. I believe that there is scarcely a single branch of scientific or technical education which is not capable of practical and remunerative pursuit in Travancore. There are minerals to be unearthed ; there is an abundant water-supply capable of being converted into different forms of energy and productiveness ; there is an infinite richness of plants and timbers and trees ; there are manifold varieties of animals and birds and insects ; there are all sorts of experiments that might be made in agriculture ; there are numerous openings for public works ; there is ample scope both for the student who prefers the laboratory, and for the out-of-door explorer or engineer.

In all these pursuits I am sure that you will meet with the warmest encouragement from the European professors of this College, and not less from His Highness the Maharaja himself. (*Cheers.*) The Maharajas of Travancore have always been distinguished for their patronage of learning. His Highness takes the keenest interest in the welfare of this College ; and I have heard with pleasure, with reference to one of the fields of study that I mentioned just now, *viz.,* that of Scientific Forestry, that he is sending four pupils to study in the Forest School of the Government of India at Dehra Dun. (*Cheers.*)

Let me urge you, therefore, students of this College, to remember that your patriotism, which is an excellent thing, should not stop at thinking or saying that there is no such

place as Travancore—otherwise it would be a rather cheap
and tawdry sentiment—but should proceed to the discovery
of independent channels by which you may each of you
render service to the State.    You have a great many
advantages offered to you in this institution.    You have
admirable tuition.    You have, I believe, the second best
library in the whole of the South of India. You have a generous and paternal Government.    You are in fact a very
highly favoured and rather a spoiled body of young men.
(*Laughter.*)  For all this you owe some return. Take therefore a line for yourselves ; get out, of the rut ; the whole of
life is not summed up in the office or in the law-courts ;
remember that while the opportunities for a career can be
and are here provided for you by others, the career itself
will be what the individual makes it ; and let the ambition
of each one of you be to say when his time is nearing its end
that, whether in a small way or in a great, he has rendered
an appreciable service to his native country. (*Loud and
prolonged cheers.*)

## ADDRESS FROM THE TANJORE RECEPTION COMMITTEE.

*29th November,* 1900.

[Leaving Trichinopoly early on Thursday morning, 29th November, the Viceregal party arrived an hour afterwards at the Tanjore Railway Station, where His Excellency was received by Mr. Andrew, the Collector, and the municipal officials of the district, and by the members of the Tanjore Reception Committee, who, on behalf of the Tanjore Municipal Council, the District Board, and the people of the district in general, presented His Excellency with an address of welcome. The address, which opened with an expression of grateful appreciation of Lord Curzon's generous sympathy with the people of India, was one of considerable length, and the points discussed in it were dealt with by His Excellency in his reply, which was as follows :—]

*Gentlemen of the Reception Committee,*—I cannot be insensible of the encouragement contained in the opening paragraphs of your address, for which I beg leave to tender to you my hearty thanks. I have received in addresses already presented elsewhere during the past few days so many generous references to the recent actions and administration of the Government of India, and I have already so frequently and gratefully acknowledged them on behalf of my colleagues as well as myself, that I will on the present occasion say no more than that the value of the tribute has been materially enhanced by the subscription to it of so important and progressive a centre as Tanjore. I will pass directly from this subject to the topics affecting your own interests and desires, which you have placed before me with much clearness and which constitute the major part of your address.

The first of these relates to the maladministration of temple endowments and funds in Southern India, which you declare to be scandalous, and concerning which legislation was recently proposed by the Madras Government, but was not accepted by the Government of India. I have not been able to refresh my memory by reference to the official documents ; but I carry very clearly in my mind the general line of reasoning which led us to this decision.

The British Government in India has always, and on principle, adopted an attitude of intense reluctance to interfere
with the religious customs or institutions of the people.
Indeed this may almost be described as a solemn pledge
that has been given before the world.  It takes a great deal
to induce us to modify this attitude ; for it must be remembered that. while the effect of such a departure may be locally
both popular and excellent, yet the departure from an established principle in one case suggests the possibility of
similar though not necessarily analogous departures in
other cases ; and the likelihood of these may produce a
wider distrust or commotion than the justifiable deviation
in a particular case may do good.  The matter cannot be
looked at solely from the point of view of a particular
set of temples or of a particular religion.  The circumstances
of other religious buildings, and the feelings of other
creeds, must also be taken into account ; and in order to
relieve Madras of an admitted scandal, we must run no
risk of shaking the public confidence in our engagements.
I remember, too, feeling some doubt as to whether the
machinery of committees that it was proposed to set up by
the Madras Bill was not open to serious objection, and might
not provoke fresh risks.  Nor was it established to our
satisfaction that full advantage is taken of the existing
machinery of the law to check a corruption which I believe
that the educated classes unite in deploring, but which is
probably regarded with greater indifference by large
sections of the population.  These were the main reasons
that induced the Government of India to withhold its assent
from the proposed legislation.

The next subject to which you have called my attention
is the recent Revenue Settlement, by which, exclusive of
local cesses, an increase of 12 lakhs has been made in
the revenue collected from the district.  I do not know
that I am called upon to say much upon the subject on
the present occasion, seeing that you promise me a full
statement of your grievances at an early date.  But I may

note, in passing, certain considerations which should, I think, not be left out of sight. In the first place, it was, I believe, a matter of common assent that the district was under-assessed before the recent settlement. Secondly, I am informed that abundant opportunities were offered by the Local Government to the landholders and to all those interested for stating their objections before the introduction of the new scheme. Thirdly, the enhanced revenue, of which you complain as excessive, has, I gather, during the years that it has been in operation, been collected without friction and without oppression. These considerations, however, even if they be beyond dispute, will not prevent me from paying respectful attention to any memorial that may reach the Government of India.

Thirdly, Gentlemen, you have expatiated upon the drawbacks arising from a defective drainage system and an imperfect distribution of water. A good deal of evidence has been placed before me in connection with this subject ; and I believe it to be true that the district stands in need of engineering works which, as regards drainage, will widen the channels in their lower reaches, and provide new drainage channels to relieve congestion ; and, as regards distribution, will reduce the number of minor branch channels, and regulate the water-supply in the remainder. Several of these works are, I understand, being taken in hand : others are in course of preparation, the most important of which is the scheme mentioned by you for bringing under cultivation parts of the Pudukotta Taluk. As soon as the engineers are agreed as to the *modus operandi*, I hope that progress may be made. It seems to me from all I have heard that there is in this neighbourhood a suitable field for extensive and remunerative irrigation works in the future.

Before I leave the subject of water, I must be allowed to congratulate you upon the good results that have ensued from the waterworks that have been constructed for this town, and which have sensibly diminished the deaths **from** choleraic attacks ; and to join in your aspiration that the Local Government may be able, by timely help, to assist other municipalities in procuring the same blessings.

Finally, as regards Light Railways, I should have been disappointed had you not furnished me with an opportunity of congratulating you upon the great success that has already attended the enterprising venture of the District Board, and upon the interesting development that is about to be taken in hand. I have always regarded the successful construction and remunerative working of the 54 miles of existing line by the Board as one of the most important displays of municipal enterprise which recent years have witnessed in India ; and I have held it up to public imitation as far away as in the remote parts of Assam. You possess a country in this neighbourhood which is peculiarly adapted to the extension of light or narrow-gauge railways ; partly because the land is so flat and construction is therefore cheap, partly because the maintenance of metalled roads is so very difficult and expensive, and still more because there are such encouraging prospects of traffic. I wish you all success in the loan that you are about to raise for the extension of your present line, and I congratulate you upon the arrangements by which, with the consent and help both of the Local Government and of the Government of India, you have come into sole possession of a property which you should find a most valuable asset in the future. I cannot give better advice to other Local Bodies who are similarly placed than to follow your example.

Gentlemen, I shall take away with me a very pleasant recollection of your assurances of profound loyalty to Her Majesty the Queen-Empress, and of friendly feeling towards Lady Curzon and myself.

ADDRESS FROM THE EURASIAN AND ANGLO-INDIAN ASSO-
CIATION OF MYSORE AND COORG.

*8th December*, 1900.

[A deputation representing the Eurasian and Anglo-Indian Association
of Mysore and Coorg waited on the Viceroy at Government House, Bangalore, at noon, on Saturday, the 8th December ( being the third of the
deputations received by His Excellency on that day), and presented him
with an address. This after offering a cordial welcome to Their Excellencies dealt generally with the position, claims, and prospects of their community, and concluded by stating that they were deeply thankful to Lord
Curzon for what he had already done for them, and were content to leave
their interests in his hands.

His Excellency replied as follows :— ]

*Gentlemen,*—I am sincerely glad, while here, to meet the
representatives of a community with whose fortunes you
are right in saying that I feel a great sympathy. In doing
justice however to me, I am afraid that you have done an
injustice to my predecessors in the Viceroyalty, in crediting
me with an " unprecedented " interest in your welfare.
No one Governor-General can fall far short of another in
the feelings of anxious consideration, which the spectacle
of a community originating as yours has done and placed as
it is, cannot fail to arouse. While, however, the opportunities
of helping you by advice have been frequent, the chances
of undertaking any practical measures for the amelioration
of your condition more rarely occur.

The first step towards either securing the favour of
Government or benefiting yourselves, is undoubtedly a
candid recognition of the weakness as well as the strength
of your own position, and of the faults as well as the virtues
of the Eurasian character. I have, therefore, been pleased
to listen to the second paragraph of your address, in which
you have, with much honesty and discrimination, defined
your own status, and admitted the conditions that tend
sometimes to isolation, sometimes to despondency, frequently
to internal discord. But I do not suppose that you will
have so correctly diagnosed your state of health without

being prepared to apply the necessary remedies : and of these you are right in pointing to greater unanimity both of opinion and action, as the most important. It is a distressing thing to see a community whose strongest point is certainly not its strength, frittering away what little it may possess in petty bickerings about microscopic things. If all the Eurasian and Anglo-Indian Associations throughout India were united together, if their members were even united among themselves, they might create a single standard of aspiration and agree upon a common programme which would materially advance the collective cause. As it is, in too many cases their energies are dissipated in fighting for different aims, or in resenting the friendly criticisms of those who wish them well.

In this neighbourhood the Eurasian question may be said to possess a special interest, owing to the experiments in agricultural colonisation that have been initiated by the late Mr. White, and by your present respected and worthy Chairman, Dr. Sausman, within a short distance of Bangalore. I have followed with much attention the histories of Whitefield and Sausmond. It will, I think, be generally admitted that the halcyon dreams of a self-contained and self-supporting community, existing by manual labour, possessing its own artificers and workmen, and excluding all competition, were over-sanguine in character, and were incapable of realisation. The original Whitefield was to be the model and pioneer of thousands of similar settlements in other parts of India. Instead it is a single community of not more than 150 souls. In the petty handicrafts and in agricultural labour it is almost impossible for the Eurasian community to compete with the Natives. The latter can work for less, and live for less, and they learn trades more easily. On the other hand, you have succeeded in providing a happy and comfortable home in the pure air and amid healthy surroundings for a limited number of Eurasian and Anglo-Indian families, and for retired pensioners of that race, where they have been able to maintain a higher standard of ease and self-respect than might elsewhere have been found possible. The weak point of the venture seems to me to consist in its restricted application. On the other hand, I see very clearly the danger that, if you expand your numbers too rapidly, you will become not a village, but a suburb, and the native bazar is certain sooner or later to creep in. Perhaps the solution may be found to lie in the repetition of small experiments, rather than in the magnifying of any single colony.

In your concluding paragraph you have expressed your willingness to leave your interests in their entirety in my hands. In so far as I can reasonably and legitimately help you, I will do so. But there are certain things that I cannot do. I cannot create special opportunities or special exemptions in your favour. I have recently seen in the papers what purports to be a reproduction of certain new rules which I am alleged to have issued for your admission to the Government of India Secretariat, as well as of certain secret instructions for excluding natives of India from particular posts for your special benefit. The Press in India knows a good many things that do exist ; but it also knows or affects to know a great many that do not. All I can say is that these rules or these instructions are unknown to me. I am also reported by the newspapers to have created a new class of Extra Assistant Commissioners in Assam to be exclusively reserved for Eurasians. This again is news to me. Some of these posts have been left open to, and may, I hope, be filled by duly qualified members of your community. But the Government of India cannot here or anywhere else constitute a special preserve, into which none but Eurasians may intrude. I have thought it advisable to make these remarks, both to remove from your minds, if it there exists, the impression that Government, in its desire to be fair to you, can anywhere consent to be unfair to others, and also to indicate to you the vehemence of public feeling that would be aroused by any partisanship in favour of one section of the population to the exclusion of another. On the other hand, opportunities have presented themselves to me, and doubtless will again, of forwarding your interests in a legitimate manner, and these, Gentlemen, you may confidently rely upon me to take.

ADDRESS FROM THE KOLAR GOLD FIELDS MINING BOARD.

*10th December,* 1900.

[On Monday, the 10th December 1900, the Viceroy, accompanied by his Staff, and Colonel Robertson, Resident in Mysore, visited the Kolar Gold Fields. Arriving at the Bowringpet Railway Station at 12-45 P.M., His Excellency was driven to the limits of the Fields, where he was met by the principal officials of the Mining Board ; and thence to Major Hancock's bungalow, where he was received and entertained at luncheon by the President and Members of the Board, and afterwards presented with an address of welcome. The Board were fully conscious, they said, that they could offer nothing in the domain of nature or art to attract a visitor, nor could they boast of magnificent scenery or ancient fanes, but they could claim to show a veritable portion of the West, planted, a rare sight, in the heart of the East. They recognised that His Excellency's visit was but one more practical manifestation of his keen and sympathetic interest in all questions connected with industry and commerce. They thanked him for the practical proof of the concern felt by his Government in the successful working of the Fields shown by the loan to the Mysore Government of experienced British officials to increase the efficiency of the Police. His Excellency's attention was drawn to the difficulties that had arisen regarding the purchase of gold by the Indian Mints, and a hope was expressed that he would look into the matter with a view to securing that transactions in gold between the Mints and the public should be conducted under the ordinary conditions of business.

The address was enclosed in a handsome silver casket, the design being in the form of an air receiver. The casket was accompanied by a gold watch-guard weighing four ounces and a half. the gold of which had been contributed by the nine producing Companies on the Fields.

His Excellency replied as follows :—]

*Gentlemen,*—It would certainly have been a great disappointment to me, had I, in visiting this part of India, been unable to include within my tour an inspection of one of the most remarkable fields of British enterprise that can be seen in any part of Asia. When one reflects that only 16 years ago this venture, after a series of disappointments, was on the verge of being abandoned, but that at that historic moment a reef was struck from which over ten millions sterling of gold have since been extracted ; when one hears that every day over 20,000 people are employed upon your mines, and that the total population of the mining camps is between 30,000 and 40,000 ; when one

reads that the output of gold from the mines has already
reached a sum not far short of £2,000,000 in the year, and
in the present year will probably exceed it ; above all, when
one sees the extraordinary sights which have passed before
my eyes this morning—what was once a barren rocky tract
converted into a busy centre of industry and population,
with its forest of chimneys, its great mounds of quartz
sand, its workshops, and engine-rooms, and assay houses
and mills, all throbbing with the measured pulse of machinery, and aglow with the red hot energy of industrial
life ; when, I say, one hears and sees all these things, one
cannot but feel a sense of proud satisfaction at the British
enterprise and capital that have created this great concern.
You have, I think, given a practical refutation to the
saying of the old Roman poet that gold was best when
undiscovered — *aurum irrepertum et sic melius situm.*
The shareholders, to whom five of the mines are now
paying dividends, will not agree with him. The Mysore
Government, which draws nearly £100,000 a year in
royalties from your enterprise, will not agree with him
(*laughter and applause*) ; and I certainly cannot do so ;
for if I did I should not have been made the recipient of
the singularly handsome chain and pendant, fabricated as I
understand from the gold of the various productive mines,
which you have just presented to me, and for which I beg
leave to return my most cordial thanks. (*Hear, hear and
applause.*)

Gentlemen, in your address you have been good enough
to express your gratitude to the Government of India and
to myself for the loan by us to the Mysore Government
of a number of experienced officials from the British service
to assist in the reorganisation of the police and detective
forces in the Gold Fields. I personally took a great interest
in the matter, as Sir John Lambert may have informed
you ; and I am glad to hear that you are satisfied with the
arrangements that have been made. I gather, however,
from what I have heard, that though by these measures

you may be able to impose a salutary and efficient check upon the theft of gold, it will be much more difficult to keep a watch upon the amalgam. Perhaps in this respect you may find it desirable to take such steps yourselves as will supplement the efforts of the Mysore Durbar.

I then come to a paragraph in your address in which you use somewhat strong language. You speak of the conditions under which the Government of India now purchases your gold as being "so inconsistent with modern commercial methods that they cannot be taken advantage of;" and again as being incompatible with "the ordinary conditions of business;" and you ask me personally to look into the matter. There is no need for me, Gentlemen, to give you any such undertaking, seeing that I have already done what you asked many months ago. The circumstance to which you refer was the substitution in the summer of the present year of payment at 60 days, for immediate payment, for the gold bullion received at our mints. Well, Gentlemen, these orders emanated, not, as you seem to imagine, from any lack of sympathy with your own industry, or from any desire to hamper it. They were the compulsory outcome of the financial situation at the period of issue. We were confronted at the time with so large an accumulation of gold in our currency reserve, and with such heavy demands for famine and other purposes upon our cash balances, all of which had to be met in rupees, that we were obliged simultaneously to take steps to reduce the redundancy of gold and to augment our stores of silver. This action was one of various measures adopted with the consent of the Secretary of State for that object; and Indian gold could not be excluded from the application of an order which applied equally to all gold. From a careful study of the correspondence I do not think that the Mining Companies had anything to complain of. The fact is that in all the discussions and arrangements about the purchase by the Government of India of your gold, your agents were trying to do the best for you, and to refrain as far as possible from

committing themselves to anything too definite. At one
moment they actually threatened to do, in your own
interests, what is now apparently represented as a hardship,
namely, to remit your gold bullion for sale to England.
If you, therefore, were so busily occupied in safeguarding
your interests, I do not think that there is any ground of
complaint that the Government of India should pay similar
attention to theirs, which I take leave to say are of an even
wider importance. I shall, however, be very glad if a time
comes when we shall be able to revert to the system of a
more speedy payment. But, Gentlemen, we cannot convert
gold bullion into gold sovereigns until our gold Mint is
established at Bombay ; and for that we have been waiting
for months and are waiting still for certain preliminary
steps that have to be taken in England, and about which
there has been very considerable delay.

In your concluding paragraph you have expressed yourselves, Gentlemen, in terms so warm-hearted and complimentary in their reference to myself, that I cannot sufficiently thank you. It is gratifying to receive the sympathy and
encouragement of a body of one's own countrymen, who,
though they are not concerned, as so many of us are in
India, in the work of Government, are engaged in the
characteristic British task of industrial exploitation. For
myself I can truthfully say, when you so kindly wish me
preferment and success after I have returned to England
later on, that I am too much absorbed in my work out here
to bother myself with thoughts or ambitions about the
future. (*Applause.*) I am quite happy where I am ; and
if during my time I can do some good in this country, and
help forward, to any appreciable extent, the noble cause in
which, in our various capacities, we are all engaged, the
cup of my contentment will be full. (*Applause.*)

Before I sit down, I should like to express my thanks
for the warm welcome that has been extended to me by the
population of the entire Settlement to-day, and particularly
to notice the charming decorations upon the route. I was

also glad to see the local volunteer force, which I understand to be a powerful and efficient body, one of whose representatives I observe at this table, and it has been especially pleasing to hear of the good relations that prevail between the different nationalities and classes who are engaged in so many various capacities upon the mines. (*Loud and continued applause.*)

## ADDRESS FROM THE MADRAS MUNICIPALITY.

### 11th December, 1900.

[Their Excellencies the Viceroy and Lady Curzon and Staff, arrived at Madras on Tuesday, the 11th December, at 8-30 A.M. Sir Arthur and Lady Havelock and the principal officials of Madras were at the Railway Station to receive them. At 11 o'clock the Viceroy, who was accompanied by Sir A. Havelock and Their Excellencies' respective Staffs, received six deputations in the Banqueting Hall of Government House, who presented addresses of welcome on behalf of the Madras Municipality; the Madras Chamber of Commerce; the Mahajana Sabha of Madras; the Anjuman-i-Mufid-i-Ahla-i-Islam on behalf of the Moslem Community of Madras; the Eurasian and Anglo-Indian Association of Southern India; and the Native Christian Community of Southern India. The subjects discussed in the various addresses are dealt with in His Excellency's replies.

Replying to the address from the Madras Municipality the Viceroy said :— ]

*Mr. President and Municipal Commissioners of Madras,*
—In the earlier part of my present tour I halted at the spot where British trade—that frequent though unthinking fore-runner of empire—first acquired a foothold on the Indian continent. It is perhaps not inappropriate that I should spend its concluding stages at the place where Englishmen first became the actual proprietors of Indian soil. Could those adventurous pioneers come to life again, and see to what a noble tree, both here and elsewhere, their precarious seed has grown, they would probably not merely be much astonished at the issue of their labours, but I expect that they would greatly prefer the conditions of modern existence at Fort St. George to the scanty amenities which they then enjoyed, and would soon settle down into excellent members of the Municipal Commission of Madras.

Just as this place is the oldest British possession in India, so also, in a sense, are you the oldest Municipality. For I learn from the records that a Mayor and Corporation were established here as long as 213 years ago. It would perhaps require a slight exercise of historical license to describe you as their lineal descendants, since, for some reason or other, the original Corporation disappeared in the middle portion of its career. But I observe striking and presumably hereditary features of resemblance between you and them in the fact that almost the first act of the Corporation when constituted in 1687 was to approach the Governor with a request to be allowed to raise various taxes, in consequence of its financial embarrassments—a faculty which, judging from the contents of your address to-day, would not appear to have grown rusty in the passage of two centuries. Here, however, I am afraid the parallelism breaks down. For whereas Governor Yale granted all the demands of the infant Corporation without the least demur—there was no Government of India and no orthodox finance in those days—I fear that it has not been possible either for Sir Arthur Havelock or myself to adopt so complacent an attitude.

Gentlemen, after taking what I believe to be perfectly legitimate and well-deserved credit to yourselves for the manner in which, with straitened means, you have conducted your Municipal duties, you proceed to lay before me the difficulties, both practical and fiscal, connected with the carrying out of your great Drainage scheme. It is perhaps scarcely incumbent upon me to follow the prolonged discussion that has been going on between the Local Government and yourselves as to the best and most appropriate sources of local taxation. The ball has been sent backwards and forwards across the net by both parties with a vigour and skill which, having studied the correspondence, I have greatly admired. But I would fain hope that the rally is now in a fair way to come to an end. As I understand, the issue has been considerably narrowed down. The cost of the drainage scheme has been somewhat reduced ; and it now only remains for you, in addition to the Rs. 1,07,000 which are already produced by the new taxes, to raise a further sum of Rs. 1,21,000 a year. Should the proposal of the Local Government to provide this sum by an increase of $2\frac{1}{2}$ per cent. in the water tax be carried into execution, the maximum local rates exacted in Madras would amount to $17\frac{3}{4}$

per cent. as compared with the 15¼ per cent. which you have mentioned in your address. The corresponding figures in Calcutta are 23 per cent., in Bombay 19¾ per cent., and in Rangoon 21 per cent. I know very well, and you know much better than I do, that your circumstances differ in many ways from those of the other Presidency towns. These differences I need not enumerate ; they may be summed up in the admission that Madras is in nearly every respect poorer than its sister cities. Nevertheless I am not sure that, considerable as they are, they are not somewhat unduly reflected in the existing disparity in the percentages of local taxation.

A second subject of discussion between the Madras Government and yourselves is your request for an increase in the Government Abkari contribution. I think that the Governor and his Colleagues are right in drawing a clear distinction between licence fees, which are all that a Municipality may properly levy, and Excise duties, which are the property of Imperial Finance. The loss of revenue which would be entailed by any surrender of the latter would therefore fall in the main, not upon Madras, but upon the Imperial Exchequer ; and I cannot see what would be the point of laying down orders prohibiting Municipalities from levying Excise duties, as the Government of India did long ago, if we were then to wink at their being infringed.

I feel hardly qualified to enter into the vexed question of a contribution to you from Provincial revenues in respect of the Coum. As far as I can see, it resolves itself into this. The Municipality contends that its beneficent activity in respect of drainage will cleanse the Coum. The Local Government contends that it will only prevent the Coum from becoming dirtier than it already is. I could not solve this vexed problem without uttering disparaging remarks about the Coum, from which I desire to refrain. I observe that you describe it in your address as "an unpleasant and unhealthy cess-pool." This language, which is permissible to those who live upon its banks, would I am afraid be regarded as insulting from an outsider. From my recollection of it when I was here 13 years ago, I should prefer to speak of it as a not too salubrious stream.

There is, however, one suggested source of taxation upon which, as it directly concerns the Imperial Government, you are, I think, entitled to my opinion. I observe that you still hanker after a terminal tax upon grain. I will not repeat here what I said upon the point at Karachi in the opening days of my present tour, although your request to-day entirely confirms my anticipations then, *viz.*, that though Karachi claimed that its circumstances and needs were absolutely exceptional, it was tolerably certain that before long I should come across some other Municipality that entertained precisely the same views as regards itself. You know very well that the ground upon which we object to this taxation is that it tends, and must tend, to become a transit duty. In Madras this would almost certainly happen; for the refund on grain exports, which is mostly in small quantities and in the hands of petty traders, would I believe in practice be found so difficult to carry out that it would probably become quite inoperative. Even, however, if this were not the case, I invite you to consider the great trouble and even cost in collection, and the friction and annoyance that would ensue from the distinction—necessary for rebate purposes—between imports of grain for consumption and imports for export. I think therefore that you will do well not to persevere with this suggestion.

Gentlemen, your last request is that I will subscribe a practical sympathy to the view that prevention of plague is an Imperial and not a purely Municipal responsibility ; in other words that, as the Local Government finds difficulty in helping you from Provincial Revenues, the Government of India will step in and relieve you of a portion of the charge. In Karachi I was asked for the whole. But I gather from the terms of your address—though I do not feel quite confident on this point—that you are more diffident and plead only for a part. However that may be, it is perhaps desirable, in view of the reiteration of these requests, that I should endeavour to state what seem to me to be the correct principles that should regulate our action. Sanitary and other measures for the prevention of plague in a Municipality are due and proper Municipal charges ; and each Municipality should be required to undertake them to the full extent of its ability. Plague has imposed heavy charges, not only on Municipal revenues (with special aid from the Government in many cases), but also on Provincial revenues, and still more, of course, on Imperial Revenues. Each must bear its share. It cannot be admitted that Imperial Revenues should entirely, or to a great extent, relieve either Provincial or Local Revenues of their proportion of the cost. On the contrary the responsibility rests first on Local, next on Provincial, and only finally on Imperial Revenues. We do what we can ; but we cannot accept an obligation the assumption of which would be unfair both to the localities affected, and to the Indian tax-payer in general—unfair because it would only spare the smaller and more responsible units in order to mulct the larger.

With these remarks, and with cordial thanks to you, Gentlemen, for your graceful reference to the presence of Lady Curzon here to-day with myself, I will pass on to the next address.

ADDRESS FROM THE CHAMBER OF COMMERCE, MADRAS.

*11th December*, 1900.

[To the address from the Chamber of Commerce, Madras, His Excellency replied as follows :—]

*Gentlemen,*—We meet upon an interesting occasion. For it is within a few days of the three hundredth anniversary of the grant of the first Charter by Queen Elizabeth to the Governor and Company of Merchants of London trading to the East Indies, that is, the first East India Company, who may I suppose be held in a certain sense to have been the progenitors of the Indian Chambers of Commerce, one of whom I am now addressing. In those days Viceroys and Chambers of Commerce were equally unknown. I daresay that the world got on very well without them. But inasmuch as we have severally been called into existence by the political and the commercial exigencies of later times, it seems to me to be a good thing that from time to time we should take advantage of such opportunities as the present to exchange views as to our respective shares in the evolution of the body politic and mercantile in India.

With much precision you have, Gentlemen, in your address tabulated the various subjects upon which you desire to appeal to me. I will follow them in the same order. First comes your protest against the existing application to this Presidency of the system of Provincial Contracts, and, as I gather from one sentence in your address, against the system itself. I cannot on the present occasion undertake either the exposition or the defence of the latter. If I did, we might still be engaged in conclave till a late hour of the afternoon. It is sufficient for me to recognise that you represent what I believe to be a widespread feeling in Madras to the effect that the system, as at present worked, takes from Madras an excessive share of its provincial revenues, and does not provide asufficient stimulus to local thrift or self-interest. This view has on several occasions been stated with great ability by the Madras Government, and has found no more vigorous or incisive advocate than your present Governor, who has more than once addressed me on the subject. To the further argument, which appears in a subsequent address from the Mahajana Sabha, that Madras is not interested in contributing to other provinces, I am less willing to subscribe ; since this is a purely separationist line of reasoning, and ignores the existence of the Imperial system. The various partners in the Empire must pay something for their share both in its glories and in its benefits. They cannot be shut off, so to speak, in water-tight compartments, each unit leading a self-centred and independent existence, and evading the responsibilities attached to the corporate life of the whole. I, therefore, am not much impressed by the argument, employed by the Mahajana Sabha, that the Madras ryot ought not to be taxed for the construction of roads in Burma or Beluchistan. This is an extreme and rhetorical method of presenting the case. The Bombay ryot might equally say that he does not see why he should be taxed to convert the Madras Harbour from a bad one into a good one. Putting aside this reasoning as specious, I would much prefer to discuss the question whether, as a factor in the Imperial system, Madras does or does not contribute more than her fair quota. This is a subject which we are now occupied in examining with the Secretary of State, and which the Government of India has no desire to approach in any but a generous spirit. But I think you should remember that Madras does not stand alone in its complaint, other provinces being similarly convinced of the hardship of the existing contracts ; and that the capacity of Imperial revenues to meet the demands made for increased expenditure in the several provinces, and on objects which have not been provincialised, such as the Army, is limited.

Gentlemen, your next heading was that of Railways. I quite agree with you as to the desirability of providing facilities for the introduction of the East Coast Railway into the city. I am informed that the total cost of the various measures that are considered necessary for this end amounts to 13½ lakhs. It is all a question of finding the money. But I hope that a beginning may be made with the more important of these works before long. I hardly think it necessary to discuss at present the agency by which the Vizagapatam-Raipur Railway should be constructed. It is unlikely that the line itself can be taken in hand for some years : and the decision may be affected by the termination of the contract of the Madras Railway. Similarly as regards the Baliapatam-Mangalore Railway, I have seen reports which speak in glowing terms of the port and the country. But while the line might be a very excellent, it would also be a very expensive one, the estimated cost of construction amounting to nearly 78 lakhs. I can see no prospect of the funds being found for this undertaking for a long time to come.

I now come to that hoary and baffling enigma, the Madras Harbour. You have expressed a hope that some comprehensive scheme may soon be decided upon. I doubt, Gentlemen, if there has been any period during the past 30 years in which what were believed to be comprehensive schemes have not been in existence. Indeed I suspect that there have been too many, rather than too few. However, I understand that the Chief Engineer of the Public Works Department is now engaged upon elaborating such a scheme as you desire, and I wish for it a better fate than its predecessors. As regards your request that your obligations to the Government of India may be diminished by a reduction in the amount of annual payments in liquidation of the loan, and also—though it is not quite clear whether you ask for one or for both favours—in the rate of interest that is now charged, I could not give a reply until I had heard the question thoroughly argued, and had been placed in possession of the opinions both of the Local Government and of my Financial advisers. I believe that the former is likely to address us on the matter. I may remark that four years ago the Government of India did make proposals that were intended to operate for your relief, since we agreed to accept repayment of the balance of the loan, and sanctioned the raising by the Harbour Trust Board of a fresh loan of 30 lakhs, bearing interest at $3\frac{1}{2}$ or $3\frac{3}{4}$ per cent., repayable in 30 years, for the purpose. But this project fell through, owing to the inability of the Board to raise the money. As regards the substitution of a Port Trust for the Harbour Board, fifteen years ago this proposal was favoured by the Government of India, but was not persevered with, owing to the hostility of the Local Government, who on administrative grounds were strongly opposed to it. Circumstances have somewhat changed since then. For I gather that under Local and Imperial Acts the Harbour Trust Board does now exercise all the more important powers of a Port Trust, with one exception, namely, the collection and expenditure of the Port Fund. These are under the control of the Local Government. But I understand that the revenues are spent entirely for the benefit of the Port, and that any surplus is credited to the Board.

Gentlemen, I am glad to receive your congratulations as to the legislation imposing countervailing duties on bounty-fed sugar, which the Government of India undertook, amid considerable criticism, last year ; and to learn that, in this Presidency, so widely interested in the industry as you have shown it to be, encouragement has been given to refiners, and the prospects are undeniably brighter. I do not know how far we may claim any credit for the remarkable change of opinion which is reported to be coming over the minds of the principal bounty-giving countries in Europe. But if these reports are correct, and if the revulsion of policy that is foreshadowed turns out to be true, perhaps our measure of last year may not have been altogether without its effect in conducing to so gratifying a result.

In conclusion, I share the satisfaction which you have expressed at the favourable rains which nearly everywhere, except in certain portions of the Bombay Deccan, where the outlook is gloomy, have relieved the terrible anxieties by which the Government of India was oppressed a few months ago. One famine is enough and too much for one Viceroyalty : and I earnestly pray that I may be spared the recurrence of any such awful visitation.

## ADDRESS FROM THE MAHAJANA SABHA, MADRAS.

### 11th *December*, 1900.

[In replying to the address from the Mahajana Sabha, the Viceroy spoke as follows :— ]

*Members of the Mahajana Subha,*—I thank you for your address, and for the agreeable words of welcome and encouragement that were contained in its opening sentences. I ought to thank you also for being so good as to curtail the reading of your address, because it is evident that if the whole of these addresses were read without any restriction at all, we should be kept here for a very long time. I share your hope that an abatement of the calamities from which India has recently suffered may enable the Government to address itself with uninterrupted energy to the many and complicated problems of internal administration that lie before us : though I am not so vain, and I hope that you are not so sanguine, as to imagine that, by any stroke of an enchanter's wand, the present Government or any Government of India can effect a revolution in the economic, social, or industrial conditions of this vast continent. It occurs to me, Gentlemen, after studying your address, that no complaint can be made, at any rate here, of undue restriction upon the absolute freedom with which you have been permitted to express your views upon an immense range of topics of the most controversial character. You seem to have profited by that liberty to use some decidedly emphatic language, which I am far from deprecating, but upon which I shall presently comment.

But first, Gentlemen, I should like to be quite certain for whom you speak. In your opening sentence you tell me that it is on behalf of the members of the Mahajana Sabha of Madras. But a little later on your representative character would appear to have acquired a wider scope, since when you come to the subject of famine prevention you " crave my permission to give expression to the views of the Indian public ;" while, when you come to an expression of your views on the subject of Judicial and Executive functions, you again present me with what you describe as " the unanimous voice of the Indian public." Now, Gentlemen, the Indian public is rather a big concern. It consists, exclusive of Mahomedans, of nearly 250,000,000 ; inclusive of Mahomedans, of some 300,000,000 persons. I am a little sceptical as to the possibility of this huge constituency being adequately represented by an association whose membership does not 1 believe extend beyond 200, and which. I gather from your rules, does not require for its general meetings a quorum of more than 15 ; and I prefer, therefore, to accept your opinions as representative of certain, and I doubt not most important, elements in Hindu society in the Madras Presidency, rather than as a pronouncement from the entire Indian continent.

Gentlemen, you tell me that you have no hesitation in saying that the policy of Land Revenue settlements has not contributed to the prosperity of the agricultural classes, who are growing poorer from year to year, and will ultimately be faced by ruin. I, on the other hand, feel a good deal of hesitation in pronouncing with complacency upon so contested a topic. I think that circumstances differ in different parts. 1 am not at all convinced that, as a general proposition, it is true that the agricultural classes are going downhill. In some districts which have been severely or repeatedly hit by drought or other visitations, there has been a positive, but not necessarily a permanent, decline in the material wellbeing of the people. But if we could raise from the dead some experienced district officer of the early years of the present century, and could send him round the scene of his former labours, I am not certain that he would discover the symptoms either of increasing penury or of impending ruin. Even if the peasant classes are growing poorer, as you contend, is it not a little rash and dogmatic to attribute it exclusively to land revenue settlements ? I think I could suggest, even from my slight know-

ledge, a good many other reasons, of which I will only name
two that appear to have escaped your notice. If the *sowkar*
were a little less exacting in the rate of interest that he
demands, and if the agriculturist could be persuaded not to
have such frequent recourse to the law-courts, and if you
would devote your influence to giving to both this prudent
advice, I think that the ryot would be a good deal better
off than he now is. (*Applause*).

Again, Gentlemen, you have pronounced with similar
confidence that the revenue demands of Government " are
excessive, increasing, and uncertain." There may be cases
in which all these propositions are correct : but I should
require a good deal evidence to convince me that they are
of universal application. If they be so, I fail to see how
we are to account for the general rise in the market value
of land. I think also that it is sometimes forgotten that an
assessment which appears to be unduly excessive in a bad
year, is often generous to a fault in a good one. If we are
to be fair, the good must be taken with the bad, and an
equation struck between the two. Instead, therefore, of
indulging in broad and dubious generalisations, it seems to
me that the case of each province and each assessment—
and one might almost descend to smaller units—demands
independent investigation. Such an examination I am now
engaged in conducting ; and I will prefer to form my opinion after I have studied the evidence that may be forthcoming, to making up my mind in advance. You express
a hope that I may be able to initiate such reforms in our
land revenue policy as will gradually redeem the agricultural
classes from poverty and distress. I wish you had told
me, Gentlemen, what they are to be. I will not now ask
you ; but I will put another question. Supposing that we
did reduce the assessment throughout India by 25 per cent.,
is there a man among you who honestly believes that there
would be no more famine, no more poverty, no more distress ;
or who would guarantee me that before 25 years had
elapsed the Mahajana Sabha of Madras would not be

repeating to some future Viceroy a verbatim reproduction of your present address ? (*Applause*).

You next refer to the Madras Irrigation Cess Act, which you say involves a violation of the rights of private property and is incapable of being worked in practice without serious injustice. I have not an idea what the former phrase may mean. Surely you do not contend that if a man grows a wet crop on land by the unquestioned use of water which has reached it by percolation from Government sources or channels, he should be at liberty to escape the water cess altogether, on the plea that he did not apply for the water which has enriched him, and that his rights of property would be violated by its exaction. If that is your conten- tion, I must frankly say that it seems to me to be an un- tenable one. There is such a thing also as the rights of the public, and it appears to me that they are the rights that would be violated, and it is upon them that serious injustice would be inflicted, if the public revenue were allowed to be defrauded by any such exemption. As to the attitude of the Government of India, it was directed to securing that the injustice which you fear to individuals should not in any circumstances take place ; for we attached as a condi- tion to our acceptance of the Bill the proviso that the water rate should only be levied when a full and constant supply of water is assured. I think, therefore, that we have suffi- ciently safeguarded the agriculturist against the perils which you anticipate.

Your next paragraph relates to the provision of industrial and technical instruction. So many platitudes are uttered upon this subject, both by those whose present addresses and by those whose duty it is to reply to them, that I will not on the present occasion add to their number. Government is bestowing its serious attention upon the matter ; and we are endeavouring to the best of our lights to create the opportunities for which you plead. But I suggest that at the other end of the scale a corresponding impetus is required. Are you quite certain that those agencies and institutions which exercise so powerful a control upon the mind of the Indian youth, are using their influence, as they might do, to encourage the particular form of education which in theory they applaud?

Your next request is that the number of seats on the Local Legislative Council that are filled by nomination from District Boards and Municipalities may be increased from five to seven. I should require a greater knowledge of the circumstances of the Presidency than I possess to be able to state exactly how the fairest representation of its many and diverse interests can be secured. But I confess that in the present stage of development the fair representation of interests and classes seems to me to be more important than the increased representation of localities : and I should be reluctant to sanction any changes that might sacrifice the former object to the latter.

As regards the Salt Tax, I am not sure that it is anything like so harsh and injurious in its incidence as you contend. But its reduction would be such a boon to the lower classes that it would be a great source of pleasure to my Colleagues and myself if we could confer it upon India during the time that I am here.

Concerning the Forest Laws you are again rather emphatic, when you speak of them as having deprived the village communities of their old communal rights. Why, Gentlemen, owing to the scandalous neglect of forestry and to widespread disafforestment, these rights had in many cases ceased to possess the smallest value. That scientific forestry under the control of Government implies some curtailment of rights that have grown up in a period of licence is true, but it does not necessarily involve their extinction. The great thing is that the Forest Laws should not be worked in an oppressive manner, and that the poor people should not be harassed by an unfeeling application of the penal clauses. In this connection I have seen a formal statement, enunciating the forest policy of the Madras Government, that was issued by the latter three years ago, and that seems to me to lay down the correct principles of administration with both justice and mercy. I happen to know that the subject is one which has forcibly appealed to the interest of your retiring Governor, and I hope that it may similarly receive the sympathy of his successor.

Gentlemen, I have now dealt with all the subjects mentioned in your address except those which I have found it more convenient to handle in reply to other addresses, either here or elsewhere ; and it only remains for me to endorse the concluding sentences in which you have spoken with just pride of the loyal and law-abiding instincts of the population in this part of India, of their progressive tendencies, and of the enterprising spirit that has taken them as emigrants to foreign lands. (*Applause.*)

## ADDRESS FROM THE ANJUMAN-I-MUFID-I-AHLA-I-ISLAM.

*11th December,* 1900.

[ In replying to the address of the Anjuman-i-Mufid-i-Ahla-i-Islam, representing the Moslem Community of Madras, the Viceroy said :—]

*Members of the Anjuman,*—It is only befitting that among the bodies from whom I have consented to receive addresses in Madras should be included a representative association of that community which in the past has played so considerable a part in the political fortunes of Southern India. The welcome that you have extended to Lady Curzon and myself on our visit to this Presidency is, I am sure, the outcome of a very deep-seated loyalty towards the Sovereign whom I have the honour to represent, as well as of a sincere interest in the task of administration with which the Government of India is charged. I gladly, therefore, accept the assurance of these sentiments which has been contained in your address.

In one respect the information that you have laid before me is indicative of the altered conditions under which the Mussulmans of Southern India now live, and of the different ideals which it is incumbent upon them to set before their eyes ; for I gather that your Anjuman exists rather to promote social and educational advancement than to further political ends. In this respect you have taken a wise initiative, which may safely be commended to your co-religionists in other parts of the country. While other communities or bodies are still occupied in talking about technical education, a phrase which seems to have an extraordinary fascination for the tongue in India, I gather that in your industrial school you are putting it into practice. I wish you success in your praiseworthy endeavour ; and I understand that the assistance which you solicit from the Madras Government towards the acquisition of a permanent habitation has long ago been promised by them, and is only dependent for fulfilment upon the possession by them of the funds with which to purchase the selected site.

Next I come to a feature in your address which I have learned from experience to regard as the inevitable concomitant of representations from Mahomedan bodies in this country. This is a complaint of your relatively ' backward position, and a request to Government to redress the balance by establishing a larger number of Mussulman scholarships in the various branches of higher education, and by giving you more posts in the higher ranks of the service. Gentlemen, if you will allow me to say so, there always seems to me to be some inconsistency between the frank admission of social or intellectual backwardness, and the claim for a larger share of the prizes that fall to social or intellectual distinction. Still I always enquire sympathetically into any proposals that may reasonably be entertained for helping you to improve your position. Figures have been placed before me showing that you are not dealt with illiberally in the matter of scholarships. As regards employment in the public service, I will not give the stereotyped answer that the statistics show you already to possess a share of offices in excess of the ratio in which you stand to the entire population of the Presidency, because I am aware that you make the reply that this result is only arrived at by including a number of purely subordinate posts, such as Police Constables and the like. Even, however, if I exclude all appointments carrying an annual salary of less than Rs. 250, and if I limit my observation to the appointments with a salary of from Rs. 250 to Rs. 10,000, I find that, in the Presidency, Mahomedans hold 438 of these posts out of a total of 8,782. This is exactly 5 per cent. ; whereas your percentage to the total population is 6·3. The disparity, therefore, even in this restricted sphere of application, does not appear to be very great. It is one, however, which I am sure that the Local Government would be only too pleased to assist you to redress, provided that candidates of the requisite capacity and training are forthcoming. For the last 30 years it has been the consistent instruction of successive Secretaries of State and Governments of India to extend fair and even generous treatment to the Mahomedans ; and the execution of this policy has already produced a vast change in your position. With the superior educational advantages now open to you, it rests to a large extent with yourselves to justify still further progress.

There are two other respects in which you have petitioned for special encouragement. They are subjects upon which I must speak with diffidence in this company, because they are matters that concern the Local rather than the Supreme Government. The first is your request that Hindustani may be recognised as an official language in the Presidency. I do not know what you mean by speaking of its non-recognition as the result of a change of policy ; since I am informed that there has been no change in this respect at all. It is for a change, in fact, that you plead. Personally I think that, while there would be a positive gain to yourselves, there might also be some advantage to the public service in such a recognition : but I should require to know more than I do of the exact proportion of Hindustani-speaking persons in different districts of the Presidency to render my opinion of any value. Your second request is that the Persian and Hindustani translatorship may be conferred upon a Mahomedan. Gentlemen, the answer is that it must be conferred upon the best man, whoever he be. There is no racial disqualification in the matter ; and the Governor of Madras, within whose patronage the appointment lies, cannot have his discretion fettered by the introduction of any other criterion than that of efficiency.

I have now dealt, Gentlemen, with all the subjects mentioned in your address, and will conclude by again thanking you for its courteous terms.

ADDRESS FROM THE EURASIAN AND ANGLO-INDIAN
ASSOCIATION OF SOUTHERN INDIA.

*11th December*, 1900.

[Replying to the address from the Eurasian and Anglo-Indian Association of Southern India, His Excellency spoke as follows :—]

*Members of the Eurasian and Anglo-Indian Association of
Southern India*,—Only a few days ago I was replying to an
address presented to me by the members of a sister Association to your own in the city of Bangalore. Some of the
observations which I ventured to make to them would be
equally pertinent in a reply to you ; but inasmuch as they
may possibly have come under your notice, I will not repeat
them on the present occasion, but will turn to the independent topics suggested by your remarks.

And first let me say that it is with no small gratification
that I meet the representatives of a society which, founded
as it was by an enthusiast, and impeded by many difficulties,
and by some ridicule in its earlier years, has persevered
to the point of attaining within the last few months its
majority. This is a creditable and should be an encouraging
landmark in your history. A second reason for my interest
in meeting you here to-day is that I believe your parent
society, with its various provincial circles and committees,
to represent a larger constituency than is to be found in any
other part of India ; though if I am right in this supposition
it seems to me a little surprising that you should not have
more than 1,877 members on your rolls. It occurs to me
that there must still be some reluctance on the part
of those whose interests you exist to promote, to come
forward and co-operate in your laudable undertaking : and
if this be so, those who stand aloof cannot fairly complain
if help does not come from others to those who do not grasp
the opportunity to help themselves.

A third cause of satisfaction to me in meeting you and
in receiving your address is that you appear to me to

entertain more prudent and sensible views of your position and work than are everywhere shown. Your address seems to me to be marked by an equal absence of false pride and of self-consciousness, and to express with admirable succinctness what I concur with you in thinking should be your aims. I am one with you when you say that you desire to keep the name Eurasian, firstly because you believe that your retention of it is the most effective method of meeting the reproach that is sometimes unworthily and undeservedly implied in its use, and secondly because there are many capable and respectable persons in that class of whom any community might justly be proud, and the credit brought by whom to the name cannot but help to shield their poorer and weaker brethren from the stigma of an unmerited reproach. I also agree with you when you lay down the indisputable proposition that your object, which is the advancement of the Eurasian community, is to be attained rather by the combined efforts of your own members than by any special privilege or concession from Government, which would give you an advantage over other races in this country. These are sound and sagacious views, and they must command the assent of every reasoning man.

Gentlemen, when in the earlier part of the present year I received a deputation from the Calcutta Society and placed my views before them at some length, I concluded by inviting them to formulate a programme, and to address to me any representations that they might choose in reply to certain friendly remarks which I had ventured to make upon their case. This invitation was accepted at the time ; but, for what reason I know not, it has hitherto failed to produce any response.

On the other hand it appears to me that your Association has entered the field with what may be a modest, but is an eminently practical programme. I understand that you possess a Central Habitation,—of which I observed a picture on the casket which you have just presented to me— with a room which may equally be used for a reading room and library, or as a hall for public meeting or the transaction of business. I have heard with interest of the institution by you of Provident and Insurance Funds, which have already dispensed to the families of subscribers no less than £20,000. Your Employment Register, by which you are enabled to secure openings in professional or domestic service for men and women of good character, is also an excellent thing. It is further gratifying to learn that on the Railways in this Presidency you are satisfied with the share of employment that you obtain for your clients.

There is one respect, however, in which I am not sure that you have not unconsciously infringed your own canon ; for after assuring me that you desire no special privilege, you proceed to ask that you should be directly, and I suppose permanently, represented upon the Legislative Councils of the various Provinces. I am afraid that the reasons, which you advance for this concession will not stand close examination. The first is that your community is small, which is the very inverse of the plea for a similar privilege that is usually addressed to me by other bodies, who are in the habit of appealing for representation on the ground that they are so large. The second is that in legislation for the country at large, your interests are liable to be overlooked. But, Gentlemen, do you not forget that you are constantly claiming that you have no class interests apart from those of Europeans, with whom your feelings and fortunes are identified ? Without weightier reasons, therefore, in its defence, your petition is not likely to meet with the acceptance of Government. As a matter of fact, I believe that there has been no reluctance in this Presidency, and for all I know elsewhere, to place capable members of your community upon the Local Legislative Council when such have been forthcoming. This is as it should be : and I doubt not that future Governors will be as liberal-minded in this respect as their predecessors have been in the past. But what may properly be conceded as a privilege in meritorious cases cannot in existing circumstances be converted into a right.

Gentlemen, I will only say in conclusion that the passage in your address with which I am in heartiest sympathy is that which you devote to education. I learn from it that scholarships and prizes have been instituted for boys and girls and that special classes exist for teaching practical acquirements to both sexes. It is in the development of this idea, which as yet appears to be in its infancy, in the provision for your young men of a business or commercial or technical training—more than in any other specific— that the future regeneration of the Eurasian community lies; and I would urge you accordingly to devote your energies and your funds in this direction. In the task with which you have charged yourselves, and which you appear to be pursuing with honesty and vigilance, permit me, Gentlemen, to wish you from the bottom of my heart every success.

## ADDRESS FROM THE NATIVE CHRISTIAN COMMUNITY
### OF SOUTHERN INDIA.

*11th December*, 1900.

[In replying to the address from the Native Christian Community of Southern India the Viceroy spoke as follows:—]

*Gentlemen*,—The list of addresses that have been presented to me this morning would have been incomplete had it not included some representation from a community so numerous, and, to one who belongs to the same faith, so necessarily interesting, as the Native Christian Community of Southern India. There has been devoted to the creation, and there is even now expended upon the development, of this striking factor in Indian life, an immense amount of pious effort, of practical philanthropy, and of unassuming work. What impression is thereby made upon the ethnological formation into which, like a wedge, this stratum of rival thought and belief has pushed its way, it is not for me to determine. It is sufficient for me to recognise its existence, to admit its claims to consideration, and to admire the practical work that it has already done.

Like the bodies whose addresses have preceded yours, you profit by the opportunity to acquaint me with what you conceive to be your reasonable grounds of grievance. The first of these is the familiar complaint that your community is inadequately represented in the higher ranks of the public service ; and while protesting that you do not ask for special treatment, you pray me to issue such instructions to the Heads of Departments as will ensure a redress of your grievance in this respect. I am not sure that there is not some inconsistency between your protest and your prayer. But you will have observed that pretty much the same complaint has been made to me here or elsewhere by the Mahomedans and the Eurasians ; and I put it to you whether it is possible to satisfy all these three communities, each of whom repudiates special privileges,

by taking steps that could scarcely admit of any other
interpretation. From the enquiries that I have made I
gather that you are not badly off in respect of your share
of Government employment. Out of the 7,240 graduates
in the Presidency, 590, or 8 per cent., are Native Christians ;
and I suspect that if you were to look closely into the
matter, you would not find your share of posts in the
public service to be in an inferior proportion.

Your next grievance arises from the existing inequality
in the incidence and administration of the succession duties,
which operate harshly upon Native Christians, as compared
with Hindus, Mahomedans, or the disciples of other religions.
I think that there are force and reason in this complaint ;
and I hope that we may be able to dispose of it in a manner
that will be satisfactory to the Madras Government, which
has ably championed your cause, and to yourselves.

Thirdly, you complain of the delay that takes place in
the dissolution of marriage between a Christian convert
and a Hindu spouse, and more particularly of the compulsory adjournment for a year after the case has reached
the Courts. If you are correct in saying that in the
majority of instances recourse is not had to a judicial
tribunal until years have been spent in fruitless negotiation
with the party who remains a Hindu, then I think that
there is much cogency in your plea that you should be saved
from the further delay that is now imposed by the law ; and
I hope that means may be devised for relieving you from it.

Fourthly, Gentlemen, the Roman Catholics among you
have asked for a recognition of the Canonical process for
the grant of the Pauline dispensation in cases where a
Christian convert seeks to be freed from his Hindu wife.
This means that a Roman Catholic convert should be permitted to dissolve his marriage by a simpler and easier
process than a Protestant, who is called upon to adopt a certain
procedure in the Civil Courts under the law. It is held both
by the Government of India and by the Secretary of State
that there is no sufficient ground for this special treatment.

Fifthly, you take up the question of the alleged civil disabilities of the Christian population in the States of Mysore, Travancore and Cochin, and you ask me to advise the rulers of those States to concede to such of their subjects as have apostasised from Hinduism and become converted to Christianity, the civil rights of inheritance, succession, and partition, as well as what you designate the primordial natural rights of the custody of children. Now, Gentlemen, this sounds very well on paper. But it requires a little further examination ; and that examination I took especial pains to devote to it when I was recently a visitor in the three States which you have named. It must be remembered that these States, or at any rate two of them, Travancore and Cochin, have a system of family life, a law of succession, and views of property, different from those that prevail for instance in British India. Under this system family property is indivisible, and members of the family are only entitled to a share in it or to maintenance from it so long as they discharge certain religious duties in which the convert to another faith cannot join. What you ask is that this corporate family system, which is the basis of the social structure on the Malabar Coast, should be broken down for the sake of the infinitesimal number of persons, nearly all of humble station and possessed of but little property—for I believe it to be quite impossible for you to sustain the opposite allegation—who secede from it to the Christian fold. I can only tell you that in the present state of development in those countries, such a change would produce infinite heart-burning and discord, and would greatly disturb both the princes and the people. Moreover, though you all join to-day in making this representation, I found when I was in the States that neither the Roman Catholics nor the Syrian Christians, who constitute the enormous majority of the Christian population, bother themselves very seriously about it, and that the demand is practically limited to the small number of European Protestants. You ask me to advise the Chiefs to alter the law and custom of their States in the interests of this minority. The Government of India might, I suppose, in the last resort insist upon their doing so ; but when it is remembered that all three rulers have earnestly protested against it, I doubt whether mere advice would go very far. A Hindu ruler may be excused for some reluctance to adopt measures that would in practice furnish a premium to proselytism from his own faith to another ; and I do not feel quite clear that our intervention would be in scrupulous accordance with the Queen's Proclamation of 1858. After all you have not very much to complain of in Travancore or Cochin. When it is remembered that in the Madras Presidency not more than $2\frac{1}{2}$ per cent. of the entire population are Christians, there can be neither any great discouragement to Christianity nor any grave disabilities to Christians, when it is found that in one of those two States they constitute $20\frac{1}{2}$ per cent. and in the other 24 per cent. of the population. I doubt not that in the passage of time even such inequalities as you now complain of will disappear. But the change is more likely to come voluntarily than in response to pressure. There is probably no sphere in which it is more unwise to go too fast, than in religious propagandism.

Finally, Gentlemen, in thanking you for your friendly words, and for the elegant and artistic casket which you have presented to me, permit me also to congratulate you upon the evidence of harmonious relations, as existing between the various branches of the great Christian Community in Southern India, that has been furnished by the joining together of Protestants and Roman Catholics in the presentation of this address.

[His Excellency in concluding his replies to the various addresses presented to him said :—]

*Gentlemen of the various bodies who have addressed me,*—I have now, to the best of my ability, replied to all the subjects contained in your addresses. I am afraid that I cannot have given satisfaction to all parties, but at least I have done a great deal of good to myself ; since the necessarily minute and laborious study of local topics to which I have been impelled by your representations, has given me a familiarity with them which I might not otherwise have acquired, and has deepened the sympathetic interest which I feel in the fortunes of this peaceful and loyal Presidency. In a few days time, Gentlemen, you will be saying good-bye to a Governor, who, coming here with great experience in the art of administration, has devoted his entire energies to the study of your needs, and has, as my predecessor and I could both testify, proved a most vigilant and patriotic champion of your interests. (*Applause.*) His place will be taken by one, of whom I may be permitted to say, since I know him, that Madras will find in him a wise head upon young shoulders, and who will devote to the service of this Presidency abilities already trained in no mean school, and a lofty and conscientious purpose. Under his *régime* I wish to Madras a continuance of prosperity and success. (*Applause.*)

## UNVEILING OF LORD LANSDOWNE'S STATUE.

### 7th January, 1901.

[The ceremony of unveiling the equestrian statue of Lord Lansdowne, which faces that of Lord Roberts on the Red Road, took place on Monday, the 7th January, at 4.30 P.M., in the presence of a large gathering of the leading officials and the principal European and Native residents of Calcutta. The Royal Irish Rifles furnished a guard of honour in the rear of the statue, while strong detachments from that regiment and the 2nd Madras and 20th Bombay Infantry were drawn up in three sides of a square with the 45th Field Battery. The Viceroy, who was accompanied by Her Excellency Lady Curzon, arrived under the escort of the Bodyguard, and was received by Sir Patrick Playfair (Chairman) and the members of the Executive Committee and conducted to a daïs facing the statue. Sir Patrick Playfair, speaking on behalf of the Executive Committee, and inviting the Viceroy to unveil the statue, said there was a general desire at the conclusion of Lord Lansdowne's term of office to commemorate the eminent services he had rendered to the Empire. A subscription was opened, and nearly Rs. 91,000 collected. The cost of the statue and pedestal was £4,650, and about Rs. 10,000 were still available, which would be utilised in placing a portrait of Lady Lansdowne in the Town Hall. Much assistance had been given by the Government who had presented eleven old bronze guns from which the statue had been cast. The speaker concluded by saying that Lord Lansdowne had not ceased to maintain a deep interest in India and its people since leaving it.

His Excellency addressed the assembly as follows :—]

*Your Honour, Your Excellency, Sir Patrick Playfair, Ladies and Gentlemen,*—Among the most agreeable but also the most delicate duties which a Viceroy can be called upon to perform in Calcutta is that of unveiling the statue of a predecessor in the same office, who has attained the distinction—in my opinion one of the highest that can be conferred upon a servant of the Crown in India—of perpetual commemoration upon this historic Maidan. The duty is agreeable, since to any of us it must be a function both of compliment and of pleasure to speak of the achievements of an eminent fellow-countryman, and all the more so if we happen to be honoured by his personal acquaintance and friendship. But it is also delicate ; inasmuch as an appreciation which is neither over-strained nor uncritical in the case of the dead, may by some be thought to be officious when applied to the living, and since a Governor-General is not perhaps the fairest judge of one of his own predecessors. I am relieved, however, from any anxiety that I might feel on this score by the consciousness that Lord Lansdowne only left India so short a time ago that his career, his services, his actions, must be even better known to many whom I am now addressing than they can be to me ; and that the officers who served under him, the friends whom he made, and the community by whom he was so greatly appreciated, must cherish a recollection of his merits and charms, so warm, and so enduring, as to stand in no need either of resuscitation or of stimulus at the hands of a successor.

There is another consideration by which I am powerfully affected. I feel that we are too near to Lord Lansdowne's Viceroyalty to pass it under final review. If the greatest of modern Governors-General, Dalhousie, could stipulate in his will that his papers were not to be published or his life written until 50 years had elapsed from his death, would it not appear to be a presumptuous thing to compose the epitaph of an administration that has only belonged to history for seven years ? Certain landmarks, however, it is permissible for us to point to as destined to affect the ultimate verdict of posterity. It was under Lord Lansdowne's administration that was secured that expansion of the constitution and functions of the Legislative Councils that has so greatly increased both their representative character and their usefulness. It was he who with infinite discretion carried into execution the policy of Imperial Service Contingents which had emanated from the ingenious brain of Lord Dufferin, and which has since borne such happy fruit. Much as the measure was denounced at the time, we now recognise in the closing of the mints, which was carried out by Lord Lansdowne's Government, the wise and indispensable prelude to the Currency reforms upon which we have since embarked. The close attention which he devoted to

Frontier questions, and to the problems of military defence, culminated in the Kabul Convention of 1893, which placed upon a happier, and it is to be hoped a durable, basis British relations with our important ally, the Amir of Afghanistan.

There was, however, a further aspect of Lord Lansdowne's personality and work which will appeal at any rate to this audience, who knew him, quite as much as any record of official achievement or of public fame. I allude to that wonderful and engaging charm of manner, that high-bred and chivalrous courtesy, and that sweetness of disposition that caused him to be loved by equals, and revered by subordinates. (*Applause.*)  Some public men attain their ends by inflexibility of character and relentless concentration of purpose.  Others pursue the same goal by the gentler agencies of suavity and conciliation.  There was no greater or more intuitive master of these humanities than Lord Lansdowne.

He would probably have been the last to deny that as Viceroy he was assisted by capable colleagues.  Some of them are still among us.  Others, like that remarkable man, the late Sir George Chesney, have passed away, or, like Sir George White and Sir H. Brackenbury, continue to serve their country in other spheres.  But it will not be disputed that the most notable of them all is he whose image confronts his former Chief from the opposite side of this roadway. (*Applause.*)  Here, as long as Calcutta lasts, the effigies of these two illustrious men, the Statesman and the Soldier, the head of the Civil and the head of the Military Administration of the Indian Empire, will face each other in chiselled bronze.  But the antithesis has a more than local application.  For the names of Lord Lansdowne and Lord Roberts will be written side by side, not merely on the page of Indian history, but on the open map of the Empire. (*Applause.*)  Little, I suspect, did either of them dream, when they left the shores of India — and little did any of you who subscribed to the erection of their statues contemplate — that within a few years' time they would be conducting, as War Minister and as Field Marshal, the first Empire war of Great Britain. In this novel field I doubt not that their old co-operation stood them and stood the country in good stead. The Commander-in-Chief, while prosecuting his arduous task, felt that he could rely upon the sagacious forethought, the administrative energy, and the loyal championship of the Minister in Pall Mall. The latter was confident from long experience of the genius and the resourcefulness of the veteran Commander. (*Applause.*) The eyes of contemporaries are apt to be fascinated by the glare of the battlefield, and the sound that vibrates in all our ears is the music of victory. But when the shouting has died down and the dusts of controversy are laid, I suspect it will be found that, with a conscientious and purposeful tenacity that never wavered, and with a dignity that stooped neither to self-exculpation nor to reproach, the War Minister pursued his thankless path, and laid the foundation of those victories which our brave soldiers were destined to win. (*Applause.*)

And now, as Sir Patrick Playfair has reminded us, Lord Lansdowne has been called to another task, one of the three greatest that can be committed to any Englishman. It is his function to guide the ship of state through the narrow and perilous shoals of the international sea. None who have not seen it at close quarters can realise how difficult is that undertaking, how great the qualities of mind and character and temper that it requires. To guard that which is the greatest of all dominions, and by its very greatness excites jealousy, to control the mysterious law that is always forcing upon the Empire a reluctant expansion, not to neglect the small things, and not to exaggerate the big — or I may equally turn it the other way, and say not to magnify the small things, and not to underrate the big — in other words to discern the true measure of imperial proportion, to keep the honour of England bright, and yet never to bluster, still less to cringe — to do this before the eyes of the whole world and amid a whirlwind of rivalry and suspicion

— this is the task of the Foreign Minister of Great Britain. (*Applause.*) Those of us who know Lord Lansdowne feel confident that he has both the skill and the urbanity, the courage and the patriotism, for the enterprise ; and we wish him well in carrying it through. (*Applause.*) Future inhabitants of Calcutta or visitors to the city, as they pass up and down this Maidan, and gaze at the figures of the great men which adorn it, will see the effigy of none who has served the Empire with greater fidelity or upon a wider field of action, than the original of the statue which I now unveil: (*Loud and continued applause.*)

[His Excellency then unveiled the statue, a salute of 31 guns being fired from the rampart of Fort William, and the troops and Guard-of-Honour presenting arms. Maharaja Bahadur Sir Jotendro Mohun Tagore, K.C.S.I., then proposed a vote of thanks to His Excelleney for presiding, and the proceedings closed. Their Excellencies were warmly cheered as they drove away.]

## DEATH OF HER MAJESTY THE QUEEN-EMPRESS.

*1st February*, 1901.

[ At the meeting of the Legislative Council held at Government House this morning His Excellency the President addressed the Hon'ble Members as follows :—]

Here, at this table, where we are met to exercise the legislative powers, for the benefit of the people of India, that have been devolved upon us by the Crown of Great Britain, we ought not, I think, to meet to-day without paying such tribute of humble respect as is open to us to the memory of the great and good sovereign who has worn that Crown for nearly two-thirds of a century, and now, in the fulness of years and honour, has passed away. The British Empire has had no such Queen, gracious, wise, dignified, symbolising all that was most enlightened and progressive in her time, of pure and stainless life. India in its long cycles, has had no such Empress, tender-hearted, large-minded, just, humane, the loving parent of her subjects of every race and clime. All the Princes of India have been proud to own their fealty to so noble an example of sovereignty, and the hearts of all the Indian peoples have been drawn together by this singular and beautiful combination of mother, woman and queen. Those of us who, in any official capacity, either here or elsewhere, have served Her Majesty have felt it to be our proudest distinction that it was her warrant that we acknowledged, her Empire that we were engaged in safe-guarding, her example that inspired us. Whether we are young or old, we shall none of us ever forget that we were honoured by wearing the uniform of Queen Victoria.

It would be easy for me to say much about the mark that this marvellous reign has left upon the history of India, and to indicate, at many points, the sagacious hand and influence of the deceased Sovereign. But perhaps the present occasion is not the best for such a purpose, while, after all, are not all her reign and character, in their relation to this country, summed up in the famous Proclamation of 1858, the Magna Charta of India, the golden guide to our conduct and aspirations?

It has been the fashion in history to designate some sovereigns by the distinguishing attributes of their personality or reign. Thus we have read of the Great, the Conqueror, the Just, the Lion-hearted, the Saintly, the Strong. Should it ever be desired to find such an appellation for the late Queen, it would be admitted by all that she deserves pre-eminently to be called by the title which she herself, I believe, gave to her own husband, namely, the Good. It is the virtue of her character, and the benignity of her influence, that her people have admired, quite as much as, if not more than, the splendour of the Victorian Era, or the unequalled glory of her reign. If blame or reproach ever fell upon her country, no shadow of it touched herself. She was above all, as well as over all. She set an example not merely to Courts and nations, but to every human hearth; and at every hearthstone in the Empire is the feeling not merely that a great monarch is dead, but that a bright and beautiful ray has been extinguished.

Nowhere, I am convinced, in the wide orbit of the British Empire is there a more genuine sorrow, or a more profound sense of loss, than in India to-day. We are truly a nation in mourning. During the past ten days, many hundreds of telegrams and letters have poured in upon me testifying to the grief of communities and individuals. The newspapers have been full of similar evidence. All these records tell the same tale. They speak of the simple emotions that spring from the heart, of the sadness with which, even when it is a throne that is left vacant, men gaze upon the parting sail " that sinks with all we love below the verge."

And yet the occasion is not one for lamentation only. We may mingle a sense of pride and of gratitude with our tears. For the Queen's life was extended far beyond the normal span. It had covered four-fifths of one century, and had crossed the threshold of another. Nature seemed for a while to have relaxed its inexorable laws in her favour, and in extreme old age, even to the end, she retained the freshness, the warmth of affections, and the energy of youth. In her more than 80 years of life, she had represented, as no other living man or woman, the higher aspects of the spirit of the age. She had shared in its trials—indeed had borne more than her portion of them—had steadied its impulses, and had sympathised with its struggles and hopes. There was left to her no public or private duty undone, no glory unattained. It may be said of her that she turned Great Britain into a world-wide Empire, with India as its corner-stone. If a part of the result is to be attributed to the statesmen who met at her Council, and part also to the movement of those unseen forces which are beyond human control, it yet remains true that her ministers were as often guided by her as she was by them, and that it was her personality and character, and the devotion which they excited, that gave to those forces the direction which they assumed. And so, having summed up in her own career the aims and achievements of the Nineteenth Century, she has now, in the very hour of the dawn of its successor, been relieved of the burden, and has handed on the trust to others. The British Empire, and the entire world, may count themselves fortunate if the new century produces any figure at all comparable with the central and shining figure of the old.

I propose, as a mark of respect, that this Council should not proceed further with its business this morning, but should stand adjourned until this day week.

## QUEEN VICTORIA MEMORIAL.

### 6th *February*, 1901.

[ The following speech was delivered by His Excellency the Viceroy at the Memorial Meeting, held in the Town Hall, Calcutta, on February 6th, 1901, for the Institution of a National Indian Memorial to Queen Victoria :—]

*Your Honour, Mr. Sheriff, and Citizens of Calcutta,—* We are met to-day upon a great and solemn occasion. For we are assembled to express, in the language, not of exaggeration or of compliment, but of the simple truth, the feelings that lie deep in the hearts of all of us. They are feelings of a threefold character, of sorrow at the death of our beloved Queen, of loyalty to her successor the new King-Emperor, Edward VII, and of our desire to commemorate the name and virtues of the deceased Sovereign by some enduring monument that shall hand down to later ages a visible memorial of our veneration and of her wonderful and glorious reign. I accept, therefore, with a mournful pride the honour which has been conferred upon me of presiding upon this historic occasion, and I will proceed to deal with the first resolution which has been committed to my care.

I have already had occasion to speak elsewhere of the character and life of the late Queen, and I need not now either repeat what I then said or encroach upon the ground of subsequent speakers. We all feel the same about her, whether we are Europeans or Indians. Our hearts are swelling with gratitude that we were fortunate enough to live under such a Sovereign, with an answering love for the great love that she bore to all of us alike, and with eagerness to preserve her memory imperishable for all time.

In India I venture to assert that there are special reasons why we should feel strongly, and act independently, and of our own initiative, in the matter. Queen Victoria loved India, as no other monarch, certainly no other monarch from another land has done. The fifteen Governors-General who served her, and of whom I shall always feel it a sad honour to have been the last, could one and all testify to her abounding regard for this country. She wrote regularly to each of them with her own hand, during the more than 60 years of her reign, 'words of wise counsel and of tender sympathy for the people whom she had charged them to rule. As we know, she learned the Indian language when already advanced in years. She was never unattended by Indian servants, and we have read that they were entrusted with the last sorrowful office of watching over her body after death. In her two Jubilee processions she claimed that the Indian Princes, and the pick of her Indian soldiers, should ride in her train. There are many of those Princes who could testify to the interest she showed in them, to the gracious welcome which she always extended to them when in England, and to the messages of congratulation or sympathy which they often received from her own hand. But it was not to the rich or the titled alone that she was gracious. She was equally a mother to the humble and the poor, Hindu and Mahomedan, man and woman, the orphan and widow, the outcast and the destitute. She spoke to them all in simple language that came straight from her heart and went straight to theirs. And these are the reasons why all India is in mourning to-day, and why I claim that there are special grounds for which we should meet together, with no loss of time, to determine what we shall do to perpetuate this precious memory and this beneficent reign.

It is not without much anxious forethought and deliberation that I venture to put before this meeting, and before the Princes and peoples of India, a definite Memorial scheme. We are all of us naturally attracted by the idea of charity. It fits in so well with what we know of Her Majesty's character, of the warmth of her heart, and the gentle sympathy that she always showed to the suffering and distressed. There is, God knows, enough of poverty and affliction in India—as indeed there must be in any great aggregation of so many millions of human beings—to appeal

to any heart, and to absorb any number of lakhs of rupees.
But, amid all the possible claimants to our support, how
should we select the favoured recipients ? I have seen in
the Press a great number of suggestions made. Some
have said that we should add a great sum to the Famine
Relief Trust that was started last year by that munificent
Prince, the Maharaja of Jaipur. Others have recommended
the claims of Hindu widows, of female education, of travelling students, of the poor ryat, of the sick and infirm, of
Technical or Industrial Schools, of Higher Research. In
fact, there is not a philanthropic or educational object, or
institution in India, that will not have its advocates for some
share in the bounty that may be evoked on behalf of an
Indian Memorial to Queen Victoria. Now, Ladies and
Gentlemen, I am the last to deny that all of these are
admirable objects fully worthy of our interest and support.
I am confident that any one of them individually would
have appealed to the heart of the late Queen. But it is
quite clear that we cannot give to them all, and that we are
not in a position to select any one of their number upon
which to concentrate the affectionate tributes of the people.
Some of them would appeal to Hindus, but not at all to
Mahomedans ; others would gratify the educated classes,
but not the unlettered ; others, again, would be confined to
a single, though numerically the largest, class of the
population.

Nor, again, would it do to pause in our appeals while
we were disputing among ourselves upon which of these
objects we should all unite. We should find that,
before we had come to an agreement, we had wasted
precious time and frittered away a golden opportunity,
and that we had disappointed the eager hopes and the burst-
ing generosity of the people. Therefore it is that I have
ventured to come forward, and, in consultation with a number
of experienced and representative gentlemen, both European
and Indian, have formulated the scheme which has appeared
in the Press. I dare to think that the conception is a not

ignoble one, and that it will not be unworthy of the great
Sovereign whom we desire to commemorate, of all the Princes
who are emulous to do her honour, and of this wonderful
country which has felt for her a loyalty aroused by no other
human being. Posterity is apt to forget in whose honour
charities were originally founded, or endowments named.
Some day in the future the endowment itself is converted to
another purpose, and the design of the original contributors
is forgotten. Who, for instance, when Queen Anne's
Bounty is annually distributed in England to augment the
incomes of the smaller clergy, spares a thought for poor
Queen Anne? On the other hand, it is different with a
concrete memorial. It remains a visible and speaking
monument to the individual or the period that is so commemorated. I venture to say that more good has been
done in arousing public interest in the Navy in England,
and in developing the lesson of patriotism in young Englishmen by the spectacle of the heroic figure of Nelson standing
on the summit of the great column in Trafalgar Square than
would have been the case had the nation founded a hundred
training ships, or endowed a score of naval hospitals in his
honour. But I can give you an even higher authority,
namely, the authority of Her Majesty the Queen herself.
When her husband, the Prince Consort, died in 1861, and
a large sum was raised by public subscription for the foundation of a National Memorial to the deceased Prince, the
Queen herself was asked what form she would prefer the
memorial to take. I will read to you the terms of her reply.
She wrote as follows to the Lord Mayor of London :—

" It would be more in accordance with the feelings of the
Queen, and she believes with those of the country in general,
that the monument should be directly personal to its object.
After giving the subject her maturest consideration, Her
Majesty had come to the conclusion that nothing would be
more appropriate, provided it was on a scale of sufficient
grandeur, than a personal memorial to be erected in Hyde
Park."

These, Ladies and Gentlemen, were the Queen's own words ; and this was the origin of that noble Albert Memorial, which no one ever goes to London without seeing, which is one of the glories of the metropolis, and which will perpetuate to hundreds of thousands of persons who will never have heard of the Albert Orphan Asylum, or the Albert Medals, or the Albert Institute, the memory of the beloved and virtuous Consort of the British Queen.

And so I ask why should we not do for the Queen herself in the capital of India what she asked to have done for her husband in the capital of Great Britain? Shall we not be carrying out what we are justified in saying would have been in accordance with her own sentiments ? Let us, therefore, have a building, stately, spacious, monumental, and grand, to which every new-comer in Calcutta will turn, to which all the resident population, European and Native, will flock, where all classes will learn the lessons of history, and see revived before their eyes the marvels of the past : and where father shall say to son and mother to daughter—" This Statue and this great Hall were erected in the memory of the greatest and best Sovereign whom India has ever known. She lived far away over the seas, but her heart was with her subjects in India, both of her own race, and of all others. She loved them both the same. In her time, and before it, great men lived, and great deeds were done. Here are their memorials. This is her monument." Gentlemen, a nation that is not aware that it has had a past will never care to possess a future ; and I believe that, if we raise such a building as has been sketched, and surround it with an exquisite garden, we shall most truly, in the words of Shakespeare, find a tongue in the trees, and a sermon in the sculptured stones, that will proclaim to later generations the glory of an unequalled epoch, and the beauty of a spotless name.

I must add that I would be the last person to desire that the erection of a National Memorial here should stand in the way of the dedication of funds, should it be so desired, to local objects elsewhere. We do not want to coerce, or to dictate to anybody. A donor is entitled to a free choice of the object for which he contributes. There may be a strong desire expressed in different parts of India for a provincial or local memorial, quite independently of ours. This seems to me quite natural. I do not see why any Presidency or Province should not please itself. They have their local standpoint and interests. They may want their memorial, whatever form it may take, all to themselves. There must be no jealousy in the matter. At the mouth of the grave all petty feelings must be extinguished ; and charity which, as our great Christian Apostle has told us " envieth not, vaunteth not itself, and is not puffed up " must quarrel with nobody, but must be permitted to seek and find its own outlet. Even in such cases, however, I hope that the local Committees may decide to transmit to us a certain proportion of their funds, so that they may have their share in the monument of the nation. But I really think that I may go further and may put it to these various communities whether, except in cases where there is an obvious opening for local commemoration they will not be acting wisely and reasonably in contributing to the Central Fund. And I say so for two reasons : partly because I want everyone—all the Princes, and all the Provinces, and all the States, to have their part and portion in this National Memorial, and partly because if they respond to the appeal on at all the scale that seems to me not unlikely, it is possible that not merely may we have funds for the erection, and equipment, and endowment of this building, but we may have a balance that may appropriately be dedicated to some object of national charity or beneficence. What it should be I cannot now say. Indeed, it would be premature to discuss an object before we have collected the money. But I make these observations in order to indicate that philanthropy is by no means excluded from our purview, and that the wider the response to our appeal, the more likely we are to be able to supplement the Victoria Hall by some object that may gratify those who have a charitable or moral purpose at heart.

Now, may I just say one word about the selection of Calcutta as a site? It is quite true that Calcutta is not the gate of India. But neither is Washington the gate of America, nor Ottawa the gate of Canada, nor Rome the gate of Italy; and yet no one would dream, or has dreamed, of erecting a great American, or Canadian, or Italian, National Memorial except at those capitals. For instance, the Washington obelisk was erected, not at New York, a city of two millions of people; but at the capital, a city of a quarter of a million. Calcutta, in the same way, quite apart from being the most populous, is also the capital city of India. This generation did not make it so; but so it is, and it is now too late for the present, or for succeeding generations, to unmake it. The seat of Government inevitably tends to acquire a metropolitan character. The presence of the Supreme Government here for five months out of every twelve cannot be gainsaid. It was from the banks of the Hugli that the orders of the Governor-General in Council were issued that bore the names of Warren Hastings and Dalhousie; and the same process will, I suppose, go on in the future.

I merely make these remarks in order to argue that if a National Monument is a desirable thing, I think that Calcutta is the inevitable site. It is said that we are rather out of the way. Perhaps we are; and yet sooner or later, just because this is the seat of Government, everybody finds his way here, whether he be an Indian Prince, or a European traveller, or an English merchant. Of course there are other cities with magnificent associations: Bombay with its splendid appearance, Delhi with its imperial memories, Agra with its majestic monuments, Madras with its historic renown. But the two seaports will probably have their own memorials: Agra is consecrated to a vanished dynasty and *régime;* while it is now too late, I sometimes wish it were not, to turn Delhi again into an imperial capital. No one will, I think, contend that we could possibly place a building of this character in a place, however famous its past, or however central its position, where the Government of India is never found, which is not even the capital of a Local Government, and where there is neither a European civil nor military population of any size. This building, if it is to be a great success, and if its contents are to be worthy of its name, will probably require the keen personal interest of the Viceroy for a number of years to come. I think that the making of the collection will thereby be a good deal facilitated. This interest I am quite prepared, and I am sure that my successors will equally be prepared, to give to it. But I doubt very much whether we could do it as well, or at all, at a distance.

Gentlemen, I am glad to be able to say that I think the prospects of a remarkable, and indeed unexampled, response to our appeal, are encouraging. Since the scheme which I ventured to propound has been put forward, it has met with a most gratifying support at the hands of all the representative organs of the Press, both European and Native, in Calcutta. I am very grateful to them for their discriminating and reasoned support. It has been communicated to the Governors and Lieutenant-Governors of the Provinces of British India, who are about to hold meetings at which its merits will be discussed. It has excited the warm sympathy of the mercantile community in Calcutta, who have come forward with their accustomed liberality, and to whose contributions I shall presently refer. And, finally, it has appealed to the enthusiastic devotion, and the boundless generosity, of the Princes of India, who have lost in the Queen a Sovereign whom they all worshipped, a mother whom they revered, and who, I prophesy, will be found to vie with each other in their desire to contribute to the immortality of her name. One of these Princes is with us to-day—His Highness the Maharaja Sindhia of Gwalior, who, if I may say so before his face, has at a comparatively early age, displayed exceptional capacities, and has already testified, with a splendid and princely munificence, his loyalty to the British Crown. It is in keeping with the generous instincts of His Highness that he should have sent me a telegram, as soon as he heard of the institution of this fund, offering me the regal donation of ten lakhs. From the Maharaja of Kashmir I have had the splendid offer of fifteen lakhs. The Maharaja of Jeypur has expressed a desire to increase his magnificent endowment of the Famine Trust by another four lakhs, and to give five lakhs in addition to the Memorial Fund. From the Mysore Durbar I have received the preliminary offer, to be increased, should the necessity arise, of one lakh. Now these offers have placed me in a position of some little embarrassment. For, while they testify to the noble instincts of their donors, they may yet be held to set a standard to which others may find it difficult to conform, and they may result in our receiving a sum largely in excess of our maximum ambitions. I have, therefore, decided to leave the matter in this way. It is too early at present to form any idea either of the sum that this National Memorial will cost—or of the extent of the contributions that are likely to be offered. I do not want at the start to stint the liberality of any man. But if a little later, we find that we are receiving sums in excess of those which we can properly spend, then I think that it will be a reasonable thing to fix a maximum, perhaps, of one lakh of rupees, beyond which we should not be willing to profit by the generosity of any individual donor, and to which we should limit our acceptance of the larger offers that had been made. There is a sort of emulation in giving for a noble object ; and it rests, I think, with those of us who are responsible for the management of this fund not to allow these instincts, however praiseworthy or honourable, to place too severe a strain upon the income of an individual or the revenues of a State.

And now I pass from the contributions of the Princes to those of the public at large. Here I rejoice to say that already the offers that have reached me have been splendid in their scale of munificence. Although [the fund has not yet been opened for more than two days, I am able to announce the following handsome subscriptions :—

|  | Rs. |
|---|---|
| Anonymous ... | 3,000 |
| The Nawab of Dacca ... | 50,000 |
| The Jute Mills of Bengal ... | 90,020 |
| The Coal Companies of Bengal ... | 14,500 |
| Mahdi Hossain Khan, Zemindar of Patna ... | 5,000 |
| Monomatha Nath Ray Chowdhury ... ... | 3,000 |
| Maharaja Monindra Chandra Nundy of Cossimbazar | 25,060 |
| H. H. Nawab Begum of Moorshedabad ... ... | 7,500 |
| Raja Ranajit Sinha, of Nashipur ... ... | 10,000 |
| Nawab, Shahar Begum, and Khan Bahadur Mirza Shujat Ali Beg ... ... ... ... | 2,500 |
| Nawab Syed Badshah ... | 5,000 |
| Maharaja Sir Jotindro Mohun Tagore ... .. | 50,000 |

I think, therefore, Gentlemen, that I may fairly claim that we have launched the ship under good auspices, and that she is sailing with a fair wind behind her.

It only remains for me to conclude my remarks with the business portion of my motion. We hope, in a very short time, to constitute a General Committee, of which it will be my privilege to act as patron, and of which I propose that the vice-patrons should be the Governors and Lieutenant-Governors of Provinces, and other Heads of Administrations, certain high officials, the leading Native Princes, and any other Prince or Chief or private donor who contributes to the fund the sum of one lakh of rupees ; while the General Committee will itself, I hope, be composed of representative men from all parts of the country. Then we shall also require a provisional Executive Committee to receive and take custody of the funds as they pour in, and inasmuch as we cannot draw here upon the inhabitants of other Provinces or States, it is inevitable that this Committee should be composed, in the main, of gentlemen resident in Calcutta, or in Bengal. We have endeavoured to constitute this Committee in a manner representative of all classes and interests in this Presidency, and

Sir Patrick Playfair, who has much experience in these matters, has very kindly consented to act as *pro tem.* Chairman of this body.

At a later date, when the money has been received, and the subscription list has been closed, and when we are aware of the different quarters from which we have received support, we shall probably require to constitute some body or bodies representative of the entire Indian community to carry the scheme in its various sections into execution.

I have now, I think, Ladies and Gentlemen, dealt with all the topics that fall under the motion assigned to me, and I will only, in conclusion, urge you, in accepting it, to give the rein to a generosity that shall be worthy of the revered and illustrious memory which we desire to honour, of Bengal and Calcutta, the capital Presidency, and the capital city of this country ; and lastly of India itself, the mightiest and the most loyal dependency of the British Crown.

## CONTENTS OF THE VICTORIA MEMORIAL HALL.

*26th February,* 1901.

[On Tuesday night, the 26th February, a special meeting of the Asiatic Society of Bengal took place at the Dalhousie Institute for the purpose of hearing an address from His Excellency the Viceroy on the subject of the contents of the proposed Memorial Hall to Queen Victoria in Calcutta. There was a large gathering of Europeans and Natives, and on the platform with His Excellency were Lady Curzon, Sir John and Lady Woodburn, the Metropolitan, the Chief Justice of Bengal and other leading officials. Their Excellencies were received on arrival by the Council of the Society, and conducted to their seats, after which the Lieutenant-Governor, in inviting the Viceroy to deliver his address, said that His Excellency had offered to address the Society on the subject of the Victoria Memorial Hall, the design of which was his own, and was a noble one. The development of His Excellency's scheme which would now be laid before them, had been awaited with expectant interest on the part of the whole community, an interest which was evidenced by the large gathering of guests of the Asiatic Society on the present occasion. The scheme was regarded by no part of the community with greater warmth than by the Society whose main concern had been in the history and traditions of India.

His Excellency the Viceroy, who on rising was very warmly received, then addressed the assembly as follows :—]

I do not think it necessary to say much about the general question of the proposed Memorial Hall to Queen Victoria in Calcutta. A good deal of the doubt or misconception that at first existed arose from ignorance of the real nature of the plan. This has been in the main dissipated by the publication of the full text of the original Memorandum, and of the proceedings at our meeting of February 6th in the Calcutta Town Hall. There only remain a few points in this connection upon which something may be added. It is quite clear, and, as I have before said, very natural and proper, that different parts of India and different localities should institute their own Memorials, although it is not always easy to determine what they shall be. The question before us, and before me in particular, was whether there should be a National Memorial as well. Now, Gentlemen, my view was that this was an occasion on which India would desire not merely to express its deep devotion to the late Queen's memory, but also to demonstrate to the world, in some striking manner, the truth of that Imperial unity which was so largely the creation of her personality and reign. Had each province been left exclusively to erect its own memorial, and had no effort been made to concentrate the public sentiment in some grander conception, we should doubtless have had, as we shall have, a number of excellent funds, and institutions, and buildings. They would have represented the feelings and the generosity of the individual province or locality, but they would not have condensed or typified the emotions of the nation. Visitors to India, and posterity in general, would hear or know little about this fund or that trust, however considerable the original endowment subscribed ; the income derived from it, whether applied to charitable objects, or to the advancement of education or research, could benefit but a small number of persons out of the population even of the province or district ; and so, in time, the name and memory of the great and good Queen would have faded out of the public mind, because there was no visible object to bring it perpetually under the eye of future generations.

The case, therefore, for a National Memorial seemed to me to be a very strong one, and nothing that I have read, or that has occurred since, has done anything to shake it. The question next arose whether, an all-Indian Memorial being accepted, it should, or should not, have assumed a concrete shape. There is much, I think, to be said on both sides of this question ; and we ourselves felt this so strongly that we decided to pronounce for neither to the exclusion of the other. All that we did was to give priority to the concrete Memorial, or, in other words, to ensure its execution as a first charge upon the Fund. No one could say, none of us can yet tell, what will be the total sum that we shall collect, or whether it would have been adequate to the constitution of a capital fund, the income accruing from which could be devoted to an object of really national service. Moveover, amid all the multiplicity of opinions, no one could inform us, and no one has yet been able to decide, what should be the non-concrete object to which an all-Indian contribution should be applied. And, if this difficulty has been felt by smaller communities, who are only called upon to express the desires or to provide for the needs of restricted areas, how much more does it apply, and on a hundredfold scale of magnitude, to the entire continent. I think, therefore, it will be conceded that, given the desirability of a National Memorial, we acted not unwisely in allowing priority to the concrete monument, leaving to subsequent discussion the allocation of the surplus funds that we may receive. Though I should not like to be too sanguine at the present stage, it seems to me to be not at all improbable that we may be presented with a total sum large enough to enable us, after building the hall, to do something substantial in the interests of charity; and no one will be better pleased than myself if this is the result. I have devoted much anxious thought to a consideration of the numerous suggestions that have been made. I have read many scores, if not hundreds, of these, and have been struck by the fact that, meritorious as many of them are, no two are identical. In other words, there is no sort of national unanimity on the subject. For the present I am disposed to think—if there be such a surplus—that we shall find it difficult to fix upon a better object to which to devote it than the Indian People's Famine Trust, which was inaugurated by that splendid donation from the Maharaja of Jaipur last year. Famine is the one great calamity that is capable of attacking the whole country. Its relief is the one great charitable boon that will affect, not isolated units, or even hundreds or thousands, but millions. Moreover, the objects of the Famine Relief Trust are outside of, and do not conflict with, the proper sphere of Government duty. These, however, are only my own ideas; and I give them for what they may be worth.

As regards Technical Education, I have not a word to say against an object in itself so admirable. It is in many ways the need of the future in India. But I have this to say about it at the present stage. The interest upon no fund that might be accumulated could possibly provide for more than the education of an infinitesimal minority, per annum, among the youths of India. The principles upon which they are to be trained, and the openings that might be found for their professional abilities and attainments, are not yet determined, and even in England, after fifteen years of struggle and discussion, are still in a fluid state. Finally, I hardly think it fair to connect the desire to commemorate the Queen's name with a task that has no definite association with her memory, and that is so pre-eminently the duty of the Government and of the community in combination, as that of providing for the education of a particular section of the population. Some people talk and write as though technical instruction were going to solve the Indian agrarian problem, and to convert millions of needy peasants into flourishing artisans. Gentlemen, long after everyone in this room has mouldered into dust, the economic problem will confront the rulers of India. It is not to be solved by a batch of Institutes or a cluster of Polytechnics. They will scarcely produce a ripple in the great ocean of social and industrial forces. Indeed, if they were to fail, or to remain empty, as might conceivably be the case at this stage of our evolution, and as has been the case with some of the premature experiments already made, where would the memory and honour of Queen Victoria be? Technical education is a problem that must be met by the patient and combined efforts of the Supreme Government, the Local Governments, Municipalities, District Boards, Chambers of Commerce, mercantile firms, and philanthropic and enterprising men. Let us all give to it that attention, but do not let us use the Queen's name to absolve us from our legitimate responsibilities.

It seems to me, therefore, that if we succeed in raising a great National Fund, which is partly devoted to the building of the Victoria Hall, and partly to the still further endowment of the Famine Trust, we shall, at the same time, have erected an impressive and enduring memorial to the name of Queen Victoria, and shall have consecrated the feelings aroused by her death to the service of the people in a manner that will beneficially affect the largest number. In the meantime, however, I have no desire to pronounce with finality upon the secondary or utilitarian object ; and, while our funds are accumulating, I shall be very glad to profit by the advice that will doubtless continue to reach me from many influential quarters.

Next I come to the question whether, presuming an all-Indian Memorial to be desirable, it was for the Viceroy to place himself at the head of the movement. I must leave this delicate question to be decided by the voice of others, not by my own. Perhaps, after all, the result will be the most conclusive answer. All I would say at this moment is that, if the position of the Viceroy is to be what, in my opinion, it ought to be, the opportunity of fusing and giving expression to the aspirations of the entire community is one that he should be proud to seize, and that, if in some quarters it be said that he should have left the movement to ferment and to come to a head as best it could, I suspect that, had this advice been followed, it would have been said in a good many other quarters that he had signally failed to realise the unique opportunities of his position, and had allowed a golden occasion to slip by of vindicating the loyalty and the devotion of the Indian Empire to the British throne.

I pass to another of the preliminary questions which it has seemed desirable to discuss. It appears to have been thought in some quarters that the scheme for a Victoria Hall in Calcutta has been snatched up, so to speak, in precipitate haste, and foisted almost without consideration upon the notice of the public. This is far from having been the case. This scheme was not for the first time conceived or matured during the fortnight that elapsed between the death of Her Majesty the Queen and the Town Hall Meeting. On the contrary, it has rarely been out of my mind during the two years in which I have been in India. I had been collecting information, consulting individuals, working out all the possible ramifications of the proposal, long before the Queen was smitten by her last fatal illness. I had, of course, no idea at that time of proposing such a building as a permanent Memorial to the Queen, because so marvellous was her vitality that such an idea as her early decease had never entered into our minds. But I had hoped, before leaving India, to carry the idea into execution as a fulfilment of what I regard as a great imperial duty, namely, the handing down to posterity of what the past has failed to provide for us, that is, a standing record of our wonderful history, a visible monument of Indian glories, and an illustration, more eloquent than any spoken address or printed page, of the lessons of public patriotism and civic duty. I had even gone so far as to talk over this scheme with friends, to prepare designs for a building, and to think of where it might be placed. Then came the death of the Queen : and then it was that, not merely in my own mind, but in that of the representative persons whom I consulted, the idea took shape that we were already in possession of the germ of a great Imperial Memorial, worthy of Queen Victoria and worthy of India. It was, therefore, no sudden or inchoate project that was submitted to the Calcutta Meeting. On the contrary, how complete it was the information that I shall presently place before you will enable you to judge.

There is only one other prefatory question to which it is necessary to advert. I have seen it asked why, instead of suggesting a scheme to others, I did not write to all the Princes and Governors, and leading men, and ask them to suggest one to me, and then decide according to the nature of their replies. Gentlemen, I invite you soberly to consider what the contents of such a postbag would have been. It needs no intuition to discern that I should have received not one scheme but one hundred, and I daresay as many more. And then a representative Committee would have had to be convened in order to discuss these schemes. It would have taken some weeks to assemble. Its deliberations would probably have taken as many months, and meanwhile where would the enthusiasm and the liberality of the people have been? We all know that even the noblest emotions are apt to dwindle, or to be chilled, if an outlet is not provided for them while they are still warm, and a course more likely to freeze the heart of the generous Indian public than that which has been suggested I cannot imagine.

From this brief discussion of what I have called preliminary questions, I now pass on to a more detailed examination of the scheme of a Victoria Hall, as it exists in the minds of those who have originated it. And the first subject to which I shall address myself is this. What will be the contents of the building when raised? I shall next ask where and how can they be procured; and, having attempted to answer both these questions, I shall, I trust, have left a clear impression in the mind of the public both as to what the scheme is and as to what it is not. Even among those who have warmly supported the idea, some doubts have been expressed on these points. " You are going to build a magnificent hall which will only be a second-class museum or an empty shell. You talk of collecting Indian relics and trophies, where are they? You want to commemorate great men and great events, who and what are they?" These are the sort of questions—and I do not regard them as unreasonable—that have been addressed to me. Indeed in some quarters there has been an attempt to throw ridicule upon the entire scheme. I shall, I hope, be able to show these critics that there is no ground for their unfriendly suspicions; and that all India may legitimately be asked to co-operate in a movement which, if its help be given, may easily be endowed with a truly cosmopolitan character, which will have a most practical as well as a sentimental side, and will contain not trash but treasures.

The building will be called the Victoria Memorial Hall. It will, therefore, I think, be befitting that a central hall or a central space should be devoted to the mementoes of Her Majesty the Queen. Whether or not the statue of the Queen that has already been executed shall be erected inside or outside this building is a matter that will remain over for subsequent decision. Probably it will remain outside. A separate representation of Her Majesty might perhaps be placed inside the hall. Around it might be grouped memorials of her reign. It might be possible to secure autograph letters from her to the various Governors-General and Viceroys who have had the honour to serve her. I at any rate shall be prepared to contribute, as the last. Some other personal relics we may be so fortunate as to secure. Upon the walls of this hall might be inscribed in letters of gold upon marble or upon bronze, both in English and in the different vernaculars, the famous Proclamation of 1858, and such other messages as the Queen has, at various times, addressed to the Indian people. If the originals are procurable, they might be placed in glass-cases below. The Emperor Asoka has spoken to posterity for 2,200 years, through his inscriptions on rock and on stone. Why should not Queen Victoria do the same?

I have, on a previous occasion, observed that the Memorial Hall would be devoted to the commemoration of notable events and remarkable men, both Indian and European, in the history of this country. I will now proceed to indicate the character of the incidents, and the personality of the individuals, who may perhaps be held worthy of this honour, and the manner in which it may be conferred. At the beginning it is almost necessary to draw a line which shall be the starting-point of our historical procession. I may say at once that the idea is not to convert this hall into an Archæological Museum, or to compete with the various institutions of that character that already exist in different parts of the country. I conceive it to be impracticable in a single building to convey a synopsis of all Indian history from the time of the Aryan immigration to the days of electric tramways and motor cars. I have not the slightest desire to accumulate here Buddhistic sculptures or implements of the bronze and stone ages. They will find their home more fitly in the Imperial and Provincial Museums. Similarly, I do not think that we can include representations of the legendary and quasi-mythological epochs of Indian history, the period in fact of the epics. Anything that dates from those days can only be a copy of originals existing elsewhere, or can have what is in the main an antiquarian, rather than a historical, interest. In practice it will, I think, be found that the earliest date from which it will be possible to accumulate any sort of original record will be the foundation of the Mogul dynasty. We may begin with Baber, and from then we may continue to the present date. Throughout the world progress seems to have taken a definite leap forward at about the same epoch ; and the situation will be much the same as though in England we began to make a collection with the Tudors, in Russia with Ivan the Terrible, in France with Francis I, in Germany with Charles V, in Turkey with Solyman the Magnificent, in Persia with the Sefavi dynasty, and in Japan with Iyeyasu.

I will first take Indian history. It ought, I think, to be possible to obtain some records of every period and every dynasty from the Moguls to the present day. These records would take the form of paintings, enamels, sculptures, manuscripts, and personal relics and belongings. I have heard of there being offered for sale in India in recent years the headdress of Akbar and the armour of Jehangir. Passing to the Mahratta ascendency, we should procure portraits of Sivaji and the leading Mahratta princes, generals, and statesmen. Then, if we turn to the Sikhs, we should have similar memorials of the leading Gurus, from Nanak to Guru Govind, of Maharajas Runjit Singh, Sher Singh, and Golab Singh of Jummu and Kashmir. All of these are, I believe, procurable. Fróm Rajputana we should collect memorials of Rana Pertab of Mewar, Raja Man Singh, and Siwai Jai Singh, the astronomer, of Jaipur, and Maharaja Jaswant Singh of Jodhpur. From Gwalior we should desire to commemorate Mahadaji Rao Sindhia and Dowlet Rao Sindhia ; from Bhopal the Nawab Sikandra Begum ; from Hyderabad Asaf Jah, the first Nizam. For my own part I should not hesitate for a moment to include those who have fought against the British, provided that their memories are not sullied with dishonour or crime. I would not admit so much as the fringe of the *pagri* of a ruffian like the Nana Sahib. But I would gladly include memorials of the brave Rani of Jhansi, and of Hyder Ali, and Tippu Sultan of Mysore. There is, I believe, a very interesting picture of the death of Tippu at Seringapatam in the palace of the Nawab of Murshidabad. If we come to more modern times, I have already collected, with the aid of those gentlemen who have been good enough to advise me, a list of the names of eminent Indian statesmen, writers, poets, administrators, judges, religious reformers and philanthropists who might be entitled to commemoration in such a Valhalla. I will mention a few typical names alone. Omichund, the great Bengal banker in the days of Lord Clive, Ali Verdi Khan, Raja Naba Kissen, Mir Jafar, Chaitanya, the founder of Vishnuism, Dwarkanath Tagore, Ram Mohun Roy, the founder of the Brahmo Somaj, who died in England, Keshub Chunder Sen, whose portrait is in the Town Hall, Rajendra Lal Mitra, the antiquarian, Raja Krishna Chandra, Sir Syed Ahmed, the founder of the Aligarh College, Romesh Chunder Mitter, the distinguished Judge. To these might be added the more eminent of the Nawabs Nazim of Bengal, and of the Talukdars of Oudh. In the memorandum previously issued were mentioned the names of well-known statesmen or public characters, such as Sir Dinkar Rao, Sir Madhava Rao, Sir Salar Jung, Sir Jamsetji Jeejheebhoy.

I now pass to British History. Here we shall endeavour to secure portraits, or busts, or mementoes—and where the originals are not forthcoming, reproductions may perhaps be available—of the long line of distinguished men who have made the British Empire in India. They will fall into several categories ; the pioneers of commerce and empire— such as Sir T. Roe, Job Charnock, Sir Josiah Child ; Governors, Governors - General, and Viceroys from Governor Holwell and Lord Clive to modern times ; famous personages, such as Sir Phillip Francis and Sir Elijah Impey ; eminent Governors or Lieutenant-Governors or Administrators of the provinces—such names, for instance, as Thomas Pitt, the grandfather of Lord Chatham, Sir Thomas Munro, and Streynsham Master from Madras ; Sir John Malcolm, Mountstuart Elphinstone, Sir Bartle Frere, Sir Richard Temple from Bombay ; Sir Henry Lawrence, James Thomason, Sir Ashley Eden, Sir Henry Ramsay, from other provinces. There will be a category of great Generals and soldiers of whom I may instance a few—Sir Eyre Coote, Sir Arthur Wellesley afterwards Duke of Wellington, Lord Lake, Lord Harris, Lord Keane, Sir David Ochterlony, Sir Charles Napier, Sir James Outram, Lord Gough, Sir Henry Havelock, Sir Colin Campbell (Lord Clyde), Sir Hugh Rose (Lord Strathnairn), Lord Roberts. There will be frontier heroes, such as Sir Herbert Edwardes, Colonel James Skinner, Colonel John Jacob, and General John Nicholson ; military adventurers such as the famous George Thomas, who rose from being a sailor and a cavalry leader to be Raja of Hansi ; and the cluster of foreigners who entered the service of Mysore, the Mahrattas, and Ranjit Singh. There will be the men of letters and science ; historians, such as Orme, Tod, Sleeman, Elliot, James Mill, Lord Macaulay, Sir John Kaye, Sir William Hunter ; students, or scholars, or antiquarians, such as Sir William Jones, James Rennell, H. H. Wilson, H. T. Colebrook, James Prinsep, Sir Alexander Cunningham, Professor Max Müller, Professor Monier Williams, Sir Henry Rawlinson, Sir Henry Yule ; financiers, such as James Wilson ; jurists, such as Sir Henry Maine and Sir James Stephen ; explorers and pioneers, such as Captain John Wood, Alexander Burnes, Moorcroft, Hayward, Sir Joseph Hooker ; reformers and philanthropists, churchmen and missionaries, such as John Clark Marshman, Carey, David Hare, Dr. Duff, Bishops Heber and Cotton. These are only a few of the names that have occurred to me, and are neither a complete nor an exhaustive list. They are merely typical instances of the service and the character that have helped to build up the fabric of British dominion in India, and that seems to me to be entitled to the honour of grateful commemoration at the hands of posterity.

And now, having specified the type of person whom it is proposed to honour, let me pass on to the methods by which it may be done. One or more of the galleries of the Victoria Hall will doubtless be devoted to sculpture. Here will be collected the life-size figures, or the busts and medallions, of great men. A large number of these memorials, as I shall show presently, are already in existence, and will, it is hoped, be available for our purpose. I shall indicate methods by which others may be procured. Cases will arise in the future in which a desire to commemorate some eminent person may not justify, either in the scope of the services rendered or in the extent of the money subscribed, the crowning honour of a statue on the *maidan.* The busts of such persons will appropriately be placed in the sculpture gallery of the Victoria Hall.

A second gallery, or galleries, will be devoted to paintings, engravings, prints, and pictorial representations in general, both of persons and of scenes. Here will be hung original pictures and likenesses, or, where these are not procurable, copies of such. There are still scattered about in Calcutta and Bengal, and 1 daresay in other parts of India, quite a number of oil-paintings, dating from the end of the last century and the beginning of this, commemorative of interesting persons and events. Now and then these find their way into the auction-room. More commonly they rot into decay. It is possible, in mezzotints, and stipple, and line engravings, to recover almost a continuous history of Anglo-Indian worthies, battles, sieges, landscapes, buildings, forts, and scenes during the last two hundred years.

While speaking of pictorial representation, it has been suggested to me that around the open corridors of the inner courts and quadrangles of the building might be depicted frescoes of memorable incidents or events. Fresco-painting is an art in which the Indian craftsman once excelled. Witness the pictured caves of Ajunta, the painted walls and ceilings of Futehpur Sikri, the decorated pavilions of Agra and Delhi, the brilliant Summer house of Tippu at Seringapatam. This art is not extinct in India, and is being fostered and revivified in Institutes and Schools of Art. I do not see why great historic scenes, such as the three battles of Panipat, or the battles of Plassey, Sobraon, Assaye, Miani, the self-immolation of Rani Pudmine and the women of Chitor, the Rahtor Queen closing the city gates against her husband when he returned defeated, the first audience of British factors with the Great Mogul, the Relief of the Residency at Lucknow, the Proclamation of the Queen at Allahabad in 1858, the Delhi Darbar of 1877, should not be thus commemorated. Precautions would have to be taken for the proper conservation of the frescoes during the rains. If pigments were found to be an unsuitable medium, however applied, recourse might be had to mosaics. Should more durable memorials still be preferred, it might be decided to fix bronze or copper plates in panels on the inner walls, containing inscriptions or bas-reliefs, dedicated to memorable scenes.

In the centre of the galleries that are occupied by paintings, or in adjoining rooms, I suggest that there should be placed stands and cases, with glass lids, containing the correspondence and handwriting, the personal relics and trophies and belongings of great men. It ought to be possible to procure autograph letters of all the Governors-General and Viceroys of India, and of the majority of those whose names have already been mentioned. Miniatures, articles of costume, objects that belonged in lifetime to the deceased, and that recall his personality or his career—all of these will fitly appear in such a collection. I may mention as an illustration the objects that are exhibited in the King's Library at the British Museum, in the Bodleian Library at Oxford, and in many kindred institutions.

A wider extension of the same principle may be applied to the commemoration of historical events. I should like to exhibit the originals, or where these cannot be procured copies, of Treaties, and Sanads, and Charters. I fancy that the original Charter of Queen Elizabeth of 31st December 1600 to the merchants of the East India Company is no longer extant, and that the earliest surviving grant is that of Charles II in 1661. Excellent facsimiles have been made in England of several of these documents. It may be noted in passing that the copy of Magna Charta which is exhibited in the British Museum is not the original, but only a reproduction. The oldest extant MS., which is itself not the original, is kept under lock and key in a fireproof safe elsewhere. A great many original documents are, however, in the possession of the Government of India, or of the India Office at home ; and a selection of the more interesting or important might be made from these. As regards earlier Indian history we may perhaps be so fortunate as to come into possession, or may be favoured with the loan, of Oriental manuscripts of which there are still a great many in this country, though, from lack of care and of means for collecting them, the majority have either perished or are fast leaving the country.

From documents or manuscripts it is a natural transition to maps and plans, both Native and European. It should not be difficult to collect, either in original or in duplicate, a complete set of all the maps of Calcutta from the beginning of the eighteenth century to the present day. Similar plans should be procurable of Fort St. George at Madras and of Bombay, and of many other factories, cities, and forts throughout the country. There is no means of studying local history and topography to compare with that of maps, and I should hope that we might acquire and exhibit a first-rate collection.

Side by side with maps I should be inclined to place newspapers. We could not hope to make any complete collection. That is the function of a library or of a museum. But a careful selection of some of the rarer or more interesting specimens might throw valuable sidelights upon the past. Coins might also be very properly included. Here we might make an exception and penetrate even further back than the Mogul days. A microcosm of the history of India through all the ages might be constructed from a classified exhibit of the different coins that have been current in India, Bactrian, Indo-Bactrian, Hindu, Afghan, Mogul, and finally British, including a specimen of every coin that has been struck in India during the Queen's reign. From the contents of a few cases we might grasp the outlines of history more vividly than from a library of books.

Among other objects that have occurred, or have been suggested, to me, I may mention musical instruments and porcelain. To some extent these are rather on the line between a historical gallery, which the Victoria Hall is intended to be, and a museum of the arts. Both, however, have a definite historical bearing. In a country where music has reached such a high pitch of development as in India, a collection of native instruments is in a certain sense a page of history. In the case of china, it may be even more so. For instance, there is no more interesting record than the few surviving pieces of the magnificent dinner-services that were used in the time of the old East India Company. We have only a few specimens left in Government House, the bulk having long ago perished. There used to be a great deal at Madras, but what little of this was left has, I believe, drifted to London.

And now I pass to what, I hope, may be a leading feature of the Victoria Hall. Several of the Indian Princes have already subscribed to the Central Memorial Fund. I have little doubt that many more will do so. I have observed in those organs of the Press which have addressed themselves

to belittling this scheme, the suggestion that pressure has
been, or will be, brought upon Princes or Darbars to contribute. This insinuation is both ungenerous and unjust.
No solicitation has been, or will be, made. It is open to a
Native Chief to join, or to stand aloof, as he pleases. He is
not likely to set before himself any other standard than the
measure of his own desire to join in a National Memorial to
the Queen. That their contributions will not be devoted to
an object in which they will bear no part or share will be
evident from what I am about to say. The wonderful
history of the Native States, the splendour of their courts,
the achievements of their great men, can only fitfully be
gathered by the visitor to India, or even by the resident in
the country, from visits to their capitals and courts. I
should like to constitute a Princes' Court or Gallery in the
Victoria Hall, where such memorials should be collected as
the Princes were willing to contribute or to lend. We
might collect pictures of leading Princes and Chiefs. We
might commemorate notable events in their dynasties and
lives. They might be willing, in some cases, to present us
from their armouries with duplicates of the large collections
that are there contained. Spears, and battle-axes, and
swords, shields and horse-trappings, and coats of mail—
these are the abundant relics, in India and elsewhere, of an
age of chivalry. Where gifts are not found possible, the
Chiefs might be prepared, as is so often done by the Royal
Family, by noblemen, and by rich collectors in England, to
allow a portion of their collections to appear on temporary
loan, the lender being of course put to no expense, and his
possessions being returned to him at the termination of such
period as he himself desired.

Whatever be our success as regards native arms, I
entertain no doubt of being able to amass a first-rate collection of British specimens. I would propose to devote one
gallery to a chronological illustration of the history of British
arms in this country. I would present in cases a complete
collection of British uniforms from the days of the earliest

sepoys of the Company to modern times.  From the various arsenals it will be a matter of ease to collect specimens of the muskets, carbines, and rifles, the powder flasks and pistols, the swords and lances, the cannons and guns of the various phases of military fashion in this country.  An enclosed verandah in the fort at Lahore is so packed at present with Sikh trophies that everything cannot be got inside.  Elsewhere military trophies are lying scattered about unhonoured and unknown.  In the same gallery I would place a complete collection of British medals that have been granted for service in this country and on its borders ; and here, too, I should hope will repose the tattered regimental banners that tell the tale of glory won, and pass on an inspiration to successors.

Another very proper adjunct of the Victoria Hall would be a collection of models.  There are many objects of immense historic interest which we either cannot procure because they have vanished, or could not introduce into our galleries because of their size and unsuitability.  These may very fitly be represented by models.  Such models might, for instance, be made of the ships that have brought European merchants and adventurers to India, from the vessel in which Vasco da Gama first cast anchor in the Harbour of Calicut on 20th May 1498, to the pioneer sloops, a century later, of Captain James Lancaster and Sir Henry Middleton, and from them to the four-masted sailing ships that still lift their spars against the sunset on the Hugli, and the ocean liners whose smoking funnels bear the colours of the British India and the P. and O.  Nor need models be confined to ships.  Nothing brings home more closely the stories of battlefields, and sieges, and assaults than well-designed models.  The storming of Chitor or Gwalior, of Bhurtpur or Seringapatam, becomes a different thing to all of us, when we have the actual scene reproduced in minia_ ture before our eyes.  I shall certainly have placed in the Gallery a model of old Fort William in Calcutta, of which I am at present engaged in identifying and demarcating the outlines. I remember when at Oxford seeing in the Bodleian Library a white marble model of the Calcutta Cathedral according to the original and uncompleted design. But why it should repose at Oxford instead of Calcutta I do not know.

I have now dealt to the best of my ability with the principal categories of objects that appear to be suitable for inclusion in the Victoria Hall. Perhaps my hearers will be inclined to agree with the friend who, after I had unbosomed myself to him on the matter, exclaimed : " Why, the danger is that you will have not too little, but too much ! " I will now proceed to point out the sources from which these and similar objects may be procured.

Two main channels of collection I have already indicated, namely, gift and loan. Many persons who would not be willing to part with cherished possessions might consent to lend them ; and, as in the Bethnal Green and other museums, we might perhaps hope for a succession of such favours. Nevertheless, for the bulk of our exhibits we must look to gift or purchase. Fortunately we already possess the admirable nucleus of such a collection as I have described in this place. Who can doubt that the fine marble statue of Warren Hastings by Westmacott, which is now effectually concealed from public view in the southern portico of the Town Hall—a building which is itself condemned— must find its way to the Victoria Hall? The same may be said of Bacon's great marble figure of Lord Cornwallis on the ground-floor of the same building, a masterpiece that is now strangely out of place amid dusty records and scribbling clerks. If the Town Hall be, as alleged, condemned, there are other portraits and busts that might very well be transferred to the new building. There are the pictures of Her Majesty Queen Victoria herself and the Prince-Consort, which I believe that she presented to the Town of Calcutta. There are portraits of Lords Clive and Lake now hanging on dark corners of the staircase ; of Dr. Duff, and Dwarkanath Tagore. There are busts of James Prinsep and the Duke of Wellington. In the High Court are two pictures of Sir Elijah Impey, one by Kettle, the other by Zoffany. Perhaps the learned Judges might spare us one. The Asiatic Society, whom I am addressing to-night, in their plethora of treasures, possess no less than one bust and three pictures of their founder, Sir William Jones. They might like to diffuse his fame. Similarly, they own portraits of four Governors-General, Warren Hastings, Lord Cornwallis, Lord Wellesley, and Lord Minto, which are now only seen by a few score of persons, and which they might be willing to place on loan for the edification of a larger public.

I may next turn to the building in which I am now speaking, and which was originally erected with very much the same object, namely, a National Valhalla, as the new hall which we are about to raise. I do not think that any one will claim that it has quite succeeded in vindicating its initial claim. Lord Dalhousie's statue, which I see opposite me, originally belonged to Government House, and was surrendered by Sir John Lawrence to this building, after its completion in 1866. Separate funds were raised for the commemoration of Havelock and Nicholson, and resulted in the busts of those two great men that we see before us. Chantrey's beautiful statue of Lord Hastings, which stands in the entrance by which we all came in, has nothing to do with this building at all, for the portico in which it was placed was raised in Lord Amherst's time to hold the statue, and the Dalhousie Institute was subsequently tacked on behind it. It will, I think, be generally conceded that all these memorials will find a more appropriate and a more worthy home in the Victoria Hall. I may carry the same line of argument and illustration further. We have three busts of Sir T. Metcalfe in the Metcalfe Hall. Having bought the place for Government, I shall be very glad to hand over one of them to the Victoria Hall. Metcalfe, the founder of a Free Press in India, ought to be commemorated there. Perhaps, too, we may appeal for some friendly assistance to the Bar Library. There, I believe, are to be

found, unless they have already perished, fourteen volumes
of the manuscript notes of cases in the handwriting of Mr.
Justice Hyde. There is his transcript of the evidence of
Warren Hastings and Barwell at the trial of Nuncomar, and
his entry of the order for the execution of that ill-fated person. I believe that there is also in the High Court the
original bond given by Bolagi Das to Nuncomar, which was
pronounced a forgery at the trial. Speaking of Warren
Hastings, I have been told that, some years ago, and I daresay still, unless they have been devoured by white ants, there
were contained in the Collector's Office at Chittagong, of
all places in the world, quite a number of official documents
in the writing of that great man and bearing his signature,
with those of Francis, Barwell, Clavering, and Monson.
Similar documents are, I doubt not, to be found, in the al-
mirahs or cupboards of many a district officer throughout
the country, and could, with a little search, be recovered
from an oblivion which in a climate such as this is sooner or
later synonymous with total destruction. I noticed a short
time ago a cry of pain from a Madras paper at the idea that
I might be going to indent upon Madras for the letters of
Sir Thomas Munro. Well, and how does Madras show its
reverence for that most interesting correspondence? By
allowing it to repose in a dingy cupboard in the Collector's
Office at Salem. I have no desire to rob any place, or any
society, or any individual, of that which may be dear to them.
But I submit that we should at least treat Sir Thomas
Munro better, for it would be difficult to treat him worse,
than his own Presidency has done.

I have said enough, I think, to indicate that in this
country, in record-rooms, in offices, and in kutcherries, will
be found a plentiful mine of documentary richness. From
the Imperial Library, and from the Foreign Office here, we
may be able to make a substantial contribution. Appeals in
the newspapers will doubtless bring to our knowledge the
existence of many objects at present lost to the public view.
In England I should make similar appeals. The India

Office might be willing to restore to us some of the objects belonging to the old East India Company which are in their possession, or to present us with copies or duplicates. I would myself undertake to write to the families, or descendants, or living representatives of the remarkable men whom we may desire to commemorate. Learned societies might be willing to contribute something to us from their abundance. Finally, there is perpetually passing through the hands of the London dealers and auctioneers a stream of interesting memorials of the Anglo-Indian past, which attract no notice, because they do not belong to celebrated collections, or because their owners are not known to fame ; but upon which a careful watch might be kept by experts appointed for the purpose. I entertain no shadow of a doubt that, within ten years of the date upon which the doors of the Victoria Hall are opened, there will, unless there be some grave and inexplicable relapse in public interest or in competent supervision in the interim, be collected therein an exhibition that will be the pride of all India, and that will attract visitors to this place from all parts of the world. I should add that if sufficient means are forthcoming, I would certainly propose adequately to endow the building, so that a sum may be annually available for adding to the contents, and maintaining them at a high standard of excellence.

I have now, I trust, said enough to show both what the Victoria Hall will be, and what it will not be. It will not be a museum of antiquities, filled with undeciphered inscriptions and bronze idols and crumbling stones. It will not be an industrial museum, stocked with samples of grains, and timbers, and manufactures. It will not be an art museum, crowded with metalware of every description, with muslins, and kinkobs, and silks, with pottery, and lacquerware, and Kashmir shawls. It will not be a geological, or ethnographical, or anthropological, or architectural museum. All these objects are served by existing institutions ; and I do not want to compete with or to denude any such fabric. The central idea of the Victoria Hall is that it should be a Historical Museum, a National Gallery, and that alone, and that it should exist, not for the advertisement of the present, but for the commemoration of that which is honourable and glorious in the past. Neither is it proposed to constitute the Victoria Hall, even while retaining its character as a Historical Gallery, a museum representative of all countries. We could not possibly collect the materials : many of them would not survive the Indian climate, and the result would be an indescribable medley, which would merely confuse instead of informing and stimulating the senses. It is, I think, essential that the art, the science, the literature, the history, the men, the events which are therein commemorated must be those of India, and of Great Britain in India, alone. That is the whole pith and marrow of the idea, and I venture to think that it would be most unwise to depart from it.

I must remove another misconception. Enquiries have been addressed to me as to whether there might not be incorporated with this building a magnificent Imperial Library, where there should be collected all the notable works, in whatever language that have been written about India, or that have been composed in the Indian vernaculars. The authors of these enquiries are perhaps unaware that I have already provided for this object. For nearly two years the negotiations have been proceeding for the acquisition of the Metcalfe Hall and its library by the Government. They are now on the verge of a happy termination. We propose to renovate and redecorate that handsome building, to transfer to it the whole of the Imperial Library at present deposited in the Home Department of the Government of India ; and to present it with an endowment sufficient to enable it, within no very lengthy space of time, to become a really representative collection of the literature that I have mentioned. We have obtained, through the good offices of the Home Government, the services of a most competent Librarian from the British Museum, and I hope, before I leave India, to have converted the Metcalfe Hall into a miniature edition of the Library and Reading Room in that great institution. a place which shall be the haven of Indian and Anglo-Indian scholars, and the nursery of writers and students.    There is obviously, therefore, no need for adding a Library to the Victoria Hall.

There is, however, one feature that might, I think, not improperly be included in the building.    Like most structures of a similar character in Europe, it should probably possess a really fine hall, distinct from the hall that is especially dedicated to the Queen.    Such a hall might be used for the Chapters of the Indian Orders, for a great darbar, or for any other ceremonial function.    An organ might be placed at one end for concerts and choral performances. Upon occasions it might supply a meeting-ground for the public, much in the same way as the Banqueting Hall is used at Madras.    As time passes on, benefactors might adorn this hall with pictures or frescoes, and with the statues of princes and great men.    I may add that, in the future, I hope that the leading Chiefs may be seen at Calcutta more frequently than in the past.    I have, for some time, been in negotiation for the purchase of Hastings House, the old country residence of Warren Hastings, at Alipore ; and if this transaction be satisfactorily concluded, I propose to utilise the house, which is a fine building, quite apart from its historical associations, for the occasional entertainment of the Princes, who are always so lavish in their hospitality to the Viceroy, as the guests of the Government of India in Calcutta.

A few details only remain to be noticed.    It is too early as yet to speak about the style of a building, when the money has not yet been subscribed with which it is to be raised.    That will have to be settled, as will most of the other points that I have raised, by a representative Committee later on.    There will probably, however, be general agreement that it should be built of the best and most solid material, white marble for choice, and that it must be so constructed as to resist the deteriorating influences of a tropical climate. There must be unity of design in the plan, but scope must be left for later generations to add to the original structure should the occasion arise. It has already been announced that it is proposed to inscribe in a prominent place in the building the names of all subscribers of half a lakh and upwards. When the collection has been made, cheap but full guide-books will be prepared, both in English and in the vernacular, so as to tell the visitor where to go, and what it is that he is about to see. Finally, the surrounding space will be converted into a beautiful garden, which, with due regard to the flowerbeds and lawns, should be accessible to all, and will be a joy and delight to the town.

Such, Ladies and Gentlemen, is the scheme of the Victoria Hall, as it presents itself to me, assisted by the able advice of the numerous authorities and scholars whom I have consulted. I hope to have shown you that it will not be a merely sentimental creation, but that it will have a most utilitarian aspect as well. There is no more practical or businesslike emotion than patriotism. I believe that this building will give to all who enter it, whether English or Indians, a pride in their country, in addition to reminding them of the veneration that all alike entertain for the great Sovereign in whose honour it was built. I believe that it will teach more history and better history than a study-full of books. I believe that it will appeal to the poor people just as directly as to the rich ; and that they will wander, wondering perhaps, but interested and receptive, through its halls. Lastly, I believe that it will do much to bind together the two races whom Providence, for its mysterious ends, has associated in the administration of this great Empire, and whose fusion has been so immeasurably enhanced by the example, the wisdom, and the influence of Queen Victoria.

I will only add that I shall be most happy now, or in the future, to receive any communication or suggestions from any who may have useful light to throw upon the

realisation of the scheme upon which we have embarked. .
(*Applause.*)

[Mr. Risley and Colonel Hendley then addressed the meeting, and a
vote of thanks to the Viceroy for presiding was proposed by the Lieutenant-
Governor. His Excellency having acknowledged the vote of thanks the
proceedings closed.]

RETURN TO the circulation desk of any
University of California Library
or to the

NORTHERN REGIONAL LIBRARY FACILITY
Bldg. 400, Richmond Field Station
University of California
Richmond, CA 94804-4698

ALL BOOKS MAY BE RECALLED AFTER 7 DAYS
2-month loans may be renewed by calling
  (415) 642-6753
1-year loans may be recharged by bringing books
  to NRLF
Renewals and recharges may be made 4 days
  prior to due date

DUE AS STAMPED BELOW

JUL 1 1 1990

YC 41209

**U.C. BERKELEY LIBRARIES**

C004064965

511666

DS480

UNIVERSITY OF CALIFORNIA LIBRARY

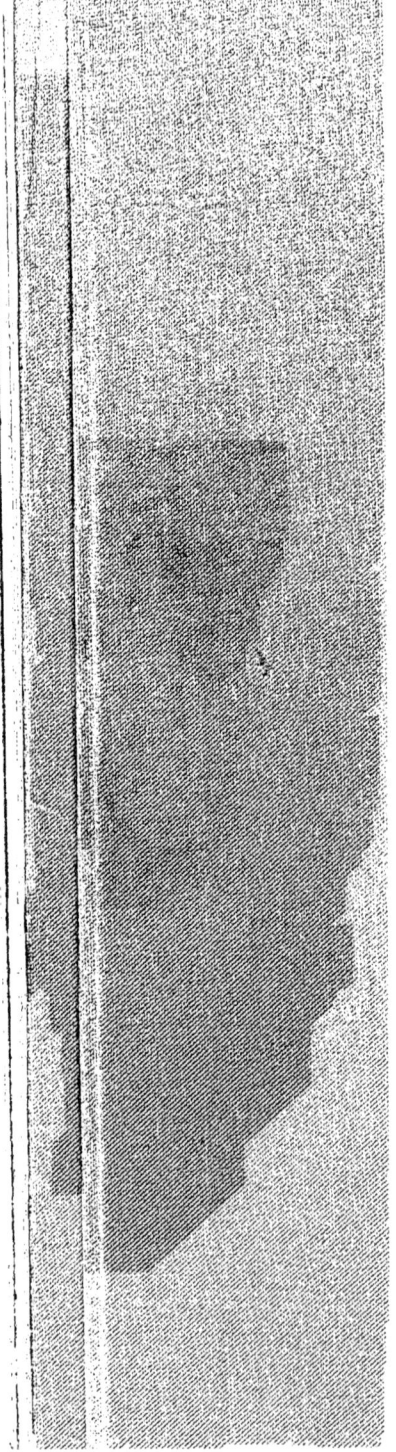

Lightning Source UK Ltd.
Milton Keynes UK
UKHW012001150119
335598UK00015B/735/P

9 781331 522720